African American English
a linguistic introduction

This authoritative introduction to African American English (AAE) is the first textbook to look at the grammar as a whole. Clearly organized, it describes patterns in the sentence structure, sound system, word formation and word use in AAE. The book uses linguistic description and data from conversation to explain that AAE is not a compilation of random deviations from mainstream English but that it is a rule-governed system. The textbook examines topics such as education, speech events in the secular and religious world, and the use of language in literature and the media to create black images. This much-needed book includes exercises to accompany each chapter and will be essential reading for students in linguistics, education, anthropology, African American studies and literature.

LISA J. GREEN is Assistant Professor in the Department of Linguistics at the University of Texas, Austin.

Lisa J. Green

African American English
a linguistic introduction

CAMBRIDGE
UNIVERSITY PRESS

PUBLISHED BY THE PRESS SYNDICATE OF THE UNIVERSITY OF CAMBRIDGE
The Pitt Building, Trumpington Street, Cambridge, United Kingdom

CAMBRIDGE UNIVERSITY PRESS
The Edinburgh Building, Cambridge CB2 2RU, UK
40 West 20th Street, New York, NY 10011-4211, USA
477 Williamstown Road, Port Melbourne, VIC 3207, Australia
Ruiz de Alarcón 13, 28014 Madrid, Spain
Dock House, The Waterfront, Cape Town 8001, South Africa

http://www.cambridge.org

First published 2002
Reprinted 2005

Printed in the United Kingdom at the University Press, Cambridge

Typefaces Times 9.5/13 pt and Quadraat Sans   *System* LATEX 2$_\varepsilon$ [TB]

A catalogue record for this book is available from the British Library

ISBN 0 521 81449 9 hardback
ISBN 0 521 89138 8 paperback

Contents

Foreword

It is difficult for me to contain my excitement at seeing this book in print! Lisa Green is one of the newest, freshest voices to contribute to the linguistic study of African American English (AAE), and this is the first theoretically informed, book-length discussion by a native speaker of what it means to know and use this beloved, belittled language. (The author is from Louisiana, a state rarely cited in previous studies of AAE.)

Although linguists have done more work on AAE than any other variety of American English, at least since the 1960s, much of this focuses on the quantitative analysis of *sociolinguistic* variation (by internal, linguistic factors as well as by external ones like social class, age, and style), the *historical* development of AAE (including its African, Creole, and English origins), and its *educational* implications (as raised, for instance, by the 1996 Oakland "Ebonics" controversy). All of this is valuable, but without a detailed understanding of the structure and patternedness of this variety in the sense that has been fundamental to modern linguistics since De Saussure and Sapir, our efforts to pursue these larger questions are limited.

Lisa Green is fully aware of the sociolinguistic issues, more so than the average theoretical linguist. (Her graduate training was at the University of Massachusetts at Amherst, but she has done postgraduate work at Stanford and regularly participates in sociolinguistic and variationist conferences.) But she wisely sets them aside in this book and provides only a brief overview of relevant historical issues. What she treats us to, instead, is a detailed, insightful exploration of the synchronic "character" or nature of AAE (its lexicon, morphosyntax and phonology) covered in the first four chapters, and a stimulating discussion of some of the "contexts" in which it is used and represented (in speech events, literature, and the media, as well as in linguistics, public attitudes, and education), the subject of the second half of the book.

Throughout, Lisa Green is insistent that AAE is systematic and rule-governed. In this respect she is similar to virtually every linguist who has previously studied this variety. But what is new is her consistent emphasis on revealing the character of AAE as a system, rather than a list of isolated features; note the extensive verbal paradigms of chapter 2, for instance, or the way that preterite *had* in chapter 3 is compared with alternative means of marking the past in AAE. Lisa Green's book also includes features (like the intrusive *d* in *light-skinded*, and AAE's distinctive intonation contours) and issues (e.g. child language acquisition and the assessment of speech disorders) that are rarely if ever treated in other texts. She often leads us to a richer, deeper understanding of the semantic subtleties and syntactic possibilities than we were aware of before this, undoubtedly related to her ability to draw on her native speaker intuitions. And her attested data is especially extensive and up-to-date, culled from natural conversations by speakers of all ages, classes, and genders, and from a wide range of sources in literature, popular culture, and the media, including the latest rap music and movies (e.g. *Bamboozled*, 2000).

Finally, I cannot close without praising Lisa Green as a teacher and pedagogue. I have had the privilege of co-teaching a course on AAE with her once (at Stanford), marveling at the skill with which she introduced students who were new to linguistics to the technical aspects of the field and the regularities and complexities of this variety. I was similarly impressed as I read this book, which will be appreciated by students and instructors alike for its clear exposition, its reference to more complex literature (by the author herself and others) for those who want to dig deeper, and for its very helpful summaries and exercises at the end of each chapter. This book will be invaluable to those of us who struggle to find an appropriate middle line between keeping students interested, and exposing them to the linguistic subtleties of AAE. It will definitely help me to teach a deeper, sweeter introduction to AAE than I have before, and it will enable my students to produce better term papers. This is one of the many reasons that I am excited to see this book in print, and to recommend my colleagues and students to this bright new scholar. She will undoubtedly continue to enrich our understanding of AAE, syntax and language in the future.

John R. Rickford

Preface

The aim of this book is to provide an introduction to the study of topics related to African American English (AAE). The focus is on presenting a description of AAE and explaining the types of rules that speakers follow when they speak it. This book evolved from plans to collaborate on a similar project with John R. Rickford, who is a leading scholar in the field and a great teacher. I gratefully acknowledge his foresight and the key role he played during the early stages of this work.

In this book and my overall research on AAE, I try to show that speakers know more than just a few unique words and phrases when they know AAE and that the variety is not a version of bad English. The book is divided into eight chapters, whose themes center on linguistic and social issues in the study of AAE. Each chapter begins with a focal point, which highlights the major thrust of the discussion, and a quote that makes a relevant point or includes an example of a linguistic construction that is addressed in the chapter. Each chapter ends with a summary and exercises that can be used in applying the material discussed in separate sections.

This book is intended for students who are taking general courses that address AAE as well as for those who want to learn about the ways in which the variety is systematic. The book may be of interest to educators and those in education-related fields. The final chapter explains how the information presented in the course of this book may be useful in developing classroom lessons and strategies for teaching mainstream English proficiency. In addition, the book may also be of interest to those who are engaged in discussions about the representation of AAE in literature and the media.

It is my good fortune to have been helped along the way by so many people. I gratefully acknowledge support from the faculty in the Department of Linguistics at the University of Massachusetts, especially during my leave there from 1997 to 1998. I am especially thankful for the feedback provided by John Baugh and Tom Wasow during the early stages of this project. I received helpful comments from students in courses I taught at The University of Texas at Austin and at the University of Massachusetts. Wali Rahman helped me with sources on the expressive language used by African Americans in the adolescent to young adult age groups. Walter Sistrunk, Ahmad Simmons, Jeremy Green and D'Andre Brown also helped in this area. I would also like to thank Michel DeGraff, Walter Edwards, Donald Winford and Joseph T. Skerrett Jr. for help with data and sources. John Tatum consulted with me on a number of issues related to church services. Helena Woodard was always willing to talk with me about African American literature and answer my many questions about everything. She is a wonderful mentor. The anonymous reviewers gave many useful and extensive comments that have helped to shape this book. They are in no way responsible for the shortcomings of this work. I gratefully acknowledge support from a University Cooperative Society Subvention Grant awarded by The University of Texas at Austin and National Science Foundation research grant BCS-0003158. I also wish to thank Andrew Winnard, editor at Cambridge University Press, for his help with the project. Copyeditor Sara Adhikari did an excellent job.

This book would certainly have not been possible without the many AAE speakers from different parts of the United States. I would also like to thank my Lake Arthur community, Pastor Melton Alfred and the ABC Reading Program for allowing me to continue to be a part of them and for continuing to keep me in their prayers. I acknowledge Pastor N. D. Lee III, for giving me permission to use his sermon. Special thanks go to my parents, Charles and Ramona Green, who have always believed in and supported me.

This book is dedicated to my husband, Vincent Jackson, who continues to hold me up on every side. Vincent's constant love, encouragement, patience and support helped me get through this project and many other day-to-day challenges.

Introduction

Goals and structure of the book

What do speakers know when they know African American English (AAE)? One of the goals of this book is to answer this question by presenting a description of AAE and explaining that it is different from but not a degraded version of classroom English (i.e., general American English, mainstream English) or the English which is the target of radio and television announcers. Researchers who study the history of AAE emphasize the importance of comparing AAE to other dialectal varieties of English, especially those spoken in the United States, because AAE is likely to be more similar to other English varieties than it is to classroom English. In this book, I will compare AAE to other English varieties and to classroom English. The comparison to classroom English is important because (1) we have a clear picture of classroom English grammar, and (2) it may be useful for those in the school systems who work with speakers of AAE to see how the variety differs systematically from classroom English.

AAE is a variety that has set phonological (system of sounds), morphological (system of structure of words and relationship among words), syntactic (system of sentence structure), semantic (system of meaning) and lexical (structural organization of vocabulary items and other information) patterns. So when speakers know AAE, they know a system of sounds, word and sentence structure, meaning and structural organization of vocabulary items and other information.

African Americans who use this variety, and not all do, use it consistently, but there are regional differences that will distinguish varieties of AAE spoken in the United States. For example, although speakers of AAE in Louisiana and Texas use very similar syntactic patterns, their vowel sounds may differ. Speakers of AAE in areas in Pennsylvania also share similar syntactic patterns with speakers in Louisiana and Texas; however, speakers in areas in Pennsylvania are not likely to share some of the patterns that the Louisiana and Texas speakers share with other speakers of southern regions. Also, speakers from the three different states have different vowel sounds. That is to say that they will all use the same or similar semantic and syntactic rules for the *be* form that indicates that some event occurs habitually (e.g., *They be running* 'They usually run'), but they will produce the vowel sounds in words such as *here* and *hair* differently, for example.

One of the ways in which this book attempts to show that AAE speakers have acquired a system is by providing extensive verbal paradigms that include verb conjugations and the environments in which certain auxiliaries and other verbal elements occur. The book also presents an overview of the system of lexical and sound patterns that speakers use. In presenting the description of the system, I note the properties that AAE shares with other varieties of English. One point that is made is that while there are superficial similarities, there are subtle differences among these varieties. In the approach that is taken here in showing that AAE is a system, the variety is characterized without addressing the question of whether it is a dialect or a language, a question that does not arise among linguists because (1) both languages and dialects are equally rule-governed, and (2) there are different views of dialects. Take the well-known Chinese case. Both Mandarin and Cantonese, though mutually unintelligible, are considered to be dialects of Chinese as they have a common writing system. Then consider the situation in Yugoslavia, given the split of Serbo-Croat into three languages (not dialects of a language): Serbian, Croatian and Bosnian. Geoffrey Pullum discusses this issue in a paper that can be summarized by its title, "African American English is not Standard English with Mistakes."

The view that I will take here is that AAE is a linguistic system that is not the same as classroom English, nor is it the same as other varieties of English although it shares features with them. This work tries to make clear what AAE is and the ways in which it is different from and similar to general American and other varieties of English. Recognizing that AAE cannot be completely defined by the syntactic, phonological, semantic and lexical patterns alone, in this study I consider speech events that are used in the linguistic system. These speech events, which follow set rules, may be used in secular as well as religious contexts.

The linguistic description of AAE is central because it helps to define the linguistic system and explain that it is based on rules. In addition it is also useful in that it has practical applications. Chapters 1–4 describe regular patterns in AAE and present examples of the types of sound and word combinations in AAE. Chapters 5–7 present an analysis of spoken and written text in which these regular patterns are used. Chapter 8 explains why being familiar with patterns of AAE would be useful in educational contexts, especially in standard English proficiency programs.

Chapter 1 considers the lexicon of AAE, in which unique meanings of words are represented. This chapter surveys the different ways in which the lexicon of AAE has been presented. In addition it also classifies and gives lexical entries for words and phrases in AAE that cross generational boundaries. It is explained that AAE is not slang but that slang plays a major role in the variety. This chapter considers slang terms for labeling people and money, and it also considers a productive process of adding elements to the lexicon.

Chapters 2 and 3 present a description of syntactic and morphological properties of AAE, as a means of describing some of the patterns that speakers know when they know the linguistic variety. Many examples are provided in these two chapters to show that speakers follow specific rules in producing sentences. These chapters explain precisely why the assessment that AAE is classroom English with mistakes is incorrect and unfounded. The positive data are often real examples from native speakers, and the negative data (flagged by an asterisk '*') are sentences that are predicted to be ungrammatical in AAE because they do not adhere to the rules of the system. The description of syntactic patterns of AAE includes a discussion of the constraints or restrictions that are placed on certain sequences in generating grammatical sentences. In these chapters, more emphasis is placed on patterns in the language system and less on characterizing AAE by a list of isolated features. For example, instead of concentrating on whether or not the copula/auxiliary *be* occurs in AAE (such as *am* in *I am here, I am running* but no *be* form in *She here, She running*), these chapters consider the syntactic and semantic distinctions between auxiliaries (e.g., *will*, inflected forms of *be* [such as *is, am, was*], *do* [*did*], *have*) and verbal markers (*be, BIN, dən*). They also address the system of past marking and a range of other constructions. In some places, technical details are included in order to give more complete descriptions of the patterns; however, it is not necessary to work through the details to understand the general AAE linguistic patterns. Realizing that some features that are presented here are shared with other varieties of English such as Alabama English and Hiberno English (Irish English), I point out similarities and explain subtle differences where possible.

The goal of chapter 4 is to present a description of the sound patterns of AAE, explaining the types of constraints that are placed on the occurrence of sounds in different positions in the word and in different linguistic environments. For example, this chapter notes properties of groups of consonants at the ends of words and preceding suffixes that begin with vowels and consonants. Some sound patterns and properties of sounds that have not been discussed extensively in the literature on AAE are discussed in this chapter. In addition this chapter reviews various arguments about the origin of AAE that have been based on the inventory of sound patterns in the variety. For instance, it has been suggested that in some contexts, the pattern of final consonant sounds in AAE is similar to the pattern of final consonant sounds in West African languages. Finally, this chapter raises some questions about the extent to which 'sounding black' is related to the different intonational and rhythmic patterns that are used by speakers of AAE. This chapter continues one of the themes in this book: AAE follows set rules.

As a means of capturing the patterns and the rules governing the occurrence of constructions in AAE, I often use descriptive statements such as the following in chapters 2, 3 and 4: In AAE, speakers say *baf* where *bath* would be used in general American English. But I go beyond such descriptive statements by discussing the linguistic environments in which such patterns occur. Of course, it should be made clear that speakers do not always say the same thing the same way or pronounce words the same way all the time, so a person who uses AAE *baf* may also use *bath* in some contexts. As I am concerned with a description of AAE, I focus more on the system of sentence structure and sounds that are different from those in general American English. To this end, structures in AAE, general American English and other varieties of English are often compared. While there is no question that general American English is accepted in the mainstream and is used in classrooms, AAE and other varieties of English are as structurally sound as general American English.

Where indicated by sex and age (e.g., bf, 30s, 'black female, age 30s'; bm, 50s, black male, age 50s), examples in this book have been taken from speakers of AAE. In some instances, the examples are labeled 'attested' if I did not record detailed information when observing and collecting them. Also, data based on my intuitions as well as the intuitions of other native speakers of AAE are included (obviously without any information about speaker, etc.), as is common in linguistic theory and practice. The data help to show how AAE differs systematically from mainstream English, and they also reflect the way speakers use a number of different rules of AAE in forming a single sentence.

Chapter 5 presents an overview of speech events, for example, the dozens, rapping, marking, signifying, loud-talking, woofing and toasting, and rules of interaction that are associated with AAE and considers the way they are used in conversation. An entire section in the chapter is dedicated to speech events and language use in African American church services. In that section, a sermon collected in 1990 is analyzed as a means of illustrating the rhetorical strategies used by the minister and the rules of interaction that the congregation and musician adhere to in engaging in verbal and musical call and response. In addition, sections of the sermon are analyzed to determine the extent to which the minister uses syntactic and phonological patterns of AAE in delivering his message. It is the case that while syntactic and phonological features are evident in passages in the sermon, rhetorical strategies outweigh these features. In subsequent sections, braggadocio style, signification and toasts are discussed in rap lyrics. These speech events are an important part of AAE, and they may be used by speakers who do not otherwise use the syntactic and phonological features that have been traditionally associated with the variety. The final section considers communicative competence and the speech of pre-school age children who are acquiring expressive language use.

Chapter 6 discusses the representation of AAE in literature and the media. This chapter considers the representation of AAE in literature to the early twentieth century, literature from the Harlem Renaissance to the mid twentieth century and literature from the mid twentieth century to the present. Literary works by authors such as William Wells Brown, Joel Chandler Harris, Zora Neale Hurston, Langston Hughes, Ralph Ellison, John Edgar Wideman and August Wilson are considered, and questions about the images of characters who are represented as using AAE are raised. Also, this chapter compares the linguistic features used to represent black characters in literature to the syntactic and semantic, phonological and lexical patterns used in current AAE and discussed in previous chapters. Some authors rely heavily on spelling conventions in the representation of the language of black characters, while others do not. The latter authors rely more on syntactic and lexical properties. For example, these authors use words such as *juba*, *womanish* and *mannish* in representing black speech.

Chapter 7 considers the use of AAE in films, and it notes that some characters who are portrayed as speaking AAE use syntactic and phonological features to mark their speech as being nonstandard or black, and others use speech events and other types of expressive language use as markers. The angle that is taken here is not one that evaluates the authenticity of the language used in the media, but it is one that attempts to determine what types of linguistic features or markers are associated with certain characters. For example, it is noted that the verbal marker *be* that indicates habitual occurrences is associated with certain types of characters in *The Best Man*, yet it is associated with adolescent street language in *Fresh*. In this chapter, I show how linguistic descriptions that have been discussed earlier in the book can be used to comment on the representation of language in the media. In addition one of the themes is that different messages are associated with the use or the approximation of AAE in these works. This point is especially relevant to the discussion of films in this chapter that portray some type of minstrel act.

Chapter 8 takes a brief look at different approaches to AAE over the years and explores issues ranging from attitudes toward AAE to classroom strategies that may be useful in teaching speakers of AAE, especially in standard English proficiency programs. Nothing in this chapter, or in this book for that matter, suggests that AAE should be taught in schools or that programs should be designed to help children learn AAE. Although educational issues have been addressed for over thirty years and progress has been made, some of the same questions regarding strategies for teaching speakers of AAE to read and become proficient in mainstream English continue to be raised. Consider the cycle of events leading to the Ann Arbor controversy in 1979, in which questions were raised about the extent to which the speech patterns of elementary school age children served as barriers to their education, and those resulting in the Oakland debates in 1996–1997. A large part of the confusion was a result of negative attitudes, very limited systematic discussions about linguistic patterns of AAE and thus not being able to distinguish the system from the expressive language that is characterized by change and used by adolescents and young adults. This chapter addresses these issues. It also discusses attitudes toward AAE from a number of viewpoints such as employer and teacher attitudes. The final section of the chapter ends with classroom strategies that take into account the type of linguistic descriptions of AAE that have been presented in this book.

Two preliminary issues that have been raised in the literature about AAE will be reviewed before moving to the main text: (1) various names for AAE and (2) historical origin of AAE.

On naming the variety

From the early 1960s, the initial period of heightened interest in AAE, to the present, many different labels have been used to refer to this variety, and the label has often been related to the social climate. For example, the period during which AAE was referred to as Negro dialect or Negro English was precisely the period during which African Americans were referred to as Negroes. To some extent, the labels have been used to link the variety to those who speak it; the same label that is used to refer to the speakers is used for the variety. The early and very general speaker-based definition is intended to establish this link. The definition refers to the variety as an ethnic and social dialect spoken by African Americans who are members of the working class. Along these same lines, the labels have served as a general description of the linguistic features that occur in the variety. Take for instance Black communications, which refers to specific communication patterns and features in the speech of black people. The features may refer to the sounds: final consonant sounds do not occur (e.g., *test* is pronounced as *tes*). They may also refer to characteristics of sentences: forms of conjugated *be* such as *is* and *are* do not always occur in AAE (e.g., *She working until 9:00 tonight* may be used instead of *She is working until 9:00 tonight.*).

'English' is included in a number of the labels for AAE, which suggests that some of its characteristics are common to or very similar to those of different varieties of English. Along these same lines, 'English' has been omitted from some of these labels in an effort to highlight African and creole relations (which will be discussed in the next section.)

A list of labels for the variety is given below, in which the last four are more commonly used today. However, those beginning with 'Black' may also be heard:

> Negro dialect
> Nonstandard Negro English
> Negro English
> American Negro speech
> Black communications
> Black dialect
> Black folk speech
> Black street speech
> Black English
> Black English Vernacular
> Black Vernacular English
> Afro American English
> African American English
> African American Language
> African American Vernacular English (AAVE)

By and large, the labels have changed over the years, but they have been used to refer to the same system. The term 'black street speech' was used by John Baugh in his 1983 book, in which he examined "one small slice of black American culture, namely, the common dialect of the black street culture" (p. 1). While the title suggested to some that the variety being referred to was used only in negotiations in street culture, Baugh was actually describing the linguistic system that is being referred to here as AAE. For the most part, the data he used were taken from speakers who participated in that culture. (See note 5 in chapter 8 for Baugh's reasons for adopting the term.) The point is that the features he distinguished are also used by speakers of AAE in small towns in which there are no inner cities and certainly no thriving street culture; in sum, the features he discussed are not limited to street culture.

Black English and African American English have been distinguished from Black English Vernacular and African American Vernacular English, respectively. William

Labov introduced the term "Black English Vernacular" in his book *Language in the Inner City: Studies in the Black English Vernacular*. He used the term to refer to "that relatively uniform grammar found in its most consistent form in the speech of black youth from 8 to 19 years old who participate fully in the street culture of the inner cities" (p. xiii). In addition he suggested that the term Black English be used as a general cover term for "the whole range of language forms used by black people in the United States" (p. xiii). Today, while some researchers choose to use African American English, others African American Vernacular English (AAVE) and still others African American Language, they are all referring to the same variety – that which I have defined in the introductory statements in this book and will discuss throughout this work. As should be clear by now, I use African American English (AAE) and do not limit the language to that used by speakers of a certain age group. It will be clear that the data presented in this book are from speakers who cover a broad range of ages, starting at six years and going all the way up to people in their eighties. Also, although I refer to African American and African American community, I do not intend to imply that this linguistic variety is associated with all African Americans – it is not – any more than I intend to suggest that all African Americans are a part of some large abstract community. My goal is to describe the linguistic system that is used by some African Americans, and I have chosen the label AAE to refer to it. As the long list shows, many other labels will work; however, slang, broken English and the like will not work because they do not characterize the variety that I am describing.

The term Ebonics, which was coined by Robert Williams in 1973, but which received considerable attention in 1996 during the Oakland case, has been left off the list of labels of AAE because Williams intended the term to cover the multitude of languages spoken by black people not just in the United States but also those spoken in the Caribbean, for example. In the introduction to *Ebonics: The True Language of Black Folks*, the following definition is given:

A two-year-old-term created by a group of black scholars, Ebonics may be defined as "the linguistic and paralinguistic features which on a concentric continuum represents the communicative competence of the West African, Caribbean, and United States slave descendant of African origin. It included the various idioms, patois, argots, idiolects, and social dialects of black people" especially those who have been forced to adapt to colonial circumstances. Ebonics derives its form from ebony (black) and phonics (sound, the study of sound) and refers to the study of the language of black people in all its cultural uniqueness.

[Williams 1975, p. vi]

The view of Williams and other scholars who discussed this issue was that the language of black people had its roots in Niger-Congo languages of Africa, not in Indo-European languages. However, during the Oakland controversy, the media and general public adopted the term "Ebonics," using it interchangeably with the labels given earlier, thus not using the term as it was intended.

Further explaining the term, Smith (1998) notes that "When the term *Ebonics* was coined it was not as a mere synonym for the more commonly used appellation *Black English*" (p. 55). He goes on to comment that a number of scholars have consistently maintained that in the hybridization process, it was the grammar of Niger-Congo African languages that was dominant and that the extensive word borrowing from the English stock does not make Ebonics a dialect of English. In fact, they argue, because it is an African Language System, it is improper to apply terminology that has been devised to describe the grammar of English to describe African American linguistic structures.

[pp. 55–56]

In commenting on the misuse of the term *Ebonics*, Smith instructs:

In sum, Ebonics is not a dialect of English. The term *Ebonics* and other Afrocentric appellations such as *Pan African Language* and *African Language Systems* all refer to the linguistic continuity of Africa in Black America. Eurocentric scholars use the term *Ebonics* as a synonym for "Black English." In doing so, they reveal an ignorance of the origin and meaning of the term *Ebonics* that is so profound that their confusion is pathetic.

[p. 57]

Smith protests against emphasizing English similarities and de-emphasizing African structure of AAE, and his points are well taken. The ongoing research on the origin of this linguistic variety is evidence that those working in this area are not oblivious to claims about African and creole contributions. The precise nature of the relationship between this variety and African languages and creoles is the topic of continued research, as only broad generalizations can be made on the basis of a few examples. In addition to labeling the linguistic variety appropriately, we should be engaged in rigorous research that presents accurate descriptions and that provides further insight into its origins.

On accounting for the origin of AAE

Research on the origin of AAE is based on comparative data from other varieties of non-standard English, varieties of English in the African diaspora and Caribbean Creoles. As more data have become available from sources such as ex-slave narratives and hoodoo texts, views about the origin of AAE have expanded. The ex-slave narratives used in linguistic research on the origin of AAE are taken from the narrative collection of the Federal Writer's Project, a collection which consists of over 2,000 interviews (from 1936–1938) with ex-slaves from seventeen states. Ewers (1996) analyzes two sets of hoodoo texts that were collected by Harry Middleton Hyatt during the period from 1936–1940 and in 1970. These texts are on the subject of witchcraft and magic, and the texts collected from 1936–1940 include interviews with 1,605 African Americans and one Caucasian, while those collected in 1970 consist of interviews with thirteen African Americans and one Caucasian. Also, see Viereck (1988) for more information on hoodoo texts.

Historical discussions about the origin of AAE often start at the point at which African slaves were thrust into a linguistic situation in which they had to learn English. Some historical accounts of the development of AAE have taken the position that the distinctive patterns of AAE are those which also occur in Niger-Congo languages such as Kikongo, Mande and Kwa. In effect, the view is that AAE is structurally related to West African languages and bears only superficial similarities to general English. See Dalby (1972) and Dunn (1976) for more discussion on this view. More recently, DeBose and Faraclas (1993) discuss AAE from this standpoint. The position is often referred to as the substratist hypothesis because it is argued that the West African or substrate languages influenced the sentence and sound structures of AAE. As Goodman (1993) notes, one characteristic of a substratum "is the subordinate social or cultural status of its speakers vis-à-vis those of the reference language" (p. 65). In this case, the reference language would be English.

One of the most hotly debated issues about the origin of AAE centers around the question of whether AAE started off as a creole such as Jamaican Creole and Gullah, which is spoken in the Sea Islands off the coast of South Carolina and Georgia. The creolist hypothesis has been offered as an explanation of the development of AAE and apparent patterns it shares with creole varieties of English (e.g., Jamaican Creole and Gullah) and with other dialects of English. On the most general account, a creole is a language that develops from a pidgin, simplified means of communication among speakers who do not speak the same languages. Creoles differ from pidgins in that they have native speakers, and they are characterized by a more extensive vocabulary and grammar.

Because of the limited amount of data available on the speech and language of African indentured servants and slaves brought to colonial America and the development of the language of their offspring, linguists have to use a number of different strategies in drawing conclusions about whether AAE was once a creole. For example, linguists have to consider sociohistorical conditions on plantations and factors such as the percentage of Africans to whites, which would have had an effect on the nature of language development. In addition, it is also necessary to study linguistic patterns of creoles and compare them to AAE.

Proponents of the Creolist view note that it is quite possible that slaves from Africa and those imported from the West Indies brought established creoles with them. Rickford (1998) presents a detailed discussion of the issues that come to bear on the creole similarities of AAE. After considering a range of data, he concludes that "there is enough persuasive evidence in these data to suggest that AAVE did have some creole roots" (p. 189). Rickford and Rickford (2000) give an overview of creole patterns in AAE. Another source is *Verb Phrase Patterns in Black English and Creole*, edited by Edwards and Winford (1991), in which one of the themes is that there are interconnections between AAE and creole languages. Also, see Holm (1984) and Singler (1991) regarding these issues.

Other accounts have been cast in an Anglicist or dialectologist frame, maintaining that the characteristic patterns of AAE are actually found in other varieties of English, especially in Southern varieties and earlier stages of English. Linguists supporting the Anglicist view have considered data from speakers in speech communities in Nova Scotia and Samaná (Dominican Republic), areas settled by African Americans during the eighteenth and nineteenth centuries. Settlers in these areas are argued to be good data sources because they may use a variety of English that is very close to the variety used by early Africans in America. Other efforts to link AAE to its original source have led linguists to ex-slave narratives, which consist of recordings of former slaves who were born between 1844 and 1861. Much of the research from this angle is based on quantitative analysis of certain features used to argue that earlier AAE was more closely related to English than to creoles. Poplack (2000) argues that "the grammatical core of contemporary AAVE developed from an English base, many of whose features have since disappeared from all but a select few varieties (African American *and* British origin), whose particular sociohistorical environments have enabled them to retain reflexes of features no longer attested in Standard English (StdE)" (p. 1). See Poplack (2000) and the bibliographies in that volume for references on this view of the origin of AAE. Also, Schneider (1989) argues against the view that earlier AAE was a creole variety.

Mufwene (2000), a work which considers sociohistorical factors, continues to raise questions about the likelihood of AAE developing from a Gullah-like creole. A theme throughout his work is that linguistic and sociohistorical evidence suggests that the language used by founders of colonial America had a large impact on the language of Africans and their descendants. In supporting this founder principle, Mufwene goes on to suggest that Africans who came to the colonies would have had the goal of adapting local norms of the area as opposed to establishing their own. He points to the segregation of community life on plantations in South Carolina and Georgia as an explanation for the development of Gullah but is skeptical about the development of AAE from such a creole. One reason is that the environment in the colonies (other than in South Carolina and Georgia) was not conducive to "the kind of ethnographic contact ecology that could foster the development of a Gullah-like Creole" (p. 245). The view set forth is that AAE and Gullah, as well as North American English varieties, developed concurrently. They selected linguistic features from North American varieties as well as from African languages.

The line in Winford (1997, 1998) is similar in some respects to the creolist view on the one hand and to the view supported by Mufwene on the other. In his words: "The position I adopt in this paper is a compromise between the traditional creolist view and the more moderate dialectologist position . . ." (1997, p. 307). The position that Winford espouses, like the creolist hypothesis, views the emergence of current AAE as a gradual affair. The changes in the language occurred during the seventeenth to nineteenth centuries as the demographics in the Southern colonies changed and as the linguistic contact situations between people of African descent and different groups of settlers changed. The argument here is that AAE was never a creole, but it was created by African slaves. Winford's view is that AAE developed out of contact between Europeans and Africans in the South during the seventeenth century. This variety continued to develop gradually in contact situations with creole varieties and varieties spoken by colonial settlers. Given this view, Africans and their descendants acquired English spoken by settlers in the area, but Winford goes on to argue that the "continuing process of adaptation resulted in a certain degree of substratum influence from other languages spoken by Africans, including African languages and restructured, especially creolized varieties of English" (p. 307). As a result, the variety that we refer to as AAE emerged. In support of this settler principle, Winford gives three kinds of explanations to account for the features that characterize AAE: (1) several features from earlier varieties of English were adopted into AAE, (2) many features appear to have resulted from imperfect second language learning, resulting in simplification or loss of segments such as certain word endings and (3) several features can be explained as a result of retention of creole structure and meaning.

The accounts summarized here are well documented and they continue to be researched. Throughout this book, I point to various linguistic data that can be considered in discussions about the history of AAE, but see the references given here for full discussions of the hypotheses about the origin of AAE and bibliographies of sources on the topic.

1 Lexicons and meaning

Focal point Certain words and phrases have a specialized or unique meaning in AAE: *saditty*, *kitchen*, *pot liquor, get my praise on*. Some of these words and phrases are used by African Americans from a range of age groups, while others are common to speakers of a particular age group. One way of adding phrases to the AAE lexicon is by the productive process in which a word of the appropriate grammatical class such as noun or verb is inserted into a template.

That evening the women brought bowls of pot liquor from black-eyed peas, from mustards, from cabbage, from kale, from collards, from turnips, from beets, from green beans. Even the juice from a boiling hog jowl.

[Toni Morrison, *The Bluest Eye*]

1.1 Introduction

A study of the lexicon and semantics of AAE should reveal information about the type of meaning that is associated with lexical items (words and phrases) in the language system, and it should also reveal information about unique meaning in the variety. The lexicon is the repository for words and phrases in a language system, and semantics refers to the ways in which sounds and meanings are related. The lexicon can be described as an abstract dictionary in which meanings and other information such as pronunciations of words can be found. When speakers know a language system, they have access to the lexicon of that system, so speakers who know AAE know the unique meanings of elements in the lexicon of that system.

The claim that the lexicon of AAE includes items that are unique to it will be explored in this chapter. It is often the case that AAE is characterized in informal terms, at least in part, by the vocabulary that is used by some African American adolescents, teenagers and young adults and that is generally not accepted in the marketplace in mainstream America.[1] This is an important part of the characterization of AAE, but by no means is it the only part. It is impossible to give an accurate description of AAE by focusing only on its unique words, phrases and meanings, but this is a good place to start because it is often easy to identify some of the vocabulary items that are used differently by African Americans.

In the wake of controversy about and interest in AAE and questions about its validity, it is beneficial to engage in a discussion about the content and structure of the lexicon in AAE. The discussions about content naturally focus on what is in an African American lexicon, and the structural description provides information about unique lexical entries and the way they may be stored in the lexicon. In addition, the description should be able to make precise statements about differences between the use of words and phrases in the African American lexicon and that of other varieties. Finally, the description should help us recognize some of the possible sources of misunderstanding that can result when speakers and listeners are not familiar with meanings associated with elements from the African American lexicon. The entries in this lexicon are also English words that occur in other varieties of American English, but they have different meanings and may be used in different linguistic environments. This unique vocabulary brings groups of people together, while it serves as a stratification device between other groups. To be sure, "One of the many fascinating features of black vocabulary is how sharply it can divide blacks and whites, and how solidly it can connect blacks from different social classes" (Rickford and Rickford 2000, p. 93). Later in this chapter, I will present an example from a large lecture class which illustrates how the black vocabulary can divide blacks and whites.

What I have found is that this unique vocabulary can be partitioned into two broad categories: words and phrases used by members of all age groups and those more likely to be identified with members of a certain age group. Class is not a major factor in categorizing the items; however, some of the words and phrases that are currently used by adolescents and young adults do vary from geographical region to region.

Characterizing the lexicon in AAE presents an interesting problem. African Americans from different regions, age groups, educational status and socioeconomic classes will know many of the words and phrases that are discussed in this chapter but may not identify themselves or be identified as AAE speakers. While they may know these unique words and phrases, they may not be as familiar with the syntactic, semantic and phonological properties of AAE. As a result, I will refer to the African American lexicon without claiming that African Americans who use words and phrases from this lexicon are speakers who necessarily use features from the sentence structure and sound systems of AAE. In effect simply using or knowing words from this lexicon does not automatically make a person an AAE speaker, but AAE speakers will necessarily know words and phrases from the black lexicon.

Some studies have been conducted on the acquisition of lexical items by speakers of mainstream English; however, to my knowledge, there are no comparable studies on the acquisition of words and phrases by speakers of AAE.[2] The result is that we have no account of the age at which speakers acquire the unique words and phrases that cross generational boundaries. I am not suggesting that African American children across the United States acquire the meanings of these words and phrases at the same time, though research on this acquisition question would contribute to the work on the African American lexicon in general and AAE in particular.

1.2   Lexicons and AAE: a review of three types

A review of the research on the lexicon of AAE reveals that it has been presented in at least three ways: (1) as a list of lexical items that occur in the variety, (2) as a list of lexical items that are subdivided into thematic topics and (3) as a repository of words, distinct from slang, that are part of the African American community. These different approaches highlight unique lexical items and the way they are used by a group of people, or they focus on the relation between the lexical items and some part of community life.

Major (1994) and Smitherman (1994) represent the first type of lexicon, and the titles of their works serve as introductions. Major compiles words and phrases under the heading of *Juba to Jive: A Dictionary of African-American Slang*, and Smitherman uses *Black Talk: Words and Phrases from the Hood to the Amen Corner*. Both titles suggest that the words and phrases that will be explicated in the books span a considerable time period and are used in secular and religious contexts. "From juba to jive" encompasses the time period from as early as the seventeenth century to the twentieth century. *Juba* refers to a dance performed by a group of slaves (1790s–1900), and *jive*, as it is still used today, refers to cool talk or talk used to put someone on. "From the hood to the amen corner" covers words and phrases that are used in the secular world as well as those used in religious contexts, and includes words and phrases that may be used in both environments. Both approaches show quite convincingly that what is referred to as black talk surpasses the boundaries of the most current lexical usage by teens.

Major classifies all of the words and phrases he lists as slang, noting that "black slang is an American language with distant roots in the ancient coastal tribes of central west Africa, as well as, indirectly, in Anglo-Irish culture and elsewhere" (pp. xxxiii–xxxiv). Anticipating that calling this type of talk slang might suggest that it should not be taken seriously as a means of communication, Major sets out "to help bring to the language we call slang a better name, a better reputation; and also to suggest, by the example of this dictionary, how intrinsic it is to the quest of human culture to express and to renew itself" (p. xxvii). The work invites the reader to consider the semantics and vocabulary of AAE as a component of the AAE grammar that is deeply rooted in African tradition, but that is also very much a part of American culture. He categorizes the vocabulary items into four groups: (1) Southern rural during slavery, (2) slang from 1900–1960 of sinner-man/black musician, (3) street culture, rap and hip-hop, (4) working class. The categorization of these items suggests that members of the AAE community who are from different backgrounds and age groups use Major's slang.

Smitherman (1994) makes a very clear statement about the relationship between participation in different parts of the African American culture and the use of "Black Talk." As she puts it,

Basic in *Black Talk*, then, is the commonality that takes us across boundaries. Regardless of job or social position, most African Americans experience some degree of participation in the life of the COMMUNITY – ... This creates in-group crossover lingo that is understood and shared by various social groups within the race ...

[p. 25].

Smitherman, like Major, emphasizes the unifying nature of "Black Talk," some aspects of which are shared by African Americans who are members of different social groups and networks.

Major (1994) and Smitherman (1994) converge on a number of issues and entries. Consider, for example, the words *ashy*, *kitchen* and *saditty*, which are used by African Americans from all age groups. These three words occur in Smitherman (1977, 1994) and two of them, *kitchen* and *saditty*, appear in Major (1994). In Smitherman (1977), *ashy* is defined as "the whitish coloration of black skin due to exposure to the Hawk (cold and wind)" (p. 67). *Kitchen* is defined as "the hair at the nape of the neck which is inclined to be very kinky" (p. 64), while *saditty* refers to "uppity-acting blacks who put on airs" (p. 68). Smitherman's (1994) update of the AAE lexicon records virtually the same meanings for these words, an indication that they are still used the way they were used when they first entered the lexicon. It should also be noted here that Smitherman (1994) is careful to label what she takes to be older terms, but *ashy*, *kitchen* and *saditty* do not bear that label, another indication that the forms are still used today. While slang is basically ephemeral, these terms have resisted change and remained in the black communities. It is understandable that *ashy* and *kitchen* have remained in black communities, as they refer to type of hair and hue of skin that are associated with blacks; however, it is not immediately clear why *saditty* has not been adopted by others.

The following is evidence that *ashy* is still used today: In June 2000, I ordered a book about natural healing and as a supplement and free gift, I received a pamphlet which explains treatment for conditions that may be specifically associated with dark skin. I randomly flipped to page 19 and found the bold title, "Get ASHY SKIN Glowing Again," with *ashy skin* in capital letters. The article begins as follows:

It's enough to make you want to hide your gorgeous legs under pants: Your shins look as if you've just stepped off a dry, dusty road, not to mention your knees that look as if they're coated with chalk. But you can shed that ashy skin and get the glow back.

THAT AWFUL ASH

'Ashy skin is really a slang term, not something I'd diagnose medically,' says Dr. Herriford. 'But it's a common concern among many of my African-American patients.' Actually, the gray, chalky film we call ash, which most commonly occurs on the arms and legs, can result from two different skin conditions ...

[Shannon Faelton, *Prevention Health Books*, 1999]

I do not know the editors of the section on ashy skin or Dr. Herriford, but I would venture as far as to say that they have had close experience with ash. Their description is vivid and on point and could certainly be used as a definition in a lexicon such as Major's or Smitherman's. The article goes on to describe the dry skin that can result from insufficient oil or accumulation of dead cells. We can infer a strong linguistic point that is made by the editors and physician: The word *ash/ashy* is specifically associated with African Americans and is not widely used outside that group. In addition, the physician labels the word slang, suggesting that, on the one hand, it is not used in the mainstream and that the word does not refer to a threatening skin condition. The article targets African American women (and other women of color) and addresses a general problem that has been labeled by African Americans and that is referred to by speakers from all classes and a range of age groups.

I also found the word *kitchen* in print in a popular magazine. Further confirmation that *kitchen* is used today comes in the form of a segment on hair, "Our Crown," in the December 1999 issue of *Essence*, a magazine for women but with particular appeal to black women. In a reminiscent tone, the relevant line reads: "And girl, if your mama could catch up your kitchen in those tiny plaits, she could find herself braiding everybody's child" (p. 24).

Returning to the discussion of Major's lexicon, we find that the entries which are given below include the part of speech (e.g., n. for noun), time period during which the lexical item was recorded, definition and geographical locations where the words and phrases were most popular.[3]

kitchen n. (1940s) nappy hair around the nape of the neck, especially on women or girls. SU.

[p. 271]

seddity n., adj. (1960s–1980s) bourgeois black person; snobbish and pretentious. SNU.

[p. 391]

Major characterizes *kitchen* as being used mostly by speakers in the South and *seddity* as being used by African Americans in the South and North. The definitions in both Major (1994) and Smitherman (1994) are virtually the same. The difference is in the spelling; Smitherman spells *saddity* with an *a* in the first syllable, while Major spells it with an *e* in the first syllable. Such variations are a result of there not being spelling conventions in AAE, a system that has been used predominantly in oral contexts.

Works such as these are important in that they serve as sources for words and phrases that entered the African American lexicon during different periods and by different methods. They also provide information about words and phrases which are used by African Americans in different parts of the United States and who are of different age groups and social backgrounds. Taken together, these works are a window into a part of the history of the semantic and lexical component of AAE, providing information that helps to draw conclusions about the ways in which parts of the lexicon have changed and remained the same throughout the centuries. On history, Major says that

Not only has there been, historically speaking, geographically determined diversity to African-American slang, but the Africans who made up the language out of Portuguese Pidgin, Bantu, and Swahili, primarily, created what was known early on as Plantation Creole. The persistence of Africanisms in the formation of black slang and African-American culture generally can be seen as a grand testimony to the strength of the human spirit and to the cultural strength of that polyglot group of Africans dumped, starting in 1619, on this continent to work the land . . . Black slang is an *American* language with distant roots in the ancient coastal tribes of central west Africa, as well as, indirectly, in Anglo-Irish culture and elsewhere.

[xxxiii–xxxiv]

One of the differences between the two lexicons is in the time periods they cover. Major's dictionary covers a time period from the seventeenth to twentieth centuries, while Smitherman's terms are argued to be "in current use by Blacks from all walks of life" (p. 39). Perhaps this is why Major includes an entry for *Crow Jane* (1900s–1920s) a black or dark complexioned woman (p. 122), *anigh* (1630s–1890s) close or near and *pot liquor* (1860s–1940s) juice from greens (but not limited to juice from greens as noted in Morrison's use at the beginning of the chapter), and Smitherman does not.

The second type of lexicon, which subdivides lexical items into thematic topics, is exemplified by the work in Folb (1980). This work is not intended to speak in general about AAE, as the research is limited to data collected from black teenagers in south central Los Angeles. Folb's research leads her to conclude that the lexicon of black teenagers has a unifying effect, serving to link teens across geographic and socioeconomic boundaries. She notes:

> My involvement with teenagers who lived in the ghetto and on the Hill suggests that being black in white America is probably the basic connection among blacks across geographic, economic, and linguistic boundaries. There is a well-formed black vernacular lexicon which is known and used by middle-class and ghetto teenagers alike. However, the day-to-day life experiences of the affluent black and the ghetto black are not the same – and even the most politically active or culturally identified young black is not going to know those words and phrases that are 'ghetto-specific' unless he or she lives there.
>
> [p. 201]

The topics that are the major focus of Folb's ethnographic work are name terms in the black community, forms of manipulation, male and female interaction and the vocabulary of drugs. They are argued to reflect the activities in which teenagers are involved and the type of relations they have. The name terms range from those for close associations (e.g., *cuz, play sister*) to outsiders such as the police (e.g., *the man*). Words and phrases that are subsumed under forms of manipulation are related to territorial control and power, and it is under this heading that words used in gang territory and other spatial phenomena fall. For example, Folb includes "throw some blows" as a descriptive term for fight. Concepts of love and sex are included in the section on male and female interaction. This section, like the one for terms in the black community, includes names for males and females alike; however, they often make reference to physical attraction. Folb's study is limited to social use and social interaction, and the factors that are argued to affect the use of these lexical items are age, gender, peer associations, experiences, socioeconomic background and region.

The goal of the third type of lexicon is to distinguish lexical items that belong to the African American community from those that are more closely associated with a particular social domain. Dillard (1977) takes such a distinction to be important and criticizes other lexicons on the basis of not making it. According to him, "To differentiate between a Black lexicon and usage of terms in domains like pimping is perhaps the most important objective not achieved by Major and the others" (p. xiv). To the extent that Dillard's lexicon arranges lexical items into categories, it is similar to the kind of lexicon presented in Folb (1980). It differs from the others in its attempt to separate those items that are a part of the linguistic system of AAE from those that are considered slang. For him, an example of the former terminology would be concepts related to religion and church such as *funeralize*, which means to conduct funeral services.[4] Dillard believes "a great deal of 'Black' slang to belong to the rackets (pimping, prostitution, narcotics hustling, general underworld activities) rather than to the Black community as such" (p. 110). In characterizing the systematic nature of the AAE lexicon, he notes that African American authors William Wells Brown and Charles W. Chesnutt give accurate representations of black vocabulary in their works.[5]

A number of other sources give information about lexical items that are argued to be part of the AAE lexicon, although they do not focus on terms used almost exclusively by African Americans. The *Dictionary of American Regional English* (*DARE*) and several volumes of the *Publication of the American Dialect Society* (*PADS*) identify lexical entries of words that were used by African Americans during certain time periods. The *DARE*, a publication of the American Dialect Society, includes in its volumes from A–O a survey of lexical items and phrases used in the various dialect areas in the United States. Some items in the *DARE* that are identified as being used or having been used by African Americans are *ashy*, *kitchen*, *get over*, *outside child* and *call and sponse* (i.e., *call and response*). *DARE* defines *ashy* as being used by Africans to refer to the whitish color of their skin resulting from dryness or exposure to the cold, and it also cites the explanation from Smitherman (1977). However, it also indicates that the word was used by whites to refer to "the greyish color of the Negro's skin when he is sick or frightened" (vol. I, p. 96). According to *DARE*, *get over* means to succeed, get by or achieve a goal by whatever means necessary and was used exclusively by African Americans in certain areas in the United States (vol. II, p. 665).[6] In addition, the *DARE* makes reference to call and response, a rhetorical strategy used in African American church services (overwhelmingly Baptist) in which the congregation responds to the preacher's call by uttering a short response. This strategy will be discussed in chapter 5, in the section on speech events and African American church services. The following entry is given under *call*: "In a song or rhyme: a solo line or stanza which is followed by a response or refrain – often used in the phrase call and sponse" (vol. I, p. 516). The *DARE* gives every indication that the call and response strategy was strictly tied to religious contexts; however, we know that it is also used in the secular world.

Each volume of the *PADS* is dedicated to some topic related to language use or dialectal patterns. These volumes are not as broad in scope as the *DARE*, but they also provide valuable information about the type of lexical items that were used by African Americans (and other groups) in certain parts of the United States. For instance, *PADS* no. 40 (Babcock 1963) considers lexical items in the works of Zora Neale Hurston that were used by African Americans in the South.[7] Such items are *color struck* or being conceited because of the color of one's skin or having an affinity for certain skin tones and *gospel bird* or chicken, so named because preachers were said to enjoy it as a meal. Other lexical items listed in *PADS* and specifically recorded as being associated with African Americans are *mind* (to mean attention, *He didn't pay me no mind.* 'He didn't pay me any attention,' [no. 6, Woodard 1946]) and *dicty*, *tief*, *ting an' ting* and *yard axe* (no. 14, Bradley 1950). The words from Number 14, as the pronunciations are represented in English orthography, are from Gullah, spoken in South Carolina. *Dicty* is synonymous with *saditty*, as it also means uppity. The verb *tief* means to steal, and the adjective *ting an' ting* means same or exactly alike, as in

Dem two chillun is ting an'ting (p. 67) 'Those children are exactly alike.' *Yard axe* is a noun that refers to a preacher of little ability. *Tote*, to carry, is also one of the words from Gullah that is listed in *PADS* no. 6. Turner (1949), in his study of the African element in Gullah records *tote* as originating from the Kikongo *tota*, which means 'to pick up.'[8]

The overlap in representation of lexical items and phrases and the convergence in meaning of these items in the three types of lexicons represented by Major (1994) and Smitherman (1994) (type 1), Folb (1980) (type 2), Dillard (1977) (type 3) and the *DARE* and *PADS* reinforce the claim that there are lexical items and phrases that are or were used almost exclusively by African Americans. These items, then, are part of the African American lexicon. But in addition to meaning, how much and what type of information should be included in the lexical entry? Should variables such as age, geographical region, socioeconomic class and thematic topic be included? Folb considers age to be an important factor – and naturally so given that her study centers around terms and inner city life – while Major includes as prominent information the time period in which the word or phrase was used in a certain geographical area. Although this information is not explicit in Smitherman's lexical entries, the thread that weaves together the entries in her lexicon is the unifying role of the vocabulary. So as the vocabulary items cross boundaries, variables such as age, class and region are not always paramount although Smitherman recognizes and elaborates on the role of rap and the hip-hop generation, specifically associated with a certain age group.

1.3   Structuring the lexicon

The picture of the African American lexicon that I will present is one that is consistent with the traditional view of lexical entries, one that involves identification of semantic and lexical properties of the linguistic system. By isolating semantic and lexical patterns and showing the environments in which lexical items occur, I will move toward presenting AAE as a system, giving a picture of the way its parts work. In response to the question raised at the end of the preceding section, I think that information indicating age, class and region is important, but it does not have to be redundantly stated for each lexical entry if it is established that the words and phrases cross age, class and regional boundaries. However, those lexical items that are restricted to a specific age group, class or region should be labeled as such.

Information about words and phrases in the AAE lexicon is stored in the brains or mental dictionaries of speakers and retrieved when necessary. African Americans will know some words and phrases that are represented in the African American lexicon, including their meanings and the environments (i.e., place in the sentence) in which they occur, but they will not necessarily know all of them. For example, I did not grow up hearing and using pot liquor, but many African Americans in my age group did.

Discussions about the structure of this mental dictionary of black vocabulary can lead to very complicated questions that would take us too far afield in this study, but it is worthwhile to raise certain issues. African Americans will know words and phrases in the African American lexicon, but they will also have access to the general

American English lexicon. In such cases, do speakers have two lexicons, one for African American-specific words and phrases and another for general American English, or do they have only one lexicon in which both groups of words and phrases are listed?[9] Whatever the structure, the African American and general American English lexicons vary in that there are lexical items that sound the same but have different meanings. For example, the word *kitchen* is used by African Americans in the same way it is used commonly by other speakers of American English, but it is also used uniquely by African Americans to refer to the hair at the nape of the neck. Other examples would be *mannish* and *womanish* which could be used to refer to characteristics of a man and characteristics of a woman, respectively, the general American English definitions. However, these words can also be used to refer to boys and girls, respectively, who are seen as behaving inappropriately for their young ages. These terms, in the sense of the African American lexicon, usually carry negative connotations in that they refer to a type of mature behavior that is unbecoming of children. But they do not always have to be negative. For example, *mannish* can be used to describe the behavior of a baby or young boy who is particularly advanced or independent for his age. A baby boy who figures out how to get his bottle from a hard-to-reach place can also be called *mannish*.

The African American lexicon includes the same type of information that is found in general American lexicons. The difference is that the former lexicon will have entries for words that sound like words in general American English; however, the meanings and perhaps other information will be different from the corresponding homonyms in general American English lexicons.

I am suggesting that the following four types of information be given in lexical entries: pronunciation, grammatical class or part of speech, linguistic environment (i.e., place in a sentence) in which the word or phrase occurs and meaning. In the examples in (1), I illustrate these four types of information by using lexical entries from the African American lexicon. Immediately following the lexical entries, I present grammatical and acceptable as well as unacceptable sentences in which the word or phrase is used. Glosses are also given to show the meaning correspondences between that in the African American lexicon and mainstream and other varieties of English. The symbol '#' indicates a possible meaning, but not the meaning that corresponds to the definition in the entry, and the symbol '*' indicates that the sentence is ill-formed; the combination of words violates the specifications in the African American lexicon. The following abbreviations are used: Prep (preposition), V (verb), V-*ing* (verb ending in -*ing*, e.g., *singing*), V-*ed* (verb ending in -*ed*, e.g., *watched* or an irregular past tense verb, e.g., *broke*), N (noun), Adj (adjective), Adv (adverb), VM (verbal marker), Asp (aspect), AspM (aspectual marker). Aspect will be mentioned later in this chapter in connection with verbal markers and discussed in chapter 2.

The lexical entries in (1) give the phonetic representations of the words, showing how they are pronounced, and the grammatical class or part of speech to which they belong.[10] They also include the linguistic environment(s) in which the term can occur, that is, whether it precedes a verb or a member of another grammatical class. The line (——) indicates where the lexical element occurs with respect to other elements. The environment is represented as being either obligatory or optional. If the following grammatical class (e.g., verb, adverb, noun) indicating the environment is in parentheses '( ),' it is optional, but if it is not in parentheses, it is obligatory. In cases in which the lexical item can precede elements from different grammatical classes, those classes are indicated in curly brackets '{}.' For example, *stay* can precede an adverb, preposition, verb or adjective, as shown in (1g). In a given sentence, it must occur in an environment in which it precedes a word from one of those classes. Finally, the lexical entries provide definitions for each word or phrase in the lexicon. I provide glosses or sentences in mainstream English for corresponding sentences with terms from the African American lexicon.

(1) Lexical entries for terms in the African American lexicon
   a. *get over* [gɪt ovə] V, — (Prep-*on*). Take advantage of, to succeed by using wit but little effort.
      (1) #The students tried to get over the teacher.
         (This sentence has an acceptable reading, but not one that is consistent with the definition in the lexical entry).
      (2) The students tried to get over on the teacher.
      (3) The students tried to get over.
         Gloss: The students tried to take advantage of the teacher. For example, the students tried to outsmart the teacher by submitting a two-page assignment that was double-spaced as opposed to single-spaced.

   The phrase *get over*, meaning to take advantage of someone or a situation, is a verb unit that is composed of a verb plus a preposition or particle element. The unit precedes the preposition *on* if it is not at the end of the sentence.

   b. *call – self* [kɔl sɛəf] V, — {V-*ing*, Noun, Adj}. In the opinion of others, making an attempt to do something (or be someone or something) but not quite doing it as the observer thinks it should be done; an observation that the person is not meeting perceived standards.
      (1) She call herself a queen.[11] (cf. #She call herself the queen.)
      (2) He call hisself cooking.
         Gloss: He thinks he's cooking, but he's merely playing around in the kitchen. That is, he isn't doing anything remarkable.
      (3) He call hisself a basketball player, and can't even dribble the ball.
      (4) They call theyselves friendly, and they won't speak to people.[12]

   In the phrase *call -self*, *my-*, *her-*, *his-*, *they-* are always attached to *-self*, depending on the subject. The pronoun (e.g., *my*, *her*, *his*, *they*) in the *call -self* phrase agrees in gender and number with the subject. This means that in the case of a plural third person subject i.e., *they*, the reflexive pronoun (pronoun which ends in *-self*) *theyself* (*theyselves*) will be used: *Them boys call theyselves playing basketball*. In the case of the singular third person feminine subject (*she*), *herself* will be used.
   In considering the meaning of *call -self*, note that the sentence #She call herself the *queen* involves a different use of *call -self*, thus it is flagged by '#.' As indicated by the meaning in the lexicon, *call herself* cannot simply be used to mean that a person uses

a particular title, such as queen, to refer to herself. In all of the grammatical sentences for this particular use of *call -self*, the phrase is used to express disapproval about a person's actions or perceived attitudes. (Also see Wolfram [1994] for a discussion of *call -self*.)

c. *come* [kʌm] VM,— V-*ing*. Expresses speaker indignation.

#They came carrying their suitcases and books.

(This sentence has a grammatical reading but not one in which *come* necessarily indicates speaker indignation.)

(1) He come walking in here like he owned the damn place. (Spears 1982, p. 852)
(2) We sitting there talking, and he come hitting on me for some money. (Spears 1982, p. 854)
(3) He come coming in here, raising all kind of hell. (Spears 1982, p. 854)
(4) Don't come telling me all those lies.
(5) I asked him if there were any other malls around here, and he come naming all those other ones that are far out. (bf, 30s)
(6) I called him in November when I was in Chicago, and he never called me back. Then like January, he come calling me. (bm, 30s)
Gloss: . . . In January, he had the nerve to call me.

The marker *come* is discussed in Spears (1982) and Baugh (1988), and it is taken to be a semi-auxiliary in that it shares at least one property with auxiliary verbs: it precedes main verbs ending in -*ing*. It is referred to here as a verbal marker. *Come* in the first sentence in (c) is used in the appropriate linguistic environment (i.e., preceding V-*ing*) specified in the entry, but it does not have the meaning in which it expresses speaker indignation. Also, *come*, in this example, is used in the past form (*came*), which is not usually the case in sentences in which it is used as a verbal marker. Here *came* simply means movement into an office, thus the sentence is flagged with '#'.

d. *mash* [mæʃ] V, — {N, Prep} to press something.
(1) Mash the button again so the elevator will come to this floor.
(2) Mash the accelerator all the way to the floor.
Gloss: Press the accelerator all the way to the floor.

The verb *mash* is used to mean press or apply light pressure to an object to achieve results, as in pressing a button to call the elevator to a certain floor. In the examples in (d), *mash* does not mean to crush or destroy. This item is used by speakers of African descent, and it is also used by white speakers in the Southern United States.[13]

e. -*own*- [on] Adj, Pronoun — self, qualifier, intensifier for reflexive pronoun.
(1) *I don't know what's wrong with herownself.
(2) She don't know what's wrong with herownself. How can she help me?
(3) He cooked his food hisownself.
(4) I don't need any help; I can do it myownself.
(5) Let them clean it theyownselves.
Gloss: Let them clean it all by themselves.

The infix *own* serves as an intensifier that expresses the independence of someone or reinforces the individuality of a person in taking responsibility for an action. The intensifier is inserted or infixed (thus it is called an infix) in the environment between the two parts of a reflexive pronoun (e.g., *her-OWN-self*). The reflexive pronoun has to agree with or match the pronoun to which it refers (see *call -self* in (b)). The reflexive *herownself* does not match the pronoun *I* in the first example sentence (instead, it matches *she*), so it is ungrammatical.

f. *some* [sʌm] Adv,— {Adj, Adv}, very; to a great extent. Southern United States.
   Note: The adverb *some* is generally pronounced with stress.
   #I really want some candy.
   (This sentence has an acceptable reading but not one in which *some* occurs in the environment above.)
   (1) Kareem Abdul Jabar is some tall.
   (2) She can cook some good.
       Gloss: She can cook very well.

As an adverb, *some* serves to indicate the extremity of a state or action; it has the meaning of *very*.

g. *stay* [ste] V, VM,— {Adv, Prep, Verb, Adj}. (1) Live; abide in a place. (2) To frequent a place. (3) To engage in activity frequently. (4) To be in some (emotional) state on most occasions.
   #They stay for a long time.
   (The sentence has an acceptable reading, but not one that is in line with the meaning above.)
   (1) I stay on New Orleans Street.
       Gloss: I live on New Orleans Street.
       Gloss: I always go on New Orleans Street.
   (2) She stay in that bathroom.
   (3) She stay running.
   (4) He stay in the air.
       Gloss: He's a frequent flyer; he travels by airplane regularly.
   (5) He stay hungry.
       Gloss: He's always hungry.

The word *stay*, a verb (or verbal marker) which precedes either an adverb, preposition, verb or adjective, can be used to mean to live in/at a place, or it can be used to express habitual meaning, as in sentences (2–4).[14] If a person says *He stay hungry*, the meaning is that the person is often hungry. *Stay*, as it is used in the first sentence (#*They stay for a long time*), has a meaning that is different from the ones given in the definition; the sentence is not acceptable given the specified meaning, so it is flagged by '#'.

h. *steady* [stɛdI], [stʌdI] VM,— V(-*ing*). Has function of indicating that an action or process specified by the verb is carried out in an intense, consistent and continuous manner.

Notes: The subject of the sentence cannot be an indefinite phrase that consists of the article *a* followed by a noun. (*A person was steady talking.)

The verb cannot indicate a state; it has to indicate an action. (*He steady having money.)

(1) Ricky Bell be steady steppin' in them number nines.[15] (Baugh 1984, p. 4)

(2) He steady be tellin' 'em how to run they lives. (Baugh 1984, p. 4)

(3) All the homeboys be rappin' steady. (Baugh 1984, p. 4)

(4) Her mouth is steady runnin'. (Baugh 1984, p. 4)

   Gloss: She is talking nonstop.

(5) When I would talk to her, she wouldn't pay me any attention.

   She would just steady drive.

Steady, a verbal marker that precedes a V-(*ing*), is used to describe the manner in which something is done. In the first ungrammatical sentence (**A person was steady* *talking*), *steady* adheres to the specification in the lexicon in that it precedes a verb that ends in -*ing*, so we must look elsewhere for the source of unacceptability. As the 'Notes' indicate, the problem is the indefinite subject with the weak determiner *a* (*a person*).[16] The second sentence in the 'Notes' (**He steady having money*) is ungrammatical because the verb *having* indicates a state and not an activity such as talking or running. Although *steady* usually precedes verbs ending in -*ing*, it can also follow them, in some cases, as shown in the third example sentence. In addition, *steady* can also precede verbs that do not end in -*ing*, as in the environment in (5). (Also, see Baugh [1984, 1999] for a discussion of *steady*.) *Steady* is like the verbal marker *come* in that it precedes V-*ing*, but it also differs from *come*, as it can occur in other environments.

Lexical entries are important because they provide necessary information for the correct pronunciation and use of words and phrases. The view is from the African American lexicon, so only items that are used 'uniquely' by African Americans are discussed here. As AAE shares patterns with other varieties of English, some words in the mental dictionaries of African Americans have the same meanings they have in other varieties of English. For example, in varieties of English, the word *steady* can be used as an adjective to mean sure in movement or lack of interruption of movement. Likewise it can have this meaning in the African American lexicon. As such African Americans may use the *steady* as in (h), and they may also use the *steady* that occurs in other varieties of English.

In a brief review of the lexical entries in (1a–h), note that only major categories have been indicated for the entries, so a number of subtle constraints and properties have been omitted or just briefly mentioned. For instance, the definiteness constraint on the subject in *steady* constructions is mentioned in a brief note under the entry for *steady* and in a footnote. Here the definiteness constraint simply refers to the preference for using *steady* with definite subjects (e.g., *the girl*) as opposed to indefinite subjects (e.g., *a girl*).

Verbal markers, which are often discussed in the literature on AAE, are not generally included in discussions of African American lexicons and dictionaries.[17] As the markers often express unique meanings, they should be indicated in the lexicon of AAE. The syntax of these markers will be discussed in chapter 2, but their lexical entries are given below. Without going into too much detail, I give some corresponding mainstream English sentences in single quotes ('') as a means of elucidating the meaning for those who are not familiar with the verbal markers. These verbal markers in AAE indicate certain properties about the way an event is carried out or completed. The markers that will be represented in the African American lexicon here are *be*, *BIN*, *dən*, *be dən* and *BIN dən*.[18]

(2)   Lexical entries for verbal markers
      a. *be* [bi], AspM— {V-*ing*, V-*ed*, Adj, Prep, N, Adv, AspM, end of sentence}. Marks the recurrence of an eventuality.[19]
         (1) *They be wake up too early.
         (2) They be waking up too early.
             'They usually wake up too early'
         (3) Half of them things that be showed on TV don't be happening.
             'It's usually the case that half of the things that are shown on TV do not happen' (Green 1998a, p. 52)
         (4) Those shoes be too expensive.
             'Those shoes are usually too expensive'
         (5) I think the puppies be in the garage sometimes.
         (6) When we play school, he be the teacher.
         (7) Call whenever you want to; they always be there.
         (8) They be den finished the aerobics session.
         (9) That's the way they be.
      b. *BIN* [bín], AspM— {V-*ing*, V-*ed*, Adj, Prep, N, Adv, AspM}. Situates the eventuality or the initiation of the eventuality in the remote past.
         Note: The verbal marker *BIN* is pronounced with stress, as indicated by the accent over the symbol 'ɪ' (í).
         (1) *They BIN is early.
         (2) They BIN waking up too early.
             'They have been waking up too early for a long time'
         (3) They BIN left.
             'They left a long time ago'
         (4) The shoes at that store BIN too expensive.
             'The shoes at that store have been too expensive for a long time'
         (5) I think the puppies BIN in the garage.
         (6) He BIN a teacher.
         (7) They BIN there.
         (8) They BIN dən left.
      c. [dən], AspM— V-*ed*, marks a completed eventuality or an eventuality that is over (occurred in the past).
         Note: The verbal marker *dən* is pronounced with an unstressed or weak vowel, which is indicated by the schwa (ə). It is distinguished from the pronunciation of *done* (in which the vowel is stressed) in the sentences *The food is done* and *She (has) done her homework*.

(1) *They dən leaving.

(2) They dən left.

d. *be dən* [bi dən], AspM— V-*ed*, (1) marks an eventuality as having ended by some point in the future. (2) marks an eventuality as habitually having ended by some time. (3) indicates a conditional meaning.

(1) *They be dən leaving.

(2) They'a be dən left by the time I get there (definition 1).

'They will have already left by the time I get there'

(3) They be dən left when I get there (definition 2).

'They have usually already left by the time I get there'

(4) They be dən stole your seat before you know it (definition 3).

'They will steal your seat as soon as they have the opportunity'

e. *BIN dən* [bín dən], AspM— V-*ed* marks an eventuality as having ended by some point in the remote past.

(1) The instructors BIN dən left.

'The instructors left a long time ago'

The lexical entries for the verbal markers in (2) provide the same type of information (phonetic representation, grammatical class, syntactic environment in which the marker occurs, meaning) that is given in the entries for the words and phrases in (1). 'AspM' stands for aspectual marker, a term that is used to characterize these markers and that will be discussed in chapter 2. Examples of grammatical and ungrammatical (flagged by '*') uses of the markers are also given. I will return to a more detailed discussion of these markers and relevant examples in chapter 2, in which their semantic and syntactic properties will be discussed. Also, in chapter 2, it will become clear that the lexical entries for *be dən* (2d) and *BIN dən* (2e) may be redundant because the second meaning of *be dən* given in definition 2 can be derived from the compositional meaning of *be* and *dən*, and the meaning of *BIN dən* can be derived from the compositional meaning of *BIN* and *dən*. In that chapter, I will explain the conditions under which the verbal marker *be* can precede a verb ending in -*ed* (e.g., *be watched*).

The section of the African American lexicon for verbal markers such as those in (2) is the locus of elements which have unique verbal properties in AAE. This is one area in which the African American lexicon differs from lexicons of other varieties of American English: it includes elements that mark the way events are carried out. For example, in AAE the verbal marker *be* can be used to show that an event occurs from time to time, and the verbal marker *BIN* can be used to talk about an event that started in the distant past. Mainstream American English and other varieties of American English use adverbs such as *always* and *usually* to convey the meaning contributed by *be*, and they use phrases such as 'a long time ago' and 'for a long time' to convey the meaning associated with *BIN*. It is interesting to note that Hiberno English (a variety of Irish English) uses *be* in ways that are similar to the uses in AAE, a point that will be explored in chapter 2.

The next section considers slang in the African American lexicon, lexical items that are associated with a particular age group and also with different geographical areas.

1.4   Slang: adding words to the lexicon

"In a culture driven by the ever-evolving slanguistics of rapspeak, 'whoa!' is to modern hip hop vernacular what prime-time game shows are to TV land: something so old fashioned that it's new again" (Mao 2000, p. 161). Black Rob, who uses the term *whoa* in his single "Whoa!" defines the word in a 2000 *Vibe* article in the following way: "There's nothin' else that you can say; when something is lookin' so good for you, it's just 'whoa!'" (p. 161). *Whoa* is one of the lexical items that is found in that part of the African American lexicon in which words and phrases are used by speakers in a particular age group, may vary from geographical region to geographical region and may be short lived. Finally, a large number of these lexical items originate in and are perpetuated through hip-hop culture, including music.

Attempting to give an account of slang in any work presents very interesting challenges. Perhaps the most formidable problem is that slang changes rapidly, so it is virtually impossible to give an accurate account of current slang items. It is certain that by the time this book is completed, many of the lexical items that are presented in this section will be obsolete. When I first started collecting information for a project related to this book in the early to mid 1990s, *phat* (adjective meaning extremely nice, good looking or of good taste) was popular among African American adolescents, teens and young adults. In 1999 and probably long before that, the word was no longer popular according to students in a large introductory lecture class in African and Afro-American studies. In the fall of 1999, I gave a guest lecture on the topic of AAE in that class and found that black and non-black students differed in their recognition and classification of words in the African American lexicon. For example, black students gave the correct definition of *saditty*, and while *phat* was taken to be in vogue by some white students, none of the black students shared this view or at least admitted to sharing it. Another point that the *saditty* and *phat* examples make is that these lexical items often divide blacks and whites, as noted by Rickford and Rickford (2000, p. 93).

The goal of this section is not to give a complete account of current slang. However, it is to use some selected examples to make two points about that part of the lexicon that constantly changes: (1) Slang items can be divided into categories and (2) new slang items can be added to the lexicon by applying productive processes of creating phrases. These two points can be illustrated just as well with items that are no longer in use, but more current words and phrases will be used in the discussion.

1.4.1   Labeling people, money, and actions

In a discussion of language used by adolescents, Teresa Labov (1992) notes three categories of slang: (1) those for labeling people, (2) those for painting people, activities and places positively or negatively and (3) those for ways of spending leisure time, focused upon having fun. Teresa Labov's data are based on responses to a questionnaire that was completed by adolescents from different high schools in the United States. In one part of her data analysis, she compared the use of slang by whites and African Americans, and found that of the thirty-three slang terms (in the speech of her informants) that show significant social difference "eight show 2.5 times or greater likelihood of African-American usage, and 25 at least three times or greater white usage. Social types account for five African-American terms (*bougies, homies, mondos, freaks,* and *rednecks*); *fresh* and *bad* in 'approval' sense; and the phrase *to be busting out* 'looking good'" (p. 351). Teresa Labov's data are consistent with Rickford and Rickford's claim that such vocabulary items serve as dividing lines between the groups.

   More current terms fit into the same types of categories discussed by Teresa Labov. One of the largest categories for slang terms today is that for referring to people. Folb (1980) also reported this finding in her ethnographic research on the use of specialized vocabulary by adolescent African Americans. The slang terms in (3) are used to refer to females, and those in (4) are used to refer to males:

(3)   Terms for females
   a. bopper
   b. dime
   c. honey
   d. hot girl
   e. ma
   f. shorty
   g. wifey

(4)   Terms for males
   a. balla
   b. cat
   c. cuz
   d. dawg (also dog)
   e. fool
   f. homes
   g. hot boy
   h. kinfolk
   i. mark
   j. money
   k. player (playa)
   l. scrub
   m. slick

The first observation is that the list for females is shorter than that for males. The term *bopper* is used to refer to a woman who is preoccupied with material gain, and a term that has come to have a similar meaning is *chickenhead*. Although women may use general terms (e.g., *girl*, in *Hey, girl*) to address each other, the names in (3) are not used in that way; they are labels for females. On the other hand, the majority of the terms in (4) are used by males as terms of address for other males. Two exceptions are the terms *balla* and *scrub*. *Balla* is used to refer to a man who has acquired money and material possessions, and *scrub*, which is derogatory, refers to a male who is not self-sufficient, so he depends on others for his livelihood. The term *dog* also has a negative connotation when it is used to refer to a male who mistreats females, but *dog/dawg* is used by males as a term of address, without negative import.

The terms for males (4) may be used as common nouns or as terms of address, and, as the latter, they share some properties of names.[20] Consider the term *money* (4j), which can be used as a common noun (5a) and as a term of address (5b).

(5)   a. That's my money (as in That's my friend).
       b. What's up, money? (as in What's up, man/Bruce?)

According to some males who use this term, *money* cannot be used in all the ways in which a common noun such as *man* can be used. For example, the following is not acceptable: #*Look at that money* (cf. *Look at that man*). The same is true for *slick* and *homes*: #*Look at that slick standing over there* (cf. *Look at that guy standing over there.*). #*Look at that homes* (cf. *Look at that guy.*). Although I have not conducted extensive research on the different constraints on uses of these items, one suggestion is that they cannot occur in this environment because they may be used most often in cases in which males are familiar with each other. As such, the sentence #*Look at that slick standing over there* may be unacceptable because it makes reference to an unfamiliar male. One possible indirect argument against this hypothesis, however, is given in Brathwaite (1992), in which it is noted that *homes* is also used in addressing someone whose name one does not know.[21] Also, the terms *dawg* and *money* (see (5a)) can be used in possessive noun phrases ('my dawg,' 'my money'):

(6)   a. That's my dog.
       b. That's my money.

But this is not a general rule that can be applied to all terms for males. The use in (7) is unacceptable:

(7)   #That's my slick.

There are also regional twists on labels for people. The members of the New Orleans-based rap group Cash Money have filled their lyrics with terms and phrases that are now associated with that geographical area. So for a member of Cash Money, his dawg or comrade is whoadie.

As is apparent in current hip-hop music, another category to which terms are frequently added is money (as in currency). One of the rappers from the hip-hop group OutKast makes his point by using three terms for money in the course of a sentence. He says, "I want greens, bills, dividends is what I'm talking about" ("Git Up, Git Out"). Other terms for money are given in (8):

(8)   Terms for money
       a. benjis (benjamins)
       b. cabbage
       c. cheese
       d. cream

    e. duckets

    f. franklins

    g. paper

    h. scrilla

Brathwaite (1992) lists at least eight terms for money, with only one being cross-listed with a term in (8): *bucks, dead presidents, dime, paper, cash money, dividends, dough* and *knot*. *Dime* and *knot* have more specialized meanings, in which the former refers to ten dollars, and the latter refers to a wad of money.

    One recurrent theme in rap and hip-hop is material gain, and to that end, terms for material possessions, in addition to money, are used robustly. Two such terms are *ice*, which refers to diamonds, and *bling bling*, which can be used broadly to refer to jewelery or platinum. The latter term is the title of a single in which the artist attests that guys wear jewelery that is "the price of a mansion round [their] neck and wrist" ("Bling Bling," B.G.).

    A very broad category that can be subdivided into groups according to topics is that for lexical items referring to actions. Included in the list of terms for actions are (1) Terms for leaving: *bounce, push off, murk*; (2) Terms for expressing or showing envy: *playa hatin* (or *hatin, hatin on*), *balla blockin*; (3) Terms for communicating or connecting: *feel, we're here* (with gesture pointing to eyes); (4) Terms for making advances toward a member of the opposite sex: *push up on, get wit(h), holler at that, sweatin*; (5) Terms for labeling that which is good, exciting, etc.: *off the hook/chain, krunk* (used in the South in the early 1990s and revived in 2000), *banging, too stupid.*

    The next subsection considers a productive process which is used to coin phrases that mean to engage in some activity.

1.4.2   Productive process of adding elements to the lexicon

A common phrase that was used in the early to mid 1990s is *get your groove on* to mean to get something going, as in dance. The phrase has become extremely productive, not necessarily by using words to mean dance, but by inserting different words in the phrase, as indicated below:

(9)   *get* – possessive pronoun – noun – *on*
        'to become engaged in some activity'
        a. get my chill on
           'to rest'
        b. get my drink/sip on
           'to drink'
        c. get my eat/grub on
           'to eat'
        d. get my mac (mack) on (usually refers to males toward females)
           'to engage in acts such as dancing with numerous partners, getting phone numbers, etc.'

e. get my praise on
  'to praise or worship'
f. get my sleep on
  'to sleep'

Forming phrases based on the template in (9) has become a productive process to create phrases used to express the meaning 'to become engaged in some activity.' The general rule is to insert a word that can be used as a verb in the position following the possessive pronoun and preceding *on*. The phrase (*get* – possessive pronoun – noun – *on*) is used as a verb and consists of four elements: the verb *get*, a possessive pronoun (usually *my* or *your*, but other possessive pronouns can occur here), the inserted verb (e.g., *sleep*) which is also used as a noun in the phrase and the preposition or particle *on*. What is of interest here are the words that name the actions and that are inserted between the possessive pronoun and *on*. The words *chill* (a), *drink/sip* (b), *eat/grub* (c), *mack* (d), *praise* (e) and *sleep* (f) are commonly used as verbs to name some type of action (e.g., *Jack **eats** apples*, *It's easy to **sip** this shake with this wide straw*, *I just want to **chill** for a minute*). But when these verbs occur in the phrase in the position of the 'X' in *get my X on*, they must be used as nouns because they follow the possessive pronoun *my*. A word that follows a possessive pronoun is a noun, as in *my **shoes***, *your **house***, *his **table*** and *her **book***.

The get-my/your-X-on phrases are attested in everyday speech and in the media such as television and radio. They also occur in print in magazines such as *Essence*. For example, the following line appears in one of the articles in the leisure section of the January 2000 issue: "Michelle chills at the Spa Atlantis, where she got her hydrotoning on" (Burford 2000, p. 116). Obviously, the reference is to a woman who engaged in the activity of hydrotoning at the Spa Atlantis. Also, the hip-hop group Cash Money plays on the productivity of this construction in the single "Get Your Roll On," a song that encourages listeners to go out and do what is pleasing to them. In the video, people get their roll on by 'rolling' in expensive cars, those that are nice or off the chain, such as the Bentley and Lamborghini.

Summary

The general picture of the African American lexicon that has been developed here is one that is broadly sectioned into three components: (1) general words and phrases that cross generational boundaries and are likely to span regional and class boundaries, (2) verbal markers and (3) current slang items used by adolescents and young adults. These components are summarized in the figure below: Each component can be further subdivided into more narrowly defined categories, and in addition to pronunciation, grammatical class, linguistic environment and meaning, specialized meaning (e.g., whether the lexical item is used in or originated in a particular region) will be indicated in the lexicon, as indicated in the entry for *whoadie*. Obviously, the African American lexicon differs from lexicons of other varieties of English in that it combines a range of lexical items or meanings that are not included in other English lexicons.

GENERAL WORDS AND PHRASES	
saditty, [sədIDi], Adj __ (N). Conceited.	(1) cross generational boundaries (2) used in religious and secular environments (3) reflect relationship between AAE and West African languages (e.g., Turner 1949)
VERBAL MARKERS	indicate way eventuality is carried out
BIN [bŒn], AspM __(V-*ing*, V-*ed*, Adj, Prep, N, Adv, AspM). Situates the eventuality or the initiation of the eventuality in the remote past.	
CURRENT SLANG	associated with age group linked to popular culture; may be associated with a particular region
whoadie [wodi], N __. Comrade (New Orleans usage).	

Sketch of the African American lexicon

However, one of the most notable differences may be the inclusion of the verbal markers (e.g., *be dən*) that indicate the way an event is carried out. An important observation is that the vocabulary can serve as sharp dividing lines between groups of people, as noted by Rickford and Rickford (2000) and Teresa Labov (1992) and exemplified in the responses from the large lecture class.

Two of the goals of this inquiry about the nature of the African American lexicon are simply to show that the lexical items which have unique meaning may be compartmentalized in certain ways and that the African American lexicon does not just consist of slang. An interesting complication is that African Americans must also have access to a lexicon that includes words in general American English, many of which are homophonous with words in the African American lexicon. The more general goal is to present AAE as a unified system with a lexical component as well as other components, and the first step to that end was to explain what is meant by the African American lexicon and to present the type of information that speakers know when they know elements from it.

Exercises

1. The *Dictionary of American Regional English* (*DARE*) presents information about regional dialect forms. Consult the *DARE* as a means of researching the following lexical items:

    a) ashy
    b) be (verbal marker)
    c) get over

Now that you have read the entries for the terms, present a general discussion (not to exceed two pages) about them. Include in your discussion meaning, geographical area in which the item was used and speakers who used the item. What types of patterns emerge from the data (e.g., Do the speakers who use the lexical items live in a certain region? Are the speakers members of certain age groups?).

2. Name another category (in addition to labels for people and money) for slang terms in AAE and give examples of the items that fall under it. Do speakers of other varieties of English use different (or any) slang items in this category? If so, what are the slang items?

3. What are other tests that can be used to determine the grammatical class of the Noun (X) in the phrase get-my-X-on? It has already been noted that nouns follow possessive pronouns. What are some other ways of proving that the element in the position of 'X' is a noun?

4. Conduct an informal survey to determine whether there are current terms for money in the AAE lexicon that are not on the list in (8) or mentioned in this chapter. What are they?

5. In this chapter, it was noted that *saditty* has basically remained in African American communities. Conduct an informal survey targeted to people who may, as well as to those who may not, have ties to African American communities to determine whether this is the case. What definitions for *saditty* did respondents in your survey give?

2 Syntax part 1: verbal markers in AAE

Focal point   Part of knowing a word involves knowing how to use it in sentences. As explained in the preceding chapter, speakers of AAE use some of the same words that occur in other varieties of English, but they may use them with different meanings. In addition, these words must occur in specific environments in a sentence. For example, the verbal marker *be* can precede words from any grammatical class such as verb (*That computer be **crashing***), adjective (*Those computers be **light***) and preposition (*Her computer be **in** her carry on bag*). On the other hand, the verbal marker *dən* can only precede verbs (*They dən **bought** all the sale books*).

Jesus is mine;
Jesus is mine;
Everywhere I go,
Everywhere I be,
Jesus is mine.

[from a gospel song]

2.1 Introduction

The preceding chapter characterizes a part of the system of AAE, the lexical component. In continuing to put the pieces together to form a complete picture of the AAE system in this chapter, I present a description of verbal markers and try to make explicit how they fit into the syntactic component. Many of the well-known features of AAE are from the syntactic component of the language system, that part of the system that deals with the way words are put together to form sentences. In many cases, words in AAE that are identical or quite similar in pronunciation to words in other varieties of English are used differently and may combine with other words in sentences in different ways. Speakers of mainstream English identify the AAE uses as being different from general English, and they label them as ungrammatical uses of English that make African Americans sound unintelligent.

Some of the defining syntactic features of AAE are argued to coincide with syntactic features of other varieties of English such as Southern States English in the United States and Hiberno English in Ireland, for example. In general, there is validity to this claim, especially if we are simply comparing a list of features from each dialect of English, such as the following: the marker *dən* is used in AAE and in Southern States English, and the verbal marker *be* is used in AAE and in Hiberno English. But in making these comparisons, it is important to move beyond listing superficial similarities between AAE and other varieties to testing whether elements such as the verbal markers *dən* and *be* exhibit the same patterns in AAE and these other varieties.

One well established syntactic feature of AAE is the use of the verbal marker *be* to signal the habitual occurrence of an event.[1] The feature is very common and has been used to show how AAE differs from other varieties of English, and it has also been used as the topic of jokes and derogatory remarks about AAE and its speakers. Ironically, this *be* is often used incorrectly by the same people who try to show that what is taken as AAE is illogical speech. Also, misleading characterizations of the verbal marker were given in newspaper and magazine articles written during discussions about the Oakland Ebonics case in 1997. In an article in *The New Yorker*, Louis Menand explains that *be* is used "to indicate a habitual condition, as in 'Johnny be good,' meaning 'Johnny is a good person'" (p. 5). The definition that Menand gives is correct, but the characterization, in particular the explanation of the example, provides little insight into the meaning indicated by *be*. In simple terms, it is unlikely that the meaning of *Johnny be good* is 'Johnny is a good person.' In spite of the inaccurate representations, this *be* is used quite systematically in AAE in sentences such as those in the focal point and in the gospel song by Donnie McClerkin referenced at the beginning of this chapter. In the song, "everywhere I be" refers to different places I go or usually am, such as home, work, the mall, gas station, school, grocery store, vacation, dentist's office, basketball games, conferences, church, etc. So the verbal marker *be* is quite effective in this song in that it helps to convey the contrast between humans and Jesus. Humans never stay in the same place and they are always changing, but Jesus is constant.

Although sentences with the verbal marker *be* adhere to rules of AAE, they are not acceptable as school or professional language. This is one of the reasons why it is important to get the meaning, use and syntactic environment of the verbal marker right. For instance, if a teacher is concerned with providing accurate mainstream English correspondences for sentences in which AAE speakers use *be*, then it is useful to know the correct properties of the verbal marker. Specific rules govern the systematic occurrence of words and phrases in AAE as they do in other languages and dialects.

This chapter discusses the properties of auxiliaries and verbal markers such as *be*, *dən* and *steady*. It explains that auxiliaries in AAE are used in the ways in which they are used in mainstream (and other varieties of) English. In addition, it gives a description of the use of verbal markers, which separates AAE and mainstream (as well as other varieties of) English.

2.2   Auxiliaries

Auxiliary verbs *have*, *do*, *be* and modals such as *will/would*, *shall/should*, *can/could* and *may/might* will be the focus of this section. Auxiliary *be* refers to the forms *is*, *am*, *are*, *was* and *were* and is distinguished from the verbal marker *be* highlighted in the introduction to this chapter. Specific properties that will be explained and illustrated in the next three subsections differentiate auxiliary verbs from main verbs such as *eat*, *run* and *rub*.

2.2.1   General description of auxiliaries

Paradigms are used to set up chart-like structures that will be helpful in exhibiting the patterns that occur with verb forms. These paradigms are especially useful in that they list the auxiliaries that occur in AAE, reflect the type of verb forms that occur in the sequences and show the 'agreement' patterns that are used. In addition the paradigms include data that represent a range of auxiliaries, and this makes it possible to show how auxiliaries listed at the beginning of section 2.2 pattern similarly.

Verbal paradigms[2]

(1)   **Present tense**

Person, number	Present	Emphatic affirmation	Negative
1st, 2nd, 3rd sg, pl	eat, run, rub	DO eat, run, rub	don't eat, run, rub

(2)   a. **Past tense**

Past	Emphatic affirmation	Negative
ate, ran, rubbed	DID eat, run, rub	din (didn't) eat, run, rub

(2)   a'. **Past tense**

		Negative
		ain('t) eat/ate, run/ran, rub/rubbed

(2)   b. **Preterite *had***

Preterite *had* (Past)	Emphatic affirmation	Negative
had ate, ran, rubbed	–	–

(3)   a. **Future tense**

Future	Emphatic affirmation	Negative
'a eat, run, rub	WILL eat, run, rub	won't eat, run, rub

(reduced *will* ('*a*) attaches to the preceding pronoun, as in *I'a, she'a*)

(3)   b. **Future tense**

Person, number	Future	Emphatic affirmation	Negative
1st sg.	I'ma eat	–	I ain't gon/ I'm not gon
2nd, 3rd sg, pl.	gon eat		ain't gon/not gon

(Note: There are also variations such as *I'm gonna/I'monna* and *you gonna*.)

(4)   a. **Present progressive (prog) (auxiliary *be*)**

Person, number	Pres prog	Emphatic affirmation	Negative
1st sg.	I'm eating	I AM eating	I'm not/ I ain('t) eating
1st pl, 2nd sg, pl, 3rd sg, pl	we, you she, they eating	IS eating	ain('t)/not eating
3nd sg neuter	it's growing	It IS eating	it's not growing it ain('t) eating

(4)   b. **Present copula *be***

Person, number	Present	Emphatic affirmation	Negative
1st sg.	I'm tall	I AM tall	I'm not tall/ I ain't tall
1st pl, 2nd sg, pl 3rd sg, pl	we, you, she, they	IS	ain('t)/not tall
3rd sg neuter	it's tall	It IS	it's not tall/ it ain('t) tall

(5)   **Past progressive**

Person, number	Past prog	Emphatic affirmation	Negative
1st, 2nd, 3rd sg, pl	was eating	WAS eating	wadn't (wasn't) eating

(6)   **Future progressive**

Future prog		Emphatic affirmation	Negative
'a be eating		WILL be eating	won('t) be eating

(7)   **Present perfect (perf)**

Person, number	Present perf	Emphatic affirmation	Negative
1st, 2nd, 3rd sg, pl	ate, ran, rubbed	HAVE ate, ran, rubbed	ain('t)/haven't ate, ran, rubbed

(8)   **Past perfect**

Past perf		Emphatic affirmation	Negative
had ate, ran, rubbed		HAD ate, ran, rubbed	hadn't ate, ran, rubbed

(9)   **Present perfect progressive**

Person, Number	Present perf prog	Emphatic affirmation	Negative
1st, 2nd, 3rd sg, pl	been eating	HAVE been eating	ain('t)/haven't been eating

(10)   **Past perfect progressive**

Past perf prog	**Emphatic affirmation**	**Negative**
had been eating	HAD been eating	hadn't been eating

(11)   **Modal perfect**

Modal perfect	**Emphatic affirmation**	**Negative**
should'a been eating	–	shouldn'a been eating

(*'a* in Paradigm (11) may correspond to a reduced form of *have*.)

The paradigms in (1–11) are similar to conjugations in general American English; however, there are some differences, which will be described here. These paradigms are representative examples of the elements that constitute the AAE auxiliary system. The first, second and third person singular and plural are given, and the emphatic affirmation and negative verb forms are indicated in that particular paradigm if they occur in the language system.

A characteristic of AAE is that a single verb form may be used with both singular and plural subjects, so in (1) the verb forms *eat*, *run* and *rub* are used with first person singular and plural (*I*, *we*), second person singular and plural (*you*, *y'all*) and third person singular and plural (*she*, *they*) in the present tense. The auxiliaries are like main verbs in this respect; a single auxiliary form is used with both singular and plural subjects. The emphatic forms *DO*, *WAS* and *HAVE* in (1), (5) and (7, 9), respectively, are used when the subject is singular (e.g., *he DO*) as well as when it is plural (e.g., *they DO*). In this way, the present tense verb forms in AAE pattern similarly with the past tense verb forms; no distinction is made between first, second and third singular and plural. So just as the main verb form *run* is used with singular and plural subjects, the past tense verb *ran* is used with singular and plural subjects.

These paradigms are intended to capture uniformity in the auxiliary system, so they do not represent the possible variation in the form and use of different verbs. That is to say that the paradigms do not reflect the extent to which social factors influence language use; so, for example, there is no indication that a single speaker may use the singular verb form (e.g., *they was*) in some linguistic and social environments and the plural verb form (e.g., *they were*) in others. Such variation is very important and has been the topic of a large amount of research on AAE.[3]

Another difference between AAE and mainstream English that is familiar even to those who have limited knowledge about AAE is the behavior of the auxiliary/copula *be*. The auxiliary *be* occurs in the environment preceding V-*ing*, as in (4a), and the copula *be* occurs in the environments preceding an adjective, adverb, noun and preposition (e.g., *She is tall/a doctor*), as in (4b). They have the same form, so I will collapse them in discussions throughout this book. The auxiliary/copula element does not obligatorily occur on the surface in all environments, as shown in the examples in (4). For the most part, it is overtly represented when it occurs with the first person singular pronoun (*I'm*) and with the third person singular neuter pronoun (*it's*). It obligatorily occurs in the past tense (*was*, in (5)) although without a singular/plural distinction. The overt auxiliary/copula form also occurs in emphatic contexts in which it is stressed (*IS*). It occurs optionally, as indicated in the paradigms for first person plural, second and third person singular and plural, in which no auxiliary/copula *be* form is given.

Another difference between the AAE and general English auxiliary systems is revealed in (2) and (7), the past and present perfect tenses, respectively. These forms show that there is no observable distinction between the simple past (2) and the present perfect (7) verb forms. In other words, the simple past and present perfect are often identical in shape (i.e., the simple past verb form is used in both); there is often no separate participle verb form such as *eaten*. In general American English, although in most cases the simple past and present perfect verb forms are identical, some verbs do take -*en* in the present perfect. (This issue will be discussed in chapter 3.) It is often the case that in AAE, the simple past and present perfect can be distinguished only in emphatic affirmation environments, cases in which the auxiliary *HAVE* is stressed and occurs on the surface in the present perfect. This observation leads to two questions:

- Do speakers actually make a distinction between the past tense and present perfect? That is, do they actually only use *DID eat* in emphatic past contexts and *HAVE ate* in emphatic present perfect contexts?
- Is there a *have* in the sense of the present perfect in AAE?

The negative categories in the paradigms in (2) and (7) suggest that the answer to the first question is yes in that the negative past tense is formed with one auxiliary and the negative present perfect is formed with another auxiliary. If there were no distinction, then we might expect the same auxiliary to occur with both forms. The second question is more difficult to answer, especially because *have* does not usually occur in regular non-emphatic present perfect sequences, and for this reason, there is no direct evidence that *have* is obligatorily used to mark the present perfect in AAE. So far the data suggest that *have* is only used in emphatic affirmation and negative contexts in present perfect sequences.

The negative forms in the present perfect are *ain't/haven't ate*. *Ain't* is the negator in other contexts, so whereas it may be used in present perfect paradigms, it is not used solely in that context. *Ain't* also occurs in past contexts such as *He ain't ate* ('He didn't eat'), in which it serves as a negative marker and is not overtly marked for tense. That is, the form *ain't* does not have distinct past and non-past forms. In the sequence *ain't ate*, the main verb is in the past form. This contrasts with *didn't eat*, in which past is marked on the auxiliary *didn't*. *Ain't* is also argued to occur in past contexts such as *He ain't eat* ('He didn't eat'), in which the main verb is in the non-past form. I have included such an example in the paradigm in (2a'); however, it is not clear that the auxiliary form preceding the verbs *eat*, *run* and *rub* is actually a full form of *ain't*. These cases raise interesting questions about tense marking and the nature of *ain't* in different environments.[4]

A final difference between the AAE and general American English systems is the use of *had* in simple past contexts. In the paradigm in (2b), the auxiliary *had* occurs in construction with a verb overtly marked for the past. As shown in the paradigm, no emphatic and negative forms occur with this use of *had*. This preterite *had* sequence is discussed in the literature in Rickford and Théberge-Rafal (1996). It will be discussed further in chapter 3.

Finally, the future marked by *will* and the modal forms in the AAE and mainstream English auxiliary systems are quite similar. As indicated in (3b), future is also marked with *gonna* or *gon*, which does not occur with first person singular (I'ma).[5] In the paradigms in (3), (6) and (11), the reduced forms of the auxiliaries have been given. It should also be noted that there is no emphatic affirmation form for the modal perfect (11). One important generalization that can be made in light of the data in (1–11) is that the auxiliaries pattern similarly by occurring in the same environments (i.e., emphatic and negative contexts).

2.2.2   Properties and processes of auxiliaries

The inflected auxiliaries or conjugated forms of *be, do, have* and modals can be characterized by a set of properties that will be discussed below. Referring once again to the paradigms in (1–11), we find that in the auxiliary + main verb sequence, tense is marked on the auxiliary (but *ain't* does not have separate past and non-past forms). In paradigms such as the past perfect (8), the main verb (*ate, ran*) is in the simple past form, but it is not marked for tense; it is in a form required in that paradigm. Past tense is marked on the auxiliary *had*. Take an example from mainstream English. The main verb (*run, eaten*) in the past perfect sequence *had run/eaten* is in the form (participle) that is required for that paradigm. Past tense is marked on the auxiliary *had*.

The second property of auxiliaries is that they can appear in a contracted, reduced or zero form such as *'s, 'm, 'll ('a), 'd* and Ø. (The symbol 'Ø' is used to show that a particular auxiliary does not occur on the surface in that position). Examples of auxiliaries in these forms are given below:

(12)   a. It's the one I like.
       b. I'm driving to Amherst.
       c. They Ø walking too fast.

(13)   You should'a made your mind up before I called you.

(14)   a. The teacher Ø got all the papers.
       b. They Ø got everything they need.

(15)   a. Bruce'a study when he get home.
       b. We'a put the cakes in the oven.
       c. He Ø be there in a minute.

(16)   a. Sometimes he'd be already sleeping.
       b. Sometimes he Ø be already sleeping.
       c. We'd be mad if they left us.

The sentences in (12) provide examples of contracted (12a, b) and zero (12c) auxiliary *be* forms. The difference between the forms *it's* and *she's* in AAE is that the former is invariable for the most part, but the latter is clearly variable. Speakers rarely ever produce sentences such as *It the one I like*, while both variants *she's* and *she* occur without question (*She's/She here.*).[6] Labov (1972) makes a slightly weaker statement on the issue of plain *it* forms. He says, "While we occasionally do get plain *it*, as in *It always somebody tougher than you are*," *it's* is "found in the great majority of cases" (p. 71).

A reduced form of the auxiliary, which corresponds to mainstream English *have*, is given in (13). In (14), no auxiliary form precedes the main verb *got*, while reduced auxiliary forms that correspond to *will* (*'a*) are in construction with the present form of the main verbs in (15a, b). The sentence in (15c) shows that the future form of the auxiliary (*will*, *'ll*) does not have to be represented overtly by a reduced form (*'a*); it can be marked by Ø. The same pattern occurs in (16) with the reduced and zero forms of *would*. If we take just a moment to look at the sentence in (16b), we find that the use of *be* there is much like the use of *be* in sentences in the focal point at the beginning of this chapter. The sentence in (16b) can have two interpretations: one like the 'usually' interpretation of the focal point sentences ('Sometimes he is already sleeping') and the one that means exactly what the sentence in (16a) means. It is the (16a) interpretation that we are interested in at the moment.

A third property of auxiliaries is that they can host the contracted negator *not* (*n't*). In other words, *n't* can 'attach' to auxiliaries. This is shown in the sentences below:

(17) a. Bruce ain't taking calculus this semester.
      b. Bruce is not taking calculus this semester.
      c. Bruce won't take calculus next semester.
      d. Bruce will not take calculus next semester.
      e. Bruce didn't (din) finish his homework last night.
      f. Bruce did not finish his homework last night.
      g. Bruce hadn't been doing his homework.
      h. Bruce had not been doing his homework.

The sentence pairs (c–d/e–f/g–h) consist of an auxiliary + contracted *not* (*n't*) sequence (c, d, e) and a full auxiliary + *not* sequence (d, f, h). In the discussion of the paradigms (1–11), I have classified *ain't* as a negator. It is different from other negated auxiliaries in that it is not formed from any particular auxiliary + contracted *not* (*n't*), although it may occur in environments in which *isn't*, *didn't* and *haven't* occur.

Auxiliaries can also be identified by their property of inverting in yes-no questions, which require a yes or no answer. Question formation in AAE, as well as in general American English, is a process by which the auxiliary assumes the position preceding the subject of the sentence. In the declarative sentence in (18a), the auxiliary *was* is in the position following the subject *Dee*, and in the yes-no question (interrogative), it is in the position preceding the subject:

(18) a. Dee **was** here.
      b. **Was** Dee here?

The property of inverting in question formation is a special property of auxiliary verbs, so auxiliaries, but not main verbs, can be placed in the position preceding subjects in yes-no questions. The sentence in (19c) is ungrammatical because the main verb *cook* has inverted preceding the subject *Bruce*:

(19)   a. Bruce can cook.
        b. Can Bruce cook?
        c. *Cook Bruce can?

An analysis of questions in AAE helps to reveal another property of auxiliaries in that variety. The fifth property of auxiliaries in AAE is that they do not occur obligatorily in questions. In cases in which auxiliaries do not occur on the surface (e.g., (20b, d)), questions are signaled by using a special question intonation, which will be discussed in chapter 4.

(20)   a. Is Bob here?
        b. Bob here?
        c. Is Bob gon' leave? ('Is Bob going to leave?')
        d. Bob gon' leave?

(21)   a. Have Bob left?
        b. Bob left?

(22)   a. Did Bob leave?
        b. Bob left?

These sentences show that, on the one hand, auxiliaries can occur at the beginning of sentences, but on the other, they can be left completely out of questions. In the (b) and (d) questions, there is no auxiliary that indicates that a question has been formed; the intonation of the sentences signals that a question is being asked. In the question in (22b), past tense is marked on the main verb (*left*). If the identical questions in (21b) and (22b) have different interpretations, they will be distinguished by the context in which they occur. The modals (e.g., *will* and *should*) cannot be left out of questions in all environments, but they can remain in the position following the subject and preceding the main verb, as in (23a, b):

(23)   a. You'a teach me how to swim? ('You'll teach me how to swim?') 'Will you teach me how to swim?'
        b. Bruce can swim?
        c. Bruce was running?

Modals and the past tense auxiliary/copula *be* (*was*) (23c) pattern similarly, in that they cannot be left out of questions, but they are not required to occur in the position preceding the subject. So note that *Bruce running* cannot be used for 'Bruce was running,' nor can it be used for 'Was Bruce running?' Question intonation is also used in these sentences to signal that the construction is a question. The claim is not that AAE is the only English variety that uses intonation to signal questions; it is that intonation can be used in this way, also. The point that will be explored in chapter 4 is that in AAE, questions can be marked by different intonational patterns that may not be commonly used in other varieties of English.

The inversion of the auxiliary in yes-no questions is the same type of inversion that results in tags, constructions in which yes-no questions are tagged onto the end of a declarative. Tag questions are formed by copying the auxiliary in a declarative sentence in the position at the end of the sentence, making it negative if its original occurrence is positive and positive if its original occurrence is negative. The pronoun corresponding to the subject of the declarative sentence is copied in the position following the copied auxiliary. This is demonstrated in (24):

(24)   Bruce WILL finish his homework, **won't he**?

Given that the auxiliary *will* is positive, its negative form (*won't*) is copied at the end of the sentence, and the pronoun (*he*), which corresponds to the subject (*Bruce*), is copied immediately following the negative auxiliary. The description of tag questions given above specifically mentions auxiliary, but as has been noted, declaratives in AAE are not necessarily formed with auxiliaries (see (12c)). In forming tag questions from declarative sentences in which there is no overt inflected *be* form, we operate as if an auxiliary is actually present:

(25)   a. Bruce Ø eating, ain't he?
       b. *Bruce Ø eating, Ø not he?
       c. Bruce not eating, is he?
       d. *Bruce Ø not eating, Ø he?

In forming the grammatical tag in (25a), the negative element (*ain't*) corresponding to the positive form of the auxiliary that would occur in the declarative if there were one is copied at the end of the sentence, and then the pronoun corresponding to *Bruce* is copied. The tag in (25c) is formed by copying the positive auxiliary (*is*) corresponding to Ø *not* in the declarative. The ungrammatical sentences in (25b) and (25d) show that the tag questions cannot be formed without placing an auxiliary in the tagged part of the sentence even if there is no overt auxiliary in the declarative. Tag question formation is an important process in the study of AAE because it can be used as a diagnostic to determine what auxiliary would occur if one were present. In short, auxiliaries that do not occur superficially in declarative sentences can be *forced* to surface by using tag questions, as in (25a, c). A final note here is that the rule for tag questions that has been presented will have to be formulated more carefully to account for the positive auxiliaries that correspond to *ain't* and *ain*, *have* and *did*, respectively, in sentences such as the following:
He ain't eating, is he?
He **ain't** ate, **have** he?
He **ain** eat, **did** he? (As noted in the previous discussion, it is not clear that the auxiliary here is actually *ain't*.)
The following will suffice for our purposes: in forming tags, if *ain't* precedes a verb in the past form in the declarative, use the auxiliary *have* (or *did* for some speakers) in the tag. In all other cases, use the auxiliary *is*.

The sixth property of auxiliaries discussed here is that they can substitute for deleted material in verb phrase-ellipsis and verb phrase-fronting. These two processes have been discussed at length in studies on auxiliaries in general American English, for the most part, to illustrate some similarities and/or differences between auxiliaries and main verbs and to show that auxiliaries do not form constituents or units with main verbs. (See Pullum and Wilson 1977, Akmajian, Steele, and Wasow 1979 and Warner 1993 for a discussion of these topics and a review of the literature.) The term VP-ellipsis is used to refer to structures in which an auxiliary is substituted for deleted material, as shown below. Recall that 'Ø' is used to indicate that an auxiliary does not occur in that position:

(26)   Bruce Ø dancing, and Dee Ø dancing, too.
       VP-ellipsis: Bruce dancing, and Dee **is**, too.

In this sentence, the auxiliary *is* substitutes for Ø *dancing*, which is omitted in the second clause of the sentence. As a result, we get … *and Dee is, too*, not *and Dee dancing, too*. VP-fronting can occur, in which the auxiliary is left behind while the verb and other material (VP) is moved forward:

(27)   Bruce said he would win the election, and win the election he **did**.

In the second clause in the sentence in (27), the whole verb phrase *win the election* moves forward to the position preceding the subject *he*, that is, fronts (as in VP-fronting); and the auxiliary (*did*) is left behind. As a result, we get *win the election* preceding, not following, the subject *he*. Again, the auxiliaries here occur in both AAE and general American English, and, furthermore, most of the processes used to demonstrate the properties of auxiliaries are common to both systems.

Generally speaking, auxiliaries in AAE bear some features that are quite similar if not identical to patterns of auxiliaries in general American English. We have seen some subtle differences between the two systems in the present perfect and in some processes in which the auxiliary does not occur on the surface in AAE. Two interesting questions that are in line with the type of research gathered in the volume *Language Variety in the South Revisted* are the following: What is the relationship between black and white speech in the South? Are the data that I have presented here on the auxiliary patterns in AAE identical to Southern white usage? I do not have corresponding paradigms for Southern American English, but I will address this question, in part, in the next section by referring to data that are available for Southern and other varieties of English. (See Labov 1969a, Baugh 1980, Holm 1984, Bailey and Schnebly 1988, Rickford, Ball, Blake, Jackson and Martin 1991, Mufwene 1992 and Green 1993, 1998a, for a discussion of auxiliaries in AAE.)

2.3   Aspectual markers (verbal markers): *be*, BIN, dən

The aspectual markers (or verbal markers) in AAE are similar in form to auxiliary verbs in general American English, and this shared identity may cause some confusion between speakers of the two language systems.[7] Because of this similarity, non-AAE speakers may expect these markers to have the same role and meaning as some auxiliary verb forms in general American English. As noted in the lexical entries in chapter 1, the verbal markers *be*, *BIN* and *dən* occur in specific environments in sentences and indicate a certain type of meaning. Due to the type of meaning these verbal markers indicate, we will refer to them as aspectual markers (more specifically tense-aspect markers).

Aspect is a complicated subject and is the topic of numerous journal articles and books (e.g., Comrie 1976, Brinton 1988, Binnick 1991, Smith 1997), but it will be helpful to give a simplified definition here. Aspect is often contrasted with tense to make useful distinctions. Tense situates an event in time, as in *Bruce ran*, in which the running took place at some past time before the sentence was uttered. Aspect, on the other hand, refers to duration, completion or habitual occurrence. The progressive or durative aspect is expressed on the verb *running* (as in *Bruce is running*), in which the running activity is durative, indicating continuing action, or that the activity is in progress. (For a more advanced analysis of aspectual markers in AAE see Déchaine 1993 and Green 1993, 2000).

2.3.1   General description of aspectual markers

The paradigms in (28–39) reflect the possible aspectual combinations. In the following paradigms, the aspectual marker is followed by a verb in the *-ing* or *-ed* forms. The following patterns are given:

(1) Column 1 – aspectual element with corresponding verb form
(2) Column 2 – aspectual element in stressed or emphatic affirmation constructions, if the form exists for that paradigm
(3) Column 3 – aspectual element in negated construction, if the form exists for that paradigm

The categories first, second, third person singular and plural are not indicated here because these distinctions are not made in the aspectual marker paradigms. The same form is used regardless of whether the subject is first, second, third person singular or plural.

(28)   **Habitual**

Habitual	Emphatic affirmation	Negative
be eating	DO be eating	don('t) be eating
'am usually/always eating'	'AM usually/always eating'	'am not usually eating'
or 'usually eats'	or 'DO usually eat'	or 'don't usually eat'

(Note: Some speakers allow *bes* in some contexts (e.g., *bes eating*)).

(29)   **Remote past (state, habit)**

Remote past	Emphatic affirmation	Negative
BIN eating	HAVE BIN eating	ain('t)/haven't BIN eating
'have been eating for a long time'	'HAVE been eating for a long time'	'hasn't/haven't been eating for a long time'

(30) **Remote past (completion)**

Remote past	Emphatic affirmation	Negative
BIN ate	HAVE BIN ate	ain('t)/haven't BIN ate
'ate a long time ago'	'DID eat a long time ago'	'didn't eat a long time ago'

(31) **Remote past perfect**

Remote past perfect	Emphatic affirmation	Negative
had BIN ate	HAD BIN ate	hadn't BIN ate
'had eaten a long time ago'	'HAD eaten a long time ago'	'hadn't eaten a long time ago'

(32) **Resultant state**

Resultant state	Emphatic affirmation	Negative
dən ate	?HAVE dən ate	ain't dən ate
'has/have already eaten'		'hasn't/haven't already eaten'

(33) **Past perfect resultant state**

Past perfect resultant state	Emphatic affirmation	Negative
had dən ate	HAD dən ate	hadn't dən ate
'had already eaten'	'HAD already eaten'	'hadn't already eaten'

(34) **Modal resultant state**

Modal resultant state	Emphatic affirmation	Negative
should'a dən ate	—	—
'should have already eaten'		

(35) **Remote past resultant state**

Remote past resultant state	Emphatic affirmation	Negative
BIN dən ate	HAVE BIN dən ate	ain't/haven't BIN dən ate
'finished eating a long time ago'	'DID finish eating a long ago'	'didn't finish eating a long time ago'

(Note: Some speakers also allow *dən BIN* (e.g., *dən BIN ate*)).

(36) **Remote past perfect resultant state**

Remote past perf resultant state	Emphatic affirmation	Negative
had BIN dən ate	—	—
'had already eaten a long time ago'		

(37) **Habitual resultant state**

Habitual resultant state	Emphatic affirmation	Negative
be dən ate	DO be dən ate	don't be dən ate
'usually have already eaten'	'usually HAVE already eaten'	'usually haven't already eaten'

(38)   **Future resultant state/conditional**

Future resultant state/ conditional	**Emphatic affirmation**	**Negative**
'a be dən ate	WILL be dən ate	won't be dən ate
'will have already eaten'	'WILL have already eaten'	'won't have already eaten'

(39)   **Modal resultant state**

Modal resultant state	**Emphatic affirmation**	**Negative**
might/may be dən ate	MIGHT/MAY be dən ate	might/may not be dən ate
'might have already eaten'	'MIGHT have already eaten'	'might not have already eaten'

Aspectual *be*

Aspectual markers denote meaning in the constructions in which they occur.[8] Generally speaking, the type of meaning (e.g., habitual, resultant state) they denote is indicated by the headings in the paradigms. Also, the meaning expressed by these aspectual markers is captured in the general American English glosses by a sequence of verbs and an adverb or adverbial phrase. Aspectual *be* (which may also be in the form of *bes* in some instances) denotes habitual or iterative meaning; therefore, the activity expressed by the verb 'eating' in (28) is characterized as recurring.[9] The adverb *usually* or *always* is used in the gloss to convey the meaning in the corresponding general English sequence. Because it denotes meaning, the aspectual marker *be* must occur in sentences in which such aspectual interpretation is intended. For example, whereas the auxiliary/copula *be* and other auxiliaries can be absent or do not have to occur obligatorily, the aspectual marker *be* cannot be left out of the sentence. If it is omitted, some sentences may receive ambiguous interpretations, or they may not receive the intended interpretation. This point is illustrated by the sentences in (40):

(40)   a. Bruce run.
   'Bruce runs on occasions' or 'Bruce doesn't have a problem with running'
   b. Bruce Ø running.
   'Bruce is running now' or 'Bruce is running these days'
   c. Bruce be running.
   'Bruce is usually running' or 'Bruce usually runs'

All of the sentences in (40) can have habitual readings, in which the running activity occurs on different occasions. The difference is that the sentence in (40c) can only have that meaning, so if a speaker leaves aspectual *be* out of the sentence, the one in (40b), in which the present progressive ('is running now' or 'is running these days') is expressed, will be produced. While the sentences in (40b) and (40c) share some superficial similarities, there is an important difference between the two. First of all, they are similar in that the verb *running* in both is in the *-ing* form, and secondly, they can both be produced with some form of *be*. In (40b), the inflected *be* form will appear on the surface in emphatic contexts (e.g., *Bruce IS running*) and in some questions

(*Is Bruce running?*). If we add an adverbial clause ('when I leave for work') that specifies a time period, we will see how the sentences differ.

(40)   b'. Bruce running when I leave for work.
       'Bruce's running is in progress when I leave for work'
       c'. Bruce be running when I leave for work.
          (1) 'It is usually the case that Bruce's running is in progress when I leave for work'
          (2) 'It is usually the case that Bruce begins to run when I leave for work'

The sentence in (40b') has one interpretation, in which the running is already in progress when I leave for work, but the sentence in (40c') has two interpretations, one in which the running is usually already in progress when I leave for work (1) and the other in which the running usually begins when I leave for work (2). This is one of the major differences between sentences such as the present progressive in (40b') and the aspectual *be* construction in (40c').

Aspectual *be* always occurs in its uninflected or bare form, so it never appears as *is*, *am* or *are*.[10] In the paradigm (28), aspectual *be* occurs in the environment preceding a verb in the *-ing* form; however, as noted in the lexical entries in the preceding chapter, it can precede elements from other grammatical classes, as illustrated in the sentences in (41):

(41)   a. She **be telling** people she eight. (Bf, 6)
          'She is always telling people she's eight' or 'she always tells people she's eight'
       b. I **be looking** for somewhere to waste time. (Bm, 30s)
          'I am usually looking for somewhere to waste time' or 'I usually look for somewhere to waste time'
       c. During the summer, they go off for two weeks, so her checks **be big**. (Bf, 50s)
          'During the summer, they go away for two weeks, so her checks are usually big then'
       d. Your phone bill **be high**, don't it. (Bf, 80s)
          'Your phone bill is usually high, isn't it?'
       e. I always **be scary** stuff. (Bm, 7)
          'I am always scary stuff'
          (Literally: I always pretend to be scary characters.)
       f. It **be knives** in here. It **be ice picks** in here. (Bf teenager, national news)
          'There are usually knives in here. There are usually ice picks in here'
       g. I **be in my office** by 7:30. (Bf, 30s)
          'I am usually in my office by 7:30'
       h. He doesn't even allow women to wear pants at women's retreats and he doesn't even **be there**. (Bf, 40s)
          'He doesn't allow women to wear pants at women's retreats and he isn't usually there'
       i. She gotta be there for 9, so they **be dən** gone to school. (Bf, 60s)
          'She has to be there at 9, so they have usually already gone to school'
          (Literally: She has to be at work at 9 AM, so the children have usually already gone to school by the time she leaves.)

j. It don't **be drove** hardly. It don't **be dogged**. I grease it and oil it. (Bm, 60s)
   'It is usually the case that it is hardly driven. It isn't usually dogged. I grease it and oil it'

In all of these cases, *be* denotes habitual or iterative meaning, so the *be* + verb/adjective/ preposition/adverb/aspectual/passive verb sequence has a 'happens on different occasions' or 'is in a certain state or place on different occasions' interpretation. In (41a) and (41b) the telling and looking events, respectively, occur on particular occasions, and in (41c) and (41d) *be* occurs with adjectives to indicate that the checks are usually big and the phone bill is usually high, and in the sentence in (41e) the speaker expresses that he pretends to be scary characters on different occasions. In (41e), the speaker is commenting on his roles during Halloween, during which he dresses as scary characters. The speaker in (41f) uses the sentence to comment on the occasional, perhaps usual presence of weapons in her school.

Aspectual *be* also precedes prepositional phrases (e.g., *in my office*, where *in* is a preposition) (41g) and adverb phrases (e.g., *there*) (41h) to indicate being in a place on particular occasions. (41g) says that it is usually the case that I am in my office by 7:30, and (41h) says that it is usually the case that he isn't there (i.e., at retreats). The aspectual marker *be* also precedes the verbal marker *dən*, which will be discussed later in this chapter. In (41i), what recurs is the event of the children having already gone to school by some particular time. Note that *be* can precede a passive verb, ending in *-ed* (41j).

In most of the cases in (41), aspectual *be* precedes a verb or other predicate phrase (such as adjective phrases, noun phrases and prepositional phrases). Here we refer to predicate phrase as a cover term for verb phrase, adjective phrase, noun phrase, adverb phrase and prepositional phrase which may name an action performed by the subject or modify the subject. The predicate phrase indicates a temporary property of an entity. For example in (41e), the scary state is temporary; the subject, the seven-year-old boy, can change his appearance from being scary back to normal.

However, in some sentences aspectual *be* precedes adjectives and prepositions that indicate permanent properties of a subject. These types of sentences are referred to as bicycle sentences in Green (2000) because the first sentence of this type that I saw in print was about bicycles.[11] The sentence in (42a) is in the 1972 book *Tense Marking in Black English* by Ralph Fasold:

(42)   a. Some of them be big and some of them be small. (Fasold 1972, p. 151)
          'It is usually/always the case that some of them are big and some of them are small' (my gloss)
          (Literally: It is usually/always the case that some of those bicycles are big and some of those bicycles are small.)
       b. Sam's wholesale stores be on the outskirts of town. (Green 2000, p. 21)
          'It is usually/always the case that Sam's wholesale stores are on the outskirts of town'
       c. Some iMacs be tangerine.
          'It is usually the case that some iMacs are tangerine'

Now when we think about the sentences in (42), we realize that their subjects can be described as having permanent properties. In particular, some bicycles are permanently big, while others are permanently small. Once built in a certain place, Sam's wholesale stores are permanently located there. Finally, some iMacs, once designed, are permanently tangerine. These states will not be changed unless some force of nature or human acts upon them. Because a bicycle is in the permanent state of being big or being small, the sentence in (42a) cannot have the interpretation in which the bicycles habitually change sizes. Likewise, because a store is permanently located in a particular place, the sentence in (42b) cannot have the interpretation in which one store habitually occurs in different places. That is to say the sentence cannot mean that Sam's stores which have been built in a certain place change locations from time to time. This explains the situations in the sentences in (42), but the cases in the sentences in (41a, b, c, e, g, h, i) are different, as the subjects are human; the subjects can volitionally participate in events that occur on different occasions, and they can participate in changing states.

The inanimate subjects of the sentences in (42) cannot volitionally participate in events, nor do they have mobility or other requirements necessary to participate in such changes. However, given the nature of aspectual *be* as a marker whose function is to give the predicate following it the interpretation that the activity happens over and over, the sentences in (42) must have some type of habitual reading even if the subjects are inanimate and cannot normally change size, color or location over and over. So the kind of interpretation we end up with in sentences such as (42) is "one in which different members of a particular group can be described by the state indicated by the predicate" (Green 2000, p. 23). As a result, the sentence *Some iMacs be tangerine* does not mean that one day the computers are tangerine and the next the same computers are grape and then finally they change their color to bondi blue. It means that out of the class of iMacs some will be tangerine, that is, some are usually tangerine. We can expect Apple to produce tangerine iMacs from time to time. Fasold (1972, p. 151) labels this use of *be* distributive, such that it is "the subject of the sentence, not the event in the predicate" that is "distributed in time," and he illustrates with the sentence in (42a). He explains that "although any given bicycle is always the same size, one encounters different bicycles at different points in time and these will be of varying sizes" (p. 151). Fasold concluded that sentences such as the ones in (42) were rare. They do, however, occur in conversation; I have collected a few of these sentences. In fact, an African American female in her 30s made the statement in (42b) as we were discussing the growing popularity of Wal-Mart stores. However, when I wrote about these sentences, I changed the name of the store to Sam's.

Aspectual *be* also occurs at the end of the sentence, as in (43a) or immediately preceding a prepositional phrase that adds additional description (43b).

(43)   a. That's how they be. (Bf, 60s)
        'That's how they usually/always are'
        (Literally: The boys' socks are always that dirty. The appearance of their socks today isn't unusual.)

b. No, that's how it be at Wal-Mart. (Bf, 60s)
   'No, that's how it usually/always is at Wal-Mart'
   (Literally: The price of aspartame sweetener is always reasonable at Wal-Mart. The reasonable price today isn't unusual.)

In these cases, aspectual *be* indicates habitual meaning, but it also attributes a property to the subjects of the sentences. For example, the property of being dirty is attributed to the socks in (43a), so they are usually dirty.

Because aspectual *be* indicates habituality, adverbs are not needed to express this meaning, but certain types of adverbs (e.g., those expressing frequency) can occur with the marker. Some examples are given in (44):

(44) a. I **always be** looking for somewhere to waste time.
          'I am always looking for somewhere to waste time'/'I always look ...'
      a'. ??I **be always** looking for somewhere to waste time.
      b. I **usually be** looking for somewhere to waste time.
          'I am usually looking for somewhere to waste time'/'I usually look ...'
      b'. ??I **be usually** looking for somewhere to waste time.
      c. I **often be** looking for somewhere to waste time.
          'I am often looking for somewhere to waste time'/'I often look ...'
      c'. ??I **be often** looking for somewhere to waste time.
      d. I **never be** looking for that.
          'I am never looking for that'/'I never look ...'
      d'. *I **be never** looking for that.

Given the meaning of aspectual *be*, we already know that the looking for somewhere to waste time activity occurs from time to time, so the adverbs in (44) specify precisely how often the looking activity occurs: always, usually, often, never. The preferred place in the sentence for these adverbs is in the position preceding aspectual *be* (44a, b, c, d), so the resulting sentences are less than perfect when the adverb follows *be* (44 a', b', c', d'). Other types of adverbs such as *probably* occur with aspectual *be*:

(45) a. They **probably be** up there laughing. (attested)
         'They are probably usually up there laughing'
      b. *They be probably up there laughing.

The sentence is bad when the adverb *probably* follows aspectual *be*.

Before moving on, let's summarize the properties of aspectual *be* in AAE:

Summary of properties of aspectual *be*

Q: What is it?
A: Aspectual *be* is a verbal or aspectual marker that is different from the auxiliary/copula *be*.
Q: What is its function?
A: Aspectual *be* indicates habitual meaning (i.e., an event occurs over and over).

Q: Where does it occur?

A: Aspectual *be* occurs before verbs, adjectives, nouns, prepositions, adverbs, *dən* and at the end of sentences.

Q: What happens when it takes a predicate that occurs with a subject that can change states?

A: The resulting interpretation is one in which the subject participates in the activity over and over.

Q: What happens when it takes a predicate that occurs with a subject that does not normally change states?

A: The resulting interpretation is not one in which a single subject undergoes change over and over. Instead it is one in which different members of the group can be described by the property indicated by the phrase following *be*.

Q: What do frequency adverbs such as *always* and *often* indicate when they occur with aspectual *be*, and where do they occur with respect to the aspectual marker?

A: Frequency adverbs specify how often the activity in the aspectual *be* construction occurs, and these adverbs usually precede aspectual *be*.

As shown in the discussion of aspectual *be*, the verbal marker has a very clear function. The types of details presented here are crucial for explaining the meaning and use of the marker; however, they are most important in that they address subtle meanings and properties that may be beneficial in developing lessons for teaching speakers of AAE to use general American English proficiently.

One challenging problem is that of explaining the difference in meaning between the type of aspectual *be* sentences in (42) and their zero *be* counterparts in (46), in which the copula *be* does not occur overtly (as indicated by 'Ø').

(46)   a. Some of them Ø big and some of them Ø small.
        'Some of them are big and some of them are small'
        (cf. Some of them be big and some of them be small.)
        b. Sam's wholesale stores Ø on the outskirts of town.
        'Sam's wholesale stores are on the outskirts of town'
        (cf. Sam's wholesale stores be on the outskirts of town.)
        c. Some iMacs Ø tangerine.
        'Some iMacs are tangerine'
        (cf. Some iMacs be tangerine.)

AAE speakers have intuitions about sentences such as (42) and (46), but it is not sufficient to use only intuition to explain the subtle meaning difference between the two groups of sentences. While the sentences in (42) and (46) are very similar (including nouns, adjectives, adverbs and prepositions which rename or describe the subjects), they do not have identical meanings. There is no aspectual *be* in the sentences in (46), so unlike the sentences in (42) they do not necessarily have the habitual interpretation that is associated with the marker.

At least two other uses of *be* in AAE resemble occurrences of aspectual *be*, in that the *be* is in its uninflected form (that is, it is not in any forms of *be* such as *is*, *am*, *are*). Examples of these two uses are in (47) and (48):

(47)   a. I'm going fishin if it don't be raining. (Bm, 60s)
       'I'm going fishing if it isn't raining'
       b. I sure hope it don't be no leak after I finish. (Bm, 60s)
       'I surely hope there isn't a leak after I finish'

In (47a), a type of conditional in which *be* precedes a verb (*raining*), the meaning is that the speaker will go fishing at some point in the future under the condition that it is not raining at that time. This sentence also has a subjunctive meaning in which it is not a fact that it will be raining, but it is a possibility. In (47b), *be* precedes a noun phrase (*no leak*), and the speaker is expressing his hope that there will not be a leak in the future.

The future meaning is given in (48) although there is no future marker *will* (or its variants, *'ll* and *'a*):

(48)   You be surprised how the Lord can use you. (attested)
       'You'll be surprised how the Lord can use you'

The speaker who used the sentence in (48) was encouraging the listener to yield to the Lord, who can and will do wonderful things. Given the context, it is clear that this occurrence of *be* is not the aspectual *be* that has been discussed in this section. The meanings are different; (48) in its intended context expresses future meaning and possibly future habitual meaning. Also, if you reconsider the paradigm in (28), you will find that aspectual *be* occurs with *do*. On the other hand, *be* in (48) would have more than likely occurred with the auxiliary *will* had the speaker stressed the point. It is likely that she would have said: 'You WILL/WOULD be surprised how the Lord can use you.' In such cases, it is necessary to hear the context in order to determine the meaning that is intended, whether aspectual *be* or some other *be* as in (46) and (47) is intended.

Aspectual *be* is also found in Hiberno English spoken in Ireland (especially in Northern Ireland), and it also occurs in varieties of English spoken by whites in the United States in some parts of the Carolinas. Both Harris (1985) and Kallen (1985) report that *be* or *do/does be* marks habituality in Hiberno English. (Note the spelling of *be's* with an apostrophe in Hiberno English.) Two examples from Harris are as follow:

(49)   a. He never be's sick or anything.
       b. They be shooting and fishing out at the Forestry lakes. (p. 76)

Kallen also discusses the role of *do* as a habitual marker and the role of *do* in *do be* sequences:

(50)   a. I do put the excess up in here.
       b. Those pancakes do be gorgeous. (p. 135)

The uses reported here are quite similar to the uses of aspectual *be* in AAE. The only difference is in the use of *do* in Hiberno English. *Do* itself can be used as a habitual marker, and it can also occur with *be*. In the latter case, Kallen suggests that habituality is doubly marked, once by *do* and another time by *be*. In contrast, *do* in this environment in AAE is limited to marking emphasis, hosting the contracted *n't* (*not*) and occurring in tag questions, ellipsis and VP-fronting. Review the AAE aspectual *be* paradigms. Neither Harris nor Kallen gives examples of *be* preceding a prepositional phrase, but, of course, it just may be the case that there are gaps in the data. The most obvious question is whether AAE aspectual *be* and Hiberno English aspectual *be* are historically related. This question is raised in Harris (1985) and discussed at length in Rickford (1986). The latter presents a number of arguments against the claim that habitual *be* represents a spread from Hiberno English to AAE.

Montgomery and Mishoe (1999) present data on the use of aspectual *be* by white speakers in the Carolinas. They give examples of *be* and *bes*, both of which can be habitual markers, as shown below:

(51)   a. Sometimes I have spells. Lately I be having more spells. (p. 247)
       b. That baby bes crying all afternoon. He's fine in the morning, but cranky in the afternoon. (p. 246)

There are clear parallels between aspectual *be* in AAE and *be* in Carolina English, but there are also some interesting differences. These *be* forms can also be used where no habitual meaning is intended:

(52)   a. I babysat your mama. Yep, I be that old. (p. 248)
       b. Lord, lord, child, you bes all grown up. (p. 247)

Be and *bes* are not limited to habitual and iterative contexts in the Carolina variety. This is one major difference between the data here and that in AAE. Another difference is that, according to Montgomery and Mishoe, *bes* is used when the subject is third person singular. Although *bes* occurs in AAE, I have not seen any hard and fast evidence suggesting that it is limited to third person singular. (Some attested examples of *bes* in AAE are in chapter 3, along with the discussion of verbal -*s*.) Based on the data and observations from Montgomery and Mishoe, it is possible to glean some interesting points about the *be* paradigms in the Carolina variety; however, time and space do not permit me to discuss them here.

Research shows that aspectual *be*, which indicates habitual meaning also occurs in other English varieties. The use and meaning of these corresponding *be* forms in AAE, Hiberno English and the English in the Carolinas overlap in significant ways. It is also the case that there are interesting differences. Historical research focusing on the origin of habitual *be* in these varieties would answer questions about the relationship among them, which goes beyond the scope of this book. Such research on origins of the marker cannot be conducted without including discussion about the influence of African languages and creoles on the language of African Americans in the United States. Issues related to historical origin are very complicated and require serious analysis and attention to detail. But see the sources in the Introduction to the book for additional references to historical research on AAE.

Remote past *BIN*[12]

BIN situates an activity or state (or some part thereof) in the remote past, and, as such, the 'eating' in the paradigm in (29) started at some point in the remote past and continues up to the moment of utterance (i.e., the point at which the speaker produces the sentence using *BIN*), while the 'eating' event in the paradigm in (30) ended at some point in the remote past, thus 'ate a long time ago.' The remote past is relative, so it can refer to a time period of fifteen minutes ago or fifteen years ago. One way to put it is that *BIN* is used to indicate that the time period referred to is longer than normal for an activity, or it can be used to affirm that a state has indeed held for a long of time. The stress (or pitch accent) distinguishes *BIN* phonetically (i.e., pronunciation) and semantically (i.e., meaning) from *been* (the unstressed form), which also occurs in AAE (cf. the present perfect progressive paradigm above in 9). *BIN* in (53a) and *been, bin* in (53b, c) have different stress patterns and different meanings; therefore, the sentences have different meanings:

(53)   a. She BIN running.
        'She has been running for a long time'
        b. She been running.
        'She has been running'
        c. She bin had him all day. (Bm, 60s)
        'She has had him all day'

One important factor is that stress is associated with meaning, such that stress on *BIN* results in the remote past interpretation. Is this *BIN* unique to AAE, or is it also shared by other varieties of English? Some speakers will recall the toothpaste commercial in which the announcer says, with stress on *been*, "Forget about the way you've *been* brushing your teeth." The first impression for some may be that the remote past *BIN* has 'crossed over' into mainstream English, but the example does not unequivocally support this claim, as the meaning that is intended is quite likely 'Forget about the way you've *been* brushing your teeth in the past.' Were this the remote past *BIN*, then the meaning would be 'Forget about the way you've been brushing your teeth for a long time.' It is not clear that the latter is the meaning that is intended in the toothpaste commercial.

In the early 1970s, linguists began to analyze the meaning that is associated with *BIN*. Rickford (1975), in presenting data from speakers in Philadelphia and the coastal Carolinas and reporting the differences in judgments about *BIN* from African American and white speakers, notes that "there is a rich arena for research in the use of *BÍN* ..." (p. 117). Some years later, Green (1998b) expanded on research on *BIN* in Labov (1972) and Rickford (1973, 1975), raising sociolinguistic questions and giving a description and semantic account of the marker and constructions in which it occurs.[13] The three types of *BIN* or environments for *BIN* are BIN_{STAT}, BIN_{HAB} and BIN_{COMP}. In what follows, I will use *BIN* labels (STAT, HAB, COMP) simply to explain the meaning of the sentences in which *BIN* occurs. The point is that there is only one *BIN*, but there are three types of meaning depending on the type of predicate with which *BIN* occurs.

In BIN_{STAT} constructions (where 'STAT' refers to state, that which holds constantly), the state started at some point in the remote past and continues to hold up to the moment of utterance or time of speech, as illustrated in the sentences below.

(54)   a. He **BIN running**.

       'He's been running for a long time'

    b. They just sent me this one, but I **BIN having** that one. (Bf, 60s)

       'They just sent me this one, but I have had that one for a long time'

    c. I **BIN knowing** he died.

       'I have known for a long time that he died'

    d. A: The police going bad.

       B: They ain't going bad. They **BIN bad**. (Bm, 40s)

       'They aren't going bad. They have been bad for a long time'

    e. He **BIN a preacher/in the kitchen/there**.[14]

       'He has been a preacher/in the kitchen/there for a long time'

In the examples in (54), *BIN* precedes a verb that ends in *-ing* (54 a, b, c) or a predicate phrase such as an adjective phrase (54d), noun phrase, prepositional phrase and adverb phrase (54e). These constructions have the 'for a long time' meaning, so in (54a) the running state has held for a long time, and in (54b) the state of having (i.e., own) has also held for a long time. The knowing state (54c) has held for a long time. As you will see in (55a), *BIN had* (in addition to *BIN having*) can also be used. The use of *having* and *knowing* in (54b) and (54c), respectively, as opposed to *BIN had* (cf. 55a) and *BIN knew* (cf. 55b) may be due to regional patterns that are used in parts of the Southern United States (Green 1998b). Janna Oetting, Ph.D., in research on AAE and nonstandard varieties of English of white speakers in southeastern Louisiana, also reports the use of *BIN having* and *BIN knowing* by African American children.[15]

    The predicates following *BIN* in the remaining sentences are not verbs, but the constructions still have a 'for a long time' reading. The term 'state' is used as a description in these constructions because the sentences refer to a situation that remains constant, unchanged. For example, according to the sentence in (54d), the police's change to a state of being bad started to hold a long time ago, and it continued to hold until the sentence was uttered (and probably after that). As noted above, certain verbs (e.g., *have*, *know*) in the BIN_{STAT} construction can be marked for past, as shown in the examples in (55):

(55)   a. A: Where'd you get that shirt?

       B: I **BIN had** it.[16] (Bf, 60s)

          'I've had it for a long time' (i.e., I've had it so long I can't remember where I bought/got it)

       A: Hunh?

       B: I BIN got it.

          'I bought/got it a long time ago'

    b. I **BIN knew** that.

       'I've know that for a long time'

Compare the sentences in (54b, c) to the sentences in (55a, b), respectively. They have the same meaning. One word of caution: It is not the case that each verb-*ing* can be used interchangeably with the corresponding past form of the verb in BIN_{STAT} constructions.

BIN running and *BIN ran* do not have the same meaning, so the sentences *She BIN running* and *She BIN ran* cannot be used interchangeably. The verbs in (54b, c) and (55a, b) are special cases because they indicate states, so they are inherently stative. They are different from a verb such as *run*, which indicates an activity. In summary, state verbs can occur in the BIN_{STAT} constructions in their *-ing* or *-ed* form without a change in meaning. We have ignored the *BIN got* sequence in B's second response in (55a), but we will return to it in the description of the BIN_{COMP} construction.

The second reading of the *BIN* construction is labeled BIN_{HAB} (where 'HAB' refers to habitual). I use habitual because the activity or state expressed by the verb begins at some point in the remote past and continues habitually, that is, on occasion or from time to time. Generally speaking, these constructions express a habit, and can be interpreted to mean 'started some time ago and continue from time to time.' The verbs in the BIN_{HAB} constructions are similar to those in the BIN_{STAT} construction in that they, too, occur in their *-ing* form, but they differ in that none of them can occur in the past form. Another difference is that only verbs can occur in BIN_{HAB} constructions (but cf. BIN_{STAT} in which other predicates such as nouns and adjectives can follow *BIN*). This is logical because these constructions are used to express habits, actions; and only verbs indicate actions, at least in this variety:

(56)   a. Bruce **BIN running**.
       'Bruce started running some time ago and he still runs from time to time'
       b. That's where I **BIN putting** my glasses.
       'That's where I started putting my glasses some time ago and I still put them there'
       c. Bruce **BIN being** a clown.
       'Bruce started acting as a clown/portraying a clown some time ago and he still acts as/portrays one from time to time'

In the sentences in (56), Bruce has had the habit of running for a long time; I have had the habit of putting my glasses in a particular place for a long time, and Bruce has had the habit of acting like a clown for a long time. The sentence in (56a) can have two readings, BIN_{STAT} and BIN_{HAB}, respectively. In principle, *BIN* verb-*ing* constructions can have the two readings. So even *BIN putting* can have a BIN_{STAT} reading if we change the sentence in (56b) slightly and think of the object (glasses) as drinking glasses.

(57)   Bruce BIN putting those glasses on the shelves.

In addition to the habitual reading, the sentence in (57) can have the BIN_{STAT} reading that means roughly that Bruce started putting those glasses on the shelves a long time ago (perhaps two hours ago) and he is still in the process of putting them there. This meaning occurs with *put* because its object (*those glasses*) is plural, so Bruce can place the glasses on the shelf one by one until he has finished the task. If glasses in (56b) refers to the object that is worn to improve sight, then the state reading is anomalous because to put a pair of glasses in a particular place requires one action, not the kind of continuous activity involved in putting drinking glasses away. (Of course this BIN_{STAT} reading also occurs when referring to plural eyeglasses.)

The third reading of the *BIN* construction is called *BIN~COMP~*. This remote past marker should not be confused with the unstressed past marker that I will represent as *bin* (also see the sentence in (53c)) in a sentence such as *I bin had this necklace 'bout fifteen, sixteen years* (Bf, 80s) 'I have had this necklace for about fifteen or sixteen years.' There are two major differences between *bin* and *BIN~COMP~*. The marker *bin* is unstressed and can occur with a time adverbial (e.g., *'bout fifteen, sixteen years*), but *BIN* is stressed and can only occur with time adverbials in specific contexts.

In *BIN~COMP~* constructions, the activity indicated by the verb ended at some point in the remote past; thus *BIN~COMP~* constructions are interpreted as meaning finished or ended 'a long time ago.' For the most part, the verbs in these constructions are in their past tense forms, but given variation and phonological processes, the *-ed* may not be pronounced, so a speaker may say either *I BIN started the car* or *I BIN start the car*. This type of variation is well documented in the literature (Wolfram 1969, Labov 1972, Wolfram and Fasold 1974, Guy 1991, Santa Ana 1992). Also, some speakers may use the present form of the verb, as in (58c).

(58)   a. I could'a **BIN went** back to work. (Bf, 60s)
        'I could have gone back to work a long time ago'
      b. A: You called her, Kaye?
        B: Yeah, I **BIN called** her. (Bf, 30s)
        'Yes, I called her a long time ago'
      c. I **BIN give** Brenda and Mr. Al they books.[17] (Bf, 60s)
        'I gave Brenda and Mr. Al their books a long time ago'
      d. I thought I would'a **BIN had** a copy of that tape. (Bf, 60s)
        'I thought that I would have gotten a copy of that tape a long time ago'

The meaning of the *BIN~COMP~* construction can be explained by referring to the example sentences in (58). In (58a), the possibility of having gone back to work is expressed as if it is in the remote past, and in (58b) *BIN called* means that the calling event was in the remote past, a long time ago. The books were given to the recipients in the remote past although the verb *give* is not overtly marked for past (58c). In the final example (58d), it is the acquisition of the copy of the tape that is in the remote past. The meaning of *BIN had* here is identical to that of *BIN got* in the second part of the example in (55a). But given the preceding discussion, this *BIN had* construction may also be interpreted as a *BIN~STAT~* sequence.

The three *BIN* readings (*BIN~STAT~*, *BIN~HAB~* and *BIN~COMP~*) have one property in common: *BIN* in all of the readings "situates the initiation of a state in the remote past, and the state continues until the moment of utterance" (Green 1998b, p. 133). In short, the use of *BIN* indicates that the state began a long time ago. All the predicates indicate some type of state, generally speaking. We have already distinguished state from activity by noting that the former remains unchanged; states are constant. In the *BIN~STAT~* and *BIN~HAB~* constructions, the state that starts in the remote past and continues up until the moment of utterance is the in-progress state. In (54a), the running event started in the remote past, and it continues, that is, it is in progress until the speaker makes the statement. This same in-progress state is applied to the running event in (56a).

The difference is that it is the habit that starts in the remote past and continues up to the moment of utterance. So in (56a), the person started the habit of running a long time ago. The state that starts in the remote past in the BIN_{COMP} reading is the resultant state, the state of an event that has ended. The resultant state simply refers to the state of an event that has ended. In (58b), the calling event is over, so it is in its resultant state.[18] (If you choose to read more about the in-progress and resultant states, see Parsons 1990). The major point is that speakers use *BIN* when they want to say that something started or happened a long time ago.

BIN does not specify the length of time that a state has been in progress or the length of time the state has been over; it just indicates that the time period a state has been in progress or over is a long one. For example, there is no indication about the number of minutes, hours, etc. that the running has been in progress in *He BIN running* or how long it has been over in *He BIN ran*. You might think that because *BIN* does not specifically note the length of time of an event, it would be possible to use an adverb that provides this information in *BIN* constructions. But *BIN* does not permit this type of additional modification, so temporal adverbial phrases (adverb phrases having to do with time) such as *for twenty minutes* and *for twenty years* are not allowed in *BIN* constructions to specify the time period. Consider the sentences below, in which the adverbial phrase is ungrammatical in the BIN_{STAT} reading but grammatical in the BIN_{HAB} reading:

(59)   John BIN running for ten minutes.

   a. **'John has been running for ten minutes' (BIN_{STAT} reading)
   b. 'John started to run for ten-minute stretches a long time ago and he still runs for ten-minute stretches' (BIN_{HAB} reading)
       ('It is the case that for a long time, John has been running for ten-minute stretches', i.e., 'for a long time John has had the habit of running for ten minutes') (Green 1998b, p. 127)

The (a) reading of the sentence in (59) is a bad one because *BIN* already gives the information that the running activity has been in progress for a long time; the additional specification "for ten minutes" is not allowed. The sentence in (59) is acceptable on the BIN_{HAB} reading (59b). In the reading in (59b), the adverbial phrase *for ten minutes* does not tell how long John has had the habit of running; instead, it modifies the duration of each of the smaller running events that together make up the habit. A scenario for the reading in (59b) could be the following: Six years ago, John jogged for ten minutes. He liked the way he felt after jogging, so he decided to do it regularly. Ever since then, he has jogged for ten minutes twice a week. So John BIN running for ten minutes.

Let us review the properties of *BIN*.

Summary of properties of *BIN*

Q: What is it?
A: *BIN* is a verbal or a tense/aspect marker.
Q: What is its special pronunciation property?
A: *BIN* is stressed.

Q: What is its function?

A: *BIN* situates something (let's call it a state) in the remote past.

Q: Where does it occur?

A: *BIN* occurs before verbs, adjectives, nouns, prepositions, adverbs and *dən*. (We will discuss *BIN* in the environment preceding *dən* shortly.)

Q: What happens when it occurs with an adverb phrase that marks a specific time period (e.g., *for ten minutes*)?

A: The time adverb has to modify the duration of each of the smaller events that combine to form the habit. The resulting interpretation is a BIN_{HAB} reading.

Q: Under what conditions do *BIN* verb *-ing* and *BIN* verb *-ed* have the same meaning?

A: This happens in the case of *BIN* occurring with verbs that indicate inherent states.

Before leaving this section, we can make an observation about the similarities between aspectual *be* and *BIN*. Both aspectual *be* and *BIN* can occur preceding verbs (ending in *-ing* and *-ed*), adjectives, nouns, adverbs, prepositions and *dən*. For linguists, this issue raises interesting questions about the relationship between *be* and *BIN*. I will not address those issues here.

Dən

The verbal marker *dən* denotes that an event has ended; it refers to events, such as having changed (60a), having finished that (60b), having done all you told me to do (60c) and having pushed it (60d), that have ended:

(60)   a. I told him you **dən changed**. (Bm, 30s)

   'I told him that you have changed'

   b. A: You through with Michael Jordan I bought you?

      (Literally: Have you finished reading the magazine that I bought you with Michael Jordan on the cover?)

      B: I dən already **finished** that. (Bm, 9)

      'I have already finished that'

   c. I **dən done** all you told me to do. I **dən visited** the sick. (Bm, 60s, 70s)

      'I have done all you told me to do. I have visited the sick'

   d. A: Push your seat.

      B: I **dən pushed** it.

      'I have (already) pushed it'

      A: Push it again.

      (elderly Bfs on Amtrak)

As shown in the paradigms in (32–39) and the sentences in (60), *dən* precedes a verb in the *-ed* form. (As you read the *dən* section of the paradigms, you will notice that there are some gaps. For example, there are no corresponding emphatic and negative forms for the modal resultant state.) The marker is pronounced with an unstressed syllable, and it is distinguished from *done*, the past participle form of the verb *do* in general American English (*She has done her homework*) and in nonstandard varieties of

English (*She done her homework.*). The two forms (*dən*, *done*) are clearly distinguished in (60c). *Dən* has the function of indicating that some eventuality has ended, but it may also indicate additional meanings such as that of recent past (61a, b) or having had some experience (61c).

(61)   a. People would say that medicine I'm taking dən made me sick. (Bm, 70s)
          'People would say that the medicine I'm taking has made me sick'
       b. I dən lost my wallet!
          'I have (just) lost my wallet!'
       c. She dən been to church. (Bf, 60s)
          'She has been to church before'

The sentence in (61a) indicates some notion of recent past in that the speaker is commenting that people would observe something strange about him, and, as a result, they would conclude that his state is due to the medicine he has been taking. The recency is in the sense that the people would have just observed the effect of the medicine. In (61b), another recent past example, the person has just lost his wallet or just realized that his wallet is lost. In (61c) *dən* indicates that the person has had the experience of attending church.

The *dən* sequence is quite similar to the present perfect in general American English, but it is not clear that it always shares the range of meanings of the present perfect:[19]

(62) | **AAE *dən*** | **General American English present perfect** |
       |---|---|
       | a. !I dən wanted to do that for five years. (special context) | a'. I have wanted to do that for five years. |
       | b. ?/*She dən always wanted to go to Liberia. | b'. She has always wanted to go to Liberia. |
       | c. ?/*His sister dən knew that for five years. | c'. His sister has known that for five years. |

The sentence in (62a) is not completely ruled out, as it can occur in a special pragmatic context. The sentence can be used in a context in which the speaker expresses surprise: I can't believe that dance class is canceled after I *dən* wanted to take dance for five years. In this context, the focus, or more precisely, the emphasis is on having wanted to take dance for five years. I have flagged the sentence with a '!' to show that it is used in a special context. Another sentence that is similar to the one in (62a) is a sentence discussed in Green (1998b, p. 48): *His sister dən been an invalid all her life*. This sentence is acceptable with the reading "How dare you offer your help now (ten years too late). She's been an invalid all her life!" The interpretation is intended to show that some special pragmatic context is required in this case, also. The sentences in (62b, c) are anomalous if not completely ruled out (thus they are marked '?/*'), and it is not clear at all whether they can occur in special contexts. However, the general American English present perfect sentences in (62a', b', c') are grammatical and do not require a special context.

A number of issues may be related to the status of the sentences in (62a, b, c). One is the type of verb that occurs in the *dən* construction, and the other is the type of adverb phrase that occurs in the sentence. *Dən* indicates that an event is over, but *know* (62b) is a state, and we have explained that states continue; they do not have ending points. As such, there appears to be an incompatibility between *dən* and the state (indicated by the verb *know*). The adverb phrase (*for five years*) refers to a time period that includes the present time, and it is allowed in present perfect contexts, as shown in (62c').[20] As shown in (58a), an adverb such as *for five years* can occur with *dən* sequences in special pragmatic contexts. Also, note that the following sentence is fine, in which the person is still in California when the sentence is uttered: *I dən been in California too long* 'I have been in California too long.' One question is whether this sentence also requires a special context. (Dayton [1996] and Labov [1998] have conducted extensive research on *dən* in AAE. See those works for further discussion, especially on their readings of new uses of *dən*. Also see Terry 2000 and Edwards 2001 on *dən* and the present perfect.)

The resultant state marker *dən* occurs with time adverbs *already* and *before*, which are compatible with an event being over:

(63)   a. **I dən** already finished that/**I dən** finished that already.
       b. **I dən** drove that car before.

Already usually occurs in the position following *dən*, but it can occur at the end of the sentence (63a). *Before* occurs at the end of the sentence (63b). Adverb phrases such as *for five years* and *too long* also occur with *dən* constructions, often in special contexts.

The properties of the verbal marker *dən* can be summarized in the following way:

Summary of properties of *dən*

Q: What is it?
A: *Dən* is a verbal or tense/aspect marker.
Q: What is its special pronunciation property?
A: *Dən* is unstressed.
Q: What is its function?
A: *Dən* indicates that an event is in the resultant state; that is, it is over. But in some contexts, it occurs with states, which do not have endpoints. (But see the last Q/A pair.)
Q: Where does it occur?
A: *Dən* usually occurs preceding verbs ending in -*ed*; however, it may precede the present form *give*, for example.
Q: What happens when it occurs with some verbs that name states?
A: In some situations, *dən* seems to be incompatible with states, so in those cases, the resulting readings are strange. In other cases (in which there are adverbials such as *for five years, too long*), *dən* and states often occur in special pragmatic contexts.

A thorough analysis of *done* in Southern white American English is given in Feagin (1979). About the marker, Feagin says: "Of all the grammatical forms in Southern White

US English which are claimed to be derived from the mesolect creole spoken by Blacks during the era of American slavery, preverbal *done* (also called quasi-modal *done*) is the most likely candidate in the verb system" (p. 159). Feagin suggests that *done* made its way to Alabama through the speech of poor whites from Georgia and the Carolinas and also through the speech of slaves. The extensive data set that Feagin provides on *done* shows that it is used in a wider range of environments by her Alabama working-class speakers than by speakers of AAE. She does not discuss any unique pronunciation properties of *done*, so I have no basis on which to compare the pronunciation of *done* in Alabama white English and *dən* in AAE. In some of its uses *done* (in Alabama) is identical to *dən* in AAE. Two examples from Feagin's data are *He done got out* (p. 128) and *Oh, I done used all my thread* (p. 129). On the other hand, at least two types of examples that Feagin presents have not been reported for current AAE, to my knowledge. In the first example, *done* occurs with an inflected form of *be* (i.e., *am* ['*m*]), and in the second example, it occurs in a sentence with an adverb that indicates past time (*yesterday*). It also precedes adjectives, as in (64c):[21]

(64) a. Lord, I'm done died! (p. 127)
   b. They done had the tables fixed yesterday, already. (p. 129)
   c. Some of em's done dead an' gone. (p. 131)

Edwards (1991) discusses similarities and differences between preverbal *don* in Guyanese Creole and *dən* in AAE. He notes that sentences such as *Dem don gat di koolii-man rom* ('They already have the Indian man's rum') in Guyanese Creole and AAE *dən* constructions are similar. One difference is that Guyanese Creole *don* is produced with significant stress, but AAE *dən* is produced as an unstressed form.

AAE *dən*, *done* in other varieties of American English and *don* in Guyanese Creole converge in their use to mark events that have ended; however, they diverge in a number of other environments in which they occur. Further research would help to determine whether the use of *done* in Alabama is representative of its use in other Southern states or whether the use of *done* in other varieties is more like that of *dən* in AAE. Also, it would be interesting to determine the extent to which the stress patterns associated with verbal markers *dən* (and *BIN*) were influenced by African languages and creoles.

Aspectual combinations with *dən*: *be dən* and *BIN dən*

The markers *be* and *BIN* can combine with *dən* to yield *be dən* and *BIN dən*, respectively. In some cases, the combination of *be* and *dən* to yield *be dən* results in the habitual resultant state compositional meaning; the newly formed unit has a meaning that is equal to the meaning of its parts, habitual *be* and resultant state *dən* that usually signals that an event is over. As we will see, there are other readings of the *be dən* sequence, in which *be* does not indicate habituality. However, *dən* has the same meaning in all *be/BIN dən* constructions. Also, *dən* is unstressed in all of the sequences in which it occurs. As such, the stress is on the first element in the sequence (on *be* and *BIN*).

Be dən (habitual resultant state)

The first *be dən* construction that will be discussed is referred to as habitual resultant state (see the habitual resultant state paradigm in (37)), in which habitual is denoted by *be* and the notion of having ended is denoted by *dən*. The verb is in the past form just as it is in the *dən* constructions that have been discussed. The meaning of these constructions can be glossed as 'have usually already.' This *be dən* sequence indicates the habitual completion of some event such as having usually already read it in the newspaper (65a).

(65)   a. A: Y'all keep up with the news, hunh?
           B: Yeah, when it come on there, we **be dən read** it in the newspaper. (Bf, 60s)
               'Yeah, when it comes on there, we have usually already read it in the newspaper'
               (Literally: Yeah, by the time the news comes on the television news show, we
               have usually already read it in the newspaper.)
       b. She gotta be there for 9, so they **be dən gone** to school. (Bf, 60s)
           'She has to be there at 9, so they have usually already gone to school by then'
           (Literally: She has to be at work at 9 AM, so the children have usually already gone
           to school by the time she leaves.)
       c. When I change the oil, I like to see how much it **be dən burned**. (Bm, 60s)
           'When I change the oil, I like to see how much it has already burned'
           (Literally: It is usually the case that when I change the oil in my truck, I like
           to see how much oil it has burned.)
       d. **Be dən told** them something before you get there. (Bm, 50s)
           '(You should) have told them something before you get there.'
           (Literally: Before you start jumping up and down as you preach, you should have
           already given the congregation a solid message.)
       e. Anybody who don' [don't] have no money and jus' **be dən got paid**, must be on
           drugs. (Bm, 30s)
           'It is usually the case that anybody who doesn't have any money but has just gotten
           paid, must be on drugs'
           (Literally: It is usually the case that a person who doesn't have money after s/he has
           just been paid must be spending money on drugs.)

This *be dən* sequence is the least discussed of all *be dən* sequences in AAE perhaps because it occurs in some geographical regions more than in others. The extent to which it occurs in inner city areas in the northeastern and western United States in which data have been collected from speakers of AAE is not clear; as such, research has not focused on descriptions of the use of habitual resultant state *be dən*, but see Dayton (1996) for examples that are compatible with this *be dən* interpretation. The sentences in (65a, b, c) are from speakers in southwestern Louisiana, but the sentence in (65d) is from an African American male in northern California, and the sentence in (65e) is from an African American male in southeastern Texas. In all of the sentences, the meaning that is conveyed is that an event has usually already occurred by the time a subsequent event takes place. In the case of (65a), speaker B notes that usually the reading event is over by the time the news comes on television. We can represent this meaning pictorially:

(66)

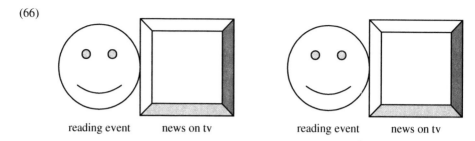

reading event   news on tv   reading event   news on tv

The smiling face represents the reading event and the square frame represents the news on television. The face precedes the frame in order to show that the reading event occurs before the news comes on television. Also, there are two groups, each of which is composed of a reading event (represented by the smiling face) and a news event (represented by the square frame). The two groups are included to show that the event of having read preceding the time the news comes on television is a habitual occurrence; it occurs from time to time.

The adverbs *usually*, *always* and *already* occur with this *be dən*. As noted earlier in this chapter, *usually* and *always* occur with aspectual *be*, and *already* occurs with *dən*. Because this sequence is composed of both *be* and *dən*, it makes sense that these adverbs occur with it.

(67)   a. I **usually be dən** read that.
       b. I **be dən already** read that./I **be dən** read that **already**.

Be dən (future resultant state)

The future resultant state *be dən* sequence is similar to the habitual resultant state in that it, too, indicates that an event is over, that the event is in the resultant state. However, the future resultant state is different in that it does not indicate habitual meaning. It is used in environments in which some activity will be completed by a future time.[22]

(68)   a. They'a **be dən growed** out that by then.
       'They will have already grown out of that by then' (Bm, 60s, Green 1993, p. 161)
       b. Five years from now, they mama be out the service. They'a **be dən got** older.
       (Bf, 50s)
       'Five years from now, their mama will be out of the service. They will have gotten older by then'
       A: Honey, what's your name?
       B: Lisa.
       A: I **be dən forgot** next week. (attested)
       'I will have forgotten by next week'

In the sentence (68a), the event of having grown out of that will have taken place before some future time, and in (68b) the event of having gotten older will have taken place before some future time. Finally, the event of having forgotten will have taken place before some event in the future (68c). As noted in an earlier discussion, *be* can be used to indicate future readings, so *be dən* here can also be regarded as being compositional. The future meaning comes from *be* and the resultant state meaning from *dən*. As indicated in the examples in (68), adverbials referring to some future time (e.g., *by then, five years from now, next week*) can occur in this *be dən* construction.

In other varieties of English, the future resultant state reading is the future perfect (*will have*) as in *He will have grown out of that by then.* In mainstream English, the verb following *will have* occurs in the participle form (*grown*), not in the simple past (*grew*).

Be dən (modal resultant state)

The *be dən* modal resultant state, as it is referred to here, is used in somewhat threatening situations, situations which are associated with veiled or mild threats or simply to express imminent actions. The constructions in which *be dən* occurs resemble conditionals in that they have an implicit and sometimes explicit *if*-clause and *then*-clause. "The *be dən* sequence, which is in the *then*-clause, is a part of the statement of the consequence. In these sentences, the speakers wish to express the fact that not only will the consequences happen if the condition is met, but they will happen immediately after it is met" (Green 1993, p. 162).

(69)

    a. Boy, I make any kind of move, this boy **be dən shot** me. (Bm, 40s)
      'If I move, this boy will shoot me'
      (Literally: If I move, then this boy will shoot me as a result of moving.)
    b. Once you put your hand on the plow, you can't be looking back, cause you **be dən dug up** something else. (Bm, 50s)
      'Once you put your hand on the plow, you can't look back, because you will dig up something else'
      (Literally: Once you put your hand on the plow, you can't look back because if you do, then you will dig up something else, that is, something you don't intend to dig up.)

In (69a, b) neither *if* nor *then* is explicitly stated, but both the statements are conditional. The sentence in (69a) would be rendered in the following way if *if* and *then* were explicitly stated: Boy, **if** I make any kind of move, **then** this boy be dən shot me. Both sentences, ([69a] and the one just stated [with the explicit *if* and *then*]) suggest that there will be some consequence as a result of some action. In (69a) the action of making any kind of move will result in the consequence of getting the speaker shot, and in (69b) the action of looking back will result in the consequence of digging up something else.

Adverbs such as *probably* and *certainly* occur with this *be dən* sequence: *Boy, I make any kind of move, this boy probably be dən shot me.*

BIN dən (remote past resultant state)

One of the most interesting characteristics of this *BIN dən* sequence is that it appears to be identical in meaning to the reading of BIN_{COMP} constructions. They both mark the remoteness of an event that ended in the past. A number of examples occur in my database; however, it is not clear how or if the sentences with *BIN dən* are different from those with BIN_{COMP}:

(70)   a. You should'a **BIN dən** called me down there. (attested)
          'You should have called me down there a long time ago'
          (cf. You should'a BIN called me down there.)
       b. He **BIN dən** put that in there. (attested)
          'He put that in there a long time ago'
          (cf. He BIN put that in there.)

The obvious question is the following: If *BIN dən* and BIN_{COMP} constructions have the same meaning, why do both occur? One response is that *dən* simply adds emphasis to the notion of the event having ended, so the difference between *He BIN dən put that in there* and *He BIN put that in there* is that the former uses *dən* to place emphasis on the resultant state of the putting that in there event, while the latter does not. The second is that in sentences such as (70) *dən* redundantly indicates the resultant state.

It is slightly misleading to refer to *be dən* and *BIN dən* as separate markers. It is probably more accurate to say that the markers *be* and *BIN* can take sequences of *dən* + verb. However, I have treated them separately as a means of being able to refer to them conveniently. Time adverbs that indicate how long ago an event has ended do not occur in *BIN dən* constructions. This is also the case with BIN_{COMP}, as noted in the discussion of *BIN*.

We have seen that *be* and *BIN* can combine with *dən*, and at this point, you are probably wondering whether *be* and *BIN* can combine to yield a compositional reading of *be BIN* or *BIN be*. Neither combination is possible, which, no doubt, raises questions about the relation between the two markers. As a result, in AAE the sentences **Bruce be BIN running* and **Bruce BIN be running* are ungrammatical. One suggestion is that the two markers cannot occur together because there is only one available place in the sentence for a *be* or *BIN* marker, and it is taken by one or the other (*be* or *BIN*), not both together. Remember that *be* indicates habituality and *BIN* situates something in the remote past. If they could occur at the same time, then we would expect to get the remote past habitual meaning. But remember from the discussion of BIN_{HAB}, that we do get this meaning with just *BIN*, so we do not need **be BIN/*BIN be* occurring together to get the remote past habitual. Also, see Green (1998b) for further details and a possible explanation for why *be* and *BIN* do not combine to yield a marker with compositional meaning.

2.3.2   Additional characteristics of aspectual markers

Referring once again to the paradigms in (28–39), we find some other important characteristics of aspectual markers. One characteristic is that aspectual markers are not
inflected for person and number, so, for example, aspectual *be* is used to indicate habitual meaning when the subject is first, second or third person singular/plural (e.g., *she
be*, *they be*). This is a point of difference between aspectual *be* and the auxiliary/copula
be in AAE. In the case of the auxiliary/copula *be* some forms are inflected, so for
example, the forms *I'm* and *is* are used. Aspectual *be*, on the other hand, is invariant
with respect to inflection for person and number; the form is always *be*.

The aspectual paradigms also show that certain auxiliaries occur with aspectual
markers in the contexts of emphatic marking and negation. For example, the auxiliary
do occurs with aspectual *be* and habitual resultant state *be dən* in emphatic affirmation
and negative environments (37). Likewise the auxiliary *have* may occur with *BIN* (29)
and *dən* (32) in emphatic affirmation environments, and *ain't* and *haven't* occur with
these markers in negative environments. (As noted in the paradigms, the judgment
about the occurrence of *have* with *dən* is somewhat questionable.) Auxiliaries also
occur with aspectual markers in some questions, as shown below:

(71)   a. **Do** they be running? (They be running?)
          *__Be__ they running?
       b. **Have** they BIN running? (They BIN running?)
          *__BIN__ they running
       c. **Do** they be dən ran? (They be dən ran?) (habitual resultant state)
          *__Be dən__ they ran?
          *__Be__ they dən ran?
       d. **Will** they be dən finished that by then? (They'a be dən finished that by then?) (future
          resultant state)
          'Will they have finished that by then?'
          *__Be dən__ they finished that by then?
          *__Be__ they dən finished that by then?

The sentences in (71) show that auxiliaries but not aspectual markers can occur at the
beginning of the sentence in questions. The sentences in which the aspectual marker
appears in inverted order with respect to the subject are ungrammatical, thus they
are flagged with '*'. As shown in parentheses following the questions formed with
auxiliaries, the questions are acceptable without auxiliaries if the aspectual marker
occurs in the position following the subject and intonation is used to signal the
question.

This same pattern of auxiliary use occurs in tag questions with aspectual markers;
an auxiliary must be copied at the end of the sentence in the tag. (You may want to
review the discussion of tag formation in the section on auxiliaries.):

(72)   Your phone bill be high, **don't** it? (Bf, 80s).
        *Your phone bill be high, **ben't** it?

The auxiliary *don't* is used in the tag because *do* occurs with the aspectual marker *be* in the declarative. *Be* cannot host *n't* (or *n't* cannot attach to *be*), so the sentence with *ben't* is ungrammatical. The auxiliaries *ain't/haven't* occur with *BIN* in tag questions:

(73)   They **BIN** left, **ain't/haven't** they?
        *They **BIN** left, **BIN't** they?

Auxiliaries are also used to support aspectual markers in verb phrase-ellipsis. (It would be a good idea to review verb phrase-ellipsis in the section on auxiliaries):

(74)   a. Bruce **be** running, and Sue **do**, too.
          *Bruce be running, and Sue **be**, too.
        b. Bruce **BIN** running, and Sue **have**, too.
          *Bruce BIN running, and Sue BIN, too.

Consider an example from natural speech:

(75)   A: I tell 'em how pretty they look.
        B: Do they be pretty?
        A: Sometime they do, and sometime they don't. I just tell 'em ALL they pretty.
        (Bf, 60s)

As we see in (74) and (75), the auxiliary *do* can substitute for deleted material, but aspectual *be* cannot. *Do* is the auxiliary that supports aspectual *be* in questions, negative constructions and emphatic constructions. Auxiliaries are used along with aspectual markers when they are needed in some environment in which an aspectual marker cannot occur.

Further examples of auxiliary support are given in (76). The auxiliary *do* occurs in the environments of questions (76a, b), negation (76c, d) and emphatic affirmation (76e, f). The sentence in (76g) expresses emphasis and negation, and the auxiliary *do* occurs in those environments. The marker *dən* receives the same type of support from *ain't* and *have* (76h, i).

(76)   a. A: You at work?
           B: Where else **do** you **be** at eight in the morning? (Bm, 30s)
           'Usually, where else are you at eight in the morning?'
        b. One day I **be** up and the next day I **be** down. **Do** you **be** like that? (attested)
           'One day I am up and the next day I am down. Are you like that sometimes?'
        c. I really **don't be** feeling too good. (Bf, 50s)
           'Usually, I really don't feel too well'
        d. He doesn't even allow women to wear pants at women's retreats and he **doesn't** even **be** there. (Bf, 40s)
           'He doesn't allow women to wear pants at women's retreats, and he isn't usually there'
        e. I **DO be** all over the place. (Bm, 30s)
           'I AM usually all over the place'

    f. At six, it **DO be** dark. (attested)
       'At six, is it usually dark?'
    g. That's all a mind game. That **DO** NOT **be** working. (Bf, 20s)
       'That's all a mind game. That does not usually work.
    h. She **dǝn** died, **ain't** she? (attested)
       'She has died, hasn't she?'
    i. When I **HAVE dǝn** come; when I **have dǝn** sung my last song, prayed my last
       prayer . . . meet me at the Jordan River. (Bm, 70s)
       'When I have come, when I have sung my last song, prayed my last prayer . . . meet
       me at the Jordan River'

Sentences such as the ones in (76) can provide valuable information about general syntactic processes in AAE, but they can also provide insight into what speakers think about language. The sentence in (76d) is especially insightful. The speaker uses a very salient property of AAE, aspectual *be*, to mark the habitual nature of being there on different occasions; however, she uses the general American English agreement pattern, *doesn't* to agree with the singular subject *he*. I do not want to suggest that general American English agreement patterns are not used in AAE, but the use of *doesn't* (as opposed to *don't*) to support aspectual *be* is rare. I have not collected any other such examples, and I do not recall seeing such examples in the literature. Overall the speaker is very careful to use general American English and probably would not consider herself an AAE speaker.

2.4   Preverbal markers: *finna, steady, come*

Markers *finna*, *steady* and *come* have been identified in AAE, but they have not been analyzed to the extent that markers such as aspectual *be*, remote past *BIN* and *dǝn* have been analyzed. There are some descriptions of them in the literature, which will be cited in the summary of each preverbal marker. Also, note that lexical entries for *steady* and *come* are given in chapter 1.

Finna

Finna (including variants *fixina*, *fixna* and *fitna*) indicates that the event is imminent; it will happen in the immediate future. It precedes non-finite verbs, which are not marked for tense and agreement. Sentences in which this marker occurs are given below:

(77)   a. I don't know about you, but I'm **finna leave**.
       'I don't know about you, but I'm getting ready/about to leave'
    b. Y'all **finna eat**?
       'Are you getting ready/about to eat?'
    c. She was **finna move** the mattress herself when I got there.
       'She was getting ready/about to move the mattress when I got there'
    d. Oh-oh they pulling they coats off. That mean they **fixna kill** us or something.
       (attested)

'Oh-oh they are pulling their coats off. That means that they are about to kill us or something'
e. They **finna do** something. (Bm, 40s)
  'They're about to do something'
  (Literally: The professional ice skaters are getting ready to make a complicated move.)

First note that the verbs following *finna* are all in their bare (non-finite) forms. For example, *move* (77c) has no tense or agreement marking. This means that the form would never be *moves* or *moved* as in *She was finna moves the mattress herself*. The word in the position preceding *finna* is glossed with some form of the auxiliary *be*. The auxiliary form of *be* occurs on the surface in the sentences in (77a) as the contracted form '*m* and in (77c) as the past form *was*, but it does not occur on the surface in the sentence in (77b). These environments (with first person singular [77a] and past [77b]) are obligatory for auxiliary *be* in AAE, so it has to appear on the surface. (See the discussion on auxiliaries presented earlier in this chapter.) Aspectual *be* can also occur in this position preceding *finna* (78):

(78)   They **be finna go** to bed when I call there.
     'They are usually getting ready/about to go to bed when I call there'

In other varieties of English, the marker is realized as *fixing to* (see Bailey, Wikle, Tillery and Sand 1991), so it appears that a major difference between the two variants is pronunciation. Rickford and Rickford (2000) include this marker under the umbrella of innovative features of AAE. In addition, they list it as one of the preverbal markers used to encode tense-aspect distinctions. DeBose and Faraclas (1993) refer to *finna* (which they represent as *finta*) as a type of modal marker used to make a weak assertion. The term they use is irrealis marker.

Steady

The marker *steady* (which may also be pronounced as 'study') precedes a verb form in the progressive (verb+-*ing*, e.g., *steady talking*, where the verb *talk* takes -*ing*). *Steady* is used to convey the meaning that an activity is carried out in an intense or consistent manner. Baugh (1984) defines the marker as "a predicate adverb" that "indicates that the activity of the corresponding progressive verb is conducted in an intense, consistent, and continuous manner" (pp. 3, 5). Because it indicates that an activity is carried out in an intense and consistent manner, it must precede a verb that names an activity. As such, *steady* does not usually precede verbs that name states such as *have*, *own* and *know*. This means that a sentence such as *They steady having money* is ungrammatical because *have* names a state, which cannot be carried out in an intense and continuous manner. States are uninterrupted; they simply hold. The source of the ungrammaticality is the semantic or meaning clash between *steady*, which functions as a marker that indicates the manner in which an activity is carried out, and the state named by *have*, which does not provide the kind of event or activity that *steady* requires. The sentence is anomalous because on the one hand, it refers to a constant state, but on the other it describes the state as occurring in a certain manner. This is a contradiction. But the sentence *They steady getting money* is good because *getting* refers to the type of activity required by *steady*.

Some sentences in which *steady* occurs are given below:

(79)   a. They want to do they own thing, and you **steady talking** to them. (attested)
          'They want to do their own thing, and you're continuing to talk to them'
       b. People be on them jobs for thirty years just **steady working**. (attested)
          'People usually stay on those jobs for thirty years, working consistently'
       c. Now that you got the new life, Satan **steady bothering** you. (Bm, 40s)
          'Now that you have a new life, Satan is consistently bothering you'
          (Literally: Now that you are a Christian, Satan is consistently trying to make you sin.)

(Also, see additional examples in the lexical entry for *steady* in chapter 1.) As shown in the sentence in (79a), the *steady* V-*ing* sequence can occur in a predicate construction in which a form of auxiliary *be* does not occur on the surface (i.e., 'and you Ø steady . . . ,' where Ø indicates that there is no overt auxiliary). Overt forms of *be* (e.g., *is, was*) can precede *steady*, as illustrated in its lexical entry in chapter 1: *That politician is/was steady talking*. The now familiar aspectual *be* can also occur in the position preceding *steady* V-*ing*, as shown in the sentence in (80):

(80)   Them students **be steady trying** to make a buck.
       'Those students are always working diligently to make money'

In such environments, *steady* has the function that has just been described, while aspectual *be* indicates habitual meaning; in sentences such as (80), *be*, not *steady*, contributes the habitual meaning.

Aspectual *be* can even combine with *know* (or any verb that expresses a state), but *steady* cannot. For this reason, the sentence *Those brothers be knowing how to fix cars* is grammatical. The verb *know* indicates a state, but it can occur with aspectual *be*, which forces a habitual reading on the state verbs that otherwise do not express this type of event reading. It expresses a meaning in which on particular occasions, the brothers do something to show that they know how to fix cars. That is, their knowledge of fixing cars is manifested on different occasions by their acts of fixing cars. Because they fix cars on different occasions, we can say that they *be knowing how to fix cars*. The sentence does not mean that they know how to fix cars on one occasion and then they forget how to fix them on others. The state of their knowing how to fix cars does not change; they always know how to fix cars. The point is that they fix cars on different occasions, which shows that those brothers have skills in the mechanics of cars. The sentence **Those brothers steady knowing how to fix cars* is not acceptable in AAE because *steady* cannot occur with a verb that expresses a state. *Steady* modifies an activity, and when it occurs with a state, the state is characterized as occurring in an intense and consistent manner. The result is a semantic clash because states cannot occur in an intense and consistent manner; they simply hold or remain constant. As noted, *have* expresses a state, so *steady having* as in **They steady having money* is ungrammatical; however, *be steady having* as in *They be steady having money* is grammatical. The latter sentence is grammatical because aspectual *be* forces *have* to take on an activity reading, and, as a result, *steady* is no longer occurring with a state. One way to put this is to say that aspectual *be* fixes *have*, gives it a reading that is compatible with the type of activity that *steady* can take.

The general properties of aspectual *be* and *steady* and compatibility with states are summarized in the chart below:

Properties of *be* and *steady*

Marker	Meaning	Compatibility with states
be	indicates activity/state recurs	compatible with states (in that it forces states to take on an activity reading)
steady	indicates activity carried out in intense/continuous manner	incompatible with states (in that it describes action associated with activities or events)

Come

Some lexical items in AAE are described as indicating or reflecting attitude, namely indignation, expressed on the part of the speaker. Whether such attitudes are always directly related to particular lexical items is an interesting issue, and research on this topic should be pursued.[23] However, it is clear that a major function of the marker *come* is to mark speaker indignation. Spears (1982, p. 850) refers to *come* as a semi-auxiliary that expresses speaker indignation. Some sentences in which this property of *come* is expressed are given below:

(81)   a. You the one come telling me it's hot. I can't believe you got your coat on. (Bm, 30s)
         'You're the one who had the nerve to tell me that it's hot. I can't believe you've got your coat on'
       b. They come walking in here like they was gon' make us change our minds.
         'They walked in here as if they were going to do or say something to make us change our minds'
       c. Don't come acting like you don't know what happened and you started the whole thing.
         'Don't try to act as if you don't know what happened, because you started the whole thing'

(Also, see additional examples in the lexical entry for *come* in chapter 1.) The viewpoint in sentences such as those above is that of the speaker, who actually sees the addressee as entering the conversation (or scene) in a manner of which the speaker does not approve. Note that in (81a), the speaker, in hindsight, disapproves of the addressee first saying it was hot and then acting differently. In all of the examples, *come* precedes verbs ending in *-ing*: *come telling, come walking* and *come acting*. In this way, the marker differs from the main verb *come*.[24] This is undoubtedly one of the reasons that Spears (1982) refers to it as a semi-auxiliary.

Summary

This chapter has presented basic verbal paradigms in AAE, pointing out general patterns in the verb forms. Throughout the discussion, the ways in which the verbal paradigms in AAE differ from those in general American English were highlighted. Some of the differences are related to person/number agreement and past and present perfect forms. Many of the major differences that were outlined are those in the aspectual paradigms. AAE uses markers *be*, BIN and *dən* to indicate specific meaning. These markers occur in well-defined environments, and they have unique stress patterns. Aspectual markers differ from auxiliaries, as shown in processes such as emphatic affirmation, negation, yes-no question formation and tag question formation. This chapter gives a description of subtle meaning and use of patterns which provide evidence that the syntactic system of these verbal markers is rule governed. The description of these markers may also be useful in developing lessons for speakers in standard English proficiency programs in that it provides numerous examples and explains how the AAE patterns differ systematically from those in general American English.

The marker *be* in AAE was compared to *be* in Hiberno English and *be* in the Carolinas, while AAE *dən* was compared to *done* in Alabama white English and *don* in Guyanese Creole. While there are similarities, there are also differences. For example, *done* in the Alabama variety is less restricted than *dən* in AAE, as the former occurs in a broader range of environments than *dən* in AAE.

The markers *finna*, *steady* and *come* were also addressed in this section. They occur with verbs in specific forms: *finna* occurs with verbs in the bare form, and *steady* and *come* occur with verbs ending in *-ing*. In addition, as has been shown, it is important to make the state/activity distinction because the marker *steady* must combine with a verb that can be understood as indicating some activity.

Exercises

1. Explain the similarities and differences between the following pairs of sentences:

    (a) They eating./They be eating.
    (b) They tall./They be tall.
    (c) They dən ate./They BIN ate.
    (d) They BIN ate./They BIN dən ate.

2. In the introduction to this chapter, I noted that in a magazine article *Johnny be good* was inaccurately glossed as 'Johnny is a good person.' What is the accurate gloss for the sentence?

3.   The example in (76) is used to illustrate *do* and *be* in ellipsis constructions. What other salient property of AAE is reflected in A's response to B's question?

4.   Consider the following sentence:

We been here for a long time.
Based on the discussion of *been* and *BIN*, tell whether the *been* in the sentence can be stressed *BIN* or whether it is the same *been* that occurs in other varieties of English (e.g., *We've been here for a long time*). Explain your answer by addressing the types of requirements that must be met in *BIN* constructions.

5.   In the discussion of *BIN*, it was noted that there are three types of *BIN* constructions. They are labeled BIN_{STAT}, BIN_{HAB} and BIN_{COMP}, due to the type of readings we get when *BIN* is used with different predicates (e.g., verbs, adjectives, nouns). The following sentence should have two meanings:
They BIN playing soccer.
What are they? (Hint: The difference in readings is related to the way we understand the length of time they have been playing soccer.)

3 Syntax Part 2: syntactic and morphosyntactic properties in AAE

Focal point For the most part, words in sentences in AAE are arranged in the same order as words in sentences in other varieties of English, but in AAE different combinations are allowed. For example, in AAE, the word order subject-auxiliary-main verb-object occurs in AAE *I didn't see nothing* just as in general American English *I didn't see anything*. The difference is that in AAE both the auxiliary and object can be negative. Also, AAE uses the same words that occur in other varieties of English, but these words can take on different meanings and functions. One case in point is that it can be used to indicate that something exists: *It be just the right amount of decoration on those birthday cakes.*

When I rose this morning, I didn't have no doubt.
[line from a song sung in African American church services]

3.1 Introduction

This chapter presents a description of patterns in the syntactic and morphological components of AAE. As in chapter 2, I will be concerned with the way words are combined to form sentences, and I will also consider morphology, that part of the system that deals with the function of smaller units of words such as suffixes. Oftentimes negative opinions are formed about AAE and the people who speak it based on the type of data that will be discussed in this chapter. Listeners understand that the AAE features differ in some way from features of general American English, but they seldom understand that the differences are based on specific rules that account for the way words are combined to form sentences in AAE. Our ears have been trained to hear and accept the sentence *There is usually just the right amount of decoration on those birthday cakes* as correct and the sentence *It be just the right amount of decoration on those birthday cakes* as incorrect and used by speakers who have a limited or low-level language repertoire.

Specific standards are established for language use in classrooms and other settings, but these standards are not based on linguistic patterns that are inherently better than other patterns. The standards are simply established norms of English use. This chapter does not attempt to debate the status of the standard language or to raise questions about the appropriateness of an established English variety. Instead it presents a general description of the rules that apply to AAE constructions and describes systematic differences between AAE and other varieties of English, including the standard.

This chapter, taken together with the syntactic properties presented in chapter 2, gives an introduction to what speakers of AAE know about syntactic patterns in the linguistic system. The syntactic patterns in this chapter range from multiple negation to patterns in question formation. The chapter also considers morphosyntactic properties related to past time marking (*-ed*), verbal *-s* and genitive marking. In addition to explaining the systematic nature of sentence formation in AAE, this chapter presents accurate general American English correspondences for AAE constructions.

Syntactic properties

3.2   Negation

Multiple negators such as *don't*, *no* and *nothing* can be used in a single negative sentence. In multiple negation constructions, negation can be marked on auxiliaries (e.g., *don't*) and indefinite nouns such as *anybody* (*nobody*) and *anything* (*nothing*). This pattern is illustrated in the examples below:

(1) a. I sure hope it **don't** be **no** leak after they finish. (Bm, 60s)
      'I hope there won't be a leak after they finish'
   b. If you **don't** do **nothing** but farm work, your social security **don't** be **nothing**. (Bm, 60s)
      'If you only do farm work, then your social security isn't usually very much'
   c. Bruce **don't** want **no** teacher telling him **nothing** about **no** books.
      'Bruce doesn't want any teacher telling him anything about (any) books'
   d. I **don't never** have **no** problems. I jus' don' like the stuff that be happening. (Bf on national news television interview)
      'I don't ever have (any) problems. I just don't like the stuff that happens from time to time'
   e. Sometimes it **didn't** have **no** chalk, **no** books, **no** teacher. (Bm, 80)
      'Sometimes there weren't any chalk, any books or any teacher'
   f. I **ain't never** seen **nobody** preach under announcements. (Bm, 50s)
      'I have never seen anyone preach while they're giving announcements'

The sentences in (1b, c, e) stop at four, but there is no limit on the number of negators that can be used. A traditional prescriptive 'rule' in general American English states that 'double' negatives are not grammatical because they make a positive. The formula multiplying two negatives yields a positive does not work for AAE. The negative meaning of the sentences in (1) is not affected by the addition of negative elements, that is, they do not become positive; so the sentence in (1e) is no less negative than the general American English gloss that accompanies it. This system of negative marking contrasts with the system in mainstream English in that it allows more than one negative element in clauses that are interpreted as negative. Researchers have referred to the 'extra' negative elements in the AAE sentences as pleonastic, suggesting that they do not contribute any additional negative meaning to the sentences. (See Labov 1972, for a discussion of multiple negation in AAE and Martin 1992, for an account of pleonastic negation in AAE and other varieties of English.) This means that in the sentence in (1e), the first negative marker *didn't* does all the work of marking negation; *no* in the following three noun phrases simply agrees with the negation on *didn't* and perhaps adds emphasis, but it does not contribute any negative meaning. According to Labov, Cohen, Robbins and Lewis (1968, p. 288), this type of negative concord or multiple negation "is strongly marked as non-standard, and therefore carries social information." Labov *et al*. do not discuss exactly what the social information is in relation to negative concord, but it could be related to such social factors as class, education and identity.

Closely related to the phenomenon of multiple negation is negative inversion, in which two sentence or clause initial elements, an auxiliary and indefinite noun phrase, are obligatorily marked for negation. In these constructions, the initial negated auxiliary is followed by a negative indefinite noun phrase, as in the example in (2a):

(2)   a. **Don't no game** last all night long. (Bf, conversation)
          'No game lasts all night'

This sentence begins with a negated auxiliary verb *don't* which is followed by a negative indefinite noun phrase *no game*. We call this noun phrase indefinite because it does not name any game in particular. Note that the two negative elements can introduce a clause (in square brackets) as in *I know [**don't no game** last all night long]*. The subject *I* begins the main sentence, but the negative inversion construction is 'embedded' (that is, it is further within the sentence) in that sentence at the beginning of a clause following the verb *know*.

       b. **Can't nobody** tell you it wasn't meant for you. (attested)
          'Nobody can tell you it wasn't meant for you'
       c. **Don't nothing** come to a sleeper but a dream. (Bf, 60s)
          'Nohing comes to a sleeper but a dream'
       d. **Ain't nothing** you can do. (attested)
          (can also be: It ain't nothing you can do.)
          'There isn't anything that you can do'
       e. **Shouldn't** be **nothing** happening you don't know about. (attested)
          (can also be: It shouldn't be nothing happening you don't know about.)
          'There shouldn't be anything happening that you don't know about'

As in the sentence in (2a), and in those in (2b, c), a negated auxiliary is followed by a negative indefinite noun phrase, which does not name anyone or anything in particular. The sentences in (2d, e) are multiple negation constructions in existential sentences, which will be discussed in section 3.3.

Negative inversion constructions are noted for their superficial resemblance to yes-no questions in that the auxiliary precedes the subject. Compare the sentences in (3), noting the similarities and differences between the negative inversion construction (3a) and the yes-no question (3b).

(3)   a. **Don't nobody** want to go to the movies.
       b. **Do anybody** want to go to the movies?

Both of the sentences are grammatical in AAE, but the first one (3a) has a negated auxiliary (*don't*) followed by a negative indefinite noun (*nobody*), whereas (3b) begins with a positive auxiliary (*do*) followed by a positive indefinite noun (*anybody*). The other major difference between the sentences is that (3a) is not a question; it makes an assertion, but (3b) asks a question. This distinction is reflected in the intonation of the sentences, such that the sentence in (3a) is uttered with declarative intonation or pitch pattern, and (3b) has question intonation, which may vary, to some extent, from the question intonation in other varieties of English. We will return to intonational patterns in AAE in chapter 4.

Set rules are followed in producing negative inversion sentences. The initial auxiliary and indefinite noun must be negative, so the sentence in (4), in which the auxiliary is positive (*do*), cannot be a negative inversion construction:

(4)   *Do nobody want to go to the movies.

Note, however, that in some special cases if the auxiliary is negative and the following noun is not negative, the sentence is still acceptable, and the meaning is basically identical to that in negative inversion constructions. Consider the following chant (5) that was once shouted in dance halls:

(5)   Freeze! **Don't another person** move! (cf. Freeze! Don't nobody move!)

At some point, while a large group of people were dancing, they would yell in unison: "Freeze!" at which point, everyone stopped in their dance steps. They would then chant, "Don't another person move!" After a few moments of being still, everyone would resume the dance steps. In this sentence, *another person*, is not in the form of a negative indefinite (*nobody*). The sentence is not a negative inversion construction, but has the same type of meaning, and it can be taken to be a variant of negative inversion constructions.

Examples of negative inversion constructions and multiple negation can be heard in songs sung in African American religious services. Consider the lines from two popular church songs, "Can't Nobody Do Me Like Jesus" (6a) and "This Morning When I Rose " (6b), also in the focal point of this chapter:

(6)   a. **Can't nobody** do me like Jesus;
          Can't nobody do me like the Lord.
          Can't nobody do me like Jesus;
          He's my friend.
       b. When I rose this morning, I **didn't** have **no doubt**.

The song in (6a), which exemplifies negative inversion, basically testifies to the greatness of the Lord, who can do what no human being can do; that is, there isn't anybody who can do me like the Lord. The line in (6b), multiple negation without inversion, explains the certainty a person has when the Lord is in her life. In effect, she didn't have any doubt about what the Lord could do. Both strategies of multiple negation, negative inversion and non-inverted negation, are robust in AAE.

The sentences in (2) can also be expressed without inversion of the negative indefinite and the auxiliary, as in the sentences in (7):

(7) a. No game don't last all night.
     b. Nobody can't tell you it wasn't meant for you.
     c. Nothing don't come to a sleeper but a dream.

According to Labov *et al.* (1968), negative inversion "is an optional process which gives additional prominence to the negative, and takes different forms in different dialects. It has a strongly affective character wherever it occurs" (p. 288). The authors suggest that negation in the inversion constructions in (2) is more prominent, but I add that a number of factors in addition to the initial placement of the negated auxiliary can determine prominence. As such, negation in the sentences in (7), in which the negative indefinite precedes the negated auxiliary, can also be prominent, and factors such as stress on the auxiliary can play a role in establishing such prominence. The word order in these sentences is that of regular declaratives in which the negative indefinite noun precedes the negated auxiliary. More advanced analyses of negation and negative inversion can be found in Martin (1992), Weldon (1994), Sells, Rickford, and Wasow (1996), Howe (1997), Howe and Walker (2000) and Green (2001). These analyses discuss the phenomenon in the context of current syntactic theory.[1]

3.3   Existential *it* and *dey*

It and *dey* occur in constructions in AAE that are used to indicate that something exists. The following six sentences called existential constructions can be used to mean 'There is some coffee in the kitchen':

(8) a. It's some coffee in the kitchen.
     b. It got some coffee in the kitchen.
     c. It have some coffee in the kitchen.
     d. Dey some coffee in the kitchen.[2]
     f. Dey got some coffee in the kitchen.
     g. Dey have some coffee in the kitchen.

The patterns are *it's* (pronounced as [Is], like *it's* without the *t* sound) (8a), *it* followed by *got* and *have* (8b, c), *dey* followed by a noun phrase (8d) and *dey* followed by *got* and *have* (8f, g). The existential constructions in (9) also occur in AAE, but they differ slightly from those in (8) in that they have an "on occasions" reading, indicated by aspectual *be*.

(9) a. It be too many cars in that parking lot.
        'There are usually/always too many cars in that parking lot'

b. It be all kinds of cakes and pies in that store.
   'There are usually/always all kinds of cakes and pies in that store'

Some restrictions are placed on the formation of these existential sentences, and they are important in showing that there is a method in producing these and other constructions in AAE. Speakers adhere to these restrictions in producing grammatical AAE sentences. I cannot stress this point enough, especially in the face of stereotypes about AAE and the concern about strategies used to teach speakers of this variety in reading and language arts courses. These existential sentences can only be constructed with an existential element (e.g., *it*) and a following obligatory form of *be* (inflected or aspectual), *have* or *got*, which will be referred to here as a linker. These elements are called linkers because they function to link the existential to the following noun phrase. The logical subject, noun phrase that the sentence is actually about (or the phrase that is linked to the existential, e.g., *too many cars* [9a]), follows the linker.

The existential constructions that we have seen so far have the following form:

Existential element – linker – logical subject

It   *be*   *too many cars*   *in that parking lot*

The sentences in (8) and (9) are models that are provided to illustrate the different parts that are used to form existential constructions in AAE, but the sentences in (10) were actually produced by speakers. They also take the form discussed above.

(10) a. **It was** a lot of things going on in this lesson. (Bm, 50s)
         'There were a lot of things going on in this lesson'
      b. **It was** seventy in the family that went down to Israel. (Bm, 50s)
         'There were seventy in the family that went to Israel'
      c. Let's stand; **it might be** somebody who need to say yes to Jesus. (Bm, 50s)
         'Let's stand; there might be somebody who needs to say yes to Jesus'
      d. You say there's a reason for it, and **it could be**. (attested)
         'You say there's a reason for it, and there could be'
         (Literally: You say there's a reason for it, and there could be a reason for it.)
      e. **It be** knives in here. **It be** ice picks in here. (Bf teenager on national news)
         'There are usually knives in here. There are usually ice picks in here'
      f. Sometimes **it didn't have** no chalk, no book, no teacher. (Bm, 80s)
         'Sometimes there wasn't any chalk, any book or any teacher'
      g. **It had** some breaded chicken sticks. **Dey had** some good French fries, too.[3] (Bf, 60s)
         'There were some breaded chicken sticks. There were some good French fries, too'

The initial existential element in (10a–g) is *it*. Of particular note here is (10d) in which *it* and the more mainstream English existential *there* are used in the same sentence. This example shows that some of the same forms and constructions that occur in general American English also occur in AAE. The sentence in (10e) was taken from a television news interview in which a student from a large inner city school in New York City was speaking about the dangerous weapons that are brought into the school frequently. She was in essence saying that it is usually/always the case that there are knives and ice picks in the school. Note also that the linker in (10f) is *have*, and it is negated with the auxiliary *didn't*. In the sentences in (10h–m), the linker (*'s*) is not a separate verbal form; instead it is attached to *it* (*it's*).

h. It's very beautiful. It's a lot of history in it. (Bf, 30s)
    'It's very beautiful. There is a lot of history in it'
i. **It's** one down there. (Bf, 40s)
    'There is one down there'
j. **It's** nothing you can do but be willing to be used by God. (Bm, 50s)
    'There is nothing you can do but be willing to be used by God'
k. **It's** a lot of people backstage who say they ready to come out and wreck shop.
    (Bm, disc jockey at 1995 birthday bash in Washington, DC)
    'There are a lot of people backstage who say they are ready to come out and wreck shop (i.e., perform)'
l. If you still sittin down by the end of this song, **it's** something wrong with you.
    (Bm, 20s)
    'If you're still sitting down by the end of this song, there's something wrong with you'
m. I don't go out like this. **It's** a shirt that go under here. (Bf, 33, on a talk show)
    'I don't go out like this. There's a shirt that goes under here'

In (10h) in the first sentence, *it's* is used as a pronoun referring to the banner that was displayed in the pulpit area and as an existential form in the second sentence. Obviously, speakers understand the different uses of *it's*; they understand when it is being used as a pronoun and as an existential element. The final existential construction (10n) is formed with an initial *dey got* sequence.

n. **Dey got** a fly messing with me. (Bf, 15).[4]
    'There is a fly messing with (i.e., bothering) me'

Let's refer to these, as in (10n), as *have/got* existentials. *Have/got* existentials are very interesting, especially when compared to *be* (i.e., all others) existentials. They are formed with an initial *dey* (or *it*) followed by the linker *have/got* and a noun.

From Feagin's (1979) extensive study on the use of language in a white community in Alabama, we find that *be* existentials are used in that variety of English. She provides a number of examples as given below, but she does not include examples of *it* existentials with aspectual *be*:

(11) a. It's all these people that – I only know through goin to Sunday school.
      b. It was some trouble here once.
      c. It's a big pole in the middle. (p. 239)

Feagin does not include any examples of *have/got* existentials in her study of the Alabama variety of English, and the extent to which such forms occur in other varieties of English is not clear.

AAE may be more similar to creoles in the formation of *have/got* existentials. Bickerton (1981) notes that many creoles express existentials and possessives by using the same lexical items. Among the creoles with this property are Guyanese Creole (GC), Haitian Creole (HC) and Hawaiian Creole English (HCE):

(12) a. dem get wan uman we get gyal-pickni. (GC)
         they have a woman who have young daughter
         'There is one woman who has a daughter'
      b. gê you fâm ki gê you petit-fi. (HC)
         have a woman who have a child girl
         'There is a woman who has a daughter'
      (Michel DeGraff [personal communication] notes that the standard spelling for the HC example is as follows: Gen yon fanm ki gen yon pitit fi.)
      c. get wan wahini shi get wandata. (HCE)
         have a woman who have a young daughter
         'There is a woman who has a daughter' (p. 66)

Note that in (12) *get* (or some form of *get*) is used as the existential linker (first occurrence of *get/have*) and as a possessive verb. In addition, Gibson (2001) includes the following example from Walter Edwards's earlier research on Guyanese Creole: ii get man a don wan bed wan dee, yu no. yu Ø pee dem faiv daala fu da dee [There are men who usually finish preparing a bed in a day, you know. You pay them five dollars for that day.] p. 195.

Compare the Creole examples above to the sentence in (10n) in AAE. Rickford (1987) gives similar examples in his study of Guyanese Creole, in which *had* is used in the first existential, while the second existential construction is formed with *gat*.

(13) a. an di ad wohn maan yuusu ad o kyaar de tu. (p. 178)
         and they had a man who used to had a car there too
         'And there was a man who had a car there too'
      b. dee gat onoao leedi laas tu. (p. 188)
         they got another lady lose two
         'There's another lady who lost two'

Before ending this section, I want to discuss an additional example of an existential construction that might raise questions about ambiguity:

(14) A: There's a brush in the bathroom.
      B: It is? (Bm, 60s)
         'There is?'

The *it* in B's response to A's statement could be interpreted as pronominal *it* that refers to brush, as in *It is in the bathroom*, or, as indicated by the gloss, *it* can be existential as in *It's a brush in the bathroom* ('There is a brush in the bathroom'). The latter interpretation is assumed here because it is not clear that B was referring to a specific brush but that rather like A he was referring to the availability of any brush.

The following section gives a description of questions in AAE.

3.4   Questions

I have already discussed yes-no and tag questions in chapter 2 in the section on auxiliaries and aspectual markers. Both types of questions were described as questions
in which the auxiliary verb precedes the subject; however, you will recall that some
yes-no questions are formed without overt auxiliaries in sentence initial position, so
the following may also be used:

(15) a. You know her name?
         'Do you know her name?'
      b. He sleeping in the car?
         'Is he sleeping in the car?'

In these examples, there are no auxiliaries in the initial position of the sentences
indicating that they are questions, but, of course, the intonational pattern used in uttering
the sentences marks them as questions. The goal here is not to give a theoretical analysis
of the process of question formation because to do so would take us too far afield, and
it would lead us into a long discussion about controversial analyses of auxiliaries. I
will briefly summarize three accounts of question formation that are relevant for the
type of questions I have discussed so far. The first account is one that is given in some
introductory linguistics texts. It says that in forming questions, we start with a regular
declarative sentence or statement.

(16) a. Bruce **can** jump.

In the declarative sentence, the auxiliary (the modal *can* in (16a)) follows the subject.
In the question, the auxiliary assumes a position in the front of the sentence preceding
the subject (16b):

      b. **Can** Bruce— jump?

This analysis works for the kind of questions that we have seen so far. In an earlier
discussion of aspectual *be*, we saw that *do* is the auxiliary that occurs at the beginning
of sentences with aspectual *be*, such as *Do you be like that?* Following the process
above illustrated with (16a, b), I explain the formation of the question in (17b):

(17) a. It **DO** be dark.
         'It IS usually dark'
      b. **Do** it be dark?
         'Is it usually dark?'

To form the question, the auxiliary *do* assumes the position preceding the subject *it*, as
in (17b).

But what about declaratives in which there is no auxiliary, such as *He sleeping in
that car* and *He be sleeping in that car*? How do we use them to form questions? We
can form corresponding questions, but auxiliaries are not necessary, as questions can
be signaled by intonation: *He sleeping in that car? He be sleeping in that car?* But to
produce questions in which auxiliaries are used, a different approach must be taken.

To get these auxiliaries, we simply insert them preceding subjects when we need them. This is exactly what I have done in (18), a third way to form questions:

(18) a. He sleeping in that car. → **Is** he sleeping in that car?
      b. He be sleeping in that car. → **Do** he be sleeping in that car?

To form the questions in (18), auxiliaries must be present because neither a main verb (i.e., *sleeping*) nor aspectual *be* can occur at the beginning of the sentence in questions. So far, three statements have been made about yes-no question formation: Statement (1): We start with a declarative sentence, locate the auxiliary and place it at the beginning of the sentence, preceding the subject.

Example: He DO be sleeping.   (Declarative with auxiliary)
          Do he be sleeping?   (Place auxiliary in front of sentence)

OR

Statement (2): We start with a declarative sentence in which there is no auxiliary, so we insert the correct one in forming the question.

He be sleeping.   (Declarative without auxiliary)
Do he be sleeping?   (Insert correct auxiliary in position in front of sentence)
OR

Statement (3): Questions without initial auxiliaries can be signaled with question intonation.

He be sleeping.   (Declarative without auxiliary)
He be sleeping?   (Questions signaled by intonation, without initial auxiliary)

   Now let's consider *wh*-questions, which are introduced by words that begin with *wh*, such as *who, what, which, why, when* and *where*. *How* does not begin with *wh*, but it is included in the group of *wh*-words. Yes-no questions and *wh*-questions differ in the content of the response or information that is requested. The former require either a yes or no response, while the latter are requests for content that will answer the *wh*-question.

(19) a. What did you eat? (Bf, 60s)
      b. What they was doing? Catching worms or something? (attested)
         'What were they doing?'
      c. What we gon get out the deal since we left everything? (attested)
         'What are we going to get out of the deal since we have left everything?'
      d. Why y'all want to treat me like this? (attested)
         'Why do y'all want to treat me like this?'
      e. Why they ain't growing? (Bm, 50s)
         'Why aren't they growing?'
      f. Why you looking like that? (attested)
         'Why are you looking like that?'
      g. Why those people don't want to take that car? (Bf, 60s)
         'Why don't those people want to take that car?'
      h. How you knew I was here? (attested)
         'How did you know I was here?'

i. How long do you be out of school? (attested)
    'How long are you usually out of school?'
j. Who you be talking to like that? (attested)
    'Who are you usually talking to like that?'
k. Where your part be at? (Bf, 20s)
    'Usually, where is your part?'
    (Literally: Where do you usually part your hair?)

Wh-questions in AAE can be formed in a number of ways. Let us illustrate one way with the sentence in (19a). The subject of that sentence is *you*; the auxiliary is *did*; the verb is *eat* and the object is *what*. The object *what* (*wh*-word) occurs in the initial position of the sentence although it is understood as the object of *eat*. We can think of the sentence in (19a) as being related to the declarative *You did eat what* (cf. *You did eat beans*), where the object *what* occurs after the verb *eat*. This related sentence differs from the *wh*-question in two ways: (1) the *wh*-word is at the end of the sentence, not at the beginning and (2) the auxiliary *did* follows the subject. In forming a *wh*-question from this fabricated declarative, in which *what* is actually represented as an object following *eat*, the following steps are taken:

Fabricated declarative: You did eat what.
Step (1): What you did eat   (*What* assumes position in front of sentence)

Step (2): What did you eat   (*Did* assumes a position immediately preceding the
                              subject)

We can do the same thing with the sentence in (19i):
Fabricated declarative: You do be out of school how long
Step (1): How long you do be out of school

Step (2): How long do you   be out of school

In the remaining *wh*-questions in (19), the auxiliary either follows the subject, or it does not occur in the sentence. The auxiliaries *was*, *ain't* and *don't* follow the subjects in (19b, e and g), respectively. Let's see what happens if we fabricate a declarative and try to form the *wh*-question in (19b) from it:

19b. What they was doing?
Fabricated declarative: They was doing what
Step (1): What they was doing (*What* assumes position in front of sentence)

Step (2): The auxiliary does not assume the position preceding the subject *they*; it retains its position following the subject. This step in which the auxiliary is placed in the position preceding the subject does not apply.

There is no overt auxiliary in (19c, d, f, h, j and k). We can try the same process for (19j):

19j. Who you be talking to like that?
Fabricated declarative: You be talking to who like that

Step (1): Who you be talking to like that (*Who* assumes position in front of sentence)

Step (2): There is no auxiliary in the fabricated declarative, so this step does not apply.

The three patterns that are associated with *wh*-questions in AAE are as follows:

(1) WH-WORD	AUXILIARY	SUBJECT		(19a)
(2) WH-WORD		SUBJECT	AUXILIARY	(19b)
(3) WH-WORD		SUBJECT		(19j)

In the first type (1), the auxiliary follows the *wh*-word and precedes the subject, and in the second type (2), the auxiliary immediately follows the subject. Finally, there is no overt auxiliary in the third type (3). AAE has three patterns for *wh*-questions, depending on the placement of the auxiliary or whether there is an auxiliary in the question. *Wh*-questions in AAE share similarities with *wh*-questions in general American English and other varieties of English. The pattern in (19b) certainly does not occur in mainstream American English, but it still needs to be determined whether other American English dialects have forms such as that.

The final questions that will be addressed in this section are indirect questions, which are introduced by question verbs and sequences of verbs such as *ask*, *wonder* and *want to see*. These sentences are like yes-no questions and *wh*-questions in that they make some type of inquiry, but they do not ask questions directly. The indirect questions are clauses themselves (because they contain a subject and a verb) that are embedded or set within the larger declarative sentence. The yes-no and *wh*-questions that we have seen are not embedded within the overall sentence; they are interrogatives that make direct requests for information. Consider the indirect or embedded questions that are set off by brackets ([ ]) below:

(20) a. I wonder [if the mailman dən passed].
         'I wonder if the mailman has already passed'
      b. It's gonna ask you [**do you** wanna make a transfer]. (attested)
         'It's going to ask you if you want to make a transfer'
      c. And we see [**can't we** make suggestions – according to what the Lord want us to do]. (attested)
         'And we will see if we can make any suggestions – according to what the Lord wants us to do'
      d. We on our way to Oklahoma. We trying to see [**can we** work out March]. (attested)
         'We are on our way to Oklahoma. We're trying to see if we can work out March'
      e. I wanted to see [**was it** the one we bought]. (attested)
         'I wanted to see if it was the one we bought'
      f. Tell me [**do it** make any sense]. (Bf, 20s)
         'Tell me if it makes any sense'
      g. They don't ask you [**did you** sit on the choir]. (attested)
         'They don't ask you if you were a member of the choir'
      h. Go over there and see [**did they** bring my car in]. (attested)
         'Go over there and see if they brought my car in'

i. I meant to ask her [**did she** want it]. (Bf, 40s)
   'I meant to ask her if she wanted it'

j. You gotta wonder [**is the fear** based on shame]. (attested)
   'You've got to wonder if the fear is based on shame'

k. I wanted to know [**could they** do it for me]. (attested)
   'I wanted to know if they could do it for me'

l. I asked Jean and them [**did they** want to eat]. (Bf, 60s)
   'I asked Jean and them if they wanted to eat'

m. I wonder [**have you** heard from heaven]. (attested)
   'I wonder if you have heard from heaven'

n. I wonder [**do it** be like the water we drink]. (attested)
   'I wonder if it is usually like the water we drink'

o. Then after the scripture, I'm gonna ask Brother Wall [**will he** come
   and play "Bless Ye the Lord" for us]. (attested)
   'Then after the scripture, I'm going to ask Brother Wall if he will come and play
   "Bless Ye the Lord" for us'

p. I wonder [**am I** helping anybody yet]. (attested)
   'I wonder if I am helping anybody yet'

q. I wonder [**what YOU** doing about it]. (attested)
   'I wonder what YOU are doing about it'

The indirect question *if the mailman dən passed* (20a) is introduced by the verb *wonder*, and the only difference between it and indirect questions in general American English is that the marker *dən* is used here. We would expect questions like this one to occur in other varieties of English such as the Alabama variety that Feagin discusses. These indirect questions are also possible with the word *whether* in place of *if*, as in *I wonder [whether the mailman dən passed]*.

The remaining questions are introduced by question verbs (e.g., *know*, *wonder*, *want to know*), and they do not contain the word *if* or *whether*; instead they are formed the same way direct yes-no questions are formed: by inverting the auxiliary. Consider the bracketed indirect questions and the inverted auxiliaries and subjects in bold print in (20b–p). Look at the question in brackets in (20n), in which the embedded question is actually identical to a yes-no question, with the auxiliary *do* preceding the subject *it*. *Wh*-questions can also be embedded, as shown in (20q). This embedded *wh*-question is identical to the root or direct *wh*-questions that were discussed in (19) (see 19f).

What we have not seen are sentences in which both *if* and the inverted auxiliary are used in indirect questions. For example, we have not seen sentences such as the following:

(21)   *It's gonna ask you [if do you wanna make a transfer].

This sentence is ungrammatical; it is predicted that speakers will not produce this sentence or sentences like it. The sentence is just another example of how AAE follows certain rules in producing constructions and if these rules are not followed, then the

resulting sentence is ill-formed in AAE. So in indirect questions either option, . . .
[**if** you wanna make a transfer] (with *if / whether*) or . . . [**do you** wanna make a transfer]
(with inverted auxiliary and subject), is used. If both options are used simultaneously,
then the resulting construction will be ungrammatical, as shown in (21).[5]

Also, we have not seen sentences in which neither *if / whether* nor an inverted auxiliary begins the embedded question, for example: **It's gonna ask you* [— *you wanna
make a transfer*]. The sentence is ruled out because either *if / whether* or an auxiliary
must occur in the initial position of the embedded question, and neither occurs. Of
course, we could say: It's gonna ask you PAUSE "You wanna make a transfer?" But in
that sentence there would be a pause before the direct quote. There is no pause before
the embedded questions in the sentences in (20). Again we see that specific rules have
to be followed in producing indirect questions to avoid ungrammatical sentences. This
is important in showing that constructions in AAE are formed according to rules.

Other varieties of English permit the inverted subject and auxiliary pattern identified
in indirect questions in AAE. Examples from these different varieties are given in
O'Grady, Dobrovolsky and Aronoff (1993, pp. 178–179), an introductory text in general
linguistics (22a, b), and Radford (1988, p. 299), an introductory text in syntax (22c):

(22)   a. The coach wondered [would the team win].
        b. A fan asked [will the team win].
        c. John wondered [would he get a degree].

The general patterns here are identical; in AAE embedded questions, the auxiliary can
precede the subject, and in the questions in (22) the auxiliaries (in these examples,
modals *would, will*) can precede the subject. I will not base any strong claims on
these three examples, especially given the fact that I do not know exactly from which
nonstandard variety of English they were taken; however, two points can be made about
them: They are introduced by either *wondered* or *asked*, which are in the past tense,
and the inverted auxiliary is a modal. In comparison, in the AAE sentences in (20),
additional verbs and sequences of verbs (e.g., *see, tell me, want to know*) can introduce
indirect questions, and auxiliaries other than modals *would* and *will* can occur in the
questions. From the sentences in (22), we see that other varieties of English share with
AAE the strategy of producing embedded questions with subject auxiliary inversion.
What is not clear is whether, in these other varieties, the verbs that can introduce
indirect questions are limited to *wonder* and *ask* and whether the auxiliaries are limited
to modals *would, will*. McCloskey (1992) discusses such constructions in Hiberno
English, and Henry (1995) discusses this inversion in embedded clauses in Belfast
English. In both varieties, a range of verbs is used to introduce the indirect clauses, but
the range is wider in Belfast English (e.g., *They couldn't work out* [**had we** *left*]. Henry
1995, p. 107).

3.5   Relative clauses

The clauses that will be discussed in this section serve as modifiers or qualifiers of a
preceding noun and are referred to as relative clauses. In AAE and in other varieties

of English, these clauses (enclosed in brackets) may be introduced by an overt relative pronoun, *that* or *who*.

(23) a. They like **the teacher** [*who* graded her assignment].
     b. That's **the person** [*who* gave me the ticket].
     c. I know **the person** [(*who*) you talking about].
     d. It was seventy in **the family** [*that* went down to Israel]. (attested)
     e. It's **one gospel** [*that* fits all people]. (attested)

The clauses in brackets modify a preceding noun phrase (in bold print) in the direct object (23a, c), predicate nominative (23b, e) or object of the preposition (23d) position. *Who* in (23c) is in parentheses because it is optional; the sentence is grammatical with or without the pronoun (e.g., *I know **the person** [— you talking about]*). In (23b), *the person* is a predicate nominative or a noun linked to the pronoun *that* by the copula *be* form *'s*.

As shown in the sentences in (24), some relative clauses modifying a noun in predicate nominative or object position are not obligatorily introduced by a relative pronoun. I follow the strategy of using the symbol 'Ø' to indicate that nothing is in the specified position, so 'Ø' indicates that there is no overt relative pronoun:

(24) a. There are many mothers [Ø don't know where their children are]. (attested)
       'There are many mothers who don't know where their children are'
     b. It's a whole lot of people [Ø don' wanna go to hell]. (Bm, 40s)
       'There are a whole lot of people who don't want to go to hell'
     c. You the one [Ø be telling me]. (Bm, 30s)
       'You're the one who usually/always tells me'
     d. You're the one [Ø ain't got no church]. (attested)
       'You're the one who doesn't have a church'
     e. It was a nurse and a nurse's aid [Ø used to stand up at the door]. (attested)
       'There was a nurse and a nurse's aid who used to stand up at the door'
     f. You the one [Ø come telling me it's hot]. I can't believe you got your coat on. (Bm, 30s).
       'You're the one who had the nerve to tell me that it's hot. I can't believe you've got your coat on'
     g. It's a whole lot of people [Ø got fire insurance]. (attested)
       'There are a whole lot of people who have fire insurance'
     h. It's nobody [Ø walk that hard].
       'There isn't anybody who walks that hard'
     i. I think Aunt M. had a daughter [Ø lived off]. (Bf, 60s)
       'I think Aunt M. had a daughter who lived far away'
     j. We got one girl [Ø be here every night]. (attested)
       'There is one girl who is usually here every night'

In the sentences in (24a–h), the relative clause introduced by a Ø relative pronoun (call it a zero relative pronoun) modifies a noun in the predicate nominative position, and the clauses in the sentences in (24i) and (24j) modify the object of the sentence, so in (24i) [lived off] modifies direct object *daughter*.[6] Relative clauses that modify nouns in the predicate nominative or object positions are not obligatorily headed by relative pronouns. (See Tottie and Harvie 2000, for a discussion of relative clauses in AAE, other varieties of English and creoles.)

3.6   Preterite *had*

One pattern in AAE that is not discussed in earlier studies is the preterite (i.e., past tense) use of *had* in certain environments. In Rickford and Théberge-Rafal (1996), preterite *had* is characterized as a new syntactic feature that is used mainly by pre-adolescents; however, data – some of which will be presented in (26) – show that this *had* also occurs in the speech of adolescents to young adults. The use of preterite *had* has sparked some interest mainly because the speakers use it in a way that is markedly different from the use of the pluperfect (past perfect) in AAE as well as in other varieties of English. The pluperfect is used to mark the past before the past, as in the following sentence (25), in which the seeing the movie event occurs at some time prior to the arriving event.

(25)   They had seen the movie by the time the large group arrived.

The preterite *had* sequence and pluperfect sequence in AAE are superficially identical; they are both formed with *had* + past tense verb form. The main difference between the two is in meaning, as will be explained in consideration of the sentences in (26):

(26)   a. That's why at W. E. we had discussed a lot. (Bm, 12)
            'That's why we discussed a lot [of information] at W. E.'
        b. The alarm at the detailing place next door had went off a few minutes ago. (Bf, 30s)
            'The alarm at the detailing place next door went off a few minutes ago'
        c. I had went to the city last night and the only Affirm they had was super, so I didn't get it. (Bf, 20s)
            'I went to the city last night and the only Affirm they had was super, so I didn't get it'
        d. I was playing basketball, and I had went up for a lay up and then I came down and sprung my ankle. (Bm, 12)
            'I was playing basketball and I went up for a lay up and then I came down and sprained my ankle'
        e. We talked about this last year. That's the test I had failed. (Bm, 13)
            'We talked about this last year. That's the test I failed'
        f. A: I don't know if Leslie coming today.
            B: Why not?
            A: I think she had left yesterday. (Bm, 13)
            'I think she left yesterday'

g. A: You had to wear jeans?
   'Did you have to wear jeans?
   B: Un un. I had wore my dickey pants. (Bm, 12)
   'No. I wore my dickey pants'
h. They ain't paid me for two days that I had took. (Bf, 20s)
   'They haven't paid me for two days that I worked'/'They didn't pay me for two
   days that I worked'
i. My mother had cooked fish last night when I had got my clothes together. (Bf, 15)
   'My mother cooked fish last night while I got my clothes together'
   (Literally: My mother was cooking fish last night when I was getting my clothes
   together, or my mother had cooked fish before I got my clothes together.)
j. I had got strep throat on the last day of school. (Bf, 11)
   'I got strep throat on the last day of school'

The general statement about these examples is that the *had* + verb (verb-*ed*) sequence
is not used to indicate action that took place in the past before the past; this sequence
basically refers to an event in the simple past. In the sentences in (26a) and (26b),
the speakers use *had* in the narration of an event that happened in the simple past.
In (26a), the speaker is conveying the point that at his school, they discussed a lot of
information in preparation for the next school year, and in (26b), a young adult begins
a telephone conversation by saying the alarm at the place next door went off a few
minutes ago. A hairdresser uses the sentence in (26c) to relay her account of having
gone to New York City the night before an appointment with a client to purchase a
hair product called Affirm. Because the supply store had super strength as opposed to
regular strength Affirm, she did not get any product at all. Here the going to New York
City event (indicated by *had went*) is not in relation to any other event, yet the speaker
uses *had* to mark the pastness of that event. The case in (26d) is also interesting in
that the speaker refers to a number of events in the sentence (playing, went up and
came down), but chooses to mark the going up event with *had*. The speaker introduces
the playing event and continues the narration with *had went*, which does not actually
precede the playing event, that is, it is not situated farther in the past than the playing
event. It is, in fact, included in the playing event.

In (26e) the adolescent notes that he failed the test, but there is no obvious event in
the conversation that the failing event precedes. He also refers to having talked about the
information, but it would appear that the talking about the information event is actually
farther in the past than the failing the test event, so **had failed** is not the pluperfect.
The same speaker uses *had* in (26f) to mark the pastness of the leaving event. It is
clear that *had* does not mark the past before the past as the other time is yesterday,
when Leslie actually left. The leaving event cannot be situated farther in the past than
yesterday. The speaker in (26g) marks the wearing event with *had* although there is no
obvious past time against which the event is evaluated. The sentence in (26h), which
is actually uttered by a young adult, might be analyzed as being ambiguous because it
could be argued that the event of having taken two days may be marked by *had*, in that
it is situated farther in the past than the event of not having been paid. The ambiguity
arises in part because of the possible interpretations of *ain't* as a perfect or simple

past marker. There are two events in the sentence (26i), the cooking fish event and the getting clothes together event, which appear to have taken place simultaneously, or the time of one has overlapped the time of the other. Finally, in (26j) the getting strep throat event is marked by *had*, but it cannot be situated farther in the past than the last day of school. The time of the getting strep throat event is situated within the time of the last day of school.

Some patterns are identified in particular as marking speakers as being associated with the African American ethnic group or being members of some African American speech community. It can be argued that one of the goals of the use of preterite *had* in the media is to mark the speaker as 'sounding black.' Montana Taylor, a comedienne (African American) who appeared regularly on *Comic View* (a comedy show on Black Entertainment Television), stated that text books will have to be written to reflect the new Ebonics. As a result, children will be able to read books with the following types of sentences:

(27)   Y'all seen how fast Jane **had ran** across the street? (*Comic View*, 1997)

The use of preterite *had* is not the only pattern, but it is definitely one of the patterns that is associated with Taylor's new language, Ebonics.

In considering the description in this and the preceding chapter, we find that AAE has a number of different types of past and different ways of marking past events. The six types of past time are indicated by simple past, preterite *had*, pluperfect (past perfect), remote past, remote past perfect and resultant state. Each type has been discussed, and I end this section with a general summary of these past categories:

(28)   **Summary of past marking**

Type of past	Marker and verb form	Meaning
Simple past (chapter 2)	*drunk*	time before the present (i.e., event culminates before now)
Preterite *had* (chapter 3)	*had drunk*	time before the present, often used in narrative contexts (i.e., event culminates before now)
Remote past (chapter 2)	*BIN drunk*	remote past
Pluperfect (past perfect) (chapter 3)	*had drunk*	past before the past
Remote past perfect (chapter 2)	*had BIN drunk*	past before the remote past
Resultant state (chapter 2)	*dən drunk*	state of having ended or having been finished, can occur with some states in special contexts

Summary

The first part of this chapter characterizes syntactic properties of negation, existential constructions, questions, relative clauses and preterite *had* in AAE. In the discussion of negative inversion, it was noted that the order of the auxiliary and subject (indefinite noun phrase) is inverted, but the construction is not interpreted as a question. Existential constructions indicate that something exists. In the general scheme, these constructions require an existential element (*it/dey*), a verbal linker and a noun. These constructions in AAE share properties with corresponding constructions in other varieties of English and in creoles. Because the *have/got* existential uses either *have* or *got* as a linker, the sentences are sometimes taken as indicating possession; but there are ways of showing that they are existential in nature. Yes-no questions, *wh*-questions and embedded or indirect questions were identified. Although one of the hallmarks of yes-no questions is subject-auxiliary inversion, in AAE such inversion does not obligatorily occur, and in these cases, questions are marked by intonation. Using intonation to mark questions is not unique to AAE; but the type of intonation in these questions might prove to be characterized by unique properties of AAE.

It was also noted that inversion occurs in indirect questions in AAE, as in varieties such as Belfast and Hiberno English. Finally, three patterns for *wh*-questions were identified. They were characterized by the position of the *wh*-word, subject and auxiliary. One of the identifying characteristics of relative clauses in AAE is the zero relative pronoun that modifies a noun in predicate nominative position or object. This section ended with a discussion of preterite *had* and its position in the six-way system of past marking in AAE. Preterite *had* constructions are identical in shape to pluperfect (past before the past) sequences, but they have different meanings.

The constructions in each of these syntactic categories must be formed in accordance with the rules of AAE. If they are not, the sentences in which they occur will be ungrammatical.

The second part of this chapter deals with morphosyntactic patterns in AAE.

Morphosyntactic properties

3.7   Morphosyntactic patterns in AAE

So far this chapter has presented a discussion of issues in the syntax or sentence structure of AAE. It will end with a brief review of related issues from the morphological and morphosyntactic component of the language system. Morphology is that part of linguistics that is concerned with morphemes, the smallest units of meaning that are put together to build words. The word *jumped* consists of two morphemes, *jump* and *-ed*. Both units contribute meaning in forming the word. *Jump* expresses the action, and *-ed* indicates that the action is in the past. The word *teacher* consists of two morphemes, and *water* consists of one. In *teacher -er* is a morpheme meaning agent or one who does something, but *-er* in *water* is not a morpheme. The focus in this section will be on suffixes that do not change the meaning or part of speech of the word but that serve some other function in the sentence, such as that of marking tense or number and genitive relations.

3.7.1   *Past morphology*

The first type of morphology that will be considered is that which is used to indicate some type of past activity. As noted in the paradigms that were discussed in chapter 2, there is usually no distinction with respect to form between simple past and past participles in AAE. For the most part, the same form or identical morphology is used in simple past and participle environments. In mainstream terminology, the participle forms are used with helping verbs such as *have*, as in *I eat, I ate, I have eaten*. The participle or *-en* form is *eaten*. Consider the summary of past marking at the end of the preceding section, in which the participle form *drunk* is used across the board, in both the simple past and the pluperfect. Likewise the participle form is often used in the past and past participle environments with the following verbs: *ring* (*rung*), *see* (*seen*), *sink* (*sunk*), and *sing* (*sung*). In these verbs, the change from non-past to participle is indicated by a change in the vowel (e.g., *i* to *u*, *drink/drunk*; *sink/sunk*). For other verbs, it is the simple past form that is used in all contexts. This is the case with *ate*, as in the simple past *I ate yesterday* and the pluperfect *I had ate a snack by the time they delivered the pizza*. Still in other verbs, the past and past participle forms are indicated by a final *-ed*, as in *jump/jumped* (*I jumped on the trampoline. I had jumped on the trampoline.*).[7]

In considering the data that have been presented, we find that many of the verbs that are used are regular verbs, so they form the past and past participle by adding *-ed* to the present form of the verb (e.g., *jumped, walked, cooked, plugged*). However, a morphological distinction is made between some past and past participle forms; that is, the past is formed by adding *-ed* to the verb, and the past participle takes some *-en* form. The past and past participle forms, respectively, of some irregular verbs are *broke/broken, grew/grown, sang/sung, sank/sunk, saw/seen, threw/thrown, took/taken, tore/torn* and *went/gone*. We can ask two questions about the situation with these verb types and forms in AAE. The first question is the following: Does AAE make a morphological distinction, using both past and past participle forms in the case of irregular verbs, or is the past form used in all environments? We have already seen that there is no past/past participle distinction in AAE for verbs such as *drink*. However, there may be a distinction where other verbs are concerned, such that both the past and past participle forms are used. Secondly, if both forms are used, is the past used in one environment and the past participle restricted to another, or are the two forms used interchangeably? There is evidence to show that both forms are used. Verb forms in *BIN* constructions that are interpreted as meaning 'for a long time' or 'a long time ago' usually take simple past morphology, but there are some instances in which the verbs are in their participle or *-en* forms.

(29)   a. . . . look like she would'a BIN called my name. (Bm, 70s)
          '. . . looks as if she would have called my name a long time ago'
       b. A: Can I take this book home?
          B: I gotta think if anyone else asked me to take it home.
          A: I BIN asked you to take it home.
          'I asked you a long time ago to take it home' (Bf, 9)

c. I'd say, "Well, Baby, she BIN passed. (Bm, 60s)
   'I'd say, "Well, Baby, she passed a long time ago" (i.e., died a long time ago)'
d. I thought they should'a BIN did that. (attested)
   'I thought (i.e., in my opinion) they should have done that a long time ago'
e. I could'a BIN went back. (attested)
   'I could have gone back a long time ago'
f. Aw, he BIN gone – married a ready-made family.
   'Aw, he's been gone for a long time . . .' or 'Aw, he left a long time ago . . .' (Bf, 60s)
g. A: They tore down Superior? So they don't have it anymore.
   B: No. That's BIN gone. (Bm, 60s)
   'No. That's been gone for a long time'

The verbs following *BIN* in (29a, b, c) are regular verbs, so they end in -*ed*. The past tense form (*did*) of the irregular verb *do* is used in (29d). The sentences in (29e, f, g) show that both past and past participle forms of *go* (*went*, *gone*, respectively) are used. Notice that some *BIN* + verb sequences modify the subjects, that is, they describe the state that the subjects have been in for a long time. This is the case in (29g), which expresses that that place has been in the state of being gone for a long time. Perhaps this is why *gone* instead of *went* is used. Now, consider additional *BIN* constructions and the verb forms and meaning.

(30)   a. The mirror BIN broke.
          (1) 'The mirror has been broken for a long time'
          (2) 'The mirror broke a long time ago'
       b. His pants BIN tore.
          (1) 'His pants have been torn for a long time'
          (2) 'His pants tore a long time ago'
       c. The soup BIN cooked.
          'The soup has been cooked for a long time'
       d. That stew BIN gone.
          'That stew has been gone for a long time'

First consider the adjectival readings in (30), in which what is being referred to is the broken state of the mirror (30a), the torn state of the pants (30b) and the cooked state of the soup (30c). The state of the stew, being no longer there, is also described in (30d). I refer to these as adjectival meanings because they describe the mirror, pants, soup and stew. The verbs *broke* (30a) and *tore* (30b) also have a use that is not descriptive, that is, one that does not focus on describing the state of the subject. This second use is more verbal in nature in that it refers to an activity. In the second reading of (30a), the activity is that the mirror broke a long time ago, and in the second reading of (30b), the activity is that the pants tore a long time ago. In these second readings, what are referred to are the breaking activity in the case of the window and the tearing activity in the case of the pants, not the description of the state of the window and pants. It is the first type of reading (descriptive/adjectival reading) that might show a preference for the past participle verb form *gone* as in (29f, g) and (30d). There is no real evidence for such a distinction with other verbs so far, but additional examples of participles will be given.

Verbs following *dən* (including *be*/*BIN dən*) bear simple past morphology as well as *-en* morphology, as is the situation with *BIN*.

(31) a. You won't even take the trash out, and she dən worked all day just like you. (Bm, 70s)
          'You won't even take the trash out, and she has worked all day just like you'

      b. We got three Dollar stores. A new one dən opened. (Bf, 60s)
          'We've got three Dollar stores. A new one has (just) opened'

      c. I say, "Now you dən lived in California and you cain' drive." (Bf, 50s)
          'I say, "Now you have lived in California before and you can't drive"'

      d. You dən got this far. (attested)
          'You have already gotten this far'

      e. That snake dən bit me again. (attested)
          'That snake has just bitten me again'

      f. I should'a dən went by now. (Bm, 30s)
          'I should have already gone by now'

      g. But He dən already said what He'a bless. (attested)
          'But He has already said what He'll bless'

      h. A: Let me know when you wash your towels.
          B: I dən washed them. (Bf, 60s)
          'I have already washed them'

      i. I dən done all you told me to do. (attested)
          'I have already done all you have told me to do'

      j. A: How many y'all got? Fifty?
          B: Oh, no. We dən progressed. (Bm, 50s)
          'Oh, no. We have progressed (i.e., made progress)'

      k. You dən been here a year. (attested)
          'Yell, you have already been here a year'

      l. I know where y'all dən come from. (Bm, 30s)
          'I know where you two have come from'

      m. I be dən drove up there, but I have to drive back. (Bf, 50s)
          'After I have driven up there, I always have to drive back' or
          'It's usually the case that I drive up there, and I have to drive back'

      n. Candy go over there every time she come, if he be dən cooked. (Bf, 50s)
          'Candy goes over there every time she comes, if he has cooked'

In all of the sentences, the meaning is quite similar to that of the present perfect in mainstream English. All the sentences in (31) indicate that some activity has ended or is in the resultant state, as in the opening activity in (31b) that has been completed. The sentence in (31k), the having been there for a year is in its resultant state.

So far it has been shown that both simple past and *-en* forms (of irregular verbs) (see 31i) are used in AAE. It is not clear that a distinction is always made such that the simple past is used in one environment while the *-en* form is always used in the other.

One verb to study in determining whether such a distinction is made is *go* (*went/gone*). It may be that in AAE *gone* is restricted to more adjectival uses and *went* is reserved for more verbal uses.

The sentences, especially those in (29) and (30), show that the combinations of aspectual markers and verbs bearing past morphology can yield a range of meanings. AAE does not regularly use past participle forms, but the language system does have a way of indicating meaning that is expressed by using the participle forms in mainstream English. For example, in some cases, a marker such as *BIN* or *dən* may be used with a verb in the past form.

Another verb that will be useful in answering the question about whether there is a past tense/past participle distinction (e.g., *saw/seen*) is *see*. One case in point is that *seen* (not *saw*) is consistently used in the past participle context in the sentence *She just want to be seen /*She just want to be saw* (Green 1993). More extensive research should be conducted on the uses of *gone* and *seen* in AAE.

There are also some environments in which the simple past tense and *-en* forms of the verb in its adjectival use occurs with aspectual *be*. Actually, the type of adjectival (descriptive) and verbal (activity) readings that are associated with the *BIN* and *dən* sequences in (30) and (31) are also available with aspectual *be* sequences. The sentences in (32), in which *be* sequences have both adjectival and verbal readings, show that the marker does indeed take the same kinds of past verb forms that occur in *BIN* and *dən* sequences:

(32) a. I be told in my sleep to go to church. (Bm, 60s)
      'I am usually told in my sleep to go to church'
      (Literally: Something tells me while I am asleep (dreaming) to go to church.)
   b. I just be broken down. I be tired. (Bf, 30s)
      'I am usually broken down. I am usually tired'
   c. It be done before I think about it. (Bf, 60s)
      'It is usually finished before I think about it'
      (Literally: The rinse cycle has already finished by the time I think about adding liquid fabric softener to the wash.)
   d. Any comments right quick before I be thrown out? (attested)
      'Are there any comments before I'm taken out of the class?'
   e. Breakfast be cooked at 8 o'clock.
      'Breakfast is usually cooked at 8 o'clock'
      Two readings are possible here:
      (1) It is the case that someone usually cooks breakfast at 8 o'clock.
      (2) Breakfast is usually in a cooked state (i.e., ready) at 8 o'clock.

The sentence in (32a) has a verbal passive reading, and the focus is on the telling event. The object (the person being told) 'I' has become the grammatical subject. Consider the corresponding active sentence *Something tells me in my sleep to go to church*, in which *something* is the subject. Note that in mainstream and other varieties of English, the past participle form is used in passive sequences, but in AAE, a simple past form can also be used (e.g., *drove*, not *driven* in (31n)). *Be broken down* in (32b) is adjectival in that it describes the state that the speaker is usually in, that of being broken down (or that of being tired). Note that the speaker uses the past participle (*broken*) not the simple past (*broke*). Likewise the sentence in (32c) has an adjectival reading, so the rinse is already in a finished state during particular times. The participle *done* (not simple past *did*) is used. The following scenario provides the context in which the sentence in (32c) was used. In this sentence, the speaker was referring to the rinse cycle that occurs when laundry is washing in a washing machine. While walking down the aisle of a large wholesale store, the speaker commented on the different laundry detergents and fabric softeners that were displayed on the shelves. In comparing the liquid fabric softeners and softener sheets, she said that, in general, she does not like the liquids because they must be put into the wash at a precise time. Fabric softener sheets, on the other hand, can be tossed right into the dryer along with the laundry. The speaker felt that the liquid fabric softener required more work because it had to be added to the washer during a particular cycle. Furthermore the liquid is an inconvenience because the washer has usually already finished the entire cycle by the time she thinks about adding the liquid softener during the rinse cycle.

In the way the sentence in (32d) was used, it has an activity reading. The lecturer who used the sentence had already exceeded his allotted time, so in a joking manner, he said that whoever was in control would have him thrown out because he didn't dismiss the class when time was up. Again, the past participle verb form (*thrown*) is used, not the simple past (*threw*). Finally, the sequence in (32e) has a verbal reading, so on the one hand, *be cooked* can mean that someone usually cooks at a certain time, while on the other, it has an adjectival reading in environments in which *cooked* modifies the state of the breakfast. In such a case, the breakfast is described as being in a cooked state. The verb *cook* is a regular verb, so it takes *-ed*.

One of the goals of this section has been to show that both simple past and past participle verb forms are used. Further research will help to determine whether past participle forms such as *seen* and *gone* are indeed restricted to certain environments. Also, as has been demonstrated, aspectual *be* and *BIN* + past verb sequences have verbal (activity) and adjectival (descriptive) readings, and *dən* + past verb sequences have verbal readings. The verb form that is used with *be, BIN* and *dən* in these environments is often identical to the simple past, but in some instances irregular verbs in the past participle form (*-en*) are used. Another point is that in AAE, both the simple past and past participle can be used in the passive. It is certain that whether or not the simple past and/or past participle form is used is related to a number of factors such as particular verb, meaning (i.e., adjectival or verbal reading) and speaker. Not much has been said about background of speakers; however, because speakers may participate in a variety of speech situations and belong to different networks, they may use verb forms in different ways.

3.7.2   Verbal -s

One point that is made in the discussion of the paradigms in chapter 2 is that number distinction between singular and plural verbs is neutralized, resulting in the use of one form in both singular and plural contexts. It is often the case that the plural verb form is used as the default form, so, for example, the plural form may occur with third person singular. As a result, speakers often produce sentences such as (33), in which the verb that occurs with the third person singular subject is not marked with an -*s* (e.g., *come* vs. *comes*):

(33)   When he come down here, I be dən talked to him. (attested)
'When he comes down here, I have usually already talked to him'

However, verbs may also be marked with verbal -*s*, which may have a number of different functions: third person singular agreement marker, narrative present marker and habitual marker. Some researchers who have considered data produced by speakers of earlier varieties of AAE have argued that the third person singular -*s* was used with verbs that occurred with third person singular subjects in much the same way that the marker is used in other varieties of English. Poplack and Tagliamonte (1989) consider verbal -*s* inflection in AAE with the goal of determining whether the variation in the use of this marker in early and modern AAE "has a precedent in the history of the language, or is rather an intrusion from another system" (p. 47).[8]

Speakers may use this verbal -*s* as a narrative present marker on verbs that occur in the narration of events. Butters (1989) and Labov (1987) address the use of verbal -*s* as a narrative marker. An example from a television court program illustrating this narrative -*s* (on *gets*) is given below. During the show, a nineteen-year-old African American female used the third person singular -*s* when she was recounting her experience with the plaintiff:

(34)   Judge: What happened?
Woman: He had called me Wednesday afternoon and asked, "Do you want to go the movies" . . . so I gets in the car. (January 2000, *Judge Joe Brown*)

In the context of answering the judge's question and telling her story, the woman uses verbal -*s* with the verb *get* although the subject is *I*, which usually takes plural verb forms (e.g., *get*). (This use of -*s* occurs in other English varieties as well.) Another environment in which verbal -*s* has been argued to occur is in habitual contexts, as illustrated below:

(35)   a. I can show you some of the stuff we tesses them on.[9] (Bf, 30s)
'I can show you some of the stuff we test them on'
b. A: You have to get your rest.
B: I dos that. (Bf, 80s)
(Note: *Dos* is pronounced as 'doos,' not as 'does.')
'I do that'
c. When I think about Palm Sunday, I gets excited. (attested)
'When I think about Palm Sunday, I get excited'
d. I sits and rides. (Bm, 60s)
'I sit and ride'
e. Nobody don't be there when it throws water everywhere? (Bf, 80s)
'Nobody is usually there when it throws water everywhere?'
(Literally: Is anybody usually there when it throws water everywhere?)

f. The devil haves us in a state of sin. (attested)
  'The devil has us in a state of sin'
g. That's really all that's important, that he come around and bes with us. (attested)
  'That's really all that's important, that he comes around and spends time with us'
h. Well, that's the way it bes. (attested)
  'Well, that's the way it usually is'

The subjects of the sentences in (35a, b, c, d) are first person plural (*we*) and first person singular (I), but the verb form still ends in -*s* (*tesses, dos, gets, sits, rides*). All of these sentences communicate some habitual meaning. Take for example (35c). The speaker begins the sentence with W*hen I think about Palm Sunday*, which expresses particular occasions (some notion of habituality) during which he gets excited. In (35b) when B says, *I dos that*, she means that she rests regularly. In the remaining sentences, the subject is third person singular (*it, the devil, he*). The -*s* morphology on *throws* (35e) may also serve as a habitual marker, in which *throws water everywhere* is an event that occurs on different occasions. The case of *throws* may be argued to be ambiguous between habitual marking and third person singular marking. Because the subject of the verb is third person singular (*it*), it is possible that the verbal -*s* morphology is also an agreement marker, dually marking number (third person singular) and habitual aspect. Consider also the case in (35f), in which *have* is actually marked with the verbal -*s*. As a habitual marker, *haves* may be used to indicate that the speaker is referring to situations in which the devil occasionally puts us in a state of sin.[10] However, -*s* on *have* may also be used to mark duration, focusing on the sinful state in which we live due to the wiles of the devil. It might also be argued that -*s* on *have* has multiple functions, including agreeing with the third person singular subject *the devil*. It would be useful to collect further data to determine whether *haves* would also occur with plural subjects. I predict that it would also occur with plural subjects.

In (35g, h), *be* forms are marked with verbal -*s*. As has been explained in the discussion of aspectual *be*, the marker is not like other verb forms in that it cannot be conjugated into different person and number forms (e.g., *is, am, are*), so it remains invariant, uninflected in its paradigm, regardless of the person and number of the subject: *I/we be, you be, he/she/it/they be*. If aspectual *be* is not marked for person or number, then what is the role of the -*s* that is attached to it in (35h)? It may very well be that the verbal -*s* is functioning here as a habitual marker, and because aspectual *be* is an inherent habitual marker, verbal -*s* is redundant; it is doing what aspectual *be* already does. It is worth noting that the sentence *It bes that way* is commonly used. In fact, the title of one of Smitherman's popular articles is "It Bees Dat Way Sometime": Sounds and Structure of Present-Day Black English" (1985). The common use of *bes* with the subject *it* may account for the sentence in (35h). The examples in (35) make good cases for arguing that the verbal -*s* also functions solely as a habitual marker in some environments in AAE. This is one difference between AAE and general American English. Verbal -*s* in general American English will always occur in third person non-past singular contexts, which may also have habitual interpretations (e.g., *Bruce runs two races* [*every week*]). Of course, in mainstream English (as well as in other varieties of English, including AAE) this habitual reading occurs with the simple present, so the verb that occurs with plural subjects can also have a habitual reading (e.g., *They handle the outgoing packages*) although it is not marked with -*s*. Also, in light of the questions that have been raised, this verbal -*s* may have other functions.

The process of marking habitual with verbal -*s* is optional in AAE, as we see in (36a, b):

(36)   a. Carl, you know what I notice about this? When it be making ice, a lot of water fall in it. (Bf, 60s)
'Carl, you know what I notice about this? When it is usually making ice, a lot of water falls into it'
     b. They be mad at me cause when the news come on, they got to get up. (Bf, 60s)
'They are usually mad at me because when the news comes on, they have to get up'

These sentences have habitual interpretations even without verbal -*s* on the verbs. In (36a) the *when* clause (*when it be making ice*) specifies the occasions on which a lot of water falls into it. The verb *fall* does not need to be marked habitual by verbal -*s*. Similarly, the verb *come* (36b) is also within a *when* clause (*when the news come on*) that specifies the occasions on which an activity occurs. *Come* does not have to be overtly marked for habitual. Note also that aspectual *be* in (36a, b) is not marked with -*s*.

3.7.3   *Genitive marking*

As has been shown, some elements are not obligatory in marking certain types of syntactic and grammatical relationships in AAE. The morphosyntactic marker genitive -*s* falls within this category in that it is not required in possessive or other genitive contexts. It has been argued that word order is sufficient for marking the possessive relationship in AAE, so possessive -'*s* need not be present (see the discussion in Smitherman 1977). In the sentences in (37), no possessive (-'*s*) marker is used, but the ownership relationship is expressed by the order, in which the possessors *my mama*, *Rolanda* and *church* precede the possessed, *house*, *bed* and *responsibility*, respectively.

(37)   a. I always get bites cause we be hanging out at my **mama house**. (Bf, 9)
'I always get bites because we usually hang out at my mama's house'
     b. Sometime **Rolanda bed** don't be made up. (Bm, 70s)
'Sometimes Rolanda's bed isn't made up'
     c. That's the **church responsibility**. (Bm, 40s)
'That's the church's responsibility'

The process of genitive marking is definitely variable in that speakers may or may not use the -'*s* in such contexts.

(38)   a. I'll be dən reached across that counter and pulled that **woman's hair** out. (Bf, 40s)
           'I'll reach across that counter and pull that woman's hair out'
           (Literally: If she takes certain actions, I will immediately reach across that counter
           and pull that woman's hair out')
        b. She say, "Y'all be so good in here and in **Miss Brown's class**, y'all be the loudest
           things in here." (Bm, 13)
           'She says, "You are usually so good in here and in Miss Brown's class,
           you are usually the loudest things in here"'
        c. I give the Lord **his money**, but it don't be from here. (Bf, 60s)
           'I give the Lord his money, but it isn't usually from here'
        d. They want to do **they own thing**, and you steady talking to them. (attested)
           'They want to do their own thing, and you're continuing to talk to them'
        e. If they wanna go out and do something else with it, that's **they business**. (attested)
           'If they want to go out and do something else with it, that's their business'

Speakers also use the -'s marker as well as pronouns such as *his*, *hers* and *they* in
genitive contexts.[11]

Summary

The focus in the final part of this chapter is on morphosyntax, in particular morphology
for marking past, habitual and genitive. AAE does not make a morphological distinction
between the past and past participle forms across the board; however, there may be a
distinction between these forms when certain verbs are used, in particular *went/gone*
and *saw/seen*. *Gone* and *seen* may be the preferred forms in adjectival or descriptive
readings.

A theme throughout this chapter is that AAE is systematic, so speakers follow set
rules in forming sentences. These rules cover areas such as verbal sequences, negation,
questions, relative clauses and existential constructions, so when speakers know AAE,
they know rules governing the use of sequences from these different categories. These
patterns have been presented separately in different sections, but speakers can put them
together to form grammatical sentences such as the following:

- That's the class that don't nobody be signing up for. (Embedded negative inversion and aspectual *be*)
- Why you think she BIN went to Texas? (*Wh*-question without subject auxiliary
  inversion, *BIN* with past verb form *went*)

Exercises

1.   In AAE genuine yes-no questions can be formed without placing an auxiliary at the begin-
      ning of the sentence. In what other way could the following question be produced: Did she
      want to go to the basketball game?

2. There are two possible tag questions for *Bruce be dən washed his car*.

    (a) What are the two tag questions?
    (b) Why are the two tag questions possible?
    (c) Explain the process you used to form the tag questions.

3. As noted, at least six distinctions in the past are made in AAE. Illustrate the examples with the verb *write*. Be sure to identify each example with the appropriate label.

4. Explain the similarities and differences between the following pairs of sentences:

    (a) Don't nothing happen in this small town./Nothing don't happen in this small town.
    (b) Nobody don't want to go to the movies./Nobody don't want to go to no movies.
    (c) I know what you talking about. That's the magazine I had read during enrichment period./I know what you talking about. That's the magazine I read during enrichment period.

5. Consider the negative inversion or near negative inversion constructions in (a–c) and the corresponding existential constructions:

    (a) Wasn't nobody there.   'Nobody was there'
        Existential: It wasn't nobody there.   'There wasn't anybody there'
    (b) Ain't nothing in that purse.   'Nothing is in that purse'
        Existential: It ain't nothing in   'There is nothing in that purse'
        that purse.
                                                'There isn't anything in that purse'
    (c) Don't be nobody on that corner.   'Nobody is usually on that corner'
        Existential: It don't be nobody on   'Usually there is nobody on that corner'
        that corner.   'Usually there isn't anybody on that corner'

    Now consider the negative inversion constructions in (d–f), which do not have corresponding existential constructions. Ungrammatical examples of existentials are provided for your information. They are flagged by '*'.

    (d) Can't nobody say nothing about that article.   'Nobody can say anything
        Existential: *It can't nobody say nothing   about that article'
        about that article
    (e) Won't nothing stop me from drinking tea.   'Nothing will stop me
        Existential: *It won't nothing stop   from drinking tea'
        me from drinking tea.
    (f) Don't nobody listen to the five o'clock news.   'Nobody listens to the
        Existential: *It don't nobody listen to   five o'clock news'
        the five o'clock news

    Explain why it is possible to form corresponding existentials for the sentences in (a–c) but not for the sentences in (d–e).

6. In our discussion of relative clauses, we noted that the relative pronoun (e.g., *who, that*) is not obligatory in all environments. Now consider the following sentences:

    (a) The dog [that bit me] is brown.

(a') *The dog [—bit me] is brown.

(b) The pens [that ran out of ink] will be put in the empty box.

(b') *The pens [— ran out of ink] will be put in the empty box.

The sentences in (a, a') and (b, b') show that the relative pronoun must be present. Why are the sentences in (a') and (b') ungrammatical; that is, why are the sentences ungrammatical when the relative pronoun is absent? You might begin by considering what the relative clause (in brackets) modifies.

4   Phonology of AAE

Focal point   The different sound patterns of AAE are reflected in the combination of sounds that are allowed in the variety. Words in AAE and general American English that have the same meanings may have different pronunciations due to constraints on sounds. For example, in AAE the th sound in general American English (and other varieties of English) *bath* is produced as f (i.e., *baf*), and the th sound in general American English *bathe* is produced as ʋ (i.e., *baʋ*). Also, as explained in the preceding chapter, yes-no questions can be produced without an initial auxiliary. Does this affect the rhythmic patterns of sentences in AAE such that they are different from those patterns in other varieties of English? This chapter addresses sound and rhythmic patterns in AAE.

It's sofer tissue!

[facial tissues television commercial]

4.1   Introduction

The unique pronunciation related to stress patterns of aspectual markers *BIN* and *dən* has been mentioned in the preceding chapters on the lexicon and syntax of AAE. Especially in the case of *BIN*, the stress pattern affects meaning. While it would seem that these patterns are significant in the study of AAE, they have not been the focus of major studies on the sound system.

The most thorough studies of phonology or sound patterns in AAE were conducted in the 1960s and 1970s (Wolfram 1969, Wolfram and Fasold 1974, Luelsdorff 1973). These studies discuss the production of word final sounds (e.g., *test* and *kind* are pronounced as *tes* and *kin*, respectively), the production of *f* in environments in which other varieties of American English produce *th* (e.g. *baf/bath*) and the vocalization of *r* and *l*, the process which results in the homophony of *court* and *coat* in some regions in the United States. A substantial amount of this research was cast in the framework of Variation Theory, in which accounts were given of the inherent variability in language.[1] In his study of the speech of African Americans in Detroit, Wolfram (1969) showed the importance of the correlation between the use of sound patterns such as the ones mentioned above and extralinguistic factors such as age, socioeconomic class and sex.

It has been noted that in different varieties of American English (including registers of standard American English), word final consonant groups such as *nd* and *st* are reduced to single consonants *n* and *s*, respectively. That is, some speakers of varieties of English may produce *kind* as *kin* (rhymes with *pine*) in certain environments, so both the AAE speaker and the speaker of another variety of general American English may at some time or another produce *kin*. Speakers may differ by using *kin* in varying environments, and they may also differ in the extent to which they reduce final consonant groups to single consonant sounds. That is, the percentage rate of reduction may be greater for some speakers than for others. It is probably this feature of consonants that has received the most attention in the phonological studies of AAE, and it has been used in comparing AAE to other varieties of American English and to West African languages. On the one hand, studies have been used to argue that the patterns of final consonants in AAE parallel those in other varieties of English. On the other hand, it has been argued that AAE may resemble West African languages that do not have final consonant clusters.

This chapter presents a descriptive summary of the system of sounds in AAE. The description will focus on the systematic nature of sound combinations and the systematic way in which sounds are produced in certain environments. Along these lines, one of the goals is to show how AAE follows rules in sound combinations. In addition to considering single segments such as consonant sounds, this chapter reports on rhythmic patterns of words and sentences in AAE. Here a general overview of research in this area, as well as further directions that related studies can take, will be presented. Generally speaking, only the surface of research on rhythmic patterns in AAE has been scratched, so study in this area offers great possibilities for contributions to the description of the language system.

4.2   Final consonant sounds

Analyses of final consonant groups or clusters in AAE have been used as evidence that the language variety is systematic and governed by rules, and they have also been used to support claims about the historical origin of AAE. Two explanations for cluster data in AAE can be summarized as follows. One explanation is that pronunciations such as *tes* ('test'), *des* ('desk') and *han* ('hand') in which the final consonant clusters *st*, *sk* and *nd* are pronounced as *s*, *s* and *n*, respectively, are a result of a process called consonant cluster reduction. A second explanation is that words such as *test*, *desk* and *hand* are pronounced as *tes*, *des* and *han*, respectively, because AAE, like African languages from which it descended, does not have final consonant clusters. In presenting a general description of the process operating on final clusters, I comment on these explanations.

Consonant cluster reduction is a process in which the final consonant group or cluster, composed of two consonant sounds, is reduced to a single consonant sound. This is illustrated in (1) below, where 'C' stands for consonant.

(1)   CC→C

    || |

    nd→n

    kind→kin

In (1) the consonant cluster *nd* (CC) is reduced to *n* (C), so the word *kind* is produced without the final *d* sound (i.e., *kin*). Under this analysis, the clusters *st* in *test* and *sk* in *desk* are reduced to the consonant sound *s*. As a result of the consonant cluster process, the words *tes* ('test') and *des* ('desk') rhyme, and are minimally different in that they contrast only in the initial *t* and *d* sounds. One property of the consonant cluster reduction analysis is that it assumes, at some level in AAE, final clusters are intact, so *tes* actually starts out as *test*, and the final *t* is deleted under certain conditions. This analysis treats a word such as *test* in AAE as being identical to *test* in mainstream English. If there are differences in the pronunciations, such that in mainstream English the word is *test* in specific environments and in AAE it is pronounced as *tes*, these different pronunciations are the result of phonological processes, and not the result of different representations of the words in the two varieties. For example, the word in AAE is *test*, but it is pronounced as *tes* because a rule, as shown in (1), reduces the final *st* cluster to *s* by deleting the final *t*. AAE, then, is just like mainstream English in this respect; the only difference is that the reduction rule applies more often to words in AAE in specific environments when certain conditions are met.

    The second account of the production of words such as *tes* ('test'), *kin* ('kind') and *contac* ('contact') is an analysis which leans toward West African origins and postulates that speakers have such pronunciations, not because the final consonant sound is deleted in some environments, but because the languages from which AAE originated do not have final consonant clusters (so there are no clusters like *nd* and *st*). Ernie Smith (1998), who takes the Africanist approach, makes the following remarks:

> For example, the scholars who view African-American speech as a dialect of English describe the absent final consonant cluster as being "lost," "weakened," "simplified," "deleted," or "omitted" consonant phoneme. But viewed as an Africanist Language system that has adopted European words, African-American speech is described by Africologists as having retained the canonical form, or shape, of the syllable structure of the Niger-Congo African languages. Thus, in Ebonics homogeneous consonant clusters tend not to occur. This is not because the final phoneme has been "lost," "weakened," "simplified," "deleted," or "omitted," but because *they never existed in the first place*. Hence it is by relexification (that is, 'the replacement of a vocabulary item in a language with a word from another, without a change in the grammar,' – see Dillard 1972) that in Ebonics English words such as *west, best, test, last* and *fast* become *wes, bes, las* and *fas*; the words *land, band, sand* and *hand* become *lan, ban, san* and *han*; the words *left, lift, drift* and *swift* become *lef, lif, drif* and *swif* – and so forth.

[p. 56]

Under the African origin view, words such as *test* start out with single final consonant sounds, not with the final consonant cluster (e.g., The form *tes* does not start off with a final *st*). So according to this view, when speakers actually produce *test* in certain environments, such as that preceding a word that begins with a vowel, they actually add the final *t* to the word. Let's illustrate with an example. In the sentence *I will test out of math*, it is argued that the word *test* is otherwise pronounced as *tes*, but the *t* is added because the word precedes *out*, which begins with a vowel. The difference is that in Smith's view, in AAE, words such as *test* and *kind* start out with single final consonant sounds (i.e., *tes* and *kin*), while in general American or mainstream English, the word starts off with final consonant clusters (i.e., *test, kind*). This view presents AAE as patterning phonologically with West African languages, as summarized in Smith's quote.

Having presented a general overview of two accounts of final consonant sounds, I want to give a description of consonant cluster phenomena which focuses on the environments in which the reduction process is said to occur and a summary of the types of analyses that have been offered to account for the reduction process. Pronunciations such as the following surface in AAE with greater or less frequency in certain environments. Greater or lesser frequency refers to cases such that some speakers may produce the words as they are given in (2) – without final clusters – more often in certain environments and less often in others. Some speakers may always use the pronunciations in (2), however. In all of the words below, *s* is pronounced instead of the clusters *st*, *sp* and *sk*, *f* is pronounced instead of the cluster *ft*, *p* instead of *pt* and *k* instead of *kt*. Finally, *n* is pronounced instead of *nd*, and *l* is pronounced instead of *ld*:

(2)   **AAE**   **Phonetic transcription**

	AAE	Phonetic transcription	
a.	pos	[pos]	'post'
b.	was	[wɔs], [was]	'wasp'
c.	mas	[mæs]	'mask'
d.	gif	[gɪf]	'gift'
e.	adop	[ədap]	'adopt'
f.	conduc	[kandʌk]	'conduct'
g.	ban	[bæn]	'band'
h.	bol	[bol]	'bold'

Key: The phonetic transcription is given for each word as a means of providing a more accurate representation of the pronunciation.[2] The vowel sounds used by AAE speakers in different regions of the United States may vary. These vowel sounds and the ones presented throughout this chapter are primarily based on the vowel sounds I have heard all my life in southwestern Louisiana.

In studying final consonant sounds, we cannot just consider words in isolation; they should also be analyzed in different environments: whether they are produced in careful or casual speech, whether the final consonant precedes a suffix that begins with a consonant or vowel and whether the final consonant precedes a word that starts with a consonant or vowel. These environments are important because speakers might be expected to retain clusters more often when they are using more careful speech. Labov (1972) discusses the effect of such conditioning factors. Also, Guy (1991) presents a detailed analysis of conditioning factors for consonant cluster reduction.

In addition to the pronunciations in (2), those in (3) also occur with varying degrees of frequency. These words, unlike those in (2) are composed of two minimal units of meaning or two morphemes:

(3)   **AAE**   **Phonetic transcription**
   a. push   [pʊʃ]   'pushed'
   b. page   [peʤ]   'paged'
   c. raise   [rez]   'raised'
   d. pick   [pɪk]   'picked'
   e. jump   [ʤʌmp]   'jumped'
   f. miss   [mɪs]   'missed'

In the general American standard variety, the morphemes in (3d) are *pick* and *ed*. In the AAE example in the appropriate context, *pick* is interpreted as if it is in the past tense. It would be understood as past in a sentence such as *Yesterday, she pick me to be on the team*. The adverb *yesterday* indicates past, so that information does not have to be redundantly stated on the verb *pick*. But in the sentence *They pick me*, we would need further contextual information to determine whether the past or non-past interpretation is intended because there are no cues within the sentence. Labov (1969b) reports that some speakers do not perceive the final *-ed* (pronounced as *t* in *picked*), in sentences such as the following:[3]

(4)   a. He pick me.
   b. I've pass my test.
   c. Last week I kick Donald in the mouth, so the teacher throwed me out the class.
      (p. 57).

In classroom correction tests in which AAE speakers were given sentences in (4), Labov notes that the speakers were not able to change the sentences into classroom English by adding *-ed* to *pick*, *pass* and *kick*. This result led him to conclude that his speakers "have little ability to detect the absence of *-ed* as a grammatical element to be corrected" (p. 57).

If you think about the general English pronunciation of the word *missed* (3f), you will realize that it sounds just like *mist*, as if it ends in *t* (although the ending is spelled with *-ed*). The final *st* sound in *missed* forms the cluster that is reduced to *s* (as in *miss* in AAE). As a result of the cluster reduction process, *missed* and *mist* will be homophonous; they will sound the same (as *miss*).

Generalizations about the data in (2) and (3) will be helpful in explaining word final consonant patterns in the phonology of AAE, and they will also be helpful in characterizing groups of sounds that are involved in the process. The cluster reduction phenomenon can be captured by a formal description that will explain where it occurs and what happens as a result of it. One particular analysis that has been used to account for the patterns in the words above can be called the *voicing generalization*. It states that a final consonant cluster (e.g., *-st* as in *mist* or the pronunciation of the final sound in *missed*) is reduced by deleting the final member if the two consonants forming the cluster have the same voicing value, in which both are [+voice] (voiced) or both are [−voice] (voiceless). Voicing is an articulatory description that is used in characterizing consonant sounds. The voicing feature is used to characterize the state of the glottis, the opening between the vocal folds. When the vocal folds – flaps covering the glottis – are apart, the air flows freely through, producing voiceless sounds (such as *p*, *t*, *k*, *s* and *f* sounds). On the other hand, when the vocal folds are together, the air forces its way through, causing vibration and subsequently producing voiced sounds (such as sounds *b*, *d*, *g*, *z*, *v*, *l*, *m*, *n*, and ŋ [representation for the *ng* sound at the end of *sing*]). (See the diagram below from McManis, Stollenwerk and Zheng-Sheng 1989.) Reprinted with permission of Ohio State University Press.

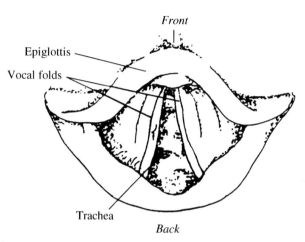

Larynx: state of the glottis

According to the voicing generalization, clusters such as *st* in *fast* and *nd* in *pound* are predicted to be reduced to *s* and *n*, respectively, because the consonants forming the clusters have the same voicing value, whereas clusters such as *nt* in *paint* and *mp* in *jump* are predicted to remain intact because the consonants forming the clusters have different voicing values. This is shown in (5), where [−v] is an abbreviation for [−voice] (voiceless) and [+v] is an abbreviation for [+voice] (voiced):

(5)   a. f   a   s   t   →   fas
                     | |
                     [−v]   [−v]
      Both *s* and *t* are [−voice].
      b. j   u   m   p   →   jump
                     | |
                     [+v]   [−v]
      m is [+voice] and *p* is [−voice].

Although they did not call it the *voicing generalization* and give it a formal characterization, Wolfram and Fasold (1974) noted this pattern of final consonant clusters in AAE.[4]

This analysis assumes that in AAE there are underlying consonant clusters, so a word such as *fast* starts off with the cluster (*st*) intact, but the cluster is reduced by deleting the final consonant (*t*) of the cluster because it has the same voicing value as the preceding consonant (*s*). This point was made above in the description of the voicing generalization (5a). Some arguments have been offered to show that this is a valid way of looking at the data and that AAE should be analyzed as having underlying consonant clusters (i.e., words in AAE actually end with final consonant clusters or groups) that are reduced when the proper conditions are met. One argument in support of this view is carried out along the following lines: We know that AAE has full final consonant clusters because when suffixes that begin with vowels (e.g. -*able*) are added to words such as *accept* to yield *acceptable*, the full cluster (*pt*) is pronounced. For some, this means that in AAE, these words must have final consonant clusters in the first place. How else would speakers pronounce the *pt* cluster? The argument goes on to say that the interaction between suffixes and consonant clusters is important. The generalization is that the cluster remains intact preceding suffixes that begin with vowels, but when clusters precede suffixes that begin with consonants (e.g., -*ly* in *friendly*), they are more likely to be reduced (*frienly*). The argument, then, is that AAE has 'underlying' clusters, but whether or not the clusters are pronounced depends on a number of factors. One is whether the cluster precedes a vowel initial or consonant initial suffix.

Now consider the examples below, which illustrate what happens when suffixes are added to words:

(6) **Consonant cluster preceding vowel initial suffix**   **Word final**
a. accept+able→accept**able**   accept→accep
b. expect+able→expect**able**   expect→expec

(7) **Consonant cluster preceding consonant initial suffix**   **Word final**
a. friend+ly→frien**ly**   friend→frien
b. soft+ness→sof**ness**   soft→sof

The words in (7) are included to provide representative examples of clusters preceding consonant initial suffixes. In (7) the *nd* cluster is reduced preceding a consonant initial suffix and at the end of the word. The major focus is on vowel initial suffixes and consonant clusters, so let's return to (6). In (6a) the *pt* cluster is retained when it precedes the vowel initial suffix (-*able*) but reduced word finally (*accep*), and the same pattern occurs with the *ct* (but formally represented as *kt*) cluster in (6b). Data collected in (Green 1991) provide evidence that the analysis is slightly more complicated in that not all vowel initial suffixes have the same effect on preceding clusters. That is, not all vowel initial suffixes are equal or behave the same. In some cases, the consonant cluster preceding vowel initial suffixes -*er* (8a) and -*ing* (8b) can also be reduced:

(8) a. cold+er→col+er→coler
b. spend+ing→spen+ing→spening

In the example in (6), the generalization is that the final cluster is more likely to be retained when it precedes a vowel initial suffix (such as -*able*) than when it precedes a consonant or ends a word, but the cluster is not necessarily retained when it precedes a vowel initial suffix. In fact, it may very well be reduced if the vowel initial suffix is -*er* or -*ing*, yielding the results in (8). The clusters preceding -*er* and -*ing* may also be retained, as in *colder* and *spending*. This means that both pronunciations *colder, coler* and *spending, spening* occur in AAE. It is not uncommon to hear speakers use the word in (8b) in the following way: *She don't mind spening a lot of money on a good pair of shoes*. The pronunciation, *spening*, is virtually indistinguishable from *spinning*, the word that is used to describe the action of a top or wheel in motion. On the one hand, *spening* is like *spinning* because the *-nd* cluster does not obligatorily occur before *-ing*. On the other, the vowel sounds in the words are pronounced the same; just as some speakers do not distinguish the vowel sounds in *pen* and *pin*, they do not distinguish them in *spend* and *spin*.

Now consider the quotation at the beginning of this chapter, in which the speaker in a television commercial of a famous brand of facial tissues presents a clear example of cluster reduction preceding the vowel initial suffix (*-er*) when he says, "It's sofer tissue." He does not produce the *ft* cluster preceding the vowel initial suffix *-er* in *softer*; only the *f* of the cluster is pronounced. Contrary to views in earlier research, the behavior of consonant clusters preceding vowel initial suffixes does not provide hard and fast evidence that words in AAE have clusters such as those in general American English. This is related to the point that Smith was trying to make about the relation between AAE and Niger-Congo languages syllable structure although he did not address suffixes. Different types of suffixes have different effects on consonant clusters.

There is also evidence that this type of reduction occurs with the *ct* (i.e., *kt*) clusters preceding the vowel initial suffix *-ing* in *acting*. When the word *acting* means performing in the strict sense, as in the case of someone on television or in a play, AAE speakers can say of the person: "She sure did a good job acting her part" (where the *ct* cluster preceding *-ing* remains intact). On the other hand, if *acting* is used to refer to behavior, it can be produced with a reduced cluster: "Stop acking like that" or "Stop acking silly," (in which the *ct* cluster preceding the *-ing* suffix is reduced).

The variation in occurrence of consonant clusters preceding suffixes *-er* and *-ing* and the invariability of retention preceding *-able* seem to be due, in part, to the type of suffix. It has been noted, in some studies in phonology, that *-er* and *-ing* are one type of suffix, and *-able* is defined as a different type. A discussion of suffix types goes beyond the scope of this chapter, but the discussion and references in Selkirk (1982) address related issues in English.

In summary, clusters preceding vowel initial suffixes *-er* and *-ing* may be reduced, but clusters preceding the vowel initial *-able* are more likely to be retained. So far, a number of pieces fit together in the explanation of consonant cluster reduction. Let's look at them as we explain *spening*. We start off with the word *spending* and given the voicing generalization, the cluster (*nd*) is reduced (to *n*) although it precedes a vowel initial suffix (*-ing*). It is interesting to note that whatever the difference between vowel initial suffixes *-ing* and *-er* on the one hand and *-able* on the other, it is reflected with consonant clusters.

To some, cluster reduction in words such as *pos* ('post'), *was* ('wasp') and *mas* ('mask') yields words that are only consistent with unintelligent speech, and to them, the pronunciation of the plural forms of these words (*posts, wasps, masks*) makes even less sense: *poses* [posɪz], *wases* [wɔɪz]/[wasɪz] and *mases* [mæsɪz], respectively. (The pronunciation of the vowel sound in *wases* may vary from region to region. The phonetic transcriptions are also given, so refer to the key in note 2.) But these pronunciations are systematic; the singular forms can be explained by reduction and the voicing generalization, and the plural forms are also governed by rules. It is true that the singular/plural forms *pos/poses, was/wases* and *mas/mases* are not the mainstream English pronunciations; nevertheless, these singular/plural pairs are based on clear patterns of sound combinations. I am not aware of current studies on the regular production of these plurals in other varieties of American English although Miller (1986) reports on the three examples of *wases* in *The Linguistic Atlas of the Middle and South Atlantic States* by whites. In order to understand the rule that describes the way the plural is formed, we have to understand that all of the singular forms end in *s* for one reason or another, either because the voicing generalization results in consonant cluster reduction or because the words were adopted into AAE without final consonant clusters, that is with just final *s*. Given that the singular forms *pos, was* and *mas* are pronounced as if they end in *s* instead of the final consonant clusters *st, sp* and *sk*, respectively, their plural endings are identical to plural endings of words that end in -*s*. That is to say that the plurals of *pos, was* and *mas* are formed in the same way that the plurals of *dose, boss* and *pass* are formed. In American English (including AAE), words that end in the *s* sound form the plural by adding -*es* (pronounced [əz] or [ɪz]). This explains why the plural for *boss* is *bosses* and *pos* ('post') is *poses*. The plural ending for both words is formed with -*es*. If the word *pos* in AAE actually ended in an *st* cluster, the plural would not likely be formed by adding -*es*.[5]

One speaker, an African American male in his 30s, was heard saying, *We having a lot of conteses at work* ('We're having a lot of contests at work'), where *conteses* [kantɛsɪz] is the plural form for general English *contests*. The point here is that, at first glance, some plural forms and other sound patterns may appear to be random, but linguistic analysis provides evidence that speakers are adhering to plural formation and other rules. The plural of words that are spelled with a final *st, sk* or *sp* cluster but pronounced with final -*s* (not the final cluster) is formed by adding -*es*, the same way plurals of other words that end in -*s* are formed.

The voicing generalization has been proposed to account for reduced clusters, but there is another possible explanation for the results that are shown in examples such as those in (2). Whereas the voicing generalization is based on the voicing value of word final consonants (e.g., *s* and *t* have the same voicing value), an alternative explanation is based on the intensity or loudness of sounds, a property referred to as sonority. Some sounds (such as *n* and *m*) are more sonorous or intense than other sounds (such as *d* and *b*). Briefly, the analysis that is based on sonority provides an account of the data in (2) by placing the consonants forming the clusters on a sonority scale and explaining that some clusters (such as *st* and *nd*) do not surface because the consonants forming them are too close in sonority. Consonant sounds are arranged from more sonorous to less sonorous on the sonority scale in (9):

(9)   Sonority scale

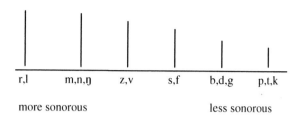

| r,l | m,n,ŋ | z,v | s,f | b,d,g | p,t,k |

more sonorous   less sonorous

I will not go into too much detail here, but I will give a general idea about how the scale works. Let's consider the final consonant clusters *st* (in *fast*) and *nd* (in *kind*), which are reduced to *s* (*fas*) and *n* (*kin*), respectively. According to the sonority scale, they are reduced because the consonants forming the clusters are too close in sonority. That is, the *s* is too close to the *t* (*st* cluster), and the *n* is too close to the *d* (*nd* cluster) in sonority. The closeness results in consonant cluster reduction. Now, consider the *nk* cluster (i.e., *ŋk*) as in *think* and *pink* and the *nt* cluster as in *paint*, which are not reduced. (Note: The final *nk* cluster in *pink* is pronounced as if it contains a *g*, *ngk*. If you pronounce the word slowly, you will hear *ng* (i.e., final sound in *sing*) before you produce *k*.) These clusters are not reduced because there is no conflict in sonority between *ŋ* and *k* and *n* and *t*; the consonants are far enough apart in sonority. A more accurate statement of the sonority analysis would also spell out what it means to be too close and far enough apart in sonority. Both the voicing generalization and the sonority analysis are ways of formally characterizing consonant cluster reduction, ways of making a formal statement about the rules that speakers use in producing combinations of sounds. Careful consideration of these consonant patterns will help to give us more insight into the AAE sound system.

In the previous discussion of the voicing generalization and sonority scale, it was noted that the *nt* cluster in words such as *paint* and *pint* remains intact. In auxiliaries, the *n't* cluster in *ain't, can't* and *don't* are not usually fully produced, so the words are pronounced as *ain', cain'* and *don'*, without the final *t*. This is not unusual for function words such as auxiliaries. Note, also, that the initial consonants, *d* and *g*, are not obligatorily produced when *don't* and *am gonna* are used in specific environments. *I don't know* may very well be produced as *I 'on know*.[6]

We have seen contexts in which the cluster is reduced such that the final *t* or *d* does not occur, for example. There are also some words in which the opposite process occurs; *t* or *d* is inserted. This is what happens with words such as *light skinned, big boned,* and *two faced*. In AAE some speakers produce these words as *light skinded* [skɪndɪd], *big boneded* [bondɪd], and *two faceted* [festɪd], respectively. In each word, a *t* or *d* sound occurs right before the *-ed* [ɪd] suffix, and the result is that the word is pronounced with an additional syllable. The final syllables in *skinded* in *light skinded* and *boneded* in *big boneded* sound like the last syllable in *candid*, and the last syllable in *faceted* in *two faceted* is like the last syllable in *rested*. In a sense, speakers treat the words *skin, bone,* and *face* as if they actually end in a *t* or *d* sound, in the way the word *bond* ends in a *d* sound and *rest* ends in a *t* sound.

When we study the words carefully, we find that speakers do not randomly insert *t* or *d* in these words; the sounds preceding the inserted *t* or *d* determine which sound (*t* or *d*) will be inserted. If the word ends in a voiced sound, as *n* in *bone* and *skin*, then *d* is inserted, but if the word ends in a voiceless sound, as the final *s* sound in *face*, *t* is inserted.[7] (Note: The end of the word *face* is spelled *ce*, but the final sound is formally or phonetically represented as *s*.) So far, we have seen that the voicing property of sounds plays a major role in the way words are pronounced. The voicing properties affect consonant cluster reduction and *t/d* insertion in some words.

4.3   Devoicing

The process of consonant devoicing, that is, making a voiced consonant voiceless, applies to some consonants at the ends of words. Words ending in the voiced *b*, *d* and *g* that undergo this process are pronounced as if they end in *p*, *t* and *k*, respectively. This process results in the pronunciation of *cab*, *feed* and *pig* as *cap*, *feet* and *pick*, respectively. In such cases, the final voiced consonant is devoiced, that is, made voiceless:

(10)   *b*   →   *p*
      voiced   voiceless
      d   →   *t*
      voiced   voiceless
      g   →   *k*
      voiced   voiceless

Baran and Seymour (1976), in early research on AAE and communication disorders, investigated children's performance in differentiating minimal word pairs in which the final consonant sound of one word was voiced and the final consonant sound of the other word in the pair was voiceless, as in *cab* and *cap*, respectively. They found that whites listening to blacks made the most errors in distinguishing the words in the pairs and that "blacks understood themselves better than they understood either other blacks or whites" (p. 470). More specifically, Baran and Seymour found that when blacks listened to these pairs produced by whites, they mistook words ending in a voiceless consonant for its counterpart ending in a voiced consonant. They explain that

> Black children had little difficulty in matching the Standard English production of *pig* with its corresponding picture, but were less certain on this task for *pick*. Since the voiceless /k/ may be used in the production of both *pig* and *pick* in Black English, standard usage of /k/ by white children seemed to create more listener confusion than did /g/.
>
> [p. 472]

The research by Baran and Seymour shows how final consonant devoicing can result in ambiguity. This type of information may be useful for educators teaching AAE speaking students who use this devoicing strategy.

The following section continues the discussion of the AAE sound system by providing a description of sound patterns that are related to *th* sounds in different parts of words.

4.4   Sound patterns and th

Another well-known pattern in the sound system of AAE is the production of *t/d* and *f/v* in environments in words in which the *th* sound occurs in general American English. The occurrence of *t/d* and *f/v* in certain environments is systematic in the sense that each sound is chosen based on phonetic properties; these sounds are not used randomly. To explain the distribution of these sounds, it is necessary to give the articulatory descriptions of them. The articulatory description of a consonant sound includes three different types of information that are used to identify or characterize them:

(a) state of the glottis in the production of the consonant (voicing, section 4.2.)
(b) place of articulation of the consonant
(c) manner of articulation of the consonant

The *t/d* and *f/v* will be described by providing the information in (a)–(c) for each sound. In defining the state of the glottis, we determine whether the sound is voiced or voiceless. The place of articulation describes the place in the mouth at which the sound is made, and the manner of articulation identifies the way the sound is made, for example, whether air is stopped at a particular point in the mouth. This information is given below for the sounds *t, d, f,* and *v*.

(11)

Sound	State of glottis	Place of articulation	Manner of articulation
t	vocal folds apart, voiceless	alveolar	stop
d	vocal folds together, voiced	alveolar	stop
f	vocal folds apart, voiceless	labiodental	fricative
v	vocal folds together, voiced	labiodental	fricative

The alveolar is the place of articulation for the *t* and *d* sounds because they are made by touching the ridge behind the top teeth (alveolar ridge) with the tip of the tongue, and labiodental is the place of articulation for *f* and *v* because they are formed by touching the bottom lip with the top teeth (i.e., labiodental, lip and teeth). The *t* and *d* are stops because the air is stopped at the alveolar ridge when they are produced, and the f and *v* are fricatives because, when these sounds are made, friction is produced, as the air escapes through the very small opening between the lip and teeth. (For an introductory discussion of the articulatory description of consonants, see Fromkin and Rodman [1998] and Ladefoged [1993].)

The *t* and *d* on the one hand and the *f* and *v* on the other differ from each other only in one respect: state of the glottis. The *t* is voiceless and the *d* is voiced, and likewise, the *f* is voiceless and the *v* is voiced. This distinction is very important, and it will be shown that speakers of AAE actually make it, as do speakers of other varieties of English and other languages. Before this distinction is discussed, it is necessary, however, to give the description of *th*, as it has been noted that *t*/*d* and *f*/*v* occur in the same environments in which *th* sounds occur in general American English. There are actually two *th* sounds, but they are both represented by one spelling *th*. Incidentally, the dictionary distinguishes these sounds by underlining the *th* (**th**) in words such as *then* and by not underlining the *th* in words such as *thin*. Can you figure out what distinguishes the two *th* sounds? Two different phonetic symbols are used to refer to these sounds.

(12)

Sound	State of glottis	Place of articulation	Manner of articulation
th (θ) (*thin*)	voiceless	interdental	fricative
th (ð) (*then*)	voiced	interdental	fricative

The *th* sounds are interdental because they are made at the point where the tongue is between the teeth, and they are fricatives because friction is caused when the air escapes through the small opening between the tongue and teeth. The *th* sound represented by /θ/ is voiceless, and the *th* sound represented by /ð/ is voiced. Voicing (i.e., state of the glottis) is the only difference between the two sounds, but it is a very important distinction.

The articulatory descriptions in (11) and (12) will be helpful is explaining the patterns that we find in the production of *t*/*d* and *f*/*v* in AAE. Consider the list below:

(13)

	AAE	Phonetic transcription	
a.	thing	[θɪŋ]	'thing'
b.	think	[θɪŋk]	'think'
c.	dese	[diz]	'these'
d.	dat	[dæt]	'that'
e.	baf	[bæf]	'bath'
f.	wif, wit	[wɪf], [wɪt]	'with'
g.	mont, monf	[mʌnt], [mʌnf]	'month'
h.	Beflehem	[bɛfləhɪm]	'Bethlehem'
i.	bave	[bev]	'bathe'
j.	smoove	[smuv]	'smooth'
k.	mova[8]	[mʌvə]	'mother'

The words in (13) show that the *t* and *d* sounds occur at the end (*wit*, *mont*) and beginning (*dese*) of words, but the *f* and *v* sounds occur in the medial position (*Beflehem*, *mova*) and at the end of words (*baf*, *bave*). Given the data in (13), the three generalizations are as follows:

Generalization 1: These sounds (*t*, *d*, *f*, *v*) occur in positions in which the *th* (i.e., [θ], [ð]) sounds occur in general American English.
Generalization 2: The voiceless sounds *t* and *f* occur in medial and final environments of words in which the voiceless *th* sound occurs in general American English. This

means that words ending in voiceless *th* in mainstream English (e.g., *baf*) will end with a voiceless *t* or *f* in AAE. But note that the voiceless *th* sound is pronounced at the beginning of words (12a, b).

Generalization 3: The voiced sounds *d* and *v* occur in the same environments in which the voiced *th* sound occurs in general American English. This means that words ending in voiced *th* in general American English will end with voiced *d* or *v* in AAE. Also, words beginning with voiced *th* in general American English (e.g., *these*) will begin with voiced *d* in AAE.

The explanation for the types of patterns that emerge in the words in (13) is that AAE speakers use the sounds consistently and adhere to set rules and patterns. It is not that speakers make lazy substitutions in using *t/f* and *d/v*; they use these sounds in well-defined environments. The distinction between the two *th* sounds is maintained in AAE when speakers use voiceless sounds in one environment and voiced sounds in the other. AAE speakers have rules that govern the occurrence of these sounds in word initial, medial and final positions.

For the reader who might be inclined to conclude that speakers of AAE make substitutions for the *th* sounds (that occur in general American English) because they cannot produce these interdental fricatives (i.e., *th* sounds) by making the so-called difficult movement of placing the tongue between the teeth, it should be noted that AAE speakers do indeed produce *th* sounds. These same speakers who produce *t/d* and *f/v* in some environments in which *th* occurs in general American English also produce the *th* sounds in some environments. They produce the voiceless *th* sound at the beginning of words, so they say words such as *thin*, *thigh*, and *thing* as they are pronounced in general American English and other varieties of English, even though they begin with the *th* sound.[9] So speakers do not use *t* in environments in which voiceless *th* begins a word in English. I have introduced a significant amount of specialized terminology in laying out descriptions that will be useful in explaining patterns in the sound system of AAE. These descriptions should be informative for those interested in AAE, but they should also be useful for educators teaching students who use such patterns. The following section discusses the production of *r* and *l* in AAE, and it explains the pronunciation of final sounds in words such as *mother* in (13k).

4.5   r and l: liquid vocalization[10]

The data in this chapter have been used to show that the sound system in AAE operates according to set rules, so speakers do not delete and add sounds haphazardly. What may sound like ignorant and uneducated speech to those who are unfamiliar with the variety or who have some preconceived notions about the people who use this variety is actually rule-governed language use. This becomes clear once systematic inquiry is made into the sound system of AAE, and descriptions are provided.

This section continues the discussion of consonants, focusing on the liquids *r* and *l*. Some patterns associated with *r* and *l* in AAE have also been recorded for other varieties of English.[11] In some environments, *r* and *l* pattern similarly in AAE. When these sounds follow vowels within words, they are not necessarily produced as liquids; instead they may be produced as an unstressed vowel (schwa ə or *uh* sound) if any sound is produced at all. Consider the examples below. (The vowel sounds may vary from region to region, so speakers in Southern regions may produce the vowel sounds in the words below differently than speakers in the Northern region although both groups of speakers may have liquid vocalization):

(14)   **AAE**   **Phonetic transcription**

a. cout   [kot]   'court'
b. bea   [bæə]   'bear'
c. brotha   [brʌðə]   'brother'
d. toe   [to]   'tore'

(15)   **AAE**   **Phonetic transcription**

a. bea   [bɛə]   'bell'
b. pia   [pɪə]   'pill'
c. coo   [ko:]   'cold'

(The *a* in the AAE representations is pronounced as the first vowel sound in *about*.)

Some generalizations can be made about the examples in (14) and (15):

Generalization 1: In all of the examples, the *r* and *l*, if they were pronounced, would follow vowel sounds.
Generalization 2: *r* and *l* may become vocalized, which means that they are pronounced more like vowel sounds than like consonant sounds, so they are represented by the unstressed vowel (ə), as in the phonetic transcription for the word *pill* (15b).
Generalization 3: *r* and *l* may become unstressed to the point to which they are not produced at all, the case with *toe* ('tore') in (14d).

The pronunciations with respect to *r* and *l* in (14) and (15), respectively, are very similar in that the sounds do not occur in the position following a vowel. Notice that in (14) and (15), a schwa (ə) is used in some positions in which r occurs in general American English and in positions in which *l* occurs in general American English. The schwa is used to indicate that the full liquid is not pronounced. This is basically the explanation of the term vocalization, which is taken to mean that the liquids in these environments take on vowel-like qualities, so instead of a full liquid (i.e., *r* and *l*), a schwa (vowel sound) is produced.

Different studies on dialects of English have noted that *r* vocalization occurs in different dialects or that the *r* is simply not produced in some dialects of English. Northern dialects such as those of Boston and New York City have been characterized as *r*-less varieties. In addition Southern English dialects have also been described as being *r*-less. AAE has this property in common with a number of English varieties, and the previous examples can also be used to show that the linguistic system patterns similarly with other varieties of English. It is interesting to note that the varieties are quite similar with respect to the vocalization of *r* and *l*, but they may differ with respect to the actual vowel sounds of the vocalized element. I made this point when I introduced (14) and (15). Linguists (Labov 1991, Wolfram 1991, Edwards 2000) have noted that, in general (not specifically regarding vowel sounds in *r* and *l* vocalization), speakers of AAE have not participated in the vowel changes that have taken place in different parts of the United States.

There is a more interesting difference in the way the vocalization process operates in AAE and in other varieties of English. In some varieties of English, there is a restriction on the vocalization of *r*, such that the sound is vocalized in the environment following a vowel, provided that the *r* is not between two vowel sounds. (The *r* in *tore* is actually not between two vowel sounds because the *o* is pronounced, but the *e* is silent.) Another way of stating this is by saying that in some varieties of English, the *r* sound cannot be vocalized when it is between two vowel sounds. In these varieties, the *r* in the word *Carol* is not vocalized because it is in the environment between two vowel sounds. On the other hand, in AAE (and perhaps in some Southern English varieties) vocalization can occur in this environment, so 'Carol' can be pronounced as *Ca'ol* [kæəl]. Wolfram and Fasold (1974) make the following observation:

> In Vernacular Black English and in some white Southern varieties, it is possible for *r* to be absent after a vowel and before another vowel within the same word. The result is pronunciation like *sto'y*, *ma'y* and *te'ific* for *story*, *marry* and *terrific*, respectively. If the vowel directly before the *r* belongs to a prefix and *r* belongs to the base, then *r* cannot be deleted, so that *be'eave* and *re'un* are not possible pronunciations for *bereave* and *rerun*
>
> [p. 140].

In vocalization cases, the *r* is not produced, but there is some schwa sound or vowel lengthening as a reflex of *r* vocalization. The point about lengthening is important in that if the liquid is not produced as an unstressed vowel, then a vowel that is already present may become longer. This is what happens in the word *coo* 'cold' (14c), as indicated by the two *o*'s and the ':' (*oo:*) in the phonetic transcription.

As has been noted above, the liquids *r* and *l* pattern similarly with respect to liquid vocalization. They do not, however, share the feature of being able to vocalize between two vowels in that the *l* must be present in this environment.

The following section summarizes some additional phonological patterns in AAE for which there is a smaller body of literature.

4.6   Additional phonological patterns

4.6.1   *-in*

The sound *ng* (ŋ) in the *-ing* suffix is realized as *n* in most contexts, so the following words end in an *n* sound:

(16)   **AAE**

    a. walkin   'walking'
    b. runnin   'running'
    c. spenin[12] 'spending'
    d. thinkin   'thinking'
    e. listnin   'listening'
    f. openin   'opening'

This pattern is restricted to the suffix -*ing*, that is to words with more than one syllable, so it never occurs in the -*ing* in words with one syllable, such as *sing* and *ring*, to yield **sin* and **rin*, respectively. The property of -*ing* (ɪŋ) as being pronounced as -*in* (ɪn) is not restricted to AAE. This pattern is actually found in nonstandard varieties of English as well as in general American English in unstressed syllables. As a result, when the final syllables of *nothing* and *something* are unstressed, the words become *nothin* and *somethin* (also *sumpm*, see Wolfram and Fasold 1974).

4.6.2   *skr*

Another phonological pattern that is mentioned from time to time, often by speech pathologists, is the occurrence of *skr* in syllable initial position where *str* occurs in general American English and other varieties of English. Presumably speech pathologists were concerned about this use of *skr* because it was not clear whether the combination of sounds was an indication of a disorder or a dialectal pattern. Still the *skr* feature has not been observed or recorded in the literature nearly as often as other sound patterns. There are three possible reasons for this: (1) One is that because *skr* only occurs in positions where *str* can occur in general American English, there will be limited opportunity to produce the sound. (2) Secondly, *skr* may be viewed as a feature of the speech of young AAE speakers that is not maintained in adult AAE. (3) Thirdly, *skr* may be associated with AAE spoken in certain regions of the United States.

    Common words in which the sequence *skr* occurs are given below:

(17)   **AAE**   **Phonetic transcription**

    a. skreet   [skrit]   'street'
    b. skrawberry [skrɔbɛri]   'strawberry'
    c. skretch   [skrɛtʃ]   'stretch'
    d. skraight   [skret]   'straight'

In summarizing her research on the cluster, Dandy (1991) notes that the form is found in Gullah and in the speech of some African Americans born in the South. She explains that the cluster is a highly stigmatized feature and that many of the students in her study who used it were referred to speech pathologists. She goes on to note the following about her research: "I also found a continuum that may indicate sound change in progress. If children said *skretch* for *stretch*, they probably used the *skr* alternation in other words that contained the feature: *skreet* for *street*, *skrong* for *strong*, *skrike* for *strike*, *skranger/deskroy* for *stranger* and *destroy*. There were some who said *skreet* but did not make the alternation on other words with that sound" (p. 44). Also, although Dandy does not make this point, it is important to note that the students' use of *skr* may have been affected by the training they were getting from speech pathologists. I will return to this feature in chapter 8 in the discussion of the interaction between a student who uses *skr* in *skreet* 'street' and a teacher who tries to 'correct' the pronunciation.

4.6.3 *oi* and other vowel sounds

The diphthong [oɪ], a two-part vowel, that occurs in some environments in which *oa* as in *coach* occurs in general American English is also used in AAE. This feature has not received very much attention, and it is similar to *skr* in that respect as well as in other ways: based on my observations, this two part vowel is used by older speakers in some Southern states. So like *skr*, it is used by AAE speakers in a certain age group, and it may be restricted to specific regions in the United States. In fact, it is not clear that it is used by children at all. It is possible that the [oɪ] is an example of an older pattern in AAE, but judgment must be reserved here until further historical research is completed in this area. Older speakers who use this pattern use the diphthong [oɪ] in words such as *coach*, *road* and *roach*. The first part of the diphthong is the *o* [o] sound in *coach*, and the second part is the *i* [ɪ] sound at the beginning of *itch*. Speakers who use this diphthong have the following pronunciations: *coach* [koɪtʃ], *road* [roɪd], *approach* [əproɪtʃ] and *roach* [roɪtʃ]. The examples here are from speakers who either live in or grew up in the South (in particular, Georgia, North Carolina and Louisiana), but it would be interesting to determine whether AAE speakers actually use this diphthong if they live in other parts of the United States and do not have close ties with the South. The most common examples of [oɪ] are in the environment of *oa* spelling in general English, but the [oɪ] sound also occurs in *porch* (i.e., [poɪtʃ]) for some speakers. Note here that *r* vocalization also occurs in this pronunciation of *porch*.

Burling (1973), in characterizing the pronunciations of words in AAE, lists different vowel patterns in the language system. He notes that in some cases, black and white speakers in different regions in the United States maintain the contrasts between the vowel sounds in different words such as *pin/pen*, *for/four* and *horse/hoarse*. In different varieties of English, the [ɪ] sound in *pick* is used in both *pin* and *pen*; there is no distinction between the vowels preceding nasal sounds *n*, *m* and *ng* (ŋ). (Recall the *spin/spend* example.) An important point is that even if contrasts are lost or maintained, they are done so according to systematic rules affecting sounds in certain environments. The processes of losing and maintaining vowel contrasts apply in the speech of all speakers including mainstream English speakers, not just in the speech of AAE speakers.

Another pattern that occurs in some regions in which AAE is spoken is the lowering of the [ɛr] sound in words such as *prepare*, *care* and *hair*. Due to lowering, the second syllable in *prepare* is affected, so that syllable almost sounds like *par*. This pattern is produced by speakers of AAE in all age groups in cities in central and northern Texas. Karen Pollock reported on her observations of this type of lowering by speakers in Memphis, Tennessee, at the American Speech-Language and Hearing Association annual meeting in San Antonio, Texas (November 1998).

4.7   Prosodic features: stress and intonation

So far in this chapter, I have focused primarily on individual segments, consonant and vowel sounds, within words. This section will consider patterns that go beyond individual consonant and vowel sounds within words and look at patterns affecting syllables, entire words, phrases and sentences. The features that will be discussed here are related to pitch of the voice and rhythm of speech, and they are called prosodic or suprasegmental features. Some specific prosodic features are stress (accentuation or emphasis placed on syllables or words) and intonation (modulation of the voice or tonal inflection).

The prosodic features of AAE are very important for a number of reasons. One reason is that research in this area may be useful in defining, at least in part, what is meant by 'sounding black,' if anything at all, and the extent to which this judgment is based on certain types of prosodic patterns. Rickford (1972) raised questions about the issue of blacks 'sounding black' and whites 'sounding white.' According to his data, listeners who heard speech samples were able to identify speakers' ethnicity with some degree of accuracy. In the study, it was suggested that a number of features such as stress patterns, pronunciation and tone of the voice are indicators of the ethnicity of speakers. Labov, et al. (1968) also conducted a study to determine the extent to which listeners could identify a speaker's ethnicity based on speech. They concluded their data showed that the listeners had the "ability to recognize the clear cases of dialects" they know "rather than any general ability to identify the ethnic background of speakers" (p. 285). Rickford (1972) and Labov et al. (1968) disagree about whether listeners can detect a speaker's ethnicity by prosodic features, and Wolfram and Fasold (1974) explain that intonation "appears to be one of the main reasons why some standard-speaking blacks may be identified ethnically" (p. 147). In effect, their claim is that even when African American speakers use mainstream English syntactic and other patterns of speaking, their intonational patterns identify them as black. Wolfram and Fasold's conclusion is strong, but it is not clear what type of evidence (e.g., experiments based on listener judgments) they have used to reach it. If Wolfram and Fasold are right, what are the features of intonation that set African American speakers apart from other speakers?

Certainly other listeners believe that it is possible to recognize ethnicity through speech patterns and voice. This must be the view that led one of the attorneys in a widely publicized court case to suggest that a speaker's race could be determined from his voice and speech. The *New York Times's* report by David Margolick the following day about the attorney's comment: "Simply by suggesting that someone's race can be gleaned from the sound and timbre of his voice, Mr. Darden opened up once more the volcanic issue of race..." (Thursday, July 13, 1995). Baugh (1999) raises questions about sensitivity to differences between AAE and general American English. Although he does not discuss suprasegmental features, it may be that he is also concerned about the role that such features play in helping listeners detect differences between types of speech.

Another reason that research in this area is important is that it can add to our understanding of the role that prosodic features play in the meaning and interpretation of phrases and sentences in AAE. In the discussion of the lexicon and syntax of AAE, it was noted that *BIN* and *dən* are produced with certain stress patterns, which are related to the way the markers are interpreted. That is to say that if *BIN* is not stressed, then it will not indicate remote past meaning.

From the discussion in the preceding chapters, we learn that the different meanings and uses of lexical items in AAE and general American English may lead to misunderstanding. In the same way, different intonational patterns, rhythm and pitch may also contribute to misunderstanding among speakers of different varieties of American English. It may be that speakers of different varieties of American English have these tones, rhythms and pitch in mind when they say that the speech of African Americans indicates that the speakers have an attitude or are angry, confrontational and rude, as well as when they say that African Americans have more expressive and soulful speech. Finally research on intonation and other prosodic features is important in that it can provide insight into what some researchers have called standard AAE, which adheres to the 'standard' rules of general American English, but incorporates intonational patterns and other types of expressive language use of AAE. That is, it is suggested that speakers of standard AAE may not use the type of syntactic patterns in chapters 2 and 3 and the sound patterns (e.g., *f/v* in *th* environments) described earlier in this chapter, but they will use intonational and rhythmic patterns associated with AAE. Standard AAE is also addressed in chapter 8 (note 13), but briefly the concept is an interesting one, and impressionistically speaking, there is no doubt that it exists. The problem in characterizing it is that a substantial amount of research has not been completed in that area. (Standard AAE has been addressed in Taylor 1971, Lewis 1981 and Spears 2000, 2001).

Comments about the way some African Americans use language and 'talk' are made in general conversation and research on AAE. For example, Kochman (1972) describes speakers as having "a fluent and lively way of talking" (p. 242). In the following passage from Fordham's (1996) ethnographic study of African Americans in a high school in the United States, a female comments on the language of her mother. In expressing her attitude toward her mother's 'telephone speech,' is the student making some implicit comment about her mother's intonational patterns and pitch?

She just talks like that on the telephone, I'll put it like that. When she talks, she puts on airs, you know, sounds White … so you can't tell whether she's White or Black. But when she's around the house, she talks, you know, regular; but when she's out around other people, anywhere out besides the house, she talks in a proper way.

[p. 114]

If we could force the daughter to expound on the way her mother "puts on airs," "sounds White," "talks regular" and "talks in a proper way," which properties would she describe? What cues lead listeners to assess speech as being "lively" and "regular?" How can these labels be translated into a more formal description of ways of talking?

Tarone (1973) asserts that "investigators have consistently recorded the impression that these suprasegmental features are probably just as distinctive in black English as the other, more carefully described, features of syntax and segmental phonology" (p. 29). Almost thirty years later, we are still relying on impression about intonation, but we have begun to make progress in this area. Still stress and intonation have not been well studied, so the unique patterns associated with them have not been defined, and they have not been formally linked to the tonal patterns of West African languages, nor have they been linked to patterns in the United States. As the debates on the origin of AAE continue, intonation and other prosodic features may prove to be useful areas of consideration. Research in this area may also shed light on the tonal properties of (stressed) *BIN* and (unstressed) *dən*. A point of departure for discussing intonational patterns in AAE and West African languages is Gullah, which has been observed as having tonal qualities that are similar to those of West African languages (Turner 1949).

Tarone's (1972, 1973) studies of intonation in AAE, are based on speech samples she collected from African American adolescents in Seattle, Washington, while they were engaged in conversation in a social setting. According to Tarone (1973), "Intonation, in its function as communicator of attitude, might therefore be expected to reflect this difference in attitude between the participants in black and white middle-class speech events" (p. 30). Some recurring patterns that she found in the speech of African American adolescents are given below:

(1)   A wider pitch range, extending into higher pitch levels than in English or formal black English, and often shifting into a falsetto register

(2)   More level and rising final pitch contours on all sentence types in an informal situation were used

(3)   Apparent greater use of falling final pitch contours with *yes-no* questions in formal, threatening situations, but level and rising final contours in informal, familiar situations

(4)   The use of non-final intonation contours, without the use of the lexical item *if*, to mark the dependent clause of some conditional sentences

Tarone gives the following as an example of the characteristic in (4): ^{2}You ^{3}a^{2}ble to ^{3}do ^{2}it, just do it (p. 34). The dependent clause (*You able to do it* 'If you're able to do it') is represented as ending in a non-final intonational contour by having 3-2 (high to medium pitch contour) assigned to it. The non-final contour simply indicates that something will follow; we are not at the end of the sentence.

Tarone suggests that "the wider pitch range may be directly traceable to the competitive nature of the black speech events" and that "the element of aggressiveness and competitiveness was reflected in a wider range of intonation" (p. 32). In other words, it may be that listeners will translate the wider range in intonation as meaning that the speakers have an attitude or are angry and confrontational. Tarone linked wider pitch range in the speech of African American adolescents in her study to the speech events in their conversations although it certainly must not be the case that wider pitch range is reflected only in speech events. In earlier and more current studies on AAE, researchers have associated aggressiveness, indignation and negativity with speech events and the use of certain lexical items. Obviously, these attitudes can be expressed in speech; however, it would also be a good idea to determine what else is associated with wider pitch range. It is not always clear to me, at least, that the listener's assessment of aggressiveness, indignation and negativity is shared by the speaker or captures what the speaker is trying to convey. Furthermore, it is not clear how insightful linking the wider pitch range to aggressiveness is, especially if wider pitch range is manifested in other environments.

The summary of characteristics in Tarone's four points are more formal descriptions of the impressionistic statements about 'sounding black.' If there is something distinctive about the rhythm and modulations of speech used by some African Americans, then some of the distinctions may be captured by the pitch range and falling and rising patterns.

Intonational patterns used by one African American are recorded in a more recent unpublished study by Scott Meredith and Caroline Henton (no date). Whereas the Tarone study, which is much earlier, tries to understand the meanings that are associated with certain contours as well as the differences between the AAE intonational patterns and those of other varieties of American English, Meredith and Henton are interested in determining the extent to which the system they have chosen to use to transcribe intonational contours can be extended to account for patterns in their African American English research. They base their data on speech samples from a 55-year-old African American female, who is "a (presumed) speaker of Black Vernacular English and who, at the time of the study lived in San Francisco, but lived in New Orleans for about 50 years." In their brief discussion, they point out that their data led them to conclude that the speaker has an extremely wide pitch range, an observation that has been made about AAE intonation in independent studies (see the summary of Tarone's research above).

The preliminary study in Green (1990) is similar to Tarone's study in that one of its goals was to determine whether certain characteristics and intonational patterns were associated with utterances in AAE. Also, like the Meredith and Henton study, the Green (1990) pilot study was designed to address questions about ways of formalizing statements about intonation. The scope of the study was narrow; it focused specifically on questions in AAE. Two goals were to determine (1) whether a special type of intonation is associated with questions (*yes-no* and *wh*-questions) in AAE and (2) whether these contours could be characterized by using a formal system. In short, the aim of the study was to determine whether unique intonational patterns occur in AAE and if they do whether they are associated with certain sentence types.

The data for this study were taken from speech samples produced by teenage and adult speakers who live in a small community in southwest Louisiana. Although the findings are preliminary, they match a significant finding in Tarone (1972), and they are in accord with preliminary findings by Tempii Champion, Ph.D., and Elisabeth Selkirk, Ph.D., in preliminary research conducted at the University of Massachusetts, Jun and Foreman (1996) and Foreman (1999).

In the Green study, the most striking pattern that recurred in *yes-no* questions was the final level tone. Think about the question *Do you want to read?* In asking the question, it is natural for some speakers to produce the word *read* with a final rise in intonation, but the yes-no questions in the data that I collected did not always have the final rise. This pattern was interesting because, for the most part, final rises have been associated with yes-no questions in English. That is not to say that questions are only produced with final rises. Cruttenden (1986) warns that "there is no such thing as 'question intonation' although some tones may be more common on questions than others" (p. 59). He goes on to suggest that high-rise and low-rise tones are more common on questions. There were a number of cases in which the final tone on the *yes-no* questions in Green (1990) was level. At the end of the question, the speaker produced neither a rising nor falling pattern; the final tone was level. The claim is not that level tones are the only contours that are associated with yes-no questions in AAE but that it is often the case that these contours are used in such sentence types.

The sentences in the study were transcribed using the model in Pierrehumbert (1980). The basic tonal units that are employed in the model are H (high) and L (low), and the tonal entities that are used in the system are the pitch accent, phrase accent and boundary tone. The pitch accent (H*, L*) is associated with the stressed syllable; the phrase accent marks the end of the phrase, and the boundary tone is realized with respect to the syllables at the edge of the domain. (I will not go into detail in summarizing Pierrehumbert's study because it requires some background in phonology.)

The ends of the questions in Green (1990) are marked by HHL, in which case the final L (low tone) is used to show that the level contour is maintained throughout the end. These final patterns were observed in sentences such as the following:

(18)   a. You can get good grades and sleep? (attested)
           'Can you get good grades and sleep?'
       b. You traded your other one in? (attested)
           'Did you trade your other one in?'
       c. You want some water too? (attested)
           'Do you want some water, too?'
       d. And you let him drink your coffee like that? (attested)
           'And do you let him drink your coffee like that?'

The questions in (18) are similar to some of the ones that were discussed in chapter 2, in which the auxiliary does not precede the subject. Instead they begin with the subject; the auxiliary is present in (18a), but subject-auxiliary inversion does not occur in any of the sentences in (18). Questions like this may be rhetorical in nature in that they will not require an answer. That is to say that the questions may be asked with an answer in mind, so all the speaker is really asking is that the listener agree with or affirm what the speaker expects to be the case. A rhetorical question might be *You took the trash out already?* after the observer notices an empty waste basket, in which case the observer strongly suspects that the listener has performed that chore. Such questions are not true *yes-no* questions in that they are not genuine requests for new information; however, it is clear that the questions that are the focus of discussion in Green (1990) are indeed 'true' yes-no questions in that they are requests for yes or no responses. The types of final level patterns that I am concerned with are represented in the sentences in (19):

(19)   Yes-no question pitch tracks (Green 1990)
   a. You traded your other one in?
       'Did you trade your other one in?'

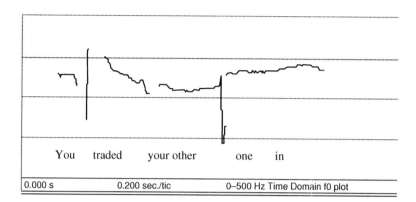

   b. Well Reverend— called y'all all one up at a time?
       'Well did Reverend— call y'all all one up at a time?'

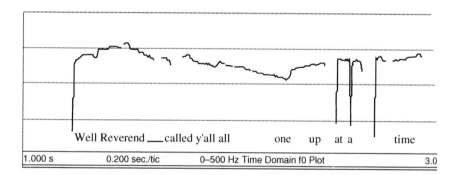

The questions in (19a) and (19b) end in a level or flat tone. In the discussion of questions in the preceding chapter, it was noted that AAE is not unique in using question intonation, but as more research is conducted in this area, we can explore issues about whether AAE uses unique intonational patterns, especially in marking questions that are not formed by subject-auxiliary inversion. The studies on question intonation in AAE strongly suggest that studying yes-no questions can yield important information about AAE intonational contours. As noted, one of the same patterns associated with the yes-no questions in Tarone's study was also found in Green's study. In addition, Foreman (1999) notes that the AAE speakers in her study did use the standard rise. However, she also found that they often used a high level or flat tone and falling tones in their yes-no questions, which are associated with declaratives. The level and falling tones are noted in Tarone (1972), and the level pattern is also associated with yes-no questions in Green (1990). The level or flat contour is used in questions and in other types of constructions in AAE. Perhaps that tone is a salient property in AAE which can be used by listeners to form opinions about the speech of AAE speakers and might be used in distinguishing the variety from other varieties of English.

The preliminary analysis of *wh*-questions in Green (1990) shows that the contours for those questions are similar to the contours for *wh*-questions in general English. Cruttenden (1986) and Pierrehumbert and Hirschberg (1987) agree that the tunes used with *wh*-questions in general American English are basically the same as those used with simple declaratives. The lowering pattern which has been called downstepping, is associated with these types of questions. This lowering occurs consistently throughout the statement, such that following low tones are lower than previous ones. This is shown in the diagrams below:

(20)   *Wh*-question pitch tracks (Green 1990)
  a. What they say?
   'What do they say?'

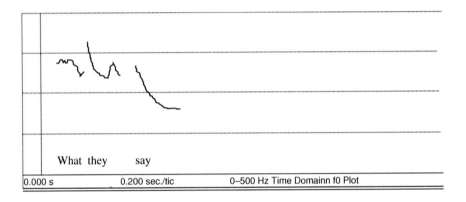

b. How you gon do on your midterm?
  'How are you going to do on your midterm?'

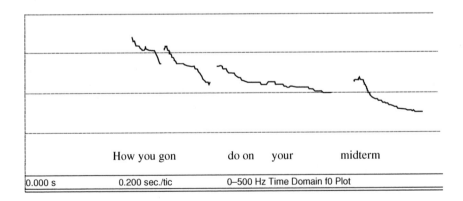

Note that the *wh*-questions are not formed with overt auxiliaries as in *What do they say?* and *How are you gon do on your midterm?*.

Research on intonational patterns may ultimately provide a body of information that can be used to give more substance to the impressionistic observations that are made about the rhythmic patterns in the variety.

In continuing the discussion of suprasegmentals, I now turn to stress patterns within the word in AAE. Investigators who have worked on AAE have commented on the stress in initial syllables of specific words in the language system. Smitherman (1977) describes this phenomenon of placing primary stress (indicated by capital letters) on the initial syllable as front shifting, and gives the following examples (p. 18):

(21)   a. PO-lice   'police'
        b. DE-troit   'Detroit'

Interestingly enough, different researchers list the syllable initial stress pattern as a common feature of AAE, and they all present the same words as examples, which suggests that the process only occurs within a limited set of words.[13] According to Baugh (1983a), this process "is limited to a portion of bisyllabic words" (p. 63). He goes on to give examples of sentences in which words (*pólice, défine, próduce, révise, pólite*) that bear initial stress occur:

(22)   a. If the pólice catch em, then he'll be sorry.
        b. But that's cause you let the man défine your problem.
        c. They can't lock . . . you . . . they better próduce some evidence first.
        d. He say he ain't coming back to work less they révise the schedule.
        e. He gots to be pólite around his moms – an like it too.

Baugh identifies this pattern as the forestressing of bisyllabic words and represents it in the following syllable structure, where stress in AAE is transferred to the first syllable. The diagram in (23) gives a general description of the differences between forestressing in bisyllabic words (note the consonants [C] and vowels [V]) in AAE and the second syllable stress in these words in general American English:

(23)   AAE   General American English
        CV   CVC   CV   CVC
        PO   l i c e   po   LIC E
    syllable 1 (stressed)   syllable 2   syllable 1   syllable 2 (stressed)

Wolfram and Fasold (1974) do not go into detail, but they note that this first syllable stress pattern is found in AAE with words such as *police, hotel, July* and *Detroit*, the same subset of words given in other studies (cf. Smitherman 1977 and Baugh 1983a). They go on to note that the stress pattern occurs in "some Southern white varieties" (p. 147), but do not go on to suggest that there are similarities between the intonational patterns in AAE and in Southern white varieties of English. The point is that while comparison between AAE and Southern white varieties have been made on a number of levels, not much has been said in relation to intonation. However, Feagin (1997) does suggest that there may be some similarities between the wide pitch ranges used by African American males and Southern white females, but to my knowledge there has not been any research on which to base this claim. These similarities, as she points out, may have "Caribbean roots as well" (p. 132).

A final note on the topic is that this stress pattern also occurs in words with more than two syllables. In data from a sermon that I recorded in 1990, the word *protector* is produced by the minister as *PROtector*, in which the first of three syllables is stressed. (A portion of that sermon is reproduced in chapter 5, section 5.5.)

Summary

In addressing sound patterns in AAE, I considered segmental and suprasegmental features. In the discussion of segmental features, I considered initial, medial and final consonant sounds and vowel sounds in certain environments. It is easy for listeners to evaluate the sounds and sound combinations that have been discussed as lazy speech, but the descriptions show the way in which combinations are very systematic and based on defined rules that make reference to specific environments in which sounds occur. The voicing value of consonant sounds plays a major role in the production of sounds and the specific sound that is used in a certain environment. For example, *f* and *v* occur in environments in which voiceless *th* and voiced *th*, respectively, occur in general American English. Data on the production of consonant sounds have been used in arguments about the origin of AAE. For instance, it has been argued that some clusters are less likely to occur due to the nature of languages from which AAE descended. In some of the discussion, technical terminology has been introduced in giving explanations for why sounds occur or do not occur in some environments. In general, one of the goals was to show that speakers do not haphazardly delete and insert sounds because they have 'lazy tongues.' The patterns in the sound system of AAE are completely regular.

Suprasegmental features such as stress and intonation have not been well studied, but they are often discussed in relation to unique features of AAE. The research in this area raises questions about the types of intonational contours that are associated with constructions in AAE. The studies that have been conducted on yes-no questions in AAE converge on the point that both level (or flat) and falling tones are used in these constructions. It may be that the types of intonational contours that speakers use mark the speech as being unique. Segmental features have been used to argue that AAE has retained features of West African languages, and they have also been used to argue that AAE is similar to other varieties of American English; however, suprasegmental features have not been brought squarely into the debate.

Exercises

1. The *ks* cluster at the end of *saks* (as in Saks Fifth Avenue) is not reduced. That is, *ks* does not become *k*, so speakers do not say *Sak Fifth Avenue. Does the *voicing generalization* make the correct prediction about *ks* clusters? Explain your response.

2. The cluster *ld* as in *build* is also reduced, so *build* in general American English can be pronounced as *buil* in AAE. As you will see, the sonority scale does not give the correct results, that is, it does not show that the *ld* cluster should be reduced. Explain how it fails to show this.

3. Now consider the verb *building* in the sentence *They building another church over there* ('They are building another church over there'). After reviewing the section on consonant cluster reduction and your response in the preceding question (number 2 above), explain how the verb *building* would be pronounced in the sentence. Also, say whether you think it is possible to get two different pronunciations. If so, what are the pronunciations? Be specific about the information you used in reaching your conclusion.

4. Consider the medial *th* in the word *birthday* in general American English. What do you think the *th* sound would become in AAE? How would the word be pronounced in AAE?

5. Think of African Americans who are in the media (e.g., Kweisi Mfume, Oprah Winfrey, Michael Jordan, etc.). Of those who come to mind, which ones (if any) would you describe as speaking what has been referred to as standard AAE? Explain your answer, and give examples to illustrate your points.

5 Speech events and rules of interaction in AAE

Focal point Syntactic and phonological patterns alone cannot sufficiently characterize AAE. Speakers manipulate common strategies of conversational interaction, and they adhere to rules of speaking in using speech events such as call and response in religious as well as secular contexts. Rhetorical strategies may be more prominent than syntactic and phonological features in speech events such as rap and sermons.

Pastor: Then he, then he, then he stops, then he stops, then he stops and he, he thinks about what happens. He says, hunh? "Through many dangers, snares I have already come. It WAS"
Congregation: Grace!

[passage from sermon]

5.1 Introduction

The purpose of chapters 2, 3 and 4 was to explain that syntactic and phonological patterns in AAE are rule-governed, so it is inaccurate to characterize the sentence and sound structures as random deviations from general American English. In presenting the range of descriptions of conditions and constraints that speakers adhere to when they use AAE, I provided examples (from conversation and data collection) that would further illustrate the features of language use. The types of examples that have been provided only reflect a part of the language use. This chapter will discuss additional ways in which language is used in AAE, focusing on speech events and rules of interaction.

Speech events, which are also governed by rules, take different forms. In some cases, their content and the way they are delivered may appear to be entertaining to some and caustic and even rude to those who are unfamiliar with them. The label 'speech event' is used here in the way in which it is presented in Hymes's (1972) discussion of units of interaction and communicative behavior in speech communities. The units of interaction are speech situation, speech event and speech act. A speech situation, for example, a ceremony, party or fight, is associated with speech but is not governed by rules of speaking. A speech event, on the other hand, is governed by rules of speaking, and takes place within a speech situation. The speech event may be a conversation that consists of smaller units or speech acts, such as a joke.

This chapter begins with an overview of speech events with brief definitions, and it discusses verbal strategies, giving examples from works in the literature on AAE, television shows and conversations. In addition it considers the use of expressive language in church services and how this language use is carried over to the secular world. This chapter also discusses verbal strategies in rap, focusing particularly on the braggadocio tone and signification that are characteristic of that speech event. The final section considers expressive language use as it relates to communicative competence. In this section, questions about the acquisition of speech events and their use in children's language are raised. In chapters 2, 3 and 4, I have indicated that in one way or another there are some similarities and subtle differences between syntactic and phonological features in AAE and other varieties of English. I do not know of any extensive studies on speech events in other varieties of English and will not be in a position to make such comparisons in this chapter. However, it is clear that the oral tradition plays a major role in the native American cultural experience. This chapter continues the themes in previous discussions in a number of ways. One way is that it addresses speech events, which may be marked by unique intonational patterns. In addressing ways of speaking and conversational interaction, a part of this chapter explains that it is necessary to look beyond the lexicon, semantics, syntax and phonology in characterizing AAE, although features from those components may very well surface in speech events.

5.2   ## Overview of speech events

Literature on speech events ranges from works in the 1930s on the dozens to the 1990's popular culture discussions of capping and snapping. I begin the discussion here with a general overview of verbal strategies, including standard definitions from Abrahams (1976), Smitherman (1977) and other investigators.

Signifying

Smitherman (1977) defines signifying as "the verbal art of insult in which a speaker humorously puts down, talks about, needles – that is, signifies on – the listener" (p. 118). This rhetorical strategy is also known as dropping lugs, joaning, capping and sounding.

Playing the dozens

A distinction is not always made between signifying and playing the dozens, but according to H. Rap Brown (1972), "The dozens is a mean game because what you try to do is totally destroy somebody else with words . . . Signifying is more humane. Instead of coming down on somebody's mother, you come down on them" (pp. 205–206). Abrahams and Smitherman take the dozens to be a form of signification. "In its indigenous folk style, the Dozens consists of set responses in versified form, usually rhymed couplets. Some refer to various sexual acts committed with "yo momma" – the mother of whoever is being addressed" (Smitherman 1977, pp. 131–132). Smitherman (1995) labels signifying and playing the dozens as two types of disses (insulting or disrespectful statements) that are actually being unified under terms such as joaning, capping and sounding.

Research on the dozens goes back to the 1930s, in which Dollard sets out to characterize this speech event, which he had observed among young males. Dollard (1939), in calling the dozens, "interactive insult," makes the following observations: (1) "It is the laughter, applause and the derision of the crowd which stirs the participants to ever renewed attempts to out-do the other in invective" (p. 11); and (2) playing the dozens with someone who is not a member of the group can result in fist fights (p. 13).

Rapping

This term has been used for different types of casual talk which include exchanges between a male and female, in which the male tries to win the favors of a female as he delivers a compliment (in his estimation) by using verbal expertise. In addition it can be used to refer to casual talk in which someone provides another with information. Smitherman (1977) notes that rap is highly stylized and may be used "to convey social and cultural information" or "for conquering foes and women" (p. 82). Prime examples of this stylized speech are the popular songs characterized by rhymes and braggadocio statements put to music.

Marking

In using the marking strategy, the speaker dramatically imitates the words and perhaps the actions of a person and makes some comment about him or her in the process. Mitchell-Kernan (1972) notes that the 'marker' reproduces "the words of the individual actors," and "affects the voice and mannerisms of the speaker" (p. 332–333).

Loud-talking

Loud-talking occurs when a speaker delivers a line that was intended for someone else loud enough for people outside of the conversation to hear. More precisely, it is used to refer "to a speaker's utterance which by virtue of its volume permits hearers other than the addressee, and is objectionable because of this" (Mitchell-Kernan 1972, p. 329).

Woofing

Woofing is defined as a strategy in which boasting is used to intimidate an opponent, thus avoiding violent confrontation. Muhammad Ali was considered to be a skilled woofer who bragged about his athletic prowess to his opponents.

Toasts

Toasts are tributes, usually poetic, to the grandeur of some character. They are narrated in first person and feature a hero who is "fearless, defiant, openly rebellious, and full of braggadocio about his masculinity, sexuality, fighting ability, and general badness" (Smitherman 1977, p. 157). Smitherman refers specifically to masculinity, but women can also deliver toasts about their extraordinary powers; consider Chaka Kahn's "I'm Every Woman," in which she says, "I can read your thoughts right now, everyone from A to Z" and also "I'm a Woman" from the 1989 musical *Black and Blue*. Given that these toasts are usually delivered in poetic form, they must be memorized, so the narrator is able to deliver them with great verbal skill.

Investigators agree that speakers must have verbal skill in order to manipulate these strategies. Dandy (1991) proposes a model, based on research by Hoover (1985) and Abrahams (1972), that is used to capture the different components of the communicative system of AAE. One component is labeled 'speech acts' and includes the verbal strategies that are listed above with the exception of signifying. In that model, signification is included in the 'style' component, which suggests that the verbal strategy is not a speech act or speech event itself but instead characterizes the style or form of the speech act.[1]

5.3   Verbal strategies

Verbal strategies or verbal acts consist of words, phrases and sentences and, in some cases, gestures which are used to impress, persuade, manipulate or even control. Some strategies require direct interaction between a speaker and listener, while others involve indirect interaction.

5.3.1   From the dozens to snaps

The history of verbal strategies in AAE goes back, according to some sources, to African communities and slavery. Some scholars have linked these speech acts and events to Africa, the middle passage and slavery. On some accounts, the term *dozens* was used to refer to the ill or old slaves who were sold in groups of twelve (Harris 1974). Under yet another account, the dozens is related to the snide remarks that were made by the field slaves as a display of hostility toward house slaves, who had some advantages (and disadvantages) that they did not have. The mother of the house slaves was said to be available to her master, as were dozens of other women. Additional sources and references to African origins of the dozens are given in Dandy (1991) and Smitherman (1995).

Simmons (1963) suggests that the dozens might be linked to West African sources such as the following: Efik tone riddles, curses, stereotyped sarcasm and retorts to curses. His tone riddle examples mention mother and father and have sexual references or refer to body parts. The examples of curses take the form of wishes of bad will such as bodily defects, and they make reference to illegitimate birth. The retorts to curses are along the same lines, in which the person being cursed replies with vulgar comments about the curser's family. Simmons summarizes by saying that "West African folkloristic retentions are definitely known to have occurred and it may well be that from the folkloristic background brought with them from Africa, the American Negroes have fashioned new forms to satisfy new needs" (p. 340). Smitherman (1995), in her discussion of playing the dozens and signifying, supports the theory that the dozens is linked to African cultures on the basis that it is the most plausible view.

Different rules must be followed by those participating in this sport of verbal repartee. During the game, which is in the call and response format, two opponents dual verbally, making derogatory remarks about each other and/or each other's family members (see section 5.5.). Participants play the game with persons they know or who are in their circle of acquaintances. To stay within the boundaries, they use exaggerated statements that do not, in reality, characterize the opponent's family members and family life. The audience judges the opponent's verbal comebacks in determining the actual winner.

Playing the dozens today is just as popular as it was years ago. Abrahams (1976) records many examples that read as if they were from data collected in the 1990s: "I can tell by your knees you mother eats surplus cheese" (p. 218). Two collections, *Snaps* (1994) and *Double Snaps* (1995) by Percelay *et al.* of lines from the dozens that have come out within the past ten years, attest to the popularity of the game even today. In the two books, the lines are referred to as snaps, and they are divided into sections such as stupid snaps, dirty snaps, house snaps and old snaps. Acknowledging that body moves and gestures are a major part of the verbal strategy, the second volume dedicates a section to "moves and stances for advanced snapping." For example, the finger hook is used to add force to the verbal snap, and eye rolling on the part of the receiver conveys the message that the speaker delivered an unimpressive snap. Also, stares and leaning stances can be used to intimidate the opponent. Although this point is not addressed, certain stress and intonational patterns are likely to be associated with snaps.

Some snaps from the Percelay *et al.* volumes are provided below:

(1) a. Your mother is so stupid, she thought a lawsuit was something you wear to court. (p. 57)
     b. Your mother's ears are so dirty, I can pull out enough wax to make candles. (p. 108)
     c. I went to your house, stepped on a cigarette, and your mother screamed, "Who turned off the heat?" (p. 112)
     d. Your mother is so old, she took her driving test on a dinosaur. (p. 106)

The lines in (1) are all extreme exaggerations that refer to "your mother." For instance, even in the most dire circumstances, we do not expect that anyone would consider using a cigarette as a household heating element. And to be sure, no one's mother who lived in the twentieth century has taken a driving test on a dinosaur. In the following exchange, taken from the sitcom *The Fresh Prince of Bel Air*, the mother signifies on the son. A character in her 70s delivered this line to her son Phil, who was upset because she had started dating again.

(2)   Phil's mother: (*to Phil*) Zee, are you ill? Your face is longer than Arsenio Hall's.

The dual role of the line here allows the mother to comment on Phil's disconsolate appearance and signify on Arsenio Hall's facial structure. The mother's retort stays within the confines of the rules of the dozens, as it is an exaggeration that comments on the son's mood by comparing it to the physical appearance of a well-known comedian.

Shirley, a restaurateur on the 1970s comedy, *What's Happening*, used the verbal strategy to send a message to a customer. She noticed that a guy at the pinball machine in the restaurant was standing in her way, as the pinball machine was very close to the telephone that she wanted to use. Shirley, with other pressing issues on her mind, became even more frustrated when she saw the guy just standing around, not being very productive. The exchange between the two goes as follows:

(3)   Shirley: Get a job! (*Looks at man on telephone in disgust*)
Male: A job? Won't you learn how to cook!
Shirley: Yo mama!

The first point to make is that in the exchange, the speakers get right to the point; one exaggerates about the other's poor cooking skills while the other implicates an abstract family member. After Shirley's initial unwelcome comment, the guy returns the serve with a timely and direct response. Anyone who has seen the sitcom knows that Shirley is not the world's best cook. Perhaps the male's comment hits too close to home, making Shirley reply with an even stronger fighting phrase: "Yo mama!" Judging from the audience's reaction, there is no doubt that Shirley is the victor. One important variation is that the male extends the game to real life when he brings Shirley's cooking expertise into question. This may be why Shirley comes down so hard on him. Because the dozens has been traditionally defined as a game that is played by males, it is significant to note that a woman delivers the scoring line. According to Dandy (1991, p. 72), "Historically, Black males have been noted for talking a particular kind of stylized talk"; and "learning how to use this talk is an essential part of passage from boyhood to manhood." Most investigators note that the strategy is used by males, but that girls also display such verbal skills. Smitherman (1995) sums it up: "As for Black women snappin, the sistas are on it like a honet, especially when there are no outsiders around" (p. 228).

Studies acknowledge that girls also play the dozens and signify, and according to Dandy (1991), girls start to play the dozens at about eleven-and-a-half years. H. Rap Brown (1972) argues that "some of the best dozens players were girls" (p. 206). Mitchell-Kernan (1972) is one of the few studies that have actually presented analyses of women's use of verbal strategies. (See, also, Smitherman's (1995) commentary on women and the dozens.) She provides examples of women signifying on other women and on men. The range of examples and explanations in that work shows how women use signification, quick wit and verbal acumen to make their points. The following exchange between Grace and Rochelle is a representative example:

(4)   Grace: After I had my little boy, I swore I was not having any more babies.
                 I thought four kids was a nice-sized family. But it didn't turn out that way.
                 I was a little bit disgusted and didn't tell anybody when I discovered I was
                 pregnant. My sister came over one day; I had started to show by that time.

       Rochelle: Girl, you sure do need to join the Metrecal for lunch bunch.

       Grace: (non-committally) Yea, I guess I am putting on a little weight.

       Rochelle: Now look here, girl, we both standing here soaking wet and you still trying
                 to tell me it ain't raining. (p. 323)

Instead of saying outright that Grace was, in no uncertain terms, pregnant, Rochelle
signifies and gets the intended message across just the same. Although the comment
can be taken to be somewhat insulting, the interlocutors focus on the humor element
in the exchange.

Morgan (1996), a study of the use of indirectness in women's conversation, is
different from previous accounts of signifying in that it analyzes the verbal strategy
as it occurs in conversation, focusing on the way in which signifying is achieved
through the use of grammatical features, stress and intonational patterns and lexical
features of AAE. According to Morgan (1996), it is important to analyze signification
in African American women's conversations because "women's interactions . . . have
been largely ignored," and "more importantly because women are often the innovators
and connoisseurs of this empowering practice" (p. 405). Two types of indirectness are
discussed in relation to signifying: pointed indirectness and baited indirectness. In
pointed indirectness, a mock target, not the actual person for which signifying is
intended, receives the message, while in baited indirectness, the signifier recounts
attributes of the target in some indirect sense while the target is present. For example, a
mock target is present during the situation in which a mother signifies on her daughter
who returned "later than expected." As the mother gazes at the mock target, she talks
directly to her and not to the daughter and then comments: "I don't have to tell you
who's grown in here" (p. 408). The mother does not have to address the daughter
directly to convey the point that she is violating her curfew.

Morgan goes on to discuss other patterns in signification in the areas of lexical
and grammatical features, prosodic features and interactional features. Indirectness
is achieved by the combination of a number of strategies that go beyond the way
the words are organized into phrases and sentences. Particular stress and intonational
patterns noted in the preceding chapter have been argued to be used in conveying the
message the signifier intends. If we analyzed passages from signification, would we
find that certain types of intonational contours and other prosodic features are used to
carry information about the signifier's attitude toward the target?

5.3.2   Loud-talking

Loud-talking, as defined earlier in this chapter, refers to the act of delivering a line,
intended for some select listener(s), loud enough for an outsider to hear. Mitchell-
Kernan (1972, p. 329) explains that "the loud-talker breaches norms of discretion; his

strategy is to use the factor of audience to achieve some desired effect on the addressee." The person delivering the statement does not have to yell, but she has to make sure the pitch is loud enough to be heard by bystanders. Because loud-talking necessarily involves a louder than normal (or necessary) pitch on the part of the addresser and often an expression of embarrassment by the addressee, it is easy to observe. Consider the situation below in which loud-talking was used to draw attention to A:

(5)   (A: Bf 32, B: Bm, 33)

Speaker B kept asking A where they should have dinner that night, but A didn't have any suggestions. After some time had elapsed, A and B had the following conversation:

A: I figured it out. Let's go to that place where I had that good veggie burger.

B: Oh yeah, American Cafe! That's a great idea.

A, B and others get ready to go to dinner.

A: *(A walks over to B and delivers the line quietly with discretion and with hands on her hips.)* I know I have great ideas, but it takes time for me to come up with them, so don't rush me.

B: *(B looks at A and delivers the line so that the other four people in the room can hear him.)* Now see, see what I have to go through!

A retreats to the door, out of sight, and waits for the others.

She running to the door. She shame now. Dən told me off, now she wanna go in the dark.

Everyone laughs.

In this exchange, speaker B violated a conversational rule by exposing parts of what speaker A intended to be a private conversation. It was clear that B's lines were heard by and intended for everyone else when B spoke louder than necessary for A to hear him. After B delivers the line that exposes A, he makes sure that the attention is drawn to A by announcing that she has committed a shameful act. At this point, everyone knew that loud-talking had taken place. As a result, A temporarily lost the face that presented her as a relatively quiet and soft-spoken person.

The intent in using the loud-talking strategy does not have to be evil or malicious, but when the event is successful, it can result in the addressee losing face. Because an interlocutor's face is at stake, he or she may often retaliate or do something to regain face in loud-talking situations. The addressee may turn the table by responding to the speaker in a matching loud voice or by surpassing the speaker's loudness and intensity. When placed in this situation, the addressee may take on the role as speaker, uttering one of the following in a louder than usual (necessary) voice:

(6)   a. Don't loud-talk me.

b. Stop loud-talking me.

c. Who you tryin to loud-talk? (rhetorical)

The examples in (6) show that members of the AAE-speaking culture recognize this verbal act as an intended violation of conversational norms and refer to it as "loud-talking," as in (6b). The speaker who uses a verbal face-saving strategy is able to come back with a quick reply and threaten the face of the interlocutor who initiated the game. However, this face-saving strategy was not an option for A in (5) because it would have been in conflict with the type of persona, quiet and non-confrontational, that she intended to display. The other speakers in the room only had secondhand evidence that she may not have been as quiet as they thought she was, but had she responded to B's statement by using the type of replies given in (6), she would have certainly sent the wrong message.

5.3.3   Marking

The verbal strategy marking may be confused with mocking for a couple of reasons. The first is that the strategy is philosophically similar to mocking, and the second is that the term *marking* is phonetically similar to the term *mocking*, so speakers, especially those who want to speak 'correctly,' may say mock to mean mark. This strategy is like mocking in that it may involve careful repetition of a person's words and mannerisms, but some implication is made about the person's attitude, character and/or disposition. It reflects the interlocutor's linguistic ability to use indirect language to report on a person's disposition.

Verbal statements in marking are accompanied by facial expressions and other body movements that help to characterize the attitudes or tendencies of the targeted person. Oftentimes people are "marked" when they are thought to speak and act 'proper.' 'Speaking proper' can, but does not necessarily, involve using what is considered by the mainstream to be standard English. In some instances, people who are characterized as 'speaking proper' are understood as repudiating and setting themselves apart from the vernacular culture. In marking these speakers, the marker exaggerates words, mannerisms, body stances and gestures that are not usually associated with the vernacular culture. The commentary that the marker makes by his actions is that the speaker shares characteristics and views of a different class or group. Along these same lines, those who appear to be entrenched in the vernacular culture may also be marked.

Speech events in AAE, in particular verbal dueling and strategic negotiating, are often from the male perspective, but increasingly the contribution by African American females to this genre is being recognized. Mitchell-Kernan (1972) explains how signifying, loud-talking and marking are used by females, and Morgan (1996) discusses different types of indirectness strategies used by women.

5.4   Expressions in nonverbal communication: eye movement and giving dap

In Morgan's example of pointed indirectness, the mother also used eye gaze in addition to verbal communication to get and hold the attention of the mock target. Nonverbal communication may carry a message that is not directly obvious from the speech, and it may reinforce the verbal message. Percelay *et al.* demonstrate nonverbal expression that communicates messages in snaps. Members of the black-speaking communities may use nonverbal communication such as eye movement, head and neck movement and hand movement as part of speech events or as the sole form of communication in conveying an attitude or impression.[2]

Different types of eye movement have been categorized under the terms 'cutting eyes' and 'rolling eyes.' Rickford and Rickford (1976) discuss the phenomenon known in Guyana as 'cut-eye' and note that "rolling the eyes" is the equivalent for African Americans. 'Cut-eye' is defined as a derogatory eye gesture that is intended to convey feelings of "hostility, displeasure, disapproval, or a general rejection of the person at whom it is directed" (p. 349). The visual gesture involves very defined eye work such that it includes at least four stages: (1) a look or short stare at the target, (2) followed by a gaze over the target, (3) and then a sharp look or 'cut' of the eyes by closing the eyelids and opening them. The sequence is usually ended by (4) turning the head away from the target in disgust or disapproval.

Similar visual gestures occur in African American communities, and speakers refer to them by name. One may comment on a person's gaze by asking rhetorically, "Who you rolling your eyes at?" The question is basically acknowledgment that the eye movement was observed; therefore, no response is required, especially if the target asked the question. In such a situation, the gazer may have looked at the target askance, moved her eyes up and down the target's body and looked away by rolling the eyeballs in another direction. It is possible that the gazer will look away in disgust or exasperation and 'turn up her nose' by slightly protruding the lips toward the nose. The nose does not move in and of itself, but the gesture is referred to as 'turning up one's nose.' A number of actions and attitudes, as far as the gazers are concerned, justify or provoke eye-rolling. A person who is believed to think that she is superior to others or who displays an attitude that may not be accepted by a particular group may be the target of eye-rolling. Also a person may roll her eyes in response to a statement that does not make any sense or that is inaccurate, in her opinion, or to an uninformed statement, as if to say, "I can't believe you said that." 'Looking down the nose' conveys basically the same meaning that is conveyed by 'turning up the nose,' but the gestures involve slightly different types of movements. Whereas turning up the nose is completed by protruding the lips upward, looking down the nose involves lowering the eyes on the target and looking downward.

Other forms of nonverbal communication involve other parts of the body such as the hands, hips, neck and head. These gestures can accompany each other, and they can also be used in conjunction with the verbal strategies that have been discussed. The actions of placing the hand on the hips and rolling the neck, moving the head back and forth, can occur simultaneously. These actions may be performed by females in situations in which they are 'telling someone off,' 'putting someone's clothes on,' 'reading someone,' 'giving a person a piece of their mind' or simply engaging in conversation. In effect, these gestures have come to be stereotypically associated with general behavior of certain African American women, and portrayals of African American women often include exaggerated movements approximating these gestures; just witness the portrayals on situation comedies and comedy shows. But not all African American women participate in these types of nonverbal communication strategies. In fact, it is not even the case that all African American women who use the lexical, syntactic and phonological features that have been discussed use these strategies. Age and other socio-related factors are correlated with the use of this type of nonverbal communication.

Not all types of notably distinct nonverbal communication in African American communities are identified as female behavior. A number of gestures and stances are associated specifically with males. African American males (and females to a lesser extent) have been noted to display different handshakes and hand movements to communicate a range of messages. Handshakes, which may change almost as often as the types of lexical and slang items that have been discussed in chapter 1, can easily consist of a sequence of hand movements. Most commonly they are used as forms of, or in conjunction with, greetings and salutations.

Related to the handshake is 'giving dap', a form of nonverbal communication that is used to express agreement about some issue in the conversation or to show solidarity. This can be carried out by a form of interaction called the pound, a process in which one person (often male) gently pounds the top of the receiver's (often male) vertical fist. The receiver responds in kind by gently pounding the top of the initiator's vertically held fist with his vertically held fist, or the participants can bring the fronts of their vertically held fists together, ending in a light tap.

The pound can be used in a number of different situations. I observed two young males either in their pre- or early teens engage in the pound during church service. In response to the acknowledgment of visitors, two young males sitting directly behind me stood up. After the formal greeting, church members, including me, immediately near the boys shook their hands. After the boys took their seats, one of their friends reached over, extending his vertically held fist and lightly pounded the fist of the male sitting to his left. The visiting member, as soon as he realized that he was about to be given dap, put his fist in position to receive the pound. Of course, in return, the visiting male responded with a pound. By extending his vertically held fist to receive the pound from the visiting member, the boy was welcoming the guest and virtually expressing his satisfaction with the way his friend presented himself to the congregation.

Another way to give dap, which has become quite common on the basketball court and football field, is to jump up (at varying heights) and touch chests, none too gently. Chest-touching, which symbolizes the type of meaning associated with the high five, is often the response to a score or tight (very nice) play. This form of giving dap, chest-touching or chest-bumping, may have been invented by males, but it is certainly used in polished forms by some college and professional women athletes. Chest-touching also seems to have crossed racial/ethnic boundaries, as it is used more and more by athletes in general. While chest-touching may have the same meaning as the high five, it is not used in all the same situations in which the high five can be used. For instance, in business settings, colleagues may use some version of the high five to acknowledge a good meeting or presentation, but chest-touching is not likely to be used in that setting.

The importance of handshakes can be seen in different facets of society. Consider for example the use of the handshake gesture by members of African American fraternities and sororities. The different fraternities and sororities have handshakes or grips as a part of their rituals, and they can be used to greet respective members of the brotherhood or sisterhood. For example, members (i.e., brothers) of the same fraternity who were pledged on different college campuses but have never met may greet each other with their special hand grip. Also, this handshake can be used by brothers who know each other but may have been out of touch for some period of time. Members of fraternities often take the opportunity to use the handshake, but sorority sisters seldom ever, if at all, use their secret handshake on such a serious level. This male-female dichotomy, of course, extends beyond fraternities and sororities, as these organizations simply mirror the greater community and society.

In the late 1980s or early 1990s, a standard handshake and grip that is reminiscent of the way fraternity men greet respective brothers became popular. It can be described as an embrace in which men proceed with the standard handshake and embrace with the free arm and hand. This type of greeting or salutation is an exchange between men who know each other well, and it may be used in contexts in which friends who may not have seen each other for some period of time get together. A variation on this shake has become more popular. In the variation, the participants grip in a hand clasp, step to each other bringing the clasped fists to the chest area and embrace by lightly bringing the fists of the free hands to each other's backs. Then they step back, extending the arms and hands into a three-part shake, which may end with a finger snap.

It is hard to comment on the extent to which handshakes are social rituals without observing the contexts in which they are used and the intensity in which participants carry them out. Handshakes or some variation of them used for acknowledgment or subtle greetings can even take place in church services, as has been illustrated with the teen pound episode. On another occasion, two African American adult males used the pound to acknowledge each other while church service was in progress. One of the males walked into the service after it had already commenced, moved to a pew directly behind a man he obviously knew, and got the acquaintance's attention. Immediately after their eyes met, they made contact with their fists, in which case the fist of one gentleman was tapped on top of the fist of the other and vice versa. This acknowledgment was done in an orderly fashion and as inconspicuously as possible to avoid distraction during the sacred service. The ritual greeting was carried out smoothly in every sense of the word: the men eased right back into the service without missing a beat, but with establishing solidarity, which is extremely important in church services. I doubt that the greeting made any impression on other members of the congregation – if they noticed it at all.

Baugh (1978) reports that for over four years, he "observed and analyzed more than six hundred handshakes performed at the Los Angeles municipal pool..." (p. 34). He also observed that participation in power handshakes in certain situations reflected the politicization of the ritualized act. The number of handshakes he observed is not overwhelming, as variations on them are developed regularly. In fact, Baugh makes this same point when he says that "the development of handshakes is similar to the use of slang words, which, as social situations change, are invented, disseminated, dropped from the vernacular, and then rediscovered" (p. 40).

5.5   Speech events and language use in African American church services[3]

Traditional African American church services, in particular Baptist, are composed of musical devotions, ritual programs and celebrations, dedications, sermons, prayers, testimonials and weekly announcements. In addition, members of the congregation, including those leading the service, may engage in nonverbal communication such as head-nodding, feet-patting, hand-waving and clapping, body-swaying and standing to express agreement with the message or acknowledgment of spiritual feeling inspired by the sermon and music.

The verbal and nonverbal participation is a unique form of expression and a tradition deeply rooted in African American culture and, by extension, African culture. To an onlooker who is not familiar with this type of service, the participation may appear to be overly exuberant. However, it is part of one's personal worship experience, which includes a connection to others who are worshipping and praising a higher being.

Members of the congregation have very personal experiences during any service, but there are ways in which they and the minister come together on one accord as participants in an extended conversation. This interaction is probably one of the most marked and distinguished characteristics of worship services, especially from the viewpoint of those interested in linguistic descriptions of patterns in the sermon genre. The minister and large congregations interact just as effectively as the minister and small congregations. I will return to a discussion of this interaction shortly.

Holt (1972) discusses the traditional black church and outlines the different segments of the church service, summarizes its history and function and explains the role and style of the minister. According to Holt, the black church "was born out of necessity," but it has developed routines and rituals that have become traditions. She goes on to say, "What developed as a necessary mode of communication has become an integral part of the language system of blacks, though the necessity is not as great as it was in the beginning. This communication behavior is more prevalent in the nonreligious society of today's blacks..." (p. 190).

Pitts (1993) provides an extensive study of African American Baptist ceremonies and their relation to African rituals in which he outlines the different segments that come together to form the worship service. One aim of that work is to show that there is an "undeniable African presence in the folk worship of African-Americans" and that this presence is felt at different levels of worship in the services (p. 6). Recognizing that there is a preponderance of focus on the linguistic patterns and distinctive preaching style of Baptist ministers, Pitts explains that the sermon is only one part of the service. Other more subdued segments such as devotions and prayer offerings are also noteworthy parts of the service. Pitts sets out "to refute the impressions, both scholarly and popular, that ritual behavior in the American black church is an ecstatic jumble ... Both somber and climactic events are required to produce the ritual structure found in the black Baptist church" (p. 8). In characterizing the events of the service and explaining how they come together, he identifies two ritual frames that "combine to create the total ritual structure" (p. 8). The first ritual frame, which includes prayer and hymns, takes place at the beginning of the worship period, and the second frame consists of the sermon. The first frame, influenced by seventeenth- and eighteenth-century English prayers and hymns, is in contrast with the second frame which "exploits the rhythms of black composers and sacred folk songs, commonly called spirituals and gospel songs" (p. 9). Pitts characterizes the importance of the juxtaposed frames in the following way:

> The variation of vernacular speech and song styles that define the two distinct frames have been crucial in preserving an oral ritual for nearly three hundred years without a written liturgy. By experiencing the contrasting moods of each frame in sequence and becoming emotionally transformed, ritual participants are restored to a state of ideological stability within a mainstream society hostile to their social, economic, and political needs.
>
> [p. 9]

The language and song styles help set the mood for the two frames, which work together to provide an atmosphere in which participants experience freedom, albeit temporary, from forces in society.

As a means of analyzing the speech styles that are used in each frame, Pitts isolated eight patterns in AAE and determined the frequency of their occurrence in prayers and sermons. He used variables such as: -in/-ing, negative concord, verbal -s, no copula, no *have* in present perfect contexts and no possessive -'s. Overall, the findings led Pitts to conclude that fewer AAE patterns associated with those variables were used in prayers than in preachers' conversational speech. The climactic sermons were marked by increased use of vernacular speech, in which the variables he considered occurred with greater frequency. In addition, the three stages of these sermons were prosaic conversation, emotional build-up and climax.

The interaction between the minister and congregation is facilitated by call and response, a traditional practice in which the minister makes a statement (a call) and members of the congregation reply (response), indicating that they agree, understand, identify with or have heard the statement, whether it be an exhortation, instruction or general information.[4] The exchange, progressing toward the end, is marked by a rhythm the preacher sets, the musician helps him keep and the congregation follow.

Smitherman (1977) sets call and response in a historical context, and explains that it is a strategy used to get participants in the church service on one accord. The inter-action between the pastor and congregation begins quite early during the service and builds with intensity as the sermon progresses. Even during the minister's conversational speech, members in the audience may be so moved to respond with a "yes" or "Aman" ("Amen"). They may respond by saying "Amen" when the minister declares, during his pastoral remarks before his sermon: "We should support our youth." As Holt puts it, "the intensity and volume of audience signals to the preacher that he is getting across, that he's telling the truth, that the audience is enjoying and appreciates how he says it" (p. 192). During the sermon, the congregation's responses may be the following: "Amen" (or some variation, "Aman," "Man"), "Come on preacher," "Go on and preach," "alright," "yes sir," "my Lord," "thank you Jesus," "I know that's right."

As I present passages from a sermon collected in a small Baptist church in Louisiana, I will highlight notable points about the order in which sections of the sermons are presented, audience interaction and strategies used by the preacher: (In the transcription of the sermon, words written in capital letters are stressed.)

The pastor begins his sermon by introducing and reading the scripture on which the sermon is based:

(7)   Pastor: ... If you please, that you would look at Philippians the third chapter the thirteenth and fourteenth verses. This is a sermon that will commit one. I think we need to be more committed the first of the year.

Congregation: Aman! Yes!

Pastor: Is that right?

Congregation: Oh yeah.

Pastor: These are words of commitment. Philippians the third chapter, Philippians the third chapter verses thirteen and fourteen. Shall we stand? (*congregation standing*)
Brethren I count not myself to have apprehended but this one thing I do forgetting those things which are behind, and reaching forth unto those things which are before, I press toward the mark for the prize of the high calling of God in Christ Jesus. The flowers fadeth and the grass withereth, but the word of God shall stand forever.

After reading the scripture, the pastor ends with Isaiah 40:8, which begins with "the flowers fadeth," a common practice by many preachers. The pastor proceeds to give a brief overview of the scripture in layperson's terms:

(8)   Pastor: Paul talks about his personal condition. Y'all wit me?

Congregation: Yeah! C'mon preacher!

Pastor: He talks about his commitment to doin' the will of the Lawd [Lord], and he says, I, I'm not gon' spend any of my TIME looking over what I HAVE done."

Congregation: Well!

Although it is always difficult to capture all congregational responses, what is shown here is that the congregation, in rhythm, utter their expressions after the preacher's phrases or full statements.[5] Holt (1972) compares the rhythmic calls and responses to another segment of African culture. They are

reminiscent of African drum ceremonies, as an illustration of the matrix out of which black communication style has evolved. It is clear, for example, that the black ministerial figure (pastor, preacher, reverend, or leader) does not deliver a message *to* his audience; he involves the audience in the message. Expressive communication (emotion, feeling) is mandatory for both speaker and receiver.

[p. 200]

As has already been noted, Smitherman (1977) makes just this point when she refers to the call and response strategy as an organizing principle.

The pastor and congregation are in rhythm in (8); he calls and the congregation responds. There are some non-rhythmic responses here, though, in that some members are so moved to offer an "all right!" at other times during the sermon. It may also be the case that because this point is early in the sermon, the members of the congregation have not yet gotten in rhythm with each other and are free to respond when they are so moved. In some cases, the responses seem to be more sporadic at the beginning of the sermon than at the end. The congregation's responses are triggered by the pastor's interpretation of the scripture, delivery and use of language. In addition, the pastor establishes a rhythm or cadence that signals the members to respond. The rhythmic prompt of the pastor's intonational patterns gives the audience the cue that he has reached a point at which they can answer, and they answer in earnest, not simply in knee-jerk fashion. The pastor also makes leading statements or asks rhetorical questions that move the congregation to respond. Look at the example in (8), in which in the first line the preacher asks the leading question, "Y'all wit me?" The rhetorical strategy of repetition also moves the congregation. Pitts (1993) explains that the verbal repetition in the sermon is used to create rhythm and audience feedback (p. 160). Consider the repetition of 'scars' in *mental scars, physical scars* and *spiritual scars* early in the sermon and the audience's response to it:

(9)   Pastor: Because the consequences of that experience have left us with some
                      MENtal scars or some PHYSICAL scars. Huhn?
       Congregation: Well! Well!
       Pastor: Even some spiritual scars. Hanh? Are you gon' pray wit me?
       Congregation: Aman [Amen]! Come on preacher!

The congregation respond to the "hunh?" and "hanh?" which can be interpreted as "Do you hear me?" or "I'm right, aren't I?" Along these same lines, rhetorical questions such as "Are you gon' pray wit me?" also help to establish the rhythm of responses. The feedback shows that the congregation is in tune with the message and is not just caught up in the manner in which the pastor uses that 'preaching' tone, sometimes appearing almost as if he is singing. Consider the interchanges below in which some members pick up on specific key words (10) and finish the preacher's sentence (11):

(10)   Pastor: That's the reason the song writer can say, "Through many dangers,
                      toils, and snares I have already come." If he had not had that experi-
                      ence, he didn't go back and say what the experiences was. He didn't
                      talk about what the snares was. He didn't even talk about the danger.
       Congregation: All right.
       Pastor: But he jus' said, "through many."
       Congregation: Through many! Aman!

In (10) members of the congregation can be heard repeating two of the pastor's key words ("through many") in their response, which are from the familiar song "Amazing Grace." In the following exchange (11), in which the pastor begins with repetition of "then he" and "then he stops," members from the audience finish the pastor's sentence without missing a beat:

(11) Pastor: Then he, then he, then he stops, then he stops, then he stops and he, he
                      thinks about what happens. He says, hunh? – "Through many dangers,
                      snares I have already come. It WAS – "
      Congregation: Grace!
      Pastor: "I din' do it by myself!"

As the pastor stresses *was*, audience members finish the statement by chiming in *grace*
from the song he is quoting.

At a later point in the sermon, the minister uses the repetition strategy as he goes
through the numbers and gives an account of events that occurred during the past ten
years:

(12) Pastor: Everybody ought to be rejoicing for the Lawd has crossed them over.
                      Is that right? The Lord has brought you safely all beginning back
                      ten years ago nineteen hundred and eighty. The Lawd brought you
                      through to one, two, three, four, five, six, seven, eight, nine an' ten.
      Congregation: Yes. All mah life!
      Pastor: Ten yeas [years] of disloyal, ten years of ups and down, ten yeas of
                      joy, ten yeas of sorrow, ten yeas of shortcoming, ten years on the
                      high side, ten yeas on the low side, ten yeas not wonderin, whatcha
                      [what you're] gon do . . .
      Congregation: Oh Lawd! Yes suh! (*clapping*)
      Pastor: Ten yeas of God days, ten yeas of sunshiny days, ten years of fool-
                      ishness and then ten years of gittin yo'self together.

The musician responds with musical expression that keeps the rhythm that has already
been established. The nonverbal responses, namely clapping, along with the musical
and verbal responses, also serve as a clue that the minister is reaching the climax,
moving to the end of the sermon.

Nonverbal expressions, for example a hand-wave or a head-nod, occur simultaneously with the congregation's verbal responses. In addition, responses to the minister's
calls can come in the form of music from various instruments in the church; however,
these musical notes are not usually played until the preacher gets well into the crescendo
to his climax. That is, just as the members of the congregation get their cue to respond
from verbal repetition or other strategies, the musician also waits for the right moment,
determined by the tone of the pastor's sermon, to answer the calls with the instrument
(usually piano or organ). One musician calls this tactic underscoring, which helps to
keep the preacher on track and on key. In effect, it helps to prevent the minister from
preaching in his rhythmic tone in the wrong key, as a musician from a Dallas, Texas,
area church explained to me.

The musician starts playing near the end of the sermon, during the minister's rise
to his finish. Toward the end of his sermon, the minister goes through the alphabet,
describing the characteristics of the Lord. He begins with an introductory statement to
the crux of his sermon:

(13)   Pastor: He IS my hos' when I don' have a friend. Ain' that right? He's alright from
         A to Z.

As the minister works through the alphabet, continuing his stylistic listing, he gets in
a rhythm that is paced more quickly than the preceding segment of the sermon. Here it
is more difficult to keep track of the congregation's responses, because there are more
of them and they are more frequent. For example, the congregation responds after the
first "Is that right?" in the passage in (14). The minister builds and the congregation
follows with more intense exchanges:

(14)   Pastor: Hmmmmm because A He is Alpha an' Omega.
                       Is that right? B He's before the beginning. Have I got a witness? An'
                       He always will be. Is that right?

                                      . . .

                       An' L the Lawd [Lord] is love. (*pause*)
        Congregation: All right! All right! C'mon now!
        Pastor: M He's a mighty God. Oh what the songwriter say?
                       "Oh what a mighty God we serve!" Have I got a witness?
                       N The Lawd is nice. Don't you hear me? The Lawd is nice to me.
                       This morning, He woke me up on time. Idn't that right? Aw Lawd!
                       An' O The Lawd is over everything. He sees the flowers abloom in
                       the spring. Idn't that right?
                       An' P You don' hear me. He IS my PROtector. You don' hear me.
                       David said, "Yea though I walk through the shadows of death, I will
                       fear no evil. For thou art wit me." You don' hear me. Aw Lawd! David
                       said, "The Lawd is my protector." Ain that right? Oh Lawd!
                       Anhan [And] Q He will not quitcha [quit you]. He'a stay witcha
                       [with you] through thick an' thin

                                      . . .

                       An' the Lawd is S because He save ya from sin.
                       (*Music begins*)

At this point, the congregation and the pianist respond to the minister's calls and
continue with him to the climax:

(15)   Pastor: . . . Lemme tell you about two mo' [more].
                       He is X because He's a X-ray technician. He can look behin' the smile you
                       have on yo' face an' see the frown in yo' heart. I'm'a, close wit this one.
                       He's Z because He is a zealyous [zealous] God.

In explanation of the Lord's X property, the minister uses comparison and contrast
when he says "smile on yo' face" and "the frown in yo' heart." The congregation
appreciates the Lord's greatness and the preacher's adept use of words and rhetorical
strategies. The pastor has reached the highest point in the sermon and begins to come

down as he returns to a key clause: "As I close this morning umhum, He said, 'I'm looking forward to the mahk [mark] of a high calling.'" At the very end of the sermon, the responses are made at every few or so words, and the minister sets up the cadence by grouping the words into rhythmic phrases and using repetition.

(16)   Pastor: Put a little joy
        Congregation: Yeah!
        Pastor: in yo' life!
        Congregation: Yeah!
        Pastor: Put a little happiness
        Congregation: Yes suh [sir]!
        Pastor: in yo' life!
        Congregation: Yes suh!
        Pastor: Turn, turn, turn you aroun', place yo' feet on higher groun'. The
                       Lawd, the Lawd, Ohhhhhh the Lawd, the Lawd!
        Congregation: Oh, yes, He will! Yes Lawd! Oh yes He will!

The minister ends the sermon on this note and takes his seat. The levels of intensity of the exchange between the minister and the congregation and the minister and musician are equally high. The exchange between the preacher and congregation is different from that in conversation between two people or among a small group of people. The exchange between the preacher and congregation is an extended interaction that involves a one-to-many situation in which there is a key speaker addressing a large congregation on the one hand, but the members of the congregation are allowed, and even expected, to talk back to the speaker, on the other. Some rules are in effect. The first is that no member of the congregation is allowed to take over the message; the minister is always the major speaker, the addresser. Another rule is that the responses from the congregation must be short in length, so if the preacher asks, "Are you gon' pray wit me?" members are not allowed to stand up and ask the preacher what he means or give some long drawn-out explanation to the question. In this situation in which "talking back" complements the segments of the address by the preacher, the rules are such that they help to facilitate the exchange, but they always define the minister as the addresser and confirm that he is getting his message across. In the case of the musician, underscoring also helps to keep the preacher on track, but even in this case, the musician is responding; it is the minister who makes the calls.

The interaction between the preacher and congregation serves as an example of the way in which certain parts of community and society are interdependent. After all is said and done, the preacher has preached to the congregation, and members have responded and ensured that they are all on one accord. The congregation have fulfilled their responsibility, talking back to the preacher thereby helping to create an environment in which everyone is involved in the sermon.

The discussion so far has been geared toward call and response and the types of strategies the preacher uses as he gets the congregation involved in the sermon. The following discussion considers some of the syntactic and phonological features of AAE that are used in the sermonic passages in this chapter. Here, I stress features because I will only refer to instances of particular constructions. The preacher does not use very many syntactic features of AAE, but he certainly uses prosodic or suprasegmental features and rhetorical strategies that are associated with preaching styles. So in analyzing such sermons, it is necessary to look beyond syntactic and segmental (phonological) features.

In the discussion of syntactic patterns, it was shown that forms of the auxiliary/copula *be* do not always occur in sentences. From a survey of the sermon, including passages that have already been presented and those that have not, it is determined that the auxiliary/copula *be* forms occur on the surface more often than not. In addition to the two instances of forms of the copula that do occur in the following, there is one case in which it does not occur on the surface (17).

(17)   Pastor: I wanna tell ya He's able to bring you through.
        Congregation: Yes!
        Pastor: Is that right?
        Congregation: Oh yes!
        Pastor: If we would talk this morning to Shadrach, Meshach, and Abinigo [Abednego], they would tell you that **He a cooling system in a fiery furnace**.

There is no occurrence of the copula in the phrase in boldface although there is one preceding the adjective in the first line of the passage ("... He's able to ... "), and the preacher uses the full form *is* in his rhetorical question in the second line ("Is that right?"). Also worth noting is the minister's use of *I'm'a* in (15), when he preaches, "I'm'a, close wit this one." As noted in chapter 2, *I'm'a* indicates future in AAE. A second variable feature that occurs more often than not in the sermon is the suffix verbal -*s* in third person singular and habitual contexts.

(18)   Pastor: Talk wit me! You ever wonder why sometime that things happen that you jus' don' understan'? **God works** in mysterious ways.

                                                ...

Pastor: An' you see the Lawd, the Lawd can do anything that **He desire** to do wit anybody that **He desire** to do it wit ...

The verbal -*s* marker occurs in *God works* but not in *He desire*. In addition there is an instance of pronominal apposition, which has been labeled as a pattern of AAE (although it is not a construction that I address in this book):

(19)   Pastor: ... So the writer the Paul he said ...

In the sequence *the writer/the Paul he*, the preacher uses the pronoun *he* to resume the function of the subject *Paul*. Also, in the passage in (14), the *wh*-question in the explanation of 'M' is formed without an overt auxiliary ("*Oh what the songwriter say?*" 'What does the songwriter say?'). *Wh*-questions were addressed in chapter 3.

Some AAE markers fall under segmental phonology such as consonant cluster reduction. This type of reduction varies; in some cases words end in clusters (*midst*), and in others, there are no final clusters (***An*** *you* ***mus'*** *believe that this God you serve is a able God.*) The pastor uses the common pronunciation *tha's* ('that's') in the sermon, also (***Tha's*** *what my uncles use to call me ol' man.*).[6] *Tha's* is also worth noting because instances in which *t* is not produced in the environment preceding *s* are common in AAE, also as in *it's* (*i's*) and *what's* (*wha's*). (If you check the discussion of expletive *it/it's* in chapter 3, you will find that the pronunciation *i's* is also used.)

More AAE markers in the sermon fall under phonology, in particular prosody. I have already alluded to the prosodic features in the sermon by pointing out the rhythmic flow, for example the phrasing or grouping of words in (16). In addition, the pastor uses the forestressing pattern in pronouncing the multisyllabic word *protector*. In the climax of the sermon in the description of 'P,' he says, "He IS my PROtector" (14), in which the auxiliary *is* and the first syllable in *protector* are stressed. Certainly, some AAE syntactic and segmental phonological features are represented in the sermon, but the overwhelming properties that characterize the speech event as AAE are rhetorical strategies such as call and response interaction, repetition and suprasegmental patterns in the rhythm and tonal contours.

What defines a speech sample as AAE? Who is or is not a speaker of AAE and what is or is not a sample of AAE cannot always be determined by tallying up the number of features in the language system such as the following and calculating their frequency of occurrence: (1) aspectual *be*, *BIN* and *dən* are used, (2) auxiliary/copula *be* is highly variable in some environments but obligatory in others, (3) *f/v* occur in some contexts in which *th* occurs in other varieties of English. In the absence of quantifiable syntactic and phonological features, there may be salient rhetorical strategies and prosodic features that are identified as part of the AAE system. The prosodic features may be used by some to classify a speaker as one who 'sounds black,' although very little stock can be put into such an identification process because, as noted in chapter 4, more research must be conducted in the area of suprasegmental properties of AAE before definitive conclusions can be drawn.

The following section is an extension of the present one, as it highlights the use of call and response in the secular world.

5.6   Extensions of call-response

The rhythmic exchange between addressers and listeners in traditional African American religious services becomes a part of the ritual order of worship. Similar exchanges, which are often referred to as backchanneling, can be heard in day-to-day informal interaction. Backchanneling occurs in the form of short responses to parts of conversations, and it encourages speakers to continue because the listeners are totally engaged in the conversation, in agreement with the speaker's point of view or in awe of it.

The type of backchanneling that can be heard in everyday speech is often modeled in the media, in movies and situation comedies that are intended to represent some part of African American life or experience.[7] During one particular scene in Spike Lee's *Jungle Fever*, a movie which addresses social issues in America, five women who are socializing in a friend's living room discuss the status of African American males and an adulterous affair between a participant's husband and an 'outside' woman. The gathering of the African American females was referred to as a war council by one of the male characters whose wife was a member of the group: "There's a war council goin' on in your livin' room."[8]

During the moment in the living room scene when one woman has the floor, the listeners give her their undivided attention and are just as focused on her speech as the congregational members are focused on the preacher's sermon that has just been analyzed. Backchanneling cues such as the following are delivered at the appropriate time in step with the rhythm the speaker has established:

(20)   a. Uhmmm, uhmmm, uhmmm!
        b. Speak the truth girl!
        c. Thank you!
        d. Girl, you know that's the truth!
        e. That's right!

The cues help to show that the participants are united by the subject matter, have had similar experiences and are in tune with each other:

(21)   A: Y'all know I'm telling the truth.
        B: I know, girl.
        C: Yes, you are!

Examples such as the following show that listeners in this secular context cue in on specific words and echo them.

(22)   A: It's not a question of responsibility. It's a fundamental disrespect.
        B: Disrespect...

The church members responded in this way on a number of occasions. Consider once again the example in (10) in which members of the congregation picked up on the pastor's words and responded verbatim, "Through many!" The call and response event (including backchanneling) is productive in AAE; it occurs in religious and secular segments of society.

The following section addresses some characteristics of language use in rap.

5.7   Language use and rap

Rap has been increasing in popularity for over twenty years, and during that time it has permeated all types of media. It is not uncommon to turn on the television only to find some character introducing a product by using rhyme scheme. For example, the familiar doughboy uses chanted lyrics to boast about his product, as does the little girl who advertises a shampoo that leaves her wet hair tangle-free, both targeting mainstream America, no doubt, not groups that have been traditionally associated with rap.

Using rap lyrics in advertisements during the National Basketball Association play-offs and in soft drink commercials is a common practice. According to George (1998), "...rap music, and hip hop style as a whole, has utterly broken through from its ghetto roots to assert a lasting influence on American clothing, magazine publishing, television, language, sexuality, and social policy as well as its obvious presence in records and movies" (p. ix). Rap has been praised and condemned by scholars, critics, and musicians alike. Also, it was once strictly associated with the secular world, but now gospel rap is played over the radio airways.

This music type, which combines different technological strategies such as scratching, sampling and punch-phrasing, has its roots in a verbal strategy employed in the African American community. Scratching refers to the rapid back and forth movement of turntables to create a deconstructed sound, and sampling involves combining a portion of a record "in the over all mix." Punch-phrasing means "to erupt into the sound of turntable #1 with a percussive sample from turntable #2 by def cuing." The use of verbal strategies is a major feature of rap: "But the most acrobatic of the technics is the verb and reverb of the human voice pushed straight out, or emulated by synthesizers, or emulating drums and falsettos, rhyming, chiming sound that is a mnemonic for black-urbanity" (Baker 1993a, p. 91).

In its resurgence, rap has been analyzed from a number of angles, including the beat that accompanies the lyrics and the themes that rappers address. The purpose here is not to provide commentary on the range of themes that recur in rap, as they are topics (e.g., social commentary, politics, misogyny) of lengthy discussion in their own right, but instead to pay more attention to the linguistic features and rhetorical strategies that help to define the speech event. One prominent feature of rap is bragging and boasting about strengths, possessions and skills in using words. The construction of messages through rhyme scheme, indirectness and crafty wording is important, and entertainers take pride in their linguistic prowess.[9]

Take, for example, the words in L. L. Cool J's rap "I Can't Live Without My Radio" (1985). He calls himself "the royal chief rocker," and goes on to profess:

(23) ...Cause it's a actual fact this jam is def
      Mos definitely created by me,
      Goin down in radio history.

The rapper establishes immediately that the rap is a hit by saying that "this jam is def," or superb, and that it will make "radio history."

Along these same lines, Wonder Mike, from Sugarhill Gang, openly mentioned bragging and boasting in the popular lyrics from the 1979 hit "Rapper's Delight":

(24) I don't mean to brag; I don't mean to boas',
      but we're like hot butter on a breakfas' toast.

In the same song, M. C. Hank boasts about his rhyming abilities:

(25) From sun to sun and from day to day
I sit down an write a bran new rhyme
Because they say that miracles never cease
I've created a devastating masterpiece
I'm gonna rock the mic, 'til you can't resist,
Everybody, I say it goes like this
Well, I was comin home late one dark afternoon
Reporter stopped me for an interview
She said she's heard stories an she's heard fables
That I'm vicious on the mic and the turntable
This young reporter I did adore.
So I rocked some vicious rhymes like I never did before.

. . .

I said, "By the way, baby, what's your name?"
Said, "I go by the name Lois Lane,
An you can be my boyfrien you surely can,
Jus let me quit my boyfrien, call Superman."
I said, "He's a fairy, I do suppose
Flyin through the air in pantyhose.
He may be very sexy, or even cute,
But he looks like a sucker in a blue an red suit."
I said, "You need a man who's got finesse
An his whole name across his ches'
He may be able to fly all through the night,
But can he rock a party 'til the early light?"

Hank advertises his skills at the outset: "I'm gonna rock the mic 'til you can't resist."
It is not only the rapper himself who thinks that he has excelled in his art; a famous
reporter, having heard stories about his ability, wants to interview him. She realizes that
not even a superhuman can compete with super M. C. Hank. Not taking anything away
from Superman, who can accomplish small feats such as "fly all through the night," the
rapper suggests that the superhuman is all right, but he probably does not have skills
in rapping. Rhetorically, as Hank puts it, "But can he rock a party 'til the early light?"

The braggadocio tone is very clear, as the rapper states outright that he can handle
a microphone, and he submits a reference in the name of a famous reporter who can
vouch for his ability. Hank establishes himself as reaching ultimate levels; the famous
superhuman, who only has the gift of flying not the art of flowing (or rapping smoothly),
dwindles by comparison. Consider the commentary by Rose (1994) which applies to
some of the rap that was popular a decade earlier: "However, rapper's [sic] rhymes
are clearly influenced by, if not a direct outgrowth of, the African-American toast
tradition" (p. 86). Speakers and rappers realize the importance of being able to use
language, and they talk about this skill in a number of contexts, one of which is rap.

The first person tribute in UTFO's "Leader of the Pack" (1984) certainly qualifies as a toast:

(26)   My superior vernacular will keep me ahead
      Most of you are cogitating what I just said
      But that's just a muscle, I'm very discrete
      An a formula for rap like this can't be beat.
      It's not the usual, it can't be condemned
      That my pre-eminent thought will lay on to the end
      Cause I'm a Zephyr in grammar, I was always a crown
      Intellectual persons like this are hard to fin.

The rapper speaks specifically about his verbal dexterity and intellectual superiority. This "zephyr in grammar" mentions his "superior vernacular," unsurpassable "formula for rap" and "pre-eminent thoughts."

More current 1990s' rap continues to display braggadocio tone (and it also focuses on social and political issues). Queen Latifah says, "I'm on a higher level with different class, another plane/ I am the Queen, that's my name, time to explain/ that I spit game with the dames" ("Bananas"). Here "spit game" obviously refers to the use of words. A Digable Planets rapper describes himself by saying, "Plus I got the platinum voice" ("The Art of Easing").

The verb 'signifying' is used just as often as 'boasting' and 'toasting' in characterizations of rap. As Baker (1993a) explains, "Fiercely competitive and hugely braggadocious in their energies, the quest of the emergent rap technologists was for the baddest toasts, boasts, and signifying possible" (p. 90). Potter (1995) also discusses signifying and double entendre in rap. This strategy is used in "I Used to Love H. E. R." (1994) by Common (Sense) when reference is made to her, a female or hip-hop. A passage from that song is given below:

(27)   And she was fun then, I'd be geeked when she'd come around
      Slim was fresh yo, when she was underground
      Original, pure untampered and down sister
      Boy I tell ya, I miss her

               . . .

      I might've failed to mention that the chick was creative
      But once the man got to her he altered her
      Told her if she got an image and a gimmick
      That she could make money, and she did it like a dummy
      Now I see her in commercials, she's universal

Given references to "her," "slim," a term for a female, and "sister," it appears that the rapper is reminiscing about a woman who is long gone. However, the reference to "underground" suggests that there is another meaning here, one in which the rapper communicates that what he is actually nostalgic about is unadulterated, that is, "pure untampered" with rap. Music that has been concocted for the mainstream market has taken the place of the art form that was once meaningful, not just about making money.

Here Common signifies on those who have allowed "the man" to alter rap, making it "universal."

In addition to the themes on language skills, rap offers a number of other themes ranging from social commentary to general experiences. Even in the rap that focuses on those themes, the braggadocio tone is apparent as well as are other properties such as signifying used in speech events.

To conclude this section, I consider some AAE syntactic features as they are used in rap lyrics. Recall from the discussion of call and response in religious contexts that passages from the minister's message exemplified features from stock sermons in the African American community such as rhythmic phrasing, crescendo leading to the climax of the sermon and strategies eliciting feedback from the congregation. In the sermon, I did note some syntactic features that occur in AAE; however, rhetorical strategies seemed to be more prominent than other linguistic features of AAE. That is not to say that a wide inventory of syntactic and phonological features does not occur in sermons because in various linguistic patterns it can, depending on the speaker. AAE speakers, including ministers, can fall anywhere on a continuum between idealized general American English and idealized AAE:

(28)   Idealized mainstream general English   Idealized African American English

$$\longleftrightarrow$$

A   B   C   D

The continuum in (28) can represent different situations. A speaker may use a variety that is closer to (e.g., D) or further away from (e.g., A) idealized AAE. Theoretically speaking, a sermon in which rhetorical strategies and linguistic features of AAE are used is closer to idealized AAE than one that has no distinctively AAE linguistic features. Different factors (e.g., speaker background, environment of speaking, etc.) determine where speakers fall on the continuum.[10]

Strictly on a linguistic feature level, a parallel can be drawn between the passages from the sermon and those from the rap lyrics. The sermon was identified as AAE to a large extent on the basis of verbal strategies although some AAE syntactic and phonological features were used in the speech event. As noted, the passage from "Rapper's Delight" (25) represents the type of braggadocio tone used in early rap. Some AAE linguistic features are used in the rap, but it is not clear that these features alone can serve to identify that rap as an African American speech event. Three examples of syntactic features in the rap are given in (29):

(29)   a. The beat don't stop until the break a dawn.

b. ... The two ladies is hypnotized.

c. Have you ever went over to a friend's house to eat, an' the food jus' ain't no good?

In the agreement pattern in (29a), the plural verb form *don't*, which can be taken to be the default form in AAE, is used with the singular noun phrase *the beat*. The opposite pattern is found in (29b), in which the singular *be* form *is* is used with the plural noun phrase *the two ladies*. Two additional AAE syntactic features are found in (29c). First the past tense form *went* is used in what is the past participle environment in mainstream English and secondly multiple negation (*ain't no good*) is used. These features are not distinctively or uniquely AAE, so other characteristics must be used to associate such speech events with AAE.

This same observation about the representation of syntactic and phonological patterns of AAE holds true for the toast from UTFO. It is necessary to look to expressive language and verbal strategies and not just to syntactic and phonological patterns to find salient patterns of AAE.

The final title that I would like to consider, "Thieves in the Night" (1999) by Black Star, addresses social issues of the time. In addition to verbal strategies, this group uses unique AAE syntactic patterns in communicating the message:

(30) Yo I'm sure that everbody out listenin agree
      That everything you see ain't really how it be
      A lot of jokers out runnin in place, chasing the style
      Be a lot goin on beneath the empty smile

In the second line in the passage in (30), aspectual *be* occurs at the end of the clause. In this environment, aspectual *be* is used to convey the meaning that it is usually the case that everything isn't really how it seems. One of the issues addressed in "Thieves in the Night" is that of producing rap that will sell in spite of the message. In the song, the rapper Talib Kweli boasts that "A lot of cats who buy records are straight broke/But my language universal they be reciting my quotes." A brief survey of the short passage reveals that a number of patterns discussed in chapter 2 are used: aspectual *be* and Ø copula/auxiliary *be* form. Both features occur in the line "But my language universal they be reciting my quotes."

Although Smitherman (1977, pp. 82, 83) was not necessarily referring to the type of rap that is the center of discussion here, her comments are still quite appropriate. She regards "black raps as stylized, dramatic, and spectacular" and boastful raps to be "used to devastate enemies." The braggadocio tone and signification used in rap can certainly be taken as being directed at rappers from other groups as well as others in society who hold different philosophical views. Smitherman is basically concerned with the rap used in regular speech as opposed to that in lyrics, but the connection between the two can be made because rap is a verbal strategy that is used in different forms of communication by speakers of the African American community.

Close readings of speech events and expressive language use reveal that AAE encompasses a broad range of speech. The speaker, addresser, minister and rapper may not always use phonological, syntactic, morphological and lexical patterns of AAE, but their speech events reflect the use of different rhetorical strategies and expressive language. In some cases, the speaker uses indirectness; in others he uses a bragging or boasting tone and signification, and in still others he uses repetition and specific rhythmic patterns. These strategies are just as important as the syntactic, phonological and lexical properties of AAE.

5.8   Speech events and communicative competence

Researchers continue to conduct studies that will help to answer questions about the acquisition of AAE. Some of these related issues are addressed in the AAE literature in speech pathology and communication disorders. One important question in that research is the following: What kinds of evaluative procedures can be used to determine whether a child is acquiring AAE normally or whether his speech is impaired? Harry Seymour, Ph.D., and his colleagues at the University of Massachusetts, Amherst, are working on an extensive project in which one of the goals is to answer this question.

Stockman and Vaughn-Cooke (1982) researched the acquisition of universal linguistic features that AAE speakers share with speakers of English and other languages. More specifically, they focused on the development of children's semantic categories such as action, existence, state, coordination and specifier possession. This type of research moved away from the discussion of general AAE features, and provided much needed information on other areas of AAE that had been ignored. The findings in the study indicated that working-class African American children ranging from ages one to four years marked the same types of semantic categories that were marked by children who were acquiring other languages. Based on their data, Stockman and Vaughn-Cooke concluded that children may code existence by using an utterance in which there is no overt form of the copula. The difference they found between African American children who are acquiring AAE and those who are acquiring other varieties of English is that the children use different systems to code the semantic categories. This means that the AAE speakers use features of the AAE syntactic, phonological and morphological system to code different categories. As such, the superficial structures of sentences that indicate something exists may be different, but they will have the same meaning. A speaker who acquires AAE may not always use an overt *be* form to code existence, but one who acquires general English will more often than not.

Researchers in the field of communication sciences and disorders have also made observations about the use of verbal strategies, such as the dozens, in the speech of African American children. Wyatt (1991, 1995) observed that children of three to five years of age manipulate strategies that resemble signification and rapping in adult speech. She gives an example of a rap produced spontaneously by two males from this age group:

(31)   DD: (Rap tempo) Everytime I see her, I'm gonna give her a kiss . . . / Ah, Ah/ Ah,
        Ah/An' I lover her! . . . An' tell her I love her . . . I lover her!

        DN: I love her . . . I'ma love her everytime . . . /

        DD: An' she can tell me everytime . . . An' I answer the phone, I say get off the phone
        mom! . . . /

        DN: She's my girl . . . and I'ma see her . . . Everytime, she call me, I say ma, get off
        the dag-gone phone . . . . I wanna talk to the girl/

        ??:   (Laughing)

        DN: Everytime, I see her . . . I'm gonna kiss her . . . I'm gonna love her and I'm gonna
        kiss her . . . /

DD: Everytime, she call me... I'ma... kiss the phone... I'm say hello... Who is it?... Ah, babes... Shut the heck up... I'ma tell my brother, get off the phone... It's my girlfriend, man!/Don't joke around with me man/ (pp. 14–15).

Wyatt concluded that the data provide evidence that such verbal strategies are acquired by AAE-speaking children at early ages.

It appears that children have been consistently demonstrating communicative competence in the use of verbal strategies, but their skills have not been discussed in terms of competence. Take for instance some of the literature in educational issues and AAE. Oftentimes researchers call for educational systems to be more open to different communicative styles of students. This is the tone in Dandy (1991) who argues that

Competence must be learned in the accepted language of the dominant culture of the United States, Standard English, for it is the language of education, politics, economics, and upward social mobility. Students must also develop competence in the language of the African American community. To be able to communicate effectively in BC [black communications] allows the speaker to achieve credibility, to promote group solidarity and ensure cultural acceptance.

[pp. 120–121]

Children acquire the rules of the AAE-speaking culture, but because they use strategies in mainstream environments in which patterns governed by such rules are neither understood nor accepted, they "are often subsequently labeled as 'behavior problems'" (Dandy 1991, p. 103). This raises the issue of having communicative competence in one variety of English, but being labeled as incompetent speakers in another. Issues such as these will be discussed in chapter 8, which looks at attitudes and education.

Summary

This chapter makes two major points: Speech events are used in religious and secular contexts and verbal strategies are as important as syntactic, phonological and lexical features in identifying AAE. The dozens and signifying, which may be historically linked to African societies, have been traditionally associated with language use of African American males, but females also use these speech events. One of the properties of signification is indirectness, which is used in conversational exchanges between individuals and in art forms such as rap.

Listener interaction and feedback are just as important when the audience is a group as it is when it is one person. The congregation responds to the preacher's calls, which may be in the form of rhythmic phrasing, rhetorical questions and stylistic listing and repetition. Call and response in conversation between two or even more people is also common.

In some cases, verbal strategies are more prominent in speech events than are linguistic features. As we have seen in passages from a sermon and early rap lyrics, verbal strategies play a major role in identifying speech events as a part of the African American vernacular culture. While much of the research on these speech events is based on teen and adult use, there is evidence that children as young as three to five years old display communicative competence in using verbal strategies in speech events in the African American vernacular.

Exercises

1.   It has been noted that the types of syntactic, morphosyntactic and phonological patterns reviewed in the preceding chapters are not always prominent in speech events. Do you notice any such patterns in B's responses in the loud-talking example in (5)? If so, what are they? Are they used according to the rules of AAE?

2.   After viewing a couple of episodes of a situation comedy, discuss the use of speech events such as signification, marking and rapping. Comment on the type of characters that use them, the messages they send and the nonverbal strategies that accompany them.

3.   Record a sermon delivered by an African American television evangelist. Analyze the recording by explaining the types of verbal strategies and other linguistic features that are used in the sermon. Do you get the idea that the verbal strategies are more prominent than the linguistic patterns? Explain your answer. Do other African American television evangelists use the same strategies? As far as you can tell, do non-African American television evangelists use the same strategies?

4.   In this chapter, the example of call and response used in conversation was from a group of females in a scene in *Jungle Fever*. Does call and response occur more often in conversation between females than in conversation between males? Is the strategy used more by African Americans than by other groups in America? Explain your response. What type of study could one develop to test this?

5.   Compare speech events in rap lyrics from a song in the 1980s to those in a song from the mid to late 1990s to the present. Explain the ways in which the verbal strategies (e.g., signification, braggadocio) used in the rap lyrics from the 1980s and the mid to late 1990s to the present are similar and different. Are the same types of syntactic, phonological and lexical patterns used in the raps?

6.   Compare the rhetorical strategies and linguistic patterns in a rap by an African American hip-hop artist to those by a non-African American hip-hop artist. In what ways are the rhetorical strategies and linguistic patterns in the raps by the two artists (or groups) similar and different? Provide examples to illustrate your points.

6   AAE in literature

Focal point   The literary representation of AAE in some authors' works is considered to be an accurate and rich representation of folk speech, while that of others is labeled stereotypical renditions of the shiftless Negro. By manipulating the spoken word, maneuvering the spelling of some and evoking symbolism and imagery, authors are able to mold characters into dialect speakers or make them appear to be dialect speakers.

> If we are to believe the majority of writers of Negro dialect and burnt-cork artists, Negro speech is a weird thing, full of 'ams' and 'Ises.' Fortunately, we don't have to believe them. We may go directly to the Negro and let him speak for himself.
>
> [Zora Neale Hurston, "Characteristics of Negro Expression"]

6.1   Introduction

Language in literature is used to achieve a number of goals: (1) to connect the character with a particular region, (2) to identify the character as a particular type (e.g., belongs to certain class) (3) to make the character more authentic and more developed, (4) to evoke some feeling within the reader. In addition, as Holloway (1978) notes in her discussion of Zora Neale Hurston's works, language use can indicate that a character is "communicating cultural understanding" (p. 118). By this Holloway means that the more deeply entrenched Hurston's characters are with their language, African American dialect, the more involved and in tune they are with each other. Literary critics and specialists have researched the use of language by African American characters and the representation of the word in many texts, Holloway (1978, 1987), Baker (1984) and Gates (1988), to name a few. Holloway investigates the link between character and language in Hurston's work, paying close attention to dialect features and patterns of language use that serve as an expression of culture and that serve to unite characters. Baker (1984) analyzes African American discourse from the standpoint of the "blues matrix" in which he gives "suggestive accounts of moments in Afro-American discourse when personae, protagonists, autobiographical narrators, or literary critics successfully negotiate an obdurate 'economics of slavery' and achieve a resonant, improvisational, expressive dignity" (p. 13). Gates's (1988) work on signification "attempts to identify a theory of criticism that is inscribed within the black vernacular tradition that in turn informs the shape of the Afro-American literary tradition" (p. xix). A common theme that is found in these studies of African American language is that which is culturally specific or unique to African American vernacular. A related theme of black identity is the topic of Favor's (1999) study, which begins by posing the questions, "Who is African American? What defines Blackness?" (p. 1). He goes on to say that "the definition of blackness is constantly being invented, policed, transgressed, and contested. When hip-hop artists remind themselves and their audiences to 'stay black' or 'keep it real,' they are implicitly suggesting that there is a recognizable, repeatable, and agreed upon thing that we might call black authenticity" (p. 1, 2).

Fishkin (1993) implies that there is something uniquely black in language, as reflected in the title of her book, *Was Huck Black?: Mark Twain and African American Voices*. In the book, she considers the representation of language in Mark Twain's *The Adventures of Huckleberry Finn*. Fishkin argues that

> This book suggests that we need to revise our understanding of the nature of the mainstream American literary tradition. The voice we have come to accept as the vernacular voice in American literature – the voice with which Twain captured our national imagination in Huckleberry Finn, and that empowered Hemingway, Faulkner, and countless other writers in the twentieth century – is in large measure a voice that is "black."
>
> [p. 4]

This chapter focuses on dialect and vernacular features of the black voice in literature. African American literature will be approached from the viewpoint of linguistic features and rhetorical strategies that have been exemplified in the previous chapters. The discussion here is not intended to be a critical analysis of the works at hand; such analysis will be better left to literary critics and theoreticians. The sections in this chapter pay particular attention to the recurrence of linguistic features that are associated with defining the black voice. The question about authenticity of linguistic features in the representation of African American characters is raised. Authenticity is concerned not only with the range of features but also with the way they are used. I refer to the discussions of linguistic patterns and rhetorical strategies presented earlier as a means of evaluating the representation of language in the literary works considered in this chapter. The linguistic description presented in the preceding chapters can be used to evaluate characters' use of language. For example, I raise questions such as the following: Are aspectual markers used in the appropriate linguistic environments? What type of social message does the use of these features send?

6.2   General overview

Holton (1984) and Brasch (1981) consider the representation of AAE in the mass media in the context of experiences of and attitudes toward African Americans and the climate of the times, political and social. Holton studies the representation of AAE in fiction from three different periods: 1790–1900, 1900–1945, 1945–1980. Brasch relates his observations about the representation of black speech to five cycles, each of which, as he argues, coincided with different periods in the study of AAE: colonial revolution, antebellum, reconstruction, Negro renaissance and civil rights. The speech represented in the colonial revolution cycle (1760s–1800) includes an approximation of the speech of runaway slaves from the perspective of those who traveled to the colonies. The antebellum cycle (early 1800s–1860), according to Brasch, saw a rise in the representation of black speech in slave narratives, and in the next cycle, the reconstruction cycle (1870s–1900), black speech continued to be used in literature by authors such as Paul Lawrence Dunbar and Joel Chandler Harris. During the Negro renaissance cycle (1920s–1940s), black themes were depicted more and more in literature, and furthermore, scholars were openly addressing the issue of African American speech in writing. Zora Neale Hurston empowered her characters with black language, and she also addressed characteristics of this language in essays. Also during that time, Lorenzo Dow Turner wrote *Africanisms in the Gullah Dialect*, which provided a data source for those interested in the African element in Gullah and the African origins of AAE. The final cycle is the civil rights period (1945–1970s), during which "the American public was reading the stories of Richard Wright, Ralph Ellison, James Baldwin, Claude Brown, and LeRoi Jones, all of whom used Black English in their stories of Black life" (p. xiv). The authors that Brasch mentions in this period were all African American. According to Brasch's hypothesis, "the only strong evidence available as to the existence of Black English historically in America is what appeared in the mass media," and "the mass media served as vehicles for presenting both fiction and nonfiction stories, poems, articles, and novels that included Black English in either narration or dialogue" (p. x). Data that appeared in the mass media were used in evaluating claims about whether black English was a separate language, a creole or a regional dialect. The works in this chapter will be from the periods during Brasch's last four cycles; the colonial revolution cycle is not represented here. We should be able to see how the representations of AAE changed over time, how the focus on particular features changed and what properties and representations remained the same.

Dillard (1972, 1992) quotes examples of speech in early literary sources and suggests that it is representative of the language of slaves and other African Americans. For example, he notes that the speech of Jupiter in Edgar Allan Poe's "The Gold Bug" (1839) may be one of the earliest attestations of Gullah. He points out two particular passages in which the character Jupiter uses tense/aspect markers *bin* (1a) and *done*, arguably *dən*, (1b) to mark past and some phonological features (e.g., consonant cluster reduction *lef'* and voiced *th/d de, det*) which have been associated with AAE:

(1) a. Somebody bin lef' him head up de tree . . .
     b. de crows done gobble every bit of det meat . . . (from Dillard 1992, p. 72)

The focus in Dillard (1992) is on the origin of AAE, so the data in (1) are intended to contribute to the understanding of its development or at least raise questions about it. One important question is the following: Can we rely on the type of data recorded in (1) to tell us something about the early stages of AAE? In answering that question, the many issues revolving around the authenticity of literary representations of speech must be addressed.

The discussion that follows will focus on some literary sources and the way African American speech is represented therein. At times it will be obvious that the speech samples at hand reveal more about the characters than the discussion indicates. At still other times, the language may be argued to be linked directly to the themes running through the works or to some other underlying issue that may not be discussed satisfactorily in this type of general study of linguistic patterns in the speech of African American characters.

6.3   Representation of AAE in literature to the early twentieth century

It is appropriate to begin the discussion of the representation of the speech of African Americans in literature with the first African American novel, William Wells Brown's *Clotel; or, the President's Daughter: A Narrative of Slave Life in the United States* (1853). In his introductory notes to a work that contains three novels that represent black fiction from the mid nineteenth to the twentieth century, Henry Louis Gates (1990) credits *Clotel* as an important work because it is the first novel written by an African American, and because it addresses a number of issues pertaining to the lives of African Americans in slavery. In addition he points out that "it is important as well because of its representation of the vernacular English that black people speak in its pages" (p. xi). Brown, then, would have been among the first black writers to approximate the black dialect that was spoken in the South. The title of the book, *Clotel; or, the President's Daughter: A Narrative of Slave Life in the United States*, is argued to make reference to the claim that Thomas Jefferson had a relationship and children with a slave. In the novel, Clotel, the mistress and mother of the child of a Virginia gentleman, takes her life after the gentleman marries a white woman who sells her and relegates her daughter Mary to slavery. The mulatto Mary fares better than her mother, as she and her slave rebel partner are able to escape the immediate holds of slavery.

The following passage is a sample of the sermon or direction the slaves in *Clotel* received from a white missionary:

(2)   "Now, when correction is given you, you either deserve it, or you do not deserve it. But whether you really deserve it or not, it is your duty, and Almighty God requires that you bear it patiently. You may perhaps think that this is hard doctrine; but, if you consider it right, you must needs think otherwise of it. Suppose, then, that you deserve correction, you cannot but say that it is just and right you should meet with it. Suppose you do not, or at least you do not deserve so much, or so severe a correction, for the fault you have committed, you perhaps have escaped a great many more, and are at last paid for all. Or suppose you are quite innocent of what is laid to your charge, and suffer wrongfully in that particular thing, is it not possible you may have done some other bad thing which was never discovered, and that Almighty God who saw you doing it would not let you escape without punishment one time or another? And ought you not, in such a case, to

give glory to him, and be thankful that he would rather punish you in this life for your wickedness than destroy your souls for it in the next life? But suppose even this was not the case (a case hardly to be imagined), and that you have by no means, known or unknown, deserved the correction you suffered, there is this comfort in it, that, if you bear it patiently, and leave your cause in the hands of God, he will reward you for it in heaven, and the punishment you suffer unjustly here shall turn to your exceeding glory hereafter." (pp. 83–84)

In contrast to the speech of the missionary, the slaves use a number of markers of AAE in their private evaluation of the sermon:

(3)   "Well," said Joe, after the three white men were out of hearing, "Marser Snyder bin try hesef to-day."
"Yes," replied Ned; "he want to show de strange gentman how good he can preach."
"Dat's a new sermon he gib us to-day," said Sandy.
"Dees white fokes is de very dibble," said Dick; "and all dey whole study is to try to fool de black people."

. . .

"I got no notion of dees white fokes, no how," returned Aunt Dafney. "Dey all de time tellin' dat de Lord made us for to work for dem, and I don't believe a word of it."
"Marser Peck give that sermon to Snyder, I know," said Uncle Simon.
"He jest de one for dat," replied Sandy.
"I think de people dat made de Bible was great fools," said Ned.
"Why?" asked Uncle Simon.
"'Caus dey made such a great big book and put nuttin' in it but servants obey yer masters."
"Oh," replied Uncle Simon, "thars more in de Bible den dat, only Snyder never reads any other part to us; I use to hear it read in Maryland, and thar was more den what Snyder lets us hear" (pp. 86–87).

Most of the features that are employed in this passage to indicate that the speakers are using a variety that is different from the mainstream English of the time, different from the language of Snyder, and, furthermore, that is associated with black slaves, fall under phonology. The initial *th* sound that occurs in other varieties of English is pronounced here as *d*, as in *dat* ('that'), *de* ('the'), *dees* ('these'), *dey* ('they'), *dem* ('them') and *den* ('than'). The pronunciation of *thars* ('there's') in the book is not represented with an initial *d*, but it does reflect a vowel change to set it off from the standard. Schneider (1989), a linguistic analysis of ex-slave narratives, provides examples from ex-slaves in which *there* is represented as being pronounced with this same vowel: *Wal,* ***thars*** *a collad girl* ***thar*** *ain't they?* ('Well, there's a colored girl there ain't they' my gloss) (p. 223).[1] Such data could suggest that the use of the vowel sound *a* in a word such as *there* was a regular part of the speaker's early AAE rule system, explaining why Brown would have used it in the nineteenth century. Or the vowel could have also been a regional marker.

Another phonological feature that Brown uses is *b* in word medial or final positions in environments in which *v* occurs in current AAE and other varieties of English. This *b* sound occurs in words such as *gib* ('give') and *dibble* ('devil'). The representation in the passage suggests that the feature is variable because it occurs in Sandy's and Dick's comments, but not in that of Uncle Simon. Brown may also be giving readers additional information about language use of characters on different levels within the slave class. Uncle Simon is also a slave as are the other members of the group, but he is more knowledgeable; he is a preacher and has heard more from the Bible than the others. As a result, his language may be slightly different from the language of the other slaves. It is interesting to note that this pattern (*b* in medial and final positions) is not listed in current descriptions of AAE, but it does occur in some of the data associated with ex-slave narratives. A number of related examples are also given in sentences in Schneider (1989): *I ain't **neber** done nothin' to nobody* ('I have never done anything to anybody' my gloss, p. 192); *One time a slave at a neighbor farm was workin' in de feel' and when he comes in, in de **ebenin's** he's wife wuz gone an' de cradle wuz empty* ('One time a slave at a neighbor farm was working in the field and when he came in, in the evening his wife was gone and the cradle was empty' my gloss) (p. 122).

The speakers in the passage from *Clotel* are also represented as using word final *n*, (*tellin'*, *nuttin'*), as opposed to the velar nasal *ŋ*, which may also occur in casual speech of speakers of other varieties of English; however, Brown chooses to use spelling notation to point out this feature. Note, also, internal vowel sound representations such as those in *jest* ('just'), *yer* ('your') and *dibble* ('devil').

In addition to phonology, some syntactic features are used to mark the black speakers. Right at the outset, one of Brown's characters comments on the person who delivered the message by saying that "Marser Snyder *bin try* . . ." Given the slaves' dis-agreeable attitude expressed in their conversation about the sermon, the reader gets the idea that the general consensus is that they were not impressed by Marser Snyder's delivery, and they were not fooled into believing the content. What we see here are discriminating characters who are able to evaluate and analyze the situation and com-ment on it by using their language. It is quite clear that *bin* is used to indicate a simple past meaning of *try*, because the time adverbial *today* is used. In all probability, the sentence can be glossed as 'Master Snyder tried (himself) today,' in which case past tense is marked on the verb *try*, but in the passage it is indicated by *bin*. As noted in chapter 2, unstressed *been* (*bin*) is used as some type of tense/aspect marker with *had*. Beyond this use, it is not clear that present-day AAE uses *bin* to mark simple past, but historical analysis might link this marker to earlier AAE. Edwards (1991) and Rickford (1977) comment on the use of *bin* in Caribbean Creoles. Rickford (1977) specifically makes some suggestions about the possible connections between the *bin* in Guyanese Creole and stressed *BIN* in AAE. Also, in Dillard's example in (1a) above (*Somebody bin lef' him head up de tree . . .*), *bin* is also used to mark simple past.

No attempt is made here to make a case for the *bin* that occurs in Brown's *Clotel*. Certainly not very much can stand on this single occurrence of the marker, but it is worth noting, and a careful analysis of the work would also be helpful in determining whether the marker occurs consistently in other environments. A suggestion here is that the marker is used on the one hand to mark a past action and on the other to identify the character as a slave and user of the black Southern speech variety.

Another identification marker is number agreement. Often speakers use one verb form with both singular and plural subjects. Here the speakers use the singular forms of the auxiliary *be* when the subject is plural. The first example is an occurrence of the present tense *be* form *is* (*Dees white fokes is the very dibble*), while the second example involves the past tense (*I think de people dat made de Bible was great fools*), in which the plural subject *dees white fokes* occurs with the singular verb form *is*, and the plural subject *de people* occurs with the singular form *was*. In other cases, the singular verb form is also used with singular subjects.

As illustrated in chapter 2, there are environments in which the copula/auxiliary *be* does not occur on the surface in AAE. One environment in which the verb form does not occur in the passage in (3) is preceding the verb -*ing* (*tellin'*) that is itself preceded by a modifier (*all de time*) as in (*Dey all de time tellin'*). Other grammatical features that occur in the passage are multiple negation as in (*no . . . notion no how*), possessive neutralization in which case the same pronominal form is used for the nominative and possessive (genitive) (*heself, dey whole study*) and the simple present tense form in past environments (*Dat's a new sermon he gib us to-day, Marser Peck give dat sermon to Snyder*, cf. *gave*). Such patterns have been recorded for current AAE in chapters 2 and 3.

The final sequence that will be highlighted is *for to* in the sentence *Dey all de time tellin' dat de Lord made us for to work for dem*. The *for to* sequence has been analyzed in Ottawa Valley English (Carroll 1983), Ozark English (Chomsky and Lasnik 1977) and Belfast English (Henry 1992, 1995), but to my knowledge, there have not been any published analyses of this sequence in AAE.[2] Different arguments have been proposed to explain why this sequence does not occur in mainstream English.[3] Analysis of literary texts and ex-slave narratives could be useful in drawing some conclusion about the history and syntax of the *for to* sequence, especially in that it is not in widespread use by African Americans throughout the United States, but, as summarized in note 1, it was used in earlier stages of English, and it is still used by some African Americans in the Southern United States.

An analysis of the speech in the entire novel would have to be completed before attempting to draw conclusions about the authenticity of the black speech in *Clotel*; however, there is enough evidence to show that Brown's speakers used features that also occur in ex-slave narratives and that are used in current AAE.

Joel Chandler Harris, who wrote in the late nineteenth and early twentieth centuries, recorded folktales of his Georgia region and plantation life. Harris notes that in writing the tales, his goal was to make accurate recordings, conveying as much as possible of the "colorful" plantation life. In his own words: "With respect to the Folk-Lore series, my purpose has been to preserve the legends in their original simplicity, and to wed them permanently to the quaint dialect – if, indeed, it can be called a dialect – through the medium of which they have become a part of the domestic history of every Southern family." He even goes on to say that his rendition of the dialect is "different also from the intolerable misrepresentations of the minstrel stage, but it is at least phonetically genuine" (Harris [1880] reprinted in 1955 *The Complete Tales of Uncle Remus*, p. xxi). Holton (1984) agrees that Harris conveys humor and realism in his representation of dialect. She notes that, "Yet it is in the figurative language and in the vocabulary and rhythmic patternings that Harris really conveys the sensitivity, humor, and poetic imagination of his black narrator" (p. 81). Dillard (1977) refers to Harris as a "sensitive observer" of black folklore and goes on to comment that "It is one of the crowning ironies that Harris has come to be taken as an extension of the minstrel show tradition" (p. 149). One way that Harris sets out to convey humor and realism is through phonetic shapes that recur in his tales. As a white author in the South during the nineteenth and twentieth centuries, Harris may very well have had a different perspective from that of African American authors during this period. In what ways and to what extent was this different perspective reflected in his representation of black speech and characters' use of features?

One way to begin to answer this question is by considering some phonological and syntactic features in passages from two of his tales, "Uncle Remus Initiates the Little Boy" (LB) and "The Wonderful Tar-Baby Story" (TB). The phonological features in the tales range from *r*, *l* vocalization to the insertion of *r* in unstressed syllables. Words from both stories are written as if they are produced with a vocalized *r* (and *l*), as shown in the examples below:

(4)   a. **mo'n** got de wuds 'more than got the words' (LB, p. 3)
      b. **sho's** you born 'sure as you're born' (TB, p. 6)
      c. **mawnin**' 'morning' (TB, p. 7)
      d. Brer Fox say to **hisse'f** '. . . says to himself' (LB, p. 3)

Given that *r* and *l* vocalization occurs in the Southern variety of speech (and other varieties of English) in general, we cannot take these features alone as indicators of AAE. The speech is also represented with the presence of *r*'s in unstressed syllables:

(5)   e. I'm monstus full **er** fleas '. . . full of . . .' (LB, p. 3)
      f. **mer**lasses jug 'molasses jug' (TB, p. 7)
      g. I wan**ter** have some 'I want to . . .' (LB, p. 3)

Also, in a number of cases, a single consonant (i.e., consonant cluster reduction) occurs in the environment in which a cluster occurs in (idealized) general American English, as in the examples below:

(6)   a. make fr'e**n**'s 'make friends' (LB, p. 3)
      b. ter bus' you wide open 'to bust . . .' (TB, p. 7)

One feature that Harris's characters use almost invariantly, at least for some words in these two stories, is *d* in environments in which *th* occurs in other varieties of English. The *d* sound occurs in word initial, medial and final positions. In AAE, in addition to *d*, the sounds *t*, *f* and *v* also occur in similar environments. As explained in chapter 4, the sound (*d*, *t*, *f*, or *v*) that occurs is determined by the position in the word and phonological properties such as voicing, place and manner of articulation. An example in which the *f* alternation is reflected in Harris's data is in *mouf* (. . . *he ain't mo'n got*

de wuds out'n his mouf twel Brer Rabbit come lopin' up de big road . . . (LB, p. 3).
Some *d* alternations are given below:

(7) a. Hol' on **d**ar 'Hold on there' (LB, p. 3)
    b. nice we**dd**er 'nice weather' (TB, p. 7)
    c. **D**en Brer Rabbit scratch one ear wid his . . .
       'Then . . . with his' (LB, p. 3)

The alternation in (7c) w*id* generally would not be predicted to occur in current AAE,
but *wid* might be possible depending on what follows the word. Normally, *wit* (and
to some extent *wif*) would be expected, at least in current AAE, because *th* in *with*
is voiceless. The extent to which *wid* is an accurate representation of a phonological
feature of the black speech that Harris is portraying is not clear. The strategy here is not
to evaluate the representations solely against the benchmark of features of present-day
AAE, but it is worthwhile to note differences (and similarities) between features in this
early literature and patterns in recent descriptions of AAE.

    Other phonological representations help to paint this variety of speech, on sight,
as being different from the narrator's and that of the little white boy's speech in "The
Wonderful Tar-Baby Story." Consider the boy's questions, especially the first line in
which *never* is stressed in the multiple negation construction:

(8) Boy: Didn't the fox *never* catch the rabbit, Uncle Remus? (p. 6)
    Boy: Did the Fox eat the Rabbit? (p. 8)

The boy's lines are in direct contrast to the dialect representation of the storyteller's
speech. There are no phonetic spellings (such as *de* for 'the' and *neber* for 'never') in
the boy's speech.

    Additional representations are the alveolar nasal *n* word finally (*pacin'* p. 6, *nothin'*
p. 7), the *ar* sound (*dar* 'there,' p. 4, *whar* 'where,' p. 5) and syllable timing, in
which case unstressed initial syllables are not produced (*skuze* 'excuse' p. 5, *'stonished*
'astonished' p. 7, *spectubble* 'respectable' p. 7). There are a number of instances in
which the author uses eye dialect or orthographic representations that are very close
to actual pronunciations to make the words look different from mainstream English
spellings (e.g., *contrapshun* 'contraption,' p. 6).[4]

    Some syntactic features that have been observed in AAE are also represented in
Harris's works. Multiple negation occurs in cases such as those below in which *ain't*
is a negator that can occur with negative auxiliary *didn't* and noun *nothing*:

(9) a. En dey keep on waitin', but **no** Brer Fox **ain't** come. (p. 4)
       'And they keep on waiting, but Brer Fox didn't come'
    b. Brer Fox, he wink his eye slow, en lay low, en de Tar-Baby, she **ain't** sayin' **nothin'**.
       (p. 7)
       'Brer Fox winks his eye slow, and lays low, and the Tar-Baby isn't saying anything'

The resultant marker *done* (perhaps *dǝn*), which also occurs in present day AAE and
(in similar and different uses) in Southern white English, is used by the storyteller in
the Uncle Remus stories.

(10)   a. **I done** got so now dat I can't eat no chicken ceppin' she's seasoned up wid calamus root. (LB, p. 5)

   b. **I done** laid in some calamus root, en I ain't gwine ter take no skuse… (TB, p. 8)

Different forms of past tense verbs are used in the stories: *seed* 'saw' (pp. 3, 4), *sot* 'sat' (pp. 4, 7), *sont* 'sent' (p. 5), *wrop* 'wrapped' (p. 5), *cotch* 'caught' (p. 5) and *mought* 'might' (p. 8). In the case of *seed*, the past tense is regularized; *see* takes an *-ed* ending, but in the remaining cases, the past is indicated by a change in the vowel within the verb.

   Given the data, *ain't* is used with the meaning of auxiliaries *isn't, don't/didn't* and *haven't*:

(11)   a. … En **I ain't** gwine ter take no skuse… (TB, p. 8)
      'and I am not going to'

   b. **I ain't** got time… (LB, p. 3)
      'I don't have time'

   c. … but he **ain't** see no dinner… (LB, p. 5)
      'but he didn't see any dinner'

   d. You **ain't** got no calamus root, is you, Brer Fox? (LB, p. 5)
      'You don't have any calamus root, do you, Brer Fox?'
      'You haven't got any calamus root, have you, Brer Fox?'

   e. En Brer Fox **ain't** never cotch 'im yet, en w'at's mo', honey,
      he ain't gwine ter. (LB, p. 6)
      'And Brer Fox hasn't ever/has never caught him yet, and what's more, honey, he isn't going to'

Before moving to the final comment on these stories, I should make one point about the tag question in (11d). In forming tag questions, at least in current AAE, the same form of the first occurrence of the auxiliary in the declarative is negated or made positive (depending on the first auxiliary) in the tag (They *do* run, *don't* they?), but in (11d), the first auxiliary *ain't* seems to be a general negator or negative marker, and, as such, *is* occurs in the tag. (See chapter 2.)

   The final issue that will be mentioned in the category of syntactic patterns is related to the copula and auxiliary *be* in the following sentences.

(12)   a. I done got so now dat I can't eat no chicken ceppin' **she's** seasoned up wid calamus root. (LB, p. 5)

   b. Better come git it while **hit's** fresh… (LB, p. 6)

   c. **Iz** you def? (TB, p. 7)

   d. You er stuck up, **dat's** w'at you **is**… en I'm gwine ter kyore you, **dat's** w'at **I'm** a gwine ter do, sezee. (TB, p. 7)

   e. Right **dar's** whar he broke his merlasses jug. (TB, p. 7)

The copula/auxiliary *be* occurs quite regularly in the stories, as shown in the examples above. If Harris's strategy was to produce an accurate representation of plantation speech and if he was successful in doing so, then the implication here is that the copula and auxiliary *be* forms by and large occurred on the surface. As has been noted in the discussion of syntactic patterns, the *be* form occurs obligatorily in environments such as (12b, d), when used with 'it's' (*hit's*), 'that's' (*dat's*) and *I'm*.

More than a few questions arise about the representation of the speech in the Uncle Remus stories. Some of them are related to the pronunciations of words such as *atter*, *hatter*, and *wedder* 'after,' 'have to,' and 'weather,' respectively. The question is whether such forms were actually attested in the speech of blacks and, if so, whether remnants of this pronunciation still exist. Along the same lines, there are questions about the pronunciation of words such as *gyarden* ('garden') and *kyarvin'* 'carving,' which are not attested in present-day AAE. The *y* indicates that the initial consonant sounds of the words are produced in part by raising the back of the tongue.

Charles W. Chesnutt, African American fiction writer, also wrote during this period. While he is known for his folktales and conjure motif, Chesnutt was careful to distinguish himself from Joel Chandler Harris. He made it clear that his works "were *artistic* creations, not folklore transcriptions" (Andrews [1980] 1992, p. 390). Andrews suggests "that Chesnutt did not want to be misrepresented as a follower of Harris, whom he considered a collector and skillful adaptor of the lore of another culture, not a truly creative figure in his own right" (p. 391). Linguist J. L. Dillard expresses a high level of respect for the representation and use of language in the works of Chesnutt (and that of William Wells Brown): "I am firmly convinced that William Wells Brown and Charles W. Chesnutt represent the vocabulary best of all" (1977, p. 155). Although Southern white writers represented the grammar and pronunciation of the vernacular, they did not have the same type of command of the vocabulary, as Dillard remarks. If this is the case, then one difference we might expect to see between works by Chesnutt and those by Joel Chandler Harris would be in the use of the AAE lexicon. Chesnutt's black characters in *The House Behind the Cedars* (1900), which addresses issues of racial intermixing, racial identity and complications of racial passing and class in the South, talk about conjuring and tell lies (where 'telling lies' refers to telling folktales and exaggerated stories). When Frank, the loyal friend of the Walden family, sees the mule with a harness and a cart, he considers explaining the gift (from the family) as being a result of some supernatural force such as witchcraft or conjuring, that is, "witchcraf er cunjin."

(13)   "Well, well!" exclaimed Frank, "ef I didn' mos' know whar dis mule, an' dis kyart, an' dis harness come from, I'd 'low dere'd be'n witchcraf er cunjin' wukkin' here." (p. 124)

In addition to using the folk motif of conjuring, Chesnutt also uses folk vocabulary, for example, *lies*, to refer to the story that the mulatto Homer Pettifoot told the guests at a party: "Homer Pettifoot related, with minute detail, an old, threadbare hunting lie, dating, in slightly differing forms, from the age of Nimrod..." (p. 144)

In *The House Behind the Cedars*, Chesnutt certainly distinguishes black and white characters, but he also makes class distinctions among blacks, especially by manipulating the language of mulattos and non-mulattos. The speech of sister and brother Rena and Warwick, the educated mulattos who have passed as whites, is clearly distinguishable from that of other mulattos and, of course, from that of black Frank in (13). Compare the lawyer Warwick's speech to their mother's:

(14)   "Well, mother, I've taken a man's chance in life, and have tried to make the most of it; and I haven't felt under any obligation to spoil it by raking up old stories that are best forgotten. There are the dear old books: have they been read since I went away?"

"No, honey, there's be'n nobody to read 'em excep' Rena, an' she don't take to books quite like you did. But I've kep' 'em dusted clean, an' kep' the moths an' the bugs out; for I hoped you'd come back some day, an' knowed you'd like to find 'em all in their places, jus' like you left 'em." (p. 12)

The mother does have some recognizable nonstandard features (e.g., consonant cluster reduction (*excep'*), regularization of past tense (*knowed*) and agreement (e.g., *she don't*), but Warwick does not.

But even given the mother's nonstandard features, her speech is clearly distinguishable from that of Frank's in (13). So Chesnutt uses different levels of speech for his black characters: educated mulattos, uneducated mulattos and non-mulattos. Another example of the speech of a non-mulatto in this book comes from Plato, "a funny darkey," who attended the "colored school." In response to the whereabouts of his teacher, he says, "Dey don' nobody know whar, suh." (p. 186). This may be an example of an existential construction, a form that is not used in current AAE.

"General Washington: a Christmas Story," the final work that will be considered from this period, is a short story by Pauline E. Hopkins. The story, which addresses social issues of the time, was written in 1900 and originally published in *Colored American Magazine*, for which Hopkins served as editor for four years. The story is about General Washington, an African American who lived in a dry goods box insulated with straw for the winter. A good dancer and a somewhat boisterous fellow, he made his living by selling chitlins (chitterlings) and peddling. One day while selling his product, General Washington was visited by Miss Fairy, a white girl, who told him all about heaven and how wonderful it was. General Washington was very excited to hear that there was plenty of heat and food in heaven because of his dire living conditions on earth. General Washington was shot while doing a good deed, and, as a result, he was able to visit heaven, a place for whites and blacks alike.

Many of the features in the works by Harris are also found in this story. Hopkins, like the other authors during this period, uses eye dialect, making words such as *bisness* 'business,' *shure* 'sure,' *wurk* 'work' and *hellow* 'hello' appear to look different from the reader's pronunciation.

Phonological features that occur in the story are the *d* and *f* in environments in which *th* usually occurs in general American English: *wid, dat, den, dis, de* (p. 73), *froo the winder* and *nufin* (p. 80), for 'with,' 'that,' 'then,' 'this,' 'the,' 'through the winter' and 'nothing,' respectively. As should be clear at this point, the overall pattern represented here is consistent with AAE, but *f* in the *th* environment in *through* is not in line with the AAE sound patterns, as initial voiceless *th* is pronounced in the variety. The pronunciation *froo* for *through* makes it appear as if General Washington has a speech impediment. Likewise in this story, the syllable timing is adjusted, so the initial unstressed syllable is not pronounced (i.e., deleted) in some words: *'pears* 'appears' (p. 70), *'clare* 'declare' (p. 72), *'casion* 'occasion' (p. 72), and *'tirely* 'entirely (p. 74).' Also, in a number of cases, unstressed syllables are represented by the *er* sound: *fellar* 'fellow' (p. 70), *yer* 'you,' *ter* 'to' (p. 73) and *er* 'a' (p. 75). This feature is shown clearly in General Washington's sentence (15) below, in which the initial unstressed syllable in *police* is pronounced *per*:

(15)   I reckon'd I'd git hyar time nuff **fer yer ter** call de **per**lice. (p. 80)
        'I reckoned I'd get here in time enough for you to call the police'

Hopkins's representation looks much like that of Harris's and Chesnutt's in this regard.

The pattern in which the bilabial stop *b* occurs in the environment in which *v* and *f* occur in general American English is also found in this story: *hab* and *ob* for *have* and *of*, respectively. Generally speaking, some of the phonological patterns in this work are similar to the ones in current AAE, but other examples have not been attested, to my knowledge. Are the representations accurate recordings of the speech of the time?

Some of the syntactic patterns found here are similar to those found in the works by Harris. The marker *done* is used by a woman in the market (16a) and by the fairy's servant, as shown in the following sentences.

(16)   a. I 'clare to de Lord, I'se **done** busted my ol' man, shure. (p. 72)
        b. I'll tell yer mawmaw how you's **done** run 'way from me to talk to dis dirty little monkey. (p. 76)

In both cases, *done* may indicate that the eventuality specified by the verb (*busted*, *run*) is over, or the sequences of *'s done* may be present perfect forms. It is also interesting to note that in both cases, a contracted form of the auxiliary precedes the marker. These sentences bear a closer resemblance to the speech recorded in Feagin's (1979) description of Alabama white English than they do to current AAE. There is no hard and fast evidence to determine the full form of the auxiliary, that is, to determine whether it is *has* or *is* because both auxiliaries have the same contracted form. Sentences with similar contractions follow:

(17)   a. . . . An **I'se** mighty onscruplus 'bout stoppin' hyar. (p. 70)
        b. . . . **I'se** got fresh aggs fer de 'casion . . . (p. 72)
        c. I want some o' de Methodess chitlins **you's** bin hollerin' 'bout. (p. 73)
        d. 'Deed, missy, **I'se** 'tirely too dirty to tech dem clos o' yourn. (p. 74)
        e. Please, sah, **I'se** gen'r'l Wash'nton. (p. 80)

Given the meaning, it is clear that the contractions in (16a), (16d) and (16e) represent the full form *is*; these are cases in which an adjective (16a), (16d) and noun (16e) follow the *be* (*'se*) auxiliary form, but it is not clear whether *I'se* in (16b) is *I* and the contracted form of *is* or *I* and the contracted form of *has*. At least given the meanings in general American English, the contracted forms in (16b) and (16c) are environments for the present perfect (forms of *have*), but of course, these forms may be different from what is expected in general American English. As such, it is possible to describe these contracted forms as *I* + *is*, although the description is not conclusive. It should be noted in passing that the forms of the copula/auxiliary *be* are overwhelmingly present in the speech of the African American characters in the story. This is another feature on which Hopkins and Harris converge. It is even the case that the first person singular form of the copula is used in third person contexts:

(18)   Bisness am mighty peart... (p. 70)

It may very well be that this is precisely one of the uses of the 'am's' against which Zora Neale Hurston protested in the passage given in the quote at the beginning of this chapter. This particular feature does not occur in present-day AAE, and the extent to which it occurred in early AAE is not clear either. But it should be noted that this use of *am* does occur in some of the ex-slave narratives. Take, for example, the following passage by an ex-slave recorded in the volume edited by Yetman (1970): "I goes back after de war to Memphis. **My mammy am** on the Kilgore place and Massa Kilgore takes her and two hundred other slaves and comes to Texas" (p. 197).

The speech of General Washington is set apart from the speech used by whites such as the fairy and the senator in the story, and this is achieved, in part, by the phonetic transformation that almost all of his words have undergone. Also, in some places the general's language seems to be exaggerated in such a way that he goes away looking pitiful. In the sentence in (17d) (*'Deed, missy, I'se 'tirely too dirty to tech dem clos o' yourn*) which the general uses to explain why he is hesitant about touching the fairy, the meaning of the words conveys his status, as he sees it, but the representation of his language says, "I'm just a poor, old, unworthy black man."

Just as in the previous works by Brown and Harris, the *for to* (*fer ter*) sequence occurs in "General Washington," in the same environment in a line from the fairy's servant.

(19)   Pickin' up sech trash **fer ter** talk to. (p. 76)

Two additional features in the story are also found in present-day AAE, and in both cases there is only one example in the text. In the first example, note that there is no overt *wh* pronoun in the relative clause (in brackets) such as *who* preceding *did*: *It's the n-----[Ø did it]*. (p. 81). (Refer to chapter 3 for a discussion of relative clauses.) The second example in the story which also occurs in some varieties of AAE features the possessive pronoun *yourn* which is formed with an *-n* ending (17d): *'Deed, missy, I'se 'tirely too dirty to tech dem clos o' yourn.*

Finally, in the story, Hopkins uses a vocabulary item from the black lexicon. As the general danced, the crowd at Dutch Dan's place chanted the following:

(20) Juba up and juba down,
     Juba all around the town;
     Can't you hyar de juba pat?
     Juba!

Juba, explained in chapter 1, refers to a dance.

In summary, the representations of AAE in the early literature presented here show that some features were definitely considered by the authors to be patterns in the language system because they occur from author to author and from work to work. As has been noted, analyzing such texts may prove to be beneficial in helping to determine the structure of early AAE, and it can also be useful in determining whether some features of AAE were prominent at an earlier period but are less prominent now. Prominent features could be those that were used more frequently or those that were stereotypically associated with the speech of African Americans. The data in these texts also show that it is not necessarily the case that the features which are taken to distinguish AAE today were the distinguishing features in the late nineteenth and early twentieth centuries. Particular representations of language are used to identify characters as being black; so their speech is contrasted with the speech of others who are not black. One final point is that even when there did not seem to be differences between pronunciations by black characters and general American English, the author makes distinctions by using eye dialect, setting black speech apart from general American English. Given that the authors in this period converge on a number of patterns, it would appear that they were capturing a number of features that were commonly associated with black speech of the time.

In the selected literature from the Harlem Renaissance to the mid twentieth century, there is a decrease in eye dialect and a broader range of linguistic patterns.

6.4   From the Harlem Renaissance to the mid twentieth century

The Harlem Renaissance (1920s and 1930s) was an important literary period during which writers used events, experiences and expressions of black life as their subjects. In Henderson's ([1973] 1999) summation, which echoes the views of other critics, "Although there were attempts at realistic depiction of Black life before they came on the scene, the writers of the Harlem Renaissance were the first to do this in a systematic manner, as even a cursory look at the period will reveal" (p. 142). For some writers during this period, black dialect represented a real part of black life, but for others, it portrayed the stereotypical, low-class black. Among writers during this period were Jean Toomer, Countee Cullen, Claude McKay, Langston Hughes and Zora Neale Hurston. The latter two, whose works will be discussed in this section, did not concern themselves so much with the mainstream English of the time; they focused more on the life and language of black folk.

6.4.1   AAE in Zora Neale Hurston's *Jonah's Gourd Vine*

The works of Zora Neale Hurston are particularly noted for the language of the characters and the use of black dialect.[5] Is her reputation as a writer who was skilled in representing the speech of the folk based, in part, on authentic renditions that are true to phonological, syntactic, semantic and lexical patterns of AAE? Should we expect to find a broader range of AAE linguistic patterns in her works? Hurston uses a fair amount of phonological, syntactic, semantic and lexical features in her representation of AAE. She does indeed use eye dialect, but not to the exclusion of consistent spellings that are intended to represent the pronunciations of African Americans in her works.

The speech in Hurston's works differs from that in some of the earlier works we have considered. One important difference is that she does not rely solely on pronunciation features to capture the folk speech; she is able to give a more realistic view of the speech by representing patterns from different components: syntax and semantics, phonology, morphology and lexicon. And then her characters use rhetorical strategies: her folk participate in call and response; her preachers flow by using the enumeration and repetition strategies that were discussed in chapter 5.

Hurston's characters spoke the language of folk, a language they could use to express their innermost thoughts, growth and connection to the culture. This language can certainly be characterized by its richness, expressiveness and metaphorical properties, but it is important to note the specifically AAE linguistic patterns Hurston used to make the speech appear to be authentic. Hurston's (1983, p. 67) position is given in the focal point. In effect she suggested that black speech went beyond the 'ams' and 'Ises' often found in renditions of black dialect. Her point would be confirmed if we listened closely to the speech actually produced by speakers of this dialect.

Hurston's first novel, *Jonah's Gourd Vine* (JGV, 1934), is a story about the tragic character John Pearson, who loses his power to use language, to some extent his rhetorical skills as a preacher, as life around him falls apart. John always uses the linguistic patterns of the speech of Hurston's folk when he speaks; however, he is not always able to express himself.

Some of the sound patterns of the black dialect that Hurston represents in this novel are the *d* and *f* sounds in alternation with voiced and voiceless *th* (*dey's* 'they's' p. 111, *bofe* 'both' and *mouf* 'mouth' p. 9), monophthongized sounds in AAE where general English has diphthongs (*mah* 'my,' *Ah* 'I' p. 111), *r* vocalization (*yeah* 'year' p. 108, *cawnbread* 'cornbread' p. 15, *cotehouse* 'courthouse' p. 163) and single final consonants (*fack* 'fact' p. 50, *jes* 'just' p. 110), which were discussed in the chapter 4. Hurston also represents *heaven* as 'heben.' Some speakers in the text pronounce 'that's', 'what's', 'let's', and 'it's' as *dass* (p. 1), *whuss* (p. 49), *less* (p. 54) and *iss* (p. 155), respectively. This pattern, which occurs in current AAE, is discussed in relation to the pronunciation of existential *it's* in chapter 3. In general, the sound patterns here are the same as those in the works that have been reviewed.

The characters also use syntactic patterns that are associated with present-day AAE. A number of sentences reflect some properties of auxiliaries in current AAE. For example, one of the characters asks, "Wonder *is* Ah done let things go too long or *is* de roots just done wore out and done turned back on me?" (p. 144). The auxiliary *is* precedes the subject (*Ah*) in embedded inversion (wonder **is** Ah . . .), and it precedes the subject (*de root*) in the conjoined question (or **is** de root . . .). This is exactly the pattern observed in embedded indirect questions in current AAE. Now consider auxiliaries in relation to the following *wh*-questions, which are used by speakers in JGV:

(21)   a. Where Ahm goin' git 'em from? (p. 145)
        b. How Ahm goin' do it? (p. 125)
        c. Whut he doin' givin' you uh present? (p. 65)
        d. Who dat callin' me? (p. 51)

The analysis of the first two sentences (21a, b) depends on the analysis of *Ahm* (*I'm*) in AAE. On the one hand, *Ahm* can be analyzed as the contracted form of Ah ('*I*') and *am*, in which case, the auxiliary does not occur in the position preceding the subject of the sentence the way it does in some questions (e.g., *How **am** I going to do it?*). On the other hand, it can be analyzed as a single morpheme, and in this case, there is no auxiliary for inversion in the question, as suggested by DeBose and Faraclas (1993). In any case, there is no inversion. Note the sentences in (21c, d) in which there is no overt auxiliary, so *whut he* not 'what is he' and *who dat* not 'who is dat.'

In the literary works to the early twentieth century discussed in the preceding section, the only verbal markers found were *dən* and perhaps *bin* in Brown's work; however, the speakers in JGV use the markers *be*, *BIN* and *dən* (written as *done* in Hurston's works), as reproduced below:

(22)   a.   Humph! Y'all think Ahm gwine put mah trunk on mah back and de tray on mah head, and dat man don't never come? Naw indeed! Ah ain't gwine tuh dress tuh marry no man 'til unless he **be's** in de house. (p. 82)

b.   He **be's** drunk when he keer on lak dat and his likker tell 'im tuh talk. Don't pay 'im no mind.

c.   Ah don't keer if he do **be** peepin' through his likkers he got tuh quit dat. Sho ez gun's iron, he got tuh quit dat. (p. 44)

d.   "Whyn't you tell John whut yuh got tuh say, Ned?" Amy slapped back, "You ***been*** tellin' 'im." (p. 45)

e.   . . . and when Ah **done** sung mah last song, **done** prayed mah last prayer, please suh, Jesus, make up mah dyin'. . . (p. 73)

f.   Don't worry 'bout me, Sister Clarke. Ah **done** been in sorrow's kitchen and Ah **done** licked out all de pots. Ah **done** died in grief and been buried in de bitter waters, and Ah **done** rose agin from de dead lak Lazarus. (p. 131)

g.   "Lawd," she cried, "you see some dem women **done** messed 'rond and spilt soap suds in mah snuff." (p. 84)

h.   He stooped and picked up mother and child and sat with them in his lap. "Lucy, Ahm sho proud uh di li'l girl chile you **done** had." (p. 93)

i.   "You been tuh de house longer'n he is," Amy said quietly. "You coulda **done been** got dat water." (p. 4)

j.   Here's dat fo' dollars Ah owe you fuh buildin' dat she-room 'fo' you went way from here. Ah could uh **been done** paid you, but Ah let talk keep me from it. (p. 195)

The passage in (22a) was spoken by Mehaley, who is in no rush to dress in her wedding attire to marry a man who is not around right at the moment. Her response is that she is not going to don her wedding clothes until the man is in the house. *Be's in the house* in (22a) takes on the meaning of 'is in the house,' in which *be* has an emphatic stative quality. Given the context and possible interpretation, this *be's* does not necessarily have the habitual reading. The sequences in (22b, c) are the more common uses of aspectual *be*, in which *be's drunk* and *do be peepin'* (in which *do* is more than likely intended to be stressed) indicate 'drunk on occasion' and 'peeping on occasion,' respectively.

The reasoning in (22b) is given by Amy as an explanation to John for his stepfather's behavior. John picks up on the 'habitual' meaning in his mother's explanation, and he responds in kind with (22c). In effect, John does not care if it is the case that his stepfather IS usually influenced by his liquor; he wants his stepfather to stop insulting him.

Been in Amy's reply (22d) is italicized, which more than likely indicates some special stress or intonation; however, it is not clear that the stress gives it the remote past reading of the marker *BIN*. It is possible that the speaker means to express that she does not understand why Ned does not say what is on his mind, because, up until the time of the utterance, he has always told John what was on his mind. In short, in the past, Ned has communicated honestly with John. Although Amy does not say, "What has changed to prevent you from telling him what is on your mind now," the reader can read this line into what Amy does say. The speech of Hurston's characters is believable and familiar to those who know something about AAE, but those who are unfamiliar with it may not get all the nuances of the linguistic markers. Holloway (1978) says that, in effect, "The speaker who does not share these features . . . but who does understand the surface . . . will therefore receive only a portion of the original message; the rest is lost in translation" (p. 87).

The marker *dən* (represented as *done* in JGV) occurs in the remaining sentences (22e–j), and in each case it indicates that an action is over. For example, the line from Emmeline's prayer (22e), can be glossed as ". . . and when I have already sung my last song, have already prayed my last prayer," expressing that the having "sung mah last song" and "prayed may mah last prayer" events are over. The prayer or conversation with God begins with a discussion about how she tried to rear her daughter in the right way, moves to disobedient children and ends the way many prayers in this tradition end – with a request for eternal blessings from God. This is the request in (22e). This familiar prayer scheme adds authenticity to the character's use of language.

Lucy expresses her condition while she is on her death bed (22f), saying that she has seen rough times and survived them. *Done* here also indicates the resultant state, the events (having been in sorrow's kitchen, having licked out all the pots and having died in grief) are over. Interestingly enough, Hurston expresses this same sentiment in her formal autobiography, *Dust Tracks on a Road*, when she says, "I have been in sorrow's kitchen and licked out all the pots" (p. 280). Hurston gives her character Lucy the language of the folk, the kind of speech that will allow her to express her innermost and deepest feelings. On the other hand, Hurston uses the medium of general English, which must have been viewed as being appropriate for her autobiography.

Some notion of recent past is associated with the sentence (20g), and this meaning comes from the marker *done*. The event, having spilled soap suds in the snuff, has already been completed, whether recently or not so recent. Mehaley's realization of the event is in the recent past, thus the use of *done* (i.e., *dən*). Knowing the full meaning of *dən* is important in understanding the message, but it is also important to understand that this marker has a specific pronunciation; it is unstressed. In (22h), the marker indicates recent past, as Lucy has recently had the baby girl.

In the sentences in (22i, j), *done* occurs with *been*. *Done* precedes *been* in (22i) and follows it in (22j). The *done been* and *been done* sequences have virtually the same meaning, completion in the remote past, so (22i) means 'You could have gotten that water a long time ago,' and (22j) means 'I could have paid you a long time ago'. In effect, what could have been completed in the remote past are the getting water event (22i) and the paying you event (22j).[6] Given that these sentences have remote past meaning, *been* must be the stressed *BIN*, which situates an event or some part of an event in the remote past. In both cases, *could* and some morpheme *a*, *uh* (perhaps an auxiliary form of *have*) precede the *done been* + verb and *been done* + verb sequences. This morpheme obligatorily occurs whenever a modal precedes a *done* or *been* sequence. (See the paradigms in chapter 2 for similar examples.) Hurston does not give any orthographical cues to hint that the *been* used here is the stressed *BIN*, the remote past marker. It seems, then, that understanding something about the AAE system would be useful in presenting a descriptive analysis of the characters' language use and linguistic patterns.

In her linguistic analysis, Holloway (1978) discusses the meaning and use of aspectual *be* and *dən*. She considers the use of habitual *be* in relation to its role of marking cultural habit that is fact, so those who are not familiar with culture-specific meanings may not get the full intent of the construction. Although I disagree with Holloway's analysis of *dən*, as a non-present form of *do*, I agree with her assessment of the meaning of the marker: "The use of *done* suggests a finality not possible with the simple past, however, not completely equivalent to the SE [Standard English] perfect" (p. 118). What Holloway is describing is the property of indicating that an event is over.

In the discussion of the sound system of AAE (chapter 4), it was noted that Tarone (1972, 1973) found that a certain intonational pattern occurred in conditional sentences without an overt *if*. This type of sentence also occurs in JGV:

(23)   Course Ah don't believe he done no sich uh hot-do, but she fool wid me tuhday Ah means tuh beat her 'til she rope lak okra, and den agin Ah'll stomp her 'til she slack lak slime. (p. 67)

If spoken, the condition, *but she fool wid me tuhday* ('but if she fools with me today'), which is not introduced by *if*, would more than likely be marked with the kind of non-final intonational contour that Tarone addresses. Of course, there is no indication that particular intonational patterns are associated with this passage, but if we are concerned about authentic representation of speech and if we know something about AAE, then it is natural to raise these questions – especially when such patterns are tied to the meaning.

In addition to other syntactic constructions, Hurston's folk also use AAE patterns of negation. There are numerous examples of multiple negation in the work: "Dey **don't** own **nobody no** mo'" (p. 14). "Ack lak '**tain't nobody** got feelings but you" (p. 68).

A few brief points will be made about the morphological representations of some lexical items in JGV. The first is that the second person singular possessive pronoun is produced as *yourn* by some speakers and *yours* by others, and the third person singular possessive feminine pronoun is *her'n* in some environments. Also, the first person plural possessive pronoun is *ourn* in some cases. Finally the first person singular possessive pronoun also takes the form *mines*. These freestanding possessive pronouns differ from possessive pronouns *his, her, your, my* and *our* in that the former do not have to precede a noun. On the other hand, the latter possessive pronouns (excluding *his*) must be followed by a noun (e.g., *her children*). By using these freestanding possessive forms and by incorporating a certain level of variation, Hurston adds to the authenticity of her characters' speech. The characters, like speakers of all languages, do not always say the same thing the same way. In addition, Hurston's characters and present-day speakers of AAE use forms that are also a part of general American English. The possessive pronoun paradigm that represents the forms Hurston's characters use and those in current AAE is given in (24):

(24)   **Freestanding possessive pronouns**   **Possessive pronouns**
           mines   my
           ourn, ours   our
           yourn, yours   your
           { hisn, hern }   his, her
           { his, hers }

Hurston basically gives all of the parts; anyone who is engaged in a linguistic description only has the task of putting them together to get a complete picture. Examples of these pronouns are given in the sentences below:

(25)   a. Yeah, John Buddy, mama know jes' how yuh feels and her heart is beatin' right wid **yourn**. (p. 40)

b. She had her birth night de day befo' **mines**. **Her'n** on December 31, and mine's January 1.

c. Eve'y chicken on dis place is **mines**.

d. We borned 'em but that didn't make 'em **ourn**.

The freestanding possessive pronouns here are quite possibly formed by analogy, based on the structure of other pronouns. *Yourn* and *her'n* (25a, b), as they take the final *n* sound, may be patterned after *mine*, and *mines* may be patterned after pronouns ending in *s, his, hers* and *yours*. Hurston distinguishes *mine's* (25b) and *mines* (25c), the former reflecting the contracted copula *be* form, it would seem.

    Hurston's characters also use lexical items from the AAE lexicon. The author herself realized that many of these items had special meanings; for instance, she included a glossary of terms at the end of *Jonah's Gourd Vine*. In chapter 1 of this book the semi-auxiliary *come* was included in the AAE lexicon and defined as a lexical marker used to indicate speaker indignation. The marker has just this meaning in JGV, and it precedes verbs ending in *-ing*:

(26)   a. Ah ain't studyin' 'bout his Exie, Mist' Alf. He better talk tuh *her*. She de one come pullin' on me. (p. 50)

b. Don't come puttin' up no po' mouf tuh me, Lucy. (p. 98)

In (26a) John is telling the judge that Exie is the one who had the audacity to make physical contact with him. In (26b) the goal of Lucy's brother's statement is to prevent her from giving him a sob story. In effect, the message her brother is conveying is "Don't even think about telling me another pitiful story; I don't want to hear it." Other AAE lexical items that occur in JGV are *mannish* and *womanish*, also noted in chapter 1: "He must smell hisself – done got so **mannish**. Some fast '**omanish** gal is grinnin' in his face and he tries to get sides hisself" (p. 45). Ned's comment refers to what he takes to be John's impudence. *Mannish* is used to refer to John, who is seen as behaving inappropriately for his age, and *'omanish* ('womanish') applies to John's girlfriend, who is also seen as getting out of her place.

Hurston's characters also use *jook* (p. 90) to refer to a dance hall in which dancing, drinking and other activities occur. *Jook* is not discussed in chapter 1; however, the term *jook joint* is still used in places in the South (perhaps not just by African Americans) to refer to establishments like the one in Hurston's novel.

Finally, the characters use the form *onliest* in environments in which *only* occurs in other varieties of English. It can be argued that the final *-est* is the superlative suffix (*only* + *est*), redundantly indicating uniqueness on the adjective. It is also possible that *onliest* is an unanalyzable whole that cannot be divided into separate morphemes. It occurs in sentences such as the following, in which someone (or something) is singled out as being unique:

(27) a. He ain't de **onliest** yaller chile in de world. (p. 9)
      b. Y'all know dat li'l gal dat trebles in de choir at Macedony – de one whut don't wrop her hair, de **onliest** one up dere dat don't wrop her hair no time wid all dat cord-string lak de rest. (p. 56)

Onliest is commonly used in current-day AAE by older speakers. I have included the form as a special vocabulary item, but it may also be used as an example of morphological properties of AAE because the *-est* may be taken to be a separate morpheme (suffix) that indicates uniqueness.

The features that have been discussed from JGV are all recognized as patterns that are used in current AAE. Some features in JGV, however, are not discussed in descriptions of present-day AAE. This does not mean that these features are inaccurate for Hurston's characters or for some variety or period of AAE, for that matter. One such example that is worth noting is the following: "Ah ain't never meant tuh marry you. Ain't got no recollection uh even tryin' tuh marry yuh, but here us is married, Hattie, how come dat" (p. 143). It has been argued that the copula *be* is obligatorily present at the end of sentences. However, the speaker does not say "How come dat is," with a sentence final obligatory copula (*is*). I have not seen any data suggesting that Hurston's sentence would occur in current AAE. At first glance, Hurston's sentence *How come dat?* ('How come that is?') seems to be quite similar to sentences such as *How long your paper?* ('How long your paper is?' or 'How long is your paper?'), which is quite common in AAE, but they are different due, in part, to the placement of the copula. Discussion of the structure of these sentences would go beyond the analysis in this book, but note that in the sentence *How long your paper?*, there are two places to put the copula, after *long* (*How long is your paper?*) or after *paper* (*How long your paper is?*). But this is not the case in Hurston's sentence *How come dat?* (*How come dat is?* but not **How come is dat?*); the copula can only go at the end of the sentence. In current AAE, the placement of the copula is related to the acceptability of *How long your paper?* and the unacceptability of **How come dat?*

While Hurston's characters would fall on the lower end of the socioeconomic scale, the language is not just a marker of class. However, because the language consists of what we understand to be nonstandard features, its speakers are automatically labeled as members of the lower class. Hurston's speakers use the language of the folk; it does not mark them as poor, pitiful unworthy blacks; it makes them appear as if they are real and sometimes makes them seem as if they are poets. Holloway (1978) notes the following about Hurston and her language: "First, she indicated that although Black speech was not a separate 'language,' it was a form of communication capable of holding the same levels and complications of thought as any 'fully-formed' languages" (p. 139). Hurston's view about this linguistic variety is communicated through the range of patterns used by her characters. In addition to phonological patterns, they use syntactic and lexical patterns. They also use specific syntactic constructions that are marked by unique intonational patterns.

6.4.2   AAE in Langston Hughes's *The Best of Simple*[8]

In his essay, "The Negro Artist and the Racial Mountain," Hughes says:

> Certainly there is, for the American Negro artist who can escape the restrictions the more advanced among his own group would put upon him, a great field of unused material ready for his art. Without going outside his race, and even among the better classes with their 'white' culture and conscious American manners, but still Negro enough to be different, there is sufficient matter to furnish a black artist with a lifetime of creative work
>
> [p. 46].

Certainly some of the "unused material" that Hughes refers to is black language.

In spite of the time span between works such as those by William Wells Brown in the earlier period and those by Hughes, some of the same features occur in their characters' speech. These similarities will become apparent during the discussion of Hughes's short stories. Along these same lines, there are differences; the immediately obvious difference is that there is a considerable decrease in eye dialect in Hughes's writing, which means less focus on spelling manipulations to convey the message that pronunciation in black speech is actually different from that in general American English.

Most of the AAE features in Hughes's Simple stories, featuring Jesse B. Simple, "part buffoon, sage, folk hero, comedian, witness, and trickster" (Ostrom 1993, p. 31) are reflected in the syntactic constructions. The stories are particularly interesting in that Simple's language, a form of 'black dialect,' is in contrast with some form of general American English, be it that used by his wife Joyce or that used by the narrator. Joyce corrects Simple's language and educates him on manners and acceptable behavior. But even during the lessons, Simple is always himself; he keeps it real. When his wife tells him why he cannot chew on a bone while he looks out of the window, he says: "People eat hot dogs in public in the Yankee Stadium... and corn on the cob at Coney Island.

So why can't I gnaw a bone in my own house?'" ("Bones, Bombs, Chicken Necks," pp. 199–200).

Simple uses multiple negation whenever necessary to make his point. In "Springtime," he says, "If I was down home, buddy-o, I would pull off my shoes and let my toes air and just set on the riverbank and dream and fish and fish and dream, and I would **not** worry about **no** job" (p. 73). Along these same lines, the character observes, "Man you know womenfolks **can't** keep **no** secret!" (p. 76) in response to the question, "How did your Aunt Lucy find out about the hen?".[7] In the same story, he goes on to say, "When she got through, I said, 'Aunt Lucy, you **ain't** gonna have to whip me **no** more. I **ain't** gonna give you **no** cause. I **do not** mind to be beat. But I **do not** *never* want to see you cry **no** more – so I am going to do my best to do right from now on and not try your soul" (p. 78). The use of negation in these illustrative sentences follows the description in chapter 3; these negative elements do not express different and separate instances of negation, the sentences are interpreted as if there is only one negation. Simple does not always use multiple negation in syntactic environments in which it can occur. In "Seven Rings" he uses single negation when he explains Joyce's good qualities: "What I like about Joyce is she would never alimony me. Joyce works and makes her own money and does not want anything out of me but love" (p. 97). Here he almost uses the elevated language of his girlfriend to lift her up, but in the fashion of Hurston's folk characters, Simple extends the grammatical class of *alimony* from noun to a verb.

The verbal marker *-s* is used in the Simple stories to mark habitual meaning. In "What Can a Man Say," Simple's landlady expresses her frustration:

(28)   a. I **tells** you roomers to pull down your windows when you leave the house. I cannot be running up and down steps looking after you-all. (p. 101)

       b. Mr. Semple, I am hurted by that last remark. I **tries** to treat everybody nice. I do! (p. 102)[9]

       c. I **likes** to go out once in a while myself. And you ain't never so much as invited me to Paddy's for a beer in all these years you been living in my house. (p. 103)

In (28a, b, c), the landlady communicates that she tells the roomers over and over, she tries over and over and she likes to go out from time to time, respectively.

The aspectual marker *done* (most likely *dən*) occurs from time to time in Simple's speech. Here, too, it is used consistently to indicate that an eventuality is over. Consider two such instances of the marker:

(29)   a. Because I had been up to devilment, and she had **done** said she was gonna whip me come Monday. ("Last Whipping," p. 75)

       b. She said, I am crying 'cause here you is a man, and don't know how to act right yet, and I **done** did my best to raise you so you would grow up good. I **done** wore out so many switches on your back, still you tries my soul. ("Last Whipping," p. 76)

In all of these cases, *done* precedes a verb that bears past tense morphology (*done said, done did, done wore*), which is a requirement of the marker. Note also that there is no past/past participle distinction in the cases of *did* and *wore*. This is consistent with the description of past marking in chapter 3. In the case of (29a), the saying event is over, while in (29b) the doing my best event is over. Finally, also in (29b) the wearing out so many switches on your back event is over. In all of these cases, *done* indicates that some event or a part of the event has already occurred.

In "Seven Rings," *done* occurs in environments in which it is supported by *has*. In this case, *done* occurs with the auxiliary *has*: Simple says, "Joyce **has done** made that woman mad at me, too. **Done** told her something" (p. 98). The auxiliary *has* precedes the first *done* here, and its occurrence is in keeping with the restrictions on auxiliaries occurring with *done* (as discussed in chapter 2). This type of data is important. Examples such as this one are important in considering the question about the existence of *has/have* in AAE. Both occurrences of *done* in the example can be glossed as 'already,' meaning the event is over and is in its resultant state.

The characters also use aspectual *be* to indicate that eventualities can occur on different occasions. In "Last Whipping," aspectual *be*, in the form of *be's*, occurs a number of times in Simple's recapitulation of Aunt Lucy's response about the devil:

(30)   She hollered, "No-ooo-oo-o! Hallelujah, no! It cannot tear your soul. Sometimes the devil comes in human form," yelled Aunt Lucy, "sometimes it **be's** born right into your own family. Sometimes the devil **be's** your own flesh and kin – and he try your soul – but your soul he cannot tear! Sometimes you **be's** forced to tear his hide before he tears your soul. Amen!" (p. 75)

(As noted in chapter 2, *bes* (*be's* in the Simple stories) has a number of different representations.) The second *be's* precedes a noun phrase, in which case the interpretation is that the devil can actually come in the appearance of people who are related to you; it is often the case that devilish people are your relatives. This means that from time to time, different people can be devils (that is, act like devils). The first and third *be's* are similar in that they take passive participles (e.g., *be's born, be's forced*). In these cases, the eventualities are activities that occur from time to time, so the devil being born into your family occurs on occasions and you being forced to tear his hide also occurs on occasion. We cannot put all of our eggs in one literary basket, but data such as these in the Simple stories can make some contribution to studies on the form and use of aspectual *be* in the early twentieth century. The data can be used in comparative studies designed to provide information on the similarities and differences between *be/bes* over the past fifty or so years.

Data such as the passage in (30) suggest that even when *bes* occurs with a third person singular subject, '*s* is not necessarily a third person singular agreement marker. In chapter 3, it was suggested that the '*s* here redundantly marks habituality on *be*, the inherent habitual marker. *Be's* also occurs with second person singular subject *you* in the passage, not just with third person singular subjects, so the *-s* cannot be a third person singular marker.

Another syntactic feature that occurs in the literature and that is discussed in current syntactic theoretical frameworks of AAE is negative inversion. Consider the following sentences from "What Can a Man Say?": "Then who will walk your dog for you? **Don't none** of your other roomers do it. Neither your husband" (p. 102). The second sentence begins with an inverted auxiliary and negative indefinite (*don't none*), the structure for negative inversion statements.

Number distinction is neutralized in one direction or the other, so the singular form is the default auxiliary *be* form. The singular form *is* is used with plural *they*, as in *They is little young snakes* ("Springtime," p. 73), and the singular form *was* is used with the plural subject *some little old birds* in *Some little old birds was flying and playing on the garbage cans down in the alley...* ("Springtime," p. 74). Also in this story, there is evidence to suggest that the default form for the verb *do* is *do*, as it is used with the first occurrence of the singular subject *it*, as in *It do not come as early in Harlem as it does down South...* ("Springtime," p. 74). However, we see that Simple uses both plural *do* and singular *does* with the singular subject *it*. The representation in this sentence, and in the Simple stories in general, reflects the variation of certain verb forms in AAE.

Some AAE lexical items are represented in the Jesse B. Simple stories. One such item is *mannish*, which Simple uses here to describe his behavior: "Oh I got all mannish, man. I said, 'Aunt Lucy, you ain't gonna whip me no more. I's a man – and you ain't gonna whip me'" ("Last Whipping," p. 76). The word *mannish* here refers to age inappropriate or disrespectful behavior for boys or for men, in the opinion of elders. As discussed in connection with Hurston's JGV, the character Ned also uses *mannish* to refer to his stepson, John. The term is included in the discussion of the lexicon in chapter 1. It is worth noting that observations such as the one made by Hurston at the beginning of this chapter also raise questions about Hughes's *I's* in *I's a man...*

A final point is that the possessive second person pronoun occurs as *yourn* on one occasion in Aunt Lucy's speech in "Last Whipping": "But it ain't *my* soul I'm thinking of, son, it's yourn" (p. 78). This is the only occurrence of the pronoun in the four stories and in fact one of the few environments for it, that is, one of the few opportunities to use it.

6.5   AAE in literature from the mid twentieth century to the present

One of the most important works in twentieth-century American literature is Ralph Ellison's *Invisible Man*, published in 1952. Ellison uses folklore and other culturally specific elements in that work:

> Well, there are certain themes, symbols and images which are based on folk material. For example, there is the old saying amongst Negroes: if you're black, stay back; if you're brown, stick around; if you're white, you're right. And there is the joke Negroes tell on themselves about their being so black they can't be seen in the dark. In my book this sort of thing was merged with the meanings which blackness and light have long had in Western mythology; evil and goodness, ignorance and knowledge, and so on.
>
> [Ellison 1955, p. 108].

Ellison uses a combination of speech events, rhetorical strategies and linguistic features to convey the language of the folk. While he does not always rely so heavily on the use of spelling manipulations to make the African American characters appear to be using a different dialect, there are some instances of eye dialect, for example *minit* 'minute' (p. 62). Features that occur in the previous works that have been discussed, especially in Hurston's *Jonah's Gourd Vine*, also occur in *Invisible Man*. The difference is that in JGV, for instance, the focus is on both phonological and syntactic properties, while in *Invisible Man*, syntactic properties are more prominent, for the most part. The level of dialect use may be directly related to a number of factors: the author's knowledge of and views about the dialect, the characters' ethnographic background, the makeup of the character's speech community and issues related to publishing. *Invisible Man* features different types of black characters who are living the black experience in America.

The trickster character Peter Wheatstraw displays verbal dexterity, rhyming and using language like that of rappers and signifiers. He packages his language in a way that allows him to conceal the meaning from outsiders. He says: "All it takes to get along in this here man's town is a little s - - - , grit and mother-wit. And man, I was bawn with all three. In fact, I'maseventhsonofaseventhsonbawnwithacauloverbotheyesandraisedon-blackcatboneshighjohntheconquerorandgreasygreens – . . . You dig me daddy?" "I'll verse you but I won't curse you – My name it Peter Wheatstraw, I'm the Devil's only son-in-law, so roll 'em" (pp. 172–173). Wheatstraw relies on speech events rather than syntactic and phonological patterns to communicate his cultural message. However, note that the form *it* in his self-introduction occurs without the *s* ("my name it Peter Wheatstraw"), which could well serve as a linguistic marker. Also, *bawn* 'born' is produced with *r* vocalization.

Three noteworthy syntactic features used by the African American characters are negative inversion, multiple functions of *ain't* and resultant state *dən*. The negative inversion constructions are introduced by negative auxiliaries such as *don'* 'don't', *ain't*, *won't* and *caint* 'can't':

(31)   a. But **don' nothin'** happen and I knows then that somethin' worse than anything I ever heard 'bout is in store for me. (p. 65)
       b. **Won't nothing** surprise me . . . (p. 298)
       c. He's the kind **caint nobody** please. (p. 426)

Note that the spellings of *don'* and *caint* clearly correspond to actual pronunciations that are different from mainstream pronunciations; they are not just trick spellings used to make the words to look different.

As in the literature from the early twentieth century and the Harlem Renaissance, *ain't* is used here in a number of different negative environments, which raises the question about whether it is a general negator or whether it has the range of meanings that are compatible with the simple past and present perfect, *didn't* and *haven't*, respectively:

(32)   a. You still up at the school, **ain't** you? (p. 75)
          'You're still up at school, aren't you?'
       b. He **ain't** been to no doctor in ten years. (p. 81)
          'He hasn't been to a doctor in ten years'
       c. A: Now you **ain't** never been to no Chicago, gal . . .
          'Now you have never been to Chicago, girl'
          B: How you know I **ain't**? (p. 88)
          'How do you know I haven't?'

In (32a) *ain't* appears in the tag even though there is no auxiliary (i.e., *be* form) in the first part of the statement. Examples such as this were presented in chapter 2 to show that auxiliaries are required to occur in tag questions. Both (32b) and (32c) are compatible with *haven't*, which occurs in present perfect contexts. The sentence in (32c) is an example of the experiential perfect in that it conveys something about the experience of having been to Chicago. *Ain't* in the second example (32b) is used in the negative environment of the present perfect in the sense that the state of being a doctor includes the time period from ten years ago to the present. In (32c) the same idea of present relevance holds here.

Done (*dən*) is also used in *Invisible Man* to refer to events that have ended. Both of the sentences in the examples are taken from a passage in which the character is relaying a dream.

(33)   a. I knowed then she was grown and I wondered how many times it'd **done** happened
          and was it that doggone boy. (pp. 56–57)
          '. . . it had already happened . . .'
        b. Then she starts screamin' and I thinks I **done** gone deaf.
          'Then she starts screaming and I think I have gone deaf'

Note that in (33a) the contracted form of the auxiliary *had* precedes the *done happened* sequence, situating it in the past before some other time. In the sentence in (33b) *done* seems to mark the recent past, in which case the speaker intends to communicate that when the girl begins to scream, he realizes that something is wrong, or he is affected by the action. In this sentence, the past participle (*gone*) versus the simple past (*went*) is used. The sentence in (33b) is also a good example of the use of the narrative -*s*, in which the speaker says "she starts" and "I thinks" in telling the story. (See Myhill and Harris 1986, Butters 1989, and comments in chapter 3 for a discussion of narrative -*s*.) This character uses narrative -*s* consistently in the nearly three pages it takes to tell his dream.

The next work from this period is Ernest Gaines's *Bloodline* (1968), a compilation of five stories. Callahan (1988) writes that "Likewise, the stories in *Bloodline* are not told in a dramatic context. No one appears to be present except the character, and the stories seem to unfold entirely inside the narrator's mind. But they are told with an accuracy of idiom, an authenticity of voice, and an economy of form worthy of Gaines's approving phrase – 'That's writing . . .' Throughout *Bloodline* Gaines makes written speech of the characters' voices" (pp. 192, 193). In this work, Gaines, an African American writer, captures the speech of his characters in a region in Louisiana. In some cases, the characters may be using patterns that are associated with southern Louisiana (and other places in the South), and not exclusively with AAE. For example, the characters use the personal dative (*me*) which has also been observed in Appalachian English (Christian 1991): *I got me all kind of boyfriend* 'I have all kinds of boyfriends' ("The Sky is Gray," p. 92).

Some lexical items that are used in the stories may also be items that are common in the South. For instance *mash*, to press or push (*Don't mash too hard*, p. 154; but see the note on *mash* in chapter 1), is used by an African American man. Another vocabulary item that occurs in one of the stories is *jugg*, which means to poke or force something into a space. The young boy in "The Sky is Gray" says, in reference to a piece of meat, "Then she wraps it up again and juggs it back in the bag and gives the bag to Mama" (p. 117). The vowel in the word sounds like the vowel sound in *pull* and *good*.

Gaines's characters are black and white speakers in a rural area in the South, and the language he assigns them shows that they share some common ground, but it is different enough to set them apart. The following line in which the marker *done* (*dən*) occurs is uttered by an African American female character:

(34)   You **done** forgot how hard cutting cane is?" Gran'mon says. You must be **done** forgot. (p. 31)
'You have already forgotten how hard cutting cane is?... You must have already forgotten'

White characters in the book also use *done*: "Y'all done ate?" and old white woman asks ("The Sky is Gray," p. 112). The black and white women in the story use the marker *done*, but the two speech patterns are different. Consider multiple negation in the black woman's speech, which does not occur in that of the white woman's:

(35)   "We **don't** take **no** handout," Mama says. (black woman)
"I'm not handing out anything," the old lady says. (white woman) (p. 113)

The black woman uses the negative auxiliary *don't* an *no*, while the white woman uses *not* and *anything*. The unstressed marker *bin* that marks simple past events is also used in one of the stories by an elderly African American woman: *What you ought to* **bin** *done was got the sheriff on him for kidnap*" ("A Long Day in November," p. 64). Basically, the grandmother means that her daughter should have taken the action (that of getting the sheriff) in the past.

Existential *dey*, represented as *they* also occurs in "A Long Day in November": *They got some books over there*... (p. 99) and in "The Sky is Gray": *They got a girl sitting 'cross from me* (p. 91). The *they* here does not refer to people; instead it is used existentially to indicate that there exist some books over there and a girl is sitting across from me. This feature is discussed in chapter 3 in the section under existential *it* and *dey*.

In "Three Men," another story in *Bloodline*, one character begins to speak of his situation by saying, "But like I'm is..." (p. 145). In this sentence, both *I'm* and *is* are used, and if *I'm* is the contracted *I* and *am*, then it is hard to explain why two forms of *be* (i.e., *am* and *is*) are used. Representations of sentences such as these in literary contexts might provide some idea about the regularity of occurrence of such sequences, which in turn might be useful in providing some insight into the question about whether to analyze *I'm* as the contracted pronominal and *be* form or as a single morpheme much like *I*. However, arguments about the *I'm is* sequence should not be based solely on literary data. And in fact, DeBose and Faraclas (1993) used data such as this from natural speech to argue that in AAE, *I'm* is not a contracted for of *I + am*; it is a single morpheme.

John Wideman's *Brothers and Keepers* (B&K, 1984) is the only non-fiction work considered in this chapter. The autobiographical work is included because of the close attention the author pays to language in representing vernacular speech. The book focuses on John Edgar Wideman, who is a college professor, and his brother, Robby, who, at the time the book was published, was a prison inmate. In explaining the different paths that the brothers took, the book reflects the different language and speech they used. From time to time, the author, who obviously knows the vernacular, switches into it, so to speak, but Robby is clearly represented as being a consistent AAE speaker. Wideman's note gives some idea about the accuracy of the details, including the authenticity of language, in the book: "The style, the voices that speak this book, are an attempt to capture a process that began in earnest about four years ago: my brother and I talking about our lives" (p. 1). There are not many instances of eye dialect to alert the reader that a particular character is a vernacular speaker. The reader will detect representations such as *mize well* (pp. 64, 93), which is used to capture the coalescence of *might* and *as* in 'might as well'; so it cannot really be considered eye dialect.

Wideman makes the following observations about Robby: "My life was relatively comfortable, pleasant, safe. I'd come west to escape the demons Robby personified. I didn't need outlaw brothers reminding me how much had been lost, how much compromised, how terribly the world still raged beyond the charmed circle of my life on the Laramie plains" (p. 11). The brothers seem to be miles apart, and their speech is one marker that helps them keep their distance.

A comparison of the works that have been discussed provides evidence to show that aspectual *be* occurs most often in B&K (but it is clearly represented in Hurston's JGV and Hughes's Simple stories). A number of factors, significant or not, may be responsible for the greater use of the marker in B&K in comparison to its use in other works. One consideration is that perhaps aspectual *be* is a later development in AAE, as argued by researchers such as Bailey and Maynor (1987), and as such, the marker occurs more in works in later periods. A component of the Bailey and Maynor argument is that the marker is an innovation in AAE and occurs in the speech of younger speakers. If Bailey and Maynor's argument is extended to the representation and use of aspectual *be* in these literary works, then one explanation is that aspectual *be* occurs more often in Wideman's B&K because the book was written in the late twentieth century, and one of the major voices in the work is that of a young adult. Aspectual *be* in B&K occurs consistently in Robby's speech. Some examples follow:

(36)   a. I still **be** performing. Read poetry in the hole. (p. 87)
       b. They say I write about the things they **be** thinking. (p. 87)
       c. I always believed we was the most alike out of all the kids. I see stuff in your books. The kinds of things I **be** thinking or feeling. (p. 87)
       d. They stone junkies, they hooked. Do anything for a hit. But me. I'm Robby. I'm cool. I **be** believing that s---, too . . . See but where it's at is you **be** doing any g----- thing for dope. You hooked and that's all it is. You a stone junkie just like the rest. (p. 94)
       e. Got to get down and dance to the tune the man **be** playing. (p. 114)
       f. It **be's** the way it always **be**. The three musketeers. Me and Cecil and Mike. (p. 150)
       g. It's real quiet in the mess hall but everybody screaming inside. That's how it is. Sometimes it **be** noon before I'm ready to talk to anybody. (p. 230)

The *be* sequences in the sentences in (36a–e) are analyzed as instances of aspectual *be*, based on the syntactic and conversational context in which they are used. For instance, although the passage in (36d) could be taken to mean "you'd be doing" (i.e., 'you would be doing'), it is more likely "you DO be doing…" (to mean 'you usually do…') because the speaker is referring to a general state of affairs, that of being hooked and being a junkie. Given this, aspectual *be* is compatible with the meaning; one who is hooked usually does anything, that is, "be doing" anything to satisfy the habit. In (36f) Robby expresses that he and two of his friends will have to do the job that needs to be done, but it is not clear whether in the statement *It be's the way it always be* he is suggesting that things at some particular moment are the same, that is, the way they usually are. If this is the case, then the first *be's* indicates moments in general (i.e., 'it is usually the case at a particular time'), and the second *be* denotes habitual meaning ('things are the way they usually are'). The *be* in (36g) is the aspectual (habitual) *be*, and the meaning of the sentence is 'Sometimes it's noon before I'm ready to talk to anybody.'

There are other instances of *be* that are compatible with both *would* and with aspectual *be* readings. Consider (37), introduced by the following sentence, which has habitual meaning: "First couple of times when I went with Smokey he'd do most the work, most the talking, and I'd just watch and listen and learn the ropes" (p. 140).

(37)   a. Carry the dude to the stone ghetto. He **be** nervous now. . . . so he's getting squirmy but you **be** bulls ------- him the whole time. You **be** in a truck or a van. Something that will hold all them TVs. You get to a house and go up the steps. Got to be a house with a back door and a front door. You **be** outside with the dude and knock on the door and somebody say, . . . Who is it? . . . See, they **be** doing all this talking and the door ain't open yet. (p. 140–141)

b. Once in a while we'd try one them big gas stations on a busy corner. They **be** steady ripping off people so they got that greed thing going too. (p. 141)

On the one hand, the *be*'s in the passage in (37a) can be understood as aspectual *be*. Take, for instance, ". . . so he's getting squirmy but you be bulls ------- him the whole time." The first clause occurs in the narrative tense (marked on *he's*), but the second clause has an adverbial, *the whole time*. The eventuality expressed by 'be bulls -------' can be interpreted as occurring throughout the time span, 'the whole time,' thus the habitual interpretation: 'keeps bulls ------- him the whole time'. This is not incompatible with the *would be* tense. It would mean 'you would be (you'd be) bulls ------- him the whole time.' The habitual interpretation is not immediately compatible with the adverbial *now* in "he be nervous now," but if the speaker is actually using *now* to refer to the time period during which the person becomes nervous, then the meaning can be a habitual one, in which case, the speaker can convey the following: It is usually the case that at this point (at which ever point he has reached in the story), the person is nervous. This reasoning is logical, but it seems more likely that the *be* sequences in (37) are *would be* + a following predicate. But in these sentences, *would* does not occur on the surface, so only *be* and the predicate are left. If this is the case, they would receive a type of past habitual meaning slightly different from that of aspectual *be*, which does not refer to habituality in the past.

In chapter 3, it was noted that relative pronouns (e.g., *who*, *that*) do not obligatorily introduce relative clauses in present-day AAE. Relative clauses that are not introduced by relative pronouns also occur in Robby's speech:

(38)   a. You know that TV of you all's [— got stolen from Mommy's]. (p. 94)

        b. You could be the one [— take Billy Sim's spot]. (p. 125)

In the sentence in (38a), the clause '—got stolen from Mommy's' refers to the TV. The '—' indicates that there is no overt relative pronoun. This sentence may look like the declarative *You know that TV of you all's got stolen from mommy's*, in which Robby would be informing his brother that their TV was stolen. However, given the context, this latter reading is not intended. The statement in (38b) is identical to the sentence type that has been discussed in chapter 3. In (38b) '—' introduces a clause that refers to the predicate nominal 'the one'.

    Multiple negation, as represented below, also occurs in Robby's speech.

(39)   a. A new day's starting and **nobody don't** like it. **Nobody don't** want to be here, (p. 230)

        b. My dream's coming true. **Ain't nothing** in the way. (p. 125)

        c. Them kids loved me. I could get them to do things nobody else could. This one named Timmy. **Ain't nobody** ever heard him say a word. (p. 136)

In (39c) the negated auxiliary (*ain't*) precedes the negative indefinite subject (*nothing, nobody*).

    Questions such as those in (40) have zero auxiliary/copula *be* forms:

(40)   a. How Ø they talking that mess? (p. 114)

        b. What Ø they gon do? (p. 151)

The auxiliary *be* may occur on the surface in the speech of vernacular speakers, so it is not surprising to find the overt form in Robby's speech as well:

(41)   a. ...I'm not liking nothing that's going down. My boys **is** gone, my piece gone, and I got this fat wad of dough in my back pocket. Now, somebody I ain't never seen in my life **is** whistling and waving me over to a place I ain't never been and it's black...(p. 123)

        b. I'm listening to every word. And it's sweet. My dream'**s** coming true. (p. 125)

In addition to contracted *be* forms on *I'm, that's* and *it's*, forms that are, for the most part, obligatorily present, the full form (*is*) and the contracted form (on *dream's*) also occur on the surface. In chapter 2, it was noted that some *be* forms (e.g., dream *is*, dream'*s*) do not always occur on the surface, but in other cases, they are more or less obligatory (*I'm, it's, that's*). As has been noted, some researchers suggest that *I'm, it's* and *that's* are single morphemes as opposed to two consisting of a pronoun and a contracted form of *be*. This is offered as an explanation for why the *-'s* form always occurs in these environments.

    Robby, who clearly uses AAE, talks about himself, and, in a sense about his use of language:

I dug being militant cause I was good. It was something I could do. Rap to people. Whip a righteous message on 'em. People knew my name. They'd listen. And I'd steady take care of business. This was when Rap Brown and Stokeley and Bobby Seale and them on TV. I identified with those cats. Malcolm and Eldridge and George Jackson. I read their books. They was Gods. That's who I thought I was when I got up on the stage and rapped at the people. It seemed like things was changing.

[p. 114]

In this passage, he comments on his linguistic prowess, his ability to "rap to people." He also uses the AAE lexical item *steady* to explain the consistent and intense manner in which he would "take care of business." (See chapter 2 for a discussion of *steady*.) Also, note the overt past tense *be* form (*was*) and the possible zero past tense *be* (*was/were*) form indicated by 'Ø' in the sentence *This was when Rap Brown and Stokeley and Bobby Seale and them Ø on TV*. In current AAE, the past tense form of *be* (e.g., *was*) is generally required to occur on the surface, but this is at least one instance in Robby's speech when it is not present.

Wideman has something different to say about experiences from his past, and he, like Robby, is concerned with using language; however, he is concerned with "good English" not with rapping to people:

Because we were brothers, holidays, family celebrations, and troubles drew us to the same rooms at the same time, but I felt uncomfortable around you. Most of what I felt was guilt. I'd made my choices. I was running away from Pittsburgh, from poverty, from blackness. To get ahead, to make something of myself, college had seemed, a logical, necessary step; my exile, my flight from home began with good grades, with good English ...

[pp. 26–27]

But Wideman felt the importance of cultural "roots" and rhetorical strategies like talking trash. The change in the subject necessitates a change in his language. Here he recalls his feelings upon returning home from school:

I was scared stiff but at the same time I needed to prove I hadn't lost my roots. Needed to boogie and drink wine ... needed to prove I could still do it all. Fight, talk trash, hoop with the best playground players at Mellon Park.

[p. 27]

Throughout the work, there is a contrast between the two brothers, partly achieved by the different styles of language. The function of language goes way beyond marking one brother as college educated and the other as streetwise. Robby uses his language to talk about the street negotiations, but he also uses it to talk seriously to people – "whip a righteous message on 'em." B&K is also linguistically interesting because it reflects variation in the use of AAE features (e.g., in some cases, Robby uses auxiliary/copula *be*, and in others he does not) and also highlights features that occur consistently in the variety but that have not been discussed in the linguistic studies of AAE. For example the infix *own* (as discussed in conjunction with the lexicon in chapter 1) has not been discussed in linguistic analyses of AAE, but it occurs in B&K from time to time, as the following examples from Robby's story illustrate:

(42)   a. They say I write about the things they be thinking. Say it's like listening to **their own self** thinking. (p. 87)

    b. We gon have to do it **our ownselves**. (p. 150)

In (42a) *own*, which is used according to the rules of AAE, is infixed between *their* and *self*, and in (42b), it is infixed between *our* and *selves*. For example, note that the pronoun *we* agrees with *our* in the reflexive pronoun. But these examples are not just linguistically interesting because they include the grammatical use of the infix *own*; they show how speakers adhere to the rules of AAE in a single sentence. For example, in (42a) Robby also uses aspectual *be* to indicate habituality, and in (42b), he does not use auxiliary *be* (*is, are*) preceding *gonna* – two salient properties of AAE.

    Ima, which also occurs in Robby's speech, is another feature that occurs in current AAE but that is not well-studied:

(43)   a. So you better believe **Ima** go for it. I'm scared and I know something ain't right, something deep down and serious ain't right, but I got to go. (p. 152)

    b. No way nobody get me inside. Almost died sitting outside so ain't no way in hell **Ima** strut up inside no police station. (p. 154)

    Finally, I will consider features of AAE in *Fences* (1986), a play by August Wilson. In an interview in 1994, Wilson explains how his view about black speech in his plays changed over the years. In telling about his 1977 play, "The Coldest Day of the Year," he says:

> It certainly was not written in the language that I write plays in now. I thought that in order to create art out of black life – because I didn't value the way that blacks speak – you had to change it. So you had lines like, 'Our lives frozen in deepest heats of spiritual turbulence.' Now, if I were going to write it, I guess the guy would just walk up to the woman and say, 'How you doing, Mama? We're out here in the cold.' . . .
>
> [Shannon [1994] 1999, p. 366]

The language in *Fences* definitely reflects Wilson's changed view about the speech of his black characters. It is clear from his later works that he allows his characters to use patterns that are associated with AAE. The main character in *Fences* is Troy Maxon, a hard-working man, who mourns his missed opportunity to become a professional baseball player. The following exchange between Troy and his friend Bono highlights some features that can be used to identify them as AAE speakers:

(44)   Bono: How you figure he **be** making out with that gal **be** up at Taylors' all the time . . . that Alberta gal?

    Troy: Same as you and me. Getting just as much as we is. Which is to say nothing.

    Bono: It is, huh? I figure you doing a little better than me . . . and I ain't saying what I'm doing.

    Troy: . . . I know you. If you had got anywhere near that gal, twenty minutes later you be looking to tell somebody. And the first one you gonna tell . . . that you gonna want to brag to . . . is gonna be me.

    Bono: I ain't saying that. I see where you **be** eyeing her.

    Troy: I eye all the women. I don't miss nothing. Don't never let nobody tell you Troy Maxon don't eye the women. (p. 3)

Aspectual *be* in Bono's first line marks the habituality of "making out with . . ." and being "up at Taylors'," so he makes out on different occasions and that gal is at Taylors' on different occasions. Troy responds to Bono's accusation about the way he "be eyeing her," (that is, he usually looks at her, probably slyly but intently) with a reference to his usual behavior ('eye all the women'). Note that Troy does not use aspectual *be* in his response, although he obviously means that he eyes them on different occasions. AAE speakers can also mark habitual meaning by using the simple (present or non-past) tense, as Troy did in "I eye all the women" by using the present plural form of *eye*. This point was made in chapter 3.

Although the *be* in Troy's statement, ". . . If you had got anywhere near that gal, twenty minutes later you *be* looking to tell somebody," is superficially identical to the previous aspectual *be* examples; it is in a conditional environment. It is in the 'then' clause of a conditional statement meaning '*then* you would (you'd) be . . .' The auxiliary that would precede this *be*, if there were one, is *would*, but the auxiliary that would precede aspectual *be* in Bono's first line is *do*. The two occurrences of *be* are different in that respect, but they are similar in that both denote habitual meaning.

The reader will observe that in the first line of the exchange, the speaker asks a question "How you figure he be making out with that gal be up at Taylors' all the time . . . that Alberta gal?" but does not use auxiliary *do* (*How do you figure* . . .) to mark it. As explained in the discussion in chapter 2, questions that are formed without auxiliaries are very productive in AAE. Note also in this statement that the speaker uses a zero relative pronoun (as opposed to *that* or *who* in the position of Ø) in *that gal [Ø be up at Taylors' all the time]*. The clause [Ø *be up at Taylors' all the time*] describes *that gal*, the object of the preposition *with* in the higher clause.

6.6   Summary

This chapter surveys the representation of AAE in literature from the mid nineteenth to late twentieth century. A number of features, especially in the phonology, were used consistently although they are not included in the feature inventory of current AAE (e.g., the patterns in chapter 4). In some cases, although the linguistic features have not been attested in current AAE, some of them have been argued to occur in the speech of ex-slaves. For example, as pointed out in the earlier discussion, selected features that are used by Brown's characters in *Clotel* are also found in ex-slave narratives. Another notable point is that some authors rely on eye dialect, which gives the visual appearance that the character's language is different from the mainstream and other varieties that may be represented in the literary work. However, dialectal representation occurs on other levels. For instance, syntactic patterns as well as rhetorical strategies are used in the speech of African American characters. As we moved to works during the Harlem Renaissance, we saw that more syntactic patterns (e.g., aspectual *be*) were used, and in later works, for example Ellison's *Invisible Man* the rhetorical strategy of indirectness was used.

The representation of AAE in literature raises questions about the authenticity of the speech patterns associated with African American characters, and it also raises questions about the types of features that are used to mark the speech of African

Americans. In addition, representations in the literature can give us more insight into what features are taken to be associated with black speech. For example, Wideman uses *ownself* in precisely the way it is explained in the lexical entries in chapter 1, although there is no discussion of this pattern in work on AAE. In Hurston's JGV, we saw examples in which there were no orthographical cues to give us information about stress on *been*. However, given the context in which it was used, the marker must be stressed *BIN*. It seems, then, that having some idea about the AAE system would be helpful (and perhaps necessary to some extent) in presenting a descriptive analysis of black speech in literature. Some suggestions have been made about using African American literature in language arts classes as a means of helping students appreciate and explaining the role and use of language in literature. Given the range of patterns used by characters in the sample works, students could learn a great deal about the use and representation of black speech.

Exercises

1. On pp. 121–127 in *American Earlier Black English*, Schneider discusses *done*. Compare the *done* that Schneider discusses to *done* (*dɔn*) as it occurs in the literary works discussed in this chapter. Make sure you include the following in your discussion: the type of main verbs that occur with it, the type of auxiliary verbs that precede it and meaning of the marker.

2. (a) The sentence in (22a) from *Jonah's Gourd Vine* is an example of the use of the marker *come*. What other AAE feature occurs in this sentence? Is the feature used in the predicted context according to the relevant discussion in chapter 2? Explain your answer.
    (b) The sentences in (28) from *Invisible Man* are examples of negative inversion. What other AAE features are reflected in the examples?

3. Consider the following passage from an ex-slave narrative by Amy Chapman, age 94: "I will tell you dough 'bout a mean man who whupped a cullid woman nearbout to death. She got so mad at him dat she tuk his baby chil whut was playin' roun' de yard and grab him up an' th'owed it in a pot of lye dat she was usin' to wash wid. His wife com a-hollin' an' run her arms down in de boilin' lye to git de chile out, an' she near 'bout burnt her arms off, but it didn't do no good 'caze when she jerked de chile out he was daid" (from A. Brown and D. Taylor, eds., *Gabr'l Blow Sof': Sumter County, Alabama Slave Narratives*, University of West Alabama, Livingston Press, 1997, p. 19).

    (a) Do the spellings used in recording this narrative strike you as eye dialect? Explain your response.
    (b) Rewrite the passage in general American classroom English.

4. (a) Give a general American English gloss for the second sentence in (37b): "They be steady ripping off people so they got that greed thing going too."
    (b) 'Ripping off' seems to be used by speakers of groups other than African Americans. Consult a slang dictionary (e.g., *New Dictionary of Slang*, Robert L. Chapman, ed., New York: Harper & Row, 1986) and trace the uses of the phrase.
    (c) Does the dictionary indicate whether 'ripping off' is associated with (or originally used by) a particular group of people? What type of information does the dictionary give regarding this issue?

5.   Consider the passage by August Wilson (preceding the discussion of *Fences* in this chapter) in which he talks about his use of language. In looking back, he says that he would have written the line in his 1977 play, "Our lives frozen in deepest heats of spiritual turbulence" as "How you doing Mama? We're out here in the cold."

   (a) How do the two lines differ?
   (b) What types of features does Wilson use in the later version? Would the line work in a play written about issues today? Why? Why not?

7 AAE in the media

Focal point   Different linguistic strategies are used in the media to mark the language of black characters. Often, current slang and lexical elements are used, especially if the characters being portrayed are in certain age groups. In addition salient features – syntactic or phonological – accurate or not may also be used.

What is virtually important is that minstrel performances reproduced not only what they supposed were racial characteristics of black Americans (minstrelsy content) but also what they supposed were their principal cultural forms: dance, music, verbal play.

[Eric Lott, *Love and Theft: Blackface Minstrelsy and the American Working Class*]

7.1   Introduction

This chapter continues the discussion of the representation of AAE, but the focus is on audiovisual media from minstrelsy to a film in the twenty-first century. This chapter presents a general overview and description of linguistic features and rhetorical strategies that recur in television shows and films about African Americans. For the most part, the linguistic patterns that I consider here are those that are addressed in the first five chapters. What does it mean for a character to 'sound black,' to use the language associated with blackness? What role does language play as viewers evaluate the images of characters in black film? In what way is it used to mark stereotypes, and how are the rhetorical strategies and syntactic, phonological and lexical patterns manipulated to mark different levels of speech, that is, different types of speech in different situations?

The question about authentic representation of black speech, I believe, is different from the question about positive and negative images of African Americans in the media, although the language may contribute to one's evaluation of images as positive or negative. For instance, the linguistic description presented in previous chapters can be used to determine the extent to which the representation of black speech in current films is authentic, but a rating of 'authentic' does not necessarily mean that the character will be perceived as being positive or negative. Language is just one of the many tools that the filmmaker uses to represent blackness. In addressing the construction of characters, Watkins (1998) comments, "We see, for example, the author's choice of costuming, makeup, movement, and environment. Also, we hear dialect and sound perspective used to provide additional layers of meaning that facilitate our 'reading' or comprehension of each character" (p. 140). Diawara (1993) considers language in film in the context of hip-hop culture. He reports that some of his students argued that characters in films such as *Boyz in the Hood* and *Straight Out of Brooklyn* "look *real* because they dress in the style of hip hop, talk the lingo of hip hop, practice its world view toward the police and women, and are played by rap stars such as Ice Cube" (p. 24). Obviously, for students in that class, hip-hop lingo is appropriate for characters in those films, who represent age groups from adolescents to young adults, and adds to their believability.

The goal of this chapter is simple: to consider the type of language that is associated with blackness and the images it is successful in creating. In the preceding chapter, I used time periods as a type of general unifying category by which to group literary works. Time is not the common theme that I used to categorize the films that I survey, and I am not sure there is one, other than the representation of blackness through language and the evaluation of linguistic patterns associated with black speech.

This chapter will not go into a discussion of even a subset of films or categories of films in which African Americans are portrayed, but the reader is referred to Bogle (1995) for an interpretation and history of African Americans in films and to other works referenced at the beginning of this section. Bogle's work covers African Americans in films from the early 1900s to the 1990s, and it treats five types of figures: tom, coon, tragic mulatto, mammy and buck.

7.2   "Chances for plenty of action and clowning"[1]

Language plays a major role in creating images of blackness so much so that animal characters may even be assigned specific linguistic features that mark them as 'sounding black'. Speech patterns, along with other attributes of characters, are intended to invoke certain images in the minds of viewers.

Images that are associated with blackness in films are deeply rooted and go back at least as far as nineteenth-century minstrelsy, in which white men and sometimes black men painted their faces black and performed caricature sketches of blacks. In addition to "minstrel devices" such as "ventriloquized dialect," "racial burlesque," (Lott 1996, p. 7), the appearance of the performer was enhanced by black face, plantation style garments, and "wide-open mouths, bulging lips, and eyes that shone like full moons" (Nathan 1996, p. 35). One minstrel, "Stop dat Knockin' at My Door," is described as having "chances for plenty of action and clowning" (Paskman 1976, p. 33). Some lines from the chorus are given below:

(1)   Oh, de furst one dat cum in de room was a dandy dressed to death.
       He looked just like de showman, what dey used to call Mackbeth.
       He said he was a Californi man, an' just arrived on shore.

I ax him whare for he cum an' rap, so hard against my door.
Wid who dar? who dar? (Paskman 1976, p. 65)

And so the language goes in the rest of the song. No description of linguistic patterns will be given here, as comments have already been made on at least some of the characteristics reflected in these lines, and then the question about authenticity does not seem to be the right one to ask about minstrels. Although the use of certain linguistic patterns signaled to the audience that the minstrel was portraying blacks, it did not accurately represent their speech. Huggins (1971) observes that "The minstrel's dialect, whatever its relationship to true Negro speech, was coarse, clumsy, ignorant, and stood at the opposite pole from the softness and grace of what was considered articulate speech" (p. 255). The first person singular present form of *be* (*am*) is used with third person singular nouns (e.g., *de moon*) and the second person singular pronoun (*you*) in the song:

(2) a. Her eyes so bright dey shine at night when de moon am gone away. (pp. 60–61)
     b. An' a who dar a-knocking at my door? Am dat you Sam? . . . (pp. 61–62)

Extension of the first person singular *be* form (*am*) to second and third person contexts may have been one of the signals indicating to the audience that the minstrel was portraying blacks, although the extent to which *am* was used in this way in actual speech remains a question.

The popular song "Dixie" was also first written as a minstrel performance. Lines from the first edition of the song are as follows:

(3) I wish I was in de land ob cotton,
     Cimmon seed, 'an sandy bottom –
     In Dixie's Land whar I was born in,
     Early on one frosty mornin.
     Look away – look 'way – Dixie Land.
     Den I wish I was in Dixie, Hooray – Hooray!
     In Dixie's Land we'll took our stand to lib and
     die in Dixie . . . (Paskman 1976, p. 185)

While "Dixie" reflects some linguistic patterns in the nineteenth-century literature reviewed in the preceding chapter, it also includes a syntactic feature that is not represented in those works, past tense verbs with auxiliary *will* (*we'll took*).

The question with regard to language in minstrel performance is not about accuracy of representation because the focus was not on depicting authentic language or other features, but instead it was on exaggerating stereotypes and creating grotesque figures. The minstrel representations perpetuated the stereotypes on which they were based, and these stereotypes, some reflected through language, were carried over into early films. Nesteby (1982) makes a general comment about the role of language by referring to the types of forms that African American characters used in early films: "Afro-Americans, regardless of class or educational distinctions, were most often expected to speak the least sophisticated forms of black English. "A drawled "Yaa-za" for "Yes, Sir," for example, was comical to Anglo-American audiences" (p. 6).

Imitation of Life (1934) is not a minstrel, but certain images in the film are reminiscent of those that must have been present in minstrels. Language certainly must have stood out in the minds of viewers as they listened to the conversations between Aunt Delilah and Miss Bea, the two main characters. The film is about a black widow, Aunt Delilah, a white widow, Miss Bea, and their two daughters. Aunt Delilah convinces Miss Bea to let her work for her, taking care of the house, Miss Bea and Miss Bea's daughter, Jessie, in exchange for a place for Aunt Delilah and her daughter, Peola, to live. Miss Bea acquiesces, so she has help, and Aunt Delilah and Peola have a home they love. Miss Bea discovers that Aunt Delilah is a superb pancake maker, and gets her to share the old family recipe with her. Miss Bea packages the recipe and offers Aunt Delilah twenty percent of the profit, but grateful and submissive Aunt Delilah turns down the money and is thankful enough that she and Peola have a wonderful place to live and the important job of taking care of Miss Bea and her daughter. How could she leave them? She tells Miss Bea, "How I gonna take care of you and Miss Jessie if I ain't here? I'se your cook. And I want to stay your cook." She uses her language of submission and gratefulness (in part marked by *I* without a *be* form and *I'se* on the one hand and intonation on the other) throughout the film. Consider some of Aunt Delilah's lines below:

(4) a. Why, she am an angel, Miss Bea.
     b. Is somebody died?
     c. Is somebody been left you money?
     d. I done put my special rabbit foot under the pillow.
     e. What is this business of hisn?

Taken together, Aunt Delilah's submissiveness, her Aunt Jemima smile and her uses of *I'se* and *am*, as in (4a), almost appear to be linguistic minstrel devices, and they may go a long way in convincing viewers that she is content with Miss Bea and in the best place she could possibly be. The features that identify Aunt Delilah's language and separate it from Miss Bea's range from *am* as the third person singular *be* form (4a) to the *-n* form of possessive pronouns as in *hisn* (4e). She uses *is* in perfect constructions (4b, c), and she also uses aspectual marker *done* (*dən*) in (4d).

Although different from linguistic devices in *Imitation of Life*, some minstrel images appear in *Bulworth*, a 1998 film starring Warren Beatty and Halle Berry. In the film, Bulworth, a white senator, was transformed from a complacent politician who told 'small' people what they wanted to hear to a politician who could be honest about why there was never very much support in the inner city. For example, when a woman in the south central Los Angeles church he visited asks him about federal funding to rebuild the community after the riots, he was forthcoming with information, and spoke the truth during his presentation to the church congregation. He explained that politicians were basically insincere, visiting the inner city communities, giving lip service and then forgetting about the people. Ironically or appropriately he begins to speak the truth in church and explain to people in that black community why they are not taken seriously.

After Bulworth meets Nina, an inner-city, streetwise girl whom he comes to admire and understand, he follows her to a nightclub, where he is exposed to a new kind of life that excites and stimulates him. Being surrounded by scenes that are assumed to be associated with inner-city black life, he dances, smokes marijuana, observes the dozens, eats ribs and spends some time scratching records in the disc jockey's booth. But the experience (or conversion) is not complete until he begins to rhyme while roaming through the dance hall looking for Nina: "What I really want to know is where did little Nina go/I'm looking here, I'm looking there, but I can't find her anywhere/Nina, Nina, has anybody seen her?" And when he finds her in one of the rooms in the nightclub, he finalizes the ditty by chanting, "Nina, Nina, where you bina?" Now he is overtaken with the 'culture' and cannot stop rhyming. "He's rhyming now . . . He's talking in rhyme. It's very, very disconcerting," observes his white male assistant. The new mode of delivery is a part of him, and he cannot bring himself to read the contrived political speeches that have been prepared for him. As a matter of fact, he speaks the truth in this new rhyme scheme. At a fundraising luncheon attended by representatives from major corporations, he delivers his message in rhyme, with backup from three hip-hop girls (including Nina), who by the way, are among the few African Americans in the audience. During his speech, he is inspired to tell the truth, and he delivers it in rhyme form: "Over here we got our friends from oil/They don't give a s--- how much wilderness they spoil." While he is most certainly being transformed, he is not believable to everyone; ironically, it is the pre-adolescent black boys out on the street who question his rhyme scheme. One of the young boys asks if that's how white people rap. At times, this film is a modern-day minstrel show, and Bulworth, like the minstrel performers, uses minstrel devices, including cool language, body language and dress intended to represent that worn by black males in the inner city. In this way, he puts on figurative blackface and does some minstrel-related tricks to convey the images that suggest that he has become a part of his surroundings. Had Bulworth put on black face literally, he would have lost all credibility as well as his face as a sincere politician who cared about the "small" people. Figurative blackface, however, made it possible for him to simulate "the culture" without seeming to cross the line of being offensive.

Senator Bulworth does not put on literal blackface, but characters in Spike Lee's *Bamboozled* (2000) do. The film features Pierre Delacroix, a writer who works for CNS network which is in desperate need of a winning show to boost its ratings. The ratings are extremely low, so, according to the white senior vice president of CNS entertainment division, Thomas Dunwitty, what the network does not need is another show about middle-class blacks because it would be "too clean," "too anti-septic" and "too white," and, furthermore, it would not entertain the audience. It is Dunwitty who gives us one of the first instances of figurative blacking up, one of the first performances. In asserting his authority on the one hand and explaining his legitimacy as a spokesperson for black America on the other, he says to Delacroix, "I am blacker than you . . . I'm keeping it real." Throughout the film, he is consistently in blackface, and it is conveyed through his language, most often by his use of slang items.

Delacroix, who is black, conspires to write an offensive show about African Americans to prove to America's viewers that the only shows about blacks that they want to see are those in which blacks act like buffoons. The show that Delacroix creates is 'Mantan: The New Millenium Minstrel Show,' which will be set in a watermelon patch. It will feature a tap dancer with educated "feets," Mantan, and his ignorant, lazy, dumb-witted, unlucky and comical sidekick, Sleep 'n' Eat. Dunwitty responds to the idea favorably: "We're gonna hit'em with the bomb diggity on this one!" He is even more enthusiastic about the dancer who will star in the show and says about him, "Yo! This kid is off the hook! This kid is off the hinges! Yo!" (As noted in chapter 1, *off the hook* is a descriptive slang phrase for that which is good.) Delacroix gets used to the idea of 'Mantan,' forgets that it is offensive and enjoys the success it brings.

There is blackface on two levels in the film: figurative blackface in *Bamboozled* on the one hand and literal blacking up in 'Mantan,' the show within *Bamboozled* on the other. Black characters actually go through the process of burning cork, rubbing the black substance on their faces and painting the fire truck red lipstick on their lips. In addition to Mantan and Sleep 'n' Eat, other familiar characters in 'Mantan' are Sambo, Aunt Jemima and Little Nigger Jim. The 'Mantan' skits are all "entertaining," either because of the fancy work of Mantan's educated "feets," some step with an oversized watermelon, the way the characters are able to act like and blend in with the chickens in the chicken coop or the way they are able to put on their hats as poor pitiful Negroes. One skit goes as follows:

(5)   Sleep 'n' Eat: I see a lot of troubles lately.
       Mantan: How be that?
       Sleep 'n' Eat: I don't know who I is.
       Audience: (*sympathetically*) Awwww!
       Mantan: Well, I'll be a Alabama porch monkey's uncle.
       Audience: (*laughter*)
       Sleep 'n' Eat: At least you know who you is.

The body movements and facial expressions are "entertaining" enough, but added images are reflected through the language. One salient feature of some people's images of black language is the uninflected *be* form, and it occurs in Mantan's first line: "How **be** that?" Rather than convey grammatical meaning in the sentence in which it occurs, the uninflected *be* form seems to serve as a marker of black speech.

Some speech events in the film, although associated with minstrelsy on a certain level, are also used by one of the characters to signify on his friend who is allowing himself to be used by the media. When Womack (portrays Sleep 'n' Eat) decides to quit the show, he says to Man Ray (portrays Mantan) in a minstrel drawl:

(6)   Yassa, Ah, what you want me to do, massa? Anything for you, suh! Ah sang for ya, I tap dance for ya, massa; I coon for you, anything just to make you laugh, massa, yassa, yes suh.

Womack uses signification, speaking what Nesteby refers to as the "least sophisticated forms of black English," to say to Man Ray that he was actually selling himself and caricaturing African Americans at all costs. Also, Delacroix's assistant signifies on him, saying, "He's not black; he's a Negro." Indirectly she suggests that Delacroix is a special African American who has arrived but is disloyal to other African Americans.

The film is linguistically interesting in that language also marks those characters who try to distance themselves from the minstrels. The Mau Mau rap group wants a revolution; the members want to take a strong stand against 'Mantan,' a stand with "some symbolism to it, some substance." They clearly have a message, but for a moment, they have problems expressing it. Virtually all the members get stuck in turn taking on the following lines when they are trying to determine what steps to take against 'Mantan': "You know what I mean?" "You know what I'm saying?" They go back and forth on these lines until one of the rappers snaps out of it and says, "We can't let this injustice go by, man."

The literal blacking up in '*Mantan*,' the show within *Bamboozled*, reveals how African Americans allow themselves to be used by the media as buffoons who entertain mainstream America. The figurative blackface in the film, in which minstrel devices are used, reflects the way blacks are seen by many in mainstream America.

7.3   Speech events in television and film

For the past twenty or so years, sitcoms centering around different aspects of the lives of African Americans, and with varying levels of accuracy and success, have been aired on different television networks. *The Fresh Prince of Bel Air*, which was aired from 1991 to 1996, features a wealthy African American couple, their three children, butler and the mother's nephew, Will, who has come to live with the family to escape his undesirable neighborhood in Philadelphia and to attend a good school in Bel Air. Invariably, Will, who is slowly adapting to the upper-class environment, uses the type of language (often exaggerated), that is typically associated with teenage to young adult African American males. In this sitcom, the language is also a marker of lower socioeconomic status, as Will, but not the children in the upper-class black family, uses it. The following is an exchange between this character and a psychologist:

(7)   Dr. Whiteman (white male psychologist): All I need to do is give you the skills
                                            you need to maintain that happiness.
      Will Smith: If you mean what I think you mean,
                                            I got *skills*.

The skills that the psychologist has in mind are strategies that people can use to solve misunderstandings in relationships and marriages. Will, however, is referring to his romantic prowess. This meaning, though never explicitly stated, is implied in the combination of the intonation and the meaning of the word as it is used in some contexts by teenagers and young adults. I am well aware that there is much in sitcoms to compare to minstrelsy, but I will not address that issue here.

Speech events in Spike Lee's *Do the Right Thing* (1989) play a major role in marking the language of black male characters. A limited number of syntactic markers are used in the speech of young adult black male characters, but they are not the major identification devices that are used to set these characters apart. For example, an uninflected form of *be* occurs in a greeting in the film, but it is not clear that this *be* is what I have been referring to as aspectual *be*, thus it is not clear that it is a grammatical feature of AAE:

(8)   A: How you be, man?
      B: Livin' large, bro.

The meaning of *be* is not transparent in this context, so it is not clear whether A is inquiring about B's general welfare or about how he is getting along at the moment. If it is the former, then the meaning of *be* is habitual, and the form itself is aspectual *be* form, but if it is the latter, then it is not habitual *be* at all; and, furthermore, it is not a *be* that is discussed in the context of current AAE. However, even if it is used to convey the second meaning, that about how B is getting along at the moment, it conveys an aura of black language. As this uninflected *be* is a highly marked element, being associated with the language of a group of people, it can conjure up images of black speech even if it is not used according to rules of AAE.

Other syntactic features that the characters use involve multiple negation (9) and various uses of auxiliaries (10). Consider multiple negation in (9):

(9)   a. **Ain't no** brothers on the wall?
      b. **Don't** call me **no** bum.
      c. Jade **don't** come here **no more**, all right?
      d. What you know bout anything – unless you, unless you dən stood in the door listening to your five hungry children cryin for bread . . . Don't call me nothing.

The sentence in (9a) includes initial multiple negation without expletive *it* or *there*, so the character makes the statement in (9a) instead of *saying it ain't no other explanation*. The sentences in (9b, c) are regular multiple negation structures in which the sequence *don't . . . no/nothing* occur. The examples related to auxiliaries are given in (10):

(10) a. What **was you** saying?
      b. I **ain'** run like that in years.
      c. Why it gotta be about jungle music? Why it gotta be about Africa?
      d. If we don't stop this and stop it now, we gon' do something we gonna regret for the rest of our lives.

In (10a) the speaker uses the singular form *was* with the second person singular pronoun, and in (10b) the speaker uses the negative marker *ain'* in a present perfect environment, both of which are common occurrences in present-day AAE. The *wh*-questions in (10c) begin with a *wh*-word but are formed without subject-auxiliary inversion, so the sentence is not produced as either of the following: *Why do it gotta be about jungle music?* or *Why does it have to be about jungle music?* In (10d), there are two possible places in which auxiliary *be* could be used, one preceding *gonna* and the other preceding *gon'*; however, it does not appear in the sentence.

The following two examples are associated with the sound component:

(11) a. Ain't gon stand for them f--- in **POlice**.
      b. Sal, my salary is two **fity** a week, all right?

In (11a) the forestressing pattern is used in the pronunciation of POlice, and in (11b) the speaker uses *fity* (i.e., without the second 'f' sound), a common pronunciation of the word *fifty* for some AAE speakers. The features in the sentences above are relatively easy to identify, but what is also notable is that there are not a significant number of sentences in which such features occur. The film clearly does not depend on syntactic and phonological features alone to help define or represent the characters as AAE users. The characters use other features that are associated with AAE. For example, they may use particular lexical items, so we find words such as *down*, which means to be in agreement with or to be supportive of a movement or plan, and they also use phrases such as *livin' large* which means to be doing well, living comfortably:

(12) a. Jade, you got to be **down**. What, you ain' **down**?
      b. A: How you be, man?
         B: **Livin' large**, bro.

Also, an older character notes that a particular brand of beer he does not like tastes like cold pot liquor. These are the types of lexical items discussed in chapter 1.

In his analysis of *Do the Right Thing*, Baker (1993b) observes that "the cultural codes of Black America make their way through the rap of Public Enemy, the dance of Rosie Perez, and the deejay work of Love Daddy, . . . They also flow energetically through the signifying of the black three-men chorus on the corner . . ." (p. 171). Baker's point is that Spike Lee uses a number of strategies in the film to relate scenes to some aspect of black America. The three porch characters in the film, referred to as the black three-men chorus by Baker, signify and use braggadocio speech. They are male characters who sit against the wall and make observations about life in general, particular situations, themselves and each other. One character signifies by commenting on his friend's limited intelligence: "You fool, you thirty cent away from having a quarter." Also, in this sentence, the speaker uses singular noun *cent* with the plural determiner (or modifier) *thirty*. This singular form *cent* also occurs with numbers greater than one in AAE, so *one cent, two cent . . . fifty cent* and so on.[2] These characters use other features, but AAE characteristics are expressed strongly in their use of speech events such as signifying.

In chapter 5, I mentioned a scene in Spike Lee's *Jungle Fever* (1991), in which a group of black women gather in a friend's living room to discuss female-male relationships. In this scene, the women use rhetorical strategies such as call and response or backchanneling. In contrast, in Malcolm Lee's *The Best Man* (1999), a group of black men gather around a card table, where they analyze and assess situations – especially male-female relationships – talk trash and signify. *The Best Man* is a story about six friends, two women and four men, who get together for a wedding and who end up resolving issues left unsettled from their college days. It is interesting to compare the women's language in the living room scene in *Jungle Fever* to the four men's in the table scene in *The Best Man*. Both groups use black speech events, but the language of the women and that of the men differ in other ways. Some of those differences are certainly gender-related, but others must be due to the relationships among the friends and to the nature of the topic of discussion.

In *The Best Man*, there are also distinctions among the men in the type of language they use. For example, two of the four men use the specialized vocabulary associated with adolescent to young adult males. In one scene in the film, Lance, the professional football player, advises his friend, the author, along the following lines:

(13)   a. I saw that she want to **git wit** you, man.
        b. For once in your life, go on and be a **dog, dawg**.

Lance uses *git wit* to intimate that the woman wants to establish a relationship with his friend, and he uses *dawg* as a term of address, a more favorable reference than the preceding use of *dog*, which refers to a male who establishes insincere relationships with women. During the table scene, he also addresses his friends as *playas*: "There's a time for everything, playas," he says. When Lance considers financial matters in relationships, he refers to money as *cheese* and *loot*:

(14)   a. And she might make more **cheese** than you someday, bro.
        b. The only way a relationship gon work is the man provide the **loot** and the woman
           takes care of the s--- at home.

Quentin, who has not committed to a single career path, is also recognized for his language use. On monogamy, a topic the friends address during the table scene, he says, using multiple negation: "**Ain't nothing** natural bout **no** monogamy... God did not intend for us to be with one person..." Quentin's friends comment on his observation:

(15)   Lance: Ok. You a philosophy major now.
        Harper: He IS a bulls--- artist.

It is Quentin who suggests that Harper take a look at himself. He says, "You my judge, right? You've always analyzed everybody's s--- and you don't do the same thing for your**own**self." Note the use of *own*, which is infixed between *your* and *self*. Of course, Quentin also uses the specialized vocabulary:

(16)   a. I still can't believe you never **hit that**.
        b. What if she did go out and **get her lil swerve on**?
           Don't you think she'd be well within her rights?

In (16a, b), Quentin makes reference to sex when he says *hit that* and *get her lil swerve on*. (The latter construction *get* – possessive pronoun – noun – *on* is discussed in chapter 1.) But these lines, uttered during the table scene, are intended to do more than make casual reference to sex, especially the one in (16b). Quentin signifies on Lance, insinuating that his fiancée would have been justified in being unfaithful because of his involvement with many different women. That statement leads to the climax, at which point Lance expresses his frustration and reveals his touched nerve by jarring the table, pulling Quentin by his shirt and walking away.

Signification during the table scene plays a major role, and it is clear that some characters are better at it than others. For example, Quentin signifies on Merchy, the law school graduate, who is characterized as being soft-spoken. He does not always have a whole lot to say during the verbal exchange at the table; however, Merchy is not an ineffective language user. He does score some points during the conversation as is evident when Lance gives him dap after one of his lines. Also, Merchy strikes back at one of Quentin's comments although he delivers an ineffectual line, "Bite it, Spivey." And to that, Quentin responds, "Grow it, Merchy," which could be interpreted to mean get a spine – to put it one way.

Aspectual *be* is not used very often in this film, but when it occurs, it is used according to grammatical patterns in AAE. The characters who use it are Lance and Quentin, the two who have already established that they can use language in certain ways; they signify and use specialized vocabulary. Certainly, I do not mean to suggest that there is a correlation between use of aspectual *be* and skill in rhetorical strategies because all that is required in using the marker is knowledge of the rules governing it. Lance's aspectual *be* constructions are in (17a, b), and Quentin's are in (17c, d, e). All of the constructions are in reference to some action with women, a major topic during the table scene. The sentences in (17b, c, d) were produced during the table scene, but those in (17a, e) were not:

(17)   a. You know you **be** kissing them babes on the forehead.
        b. They **be** making breakfast for this fool, buying him jewelery and then they try to figure why they do the s--- cause they really hate his yellow a--.
        c. That's what I **be** putting on the ladies when I do my thang.
        d. ... You **be** having these girlfriends.
        e. You know you don't like the way she **be** carrying you.

Lance's use of aspectual *be* as well as Quentin's are grammatical uses of the marker, in which it precedes verbs ending in *-ing*. So (17a) refers to kissing women on the forehead on different occasions, and (17b) refers to making breakfast on different occasions. (17c) refers to Quentin's act of putting something on the ladies on different occasions. In particular, Quentin is alluding to the **mojo** he puts on the ladies which he mentions in his previous statement. *Mojo* is defined in Smitherman's (1994, p. 162) lexicon as a magical charm and (17d) is used to suggest that Harper has different girlfriends from time to time. Finally, *be carrying* (17e) actually refers to the way Merchy's girlfriend usually manipulates him and orders him around. I should note that some researchers have suggested that aspectual *be* is used to express negative feelings and actions, but the sentences in (17a, b, c) are not negative (at least not from the speakers' points of view). It is not the case that aspectual *be* can only *be* used to talk about action with women; the characters who use aspectual *be* happen to be engaged in a conversation about recurring action related to women.

The use of aspectual *be* cannot be accidental; it is used by the two male characters who seem to be more 'worldly' and thus who may be expected to have a broader language repertoire. But worldly here does not mean of 'the street'. Then it is no surprise that Quentin, who uses aspectual *be*, also says the following:

(18)   a. Now a handsome gentleman playa like myself,
I'ma pimp this baby right here.
b. Pops, uh, gave me the key to the penthouse suite tonight.
I'm talking about this s--- is about to be ignant [ignorant] off the hook!

In (18a), Quentin is admiring himself in the designer tuxedo he plans to wear as a groomsman in Lance's wedding. Expressing approval of what he sees, he concludes that he will wear the suit well, "pimp this baby right here." Also, note the use of *I'ma*. When he says, "…this s--- is about to be ignant off the hook," he is referring to the exciting, fabulous and well-planned bachelor party that will be held in the penthouse suite in his father's hotel. That is to say that it will be a party to end all parties.

One reason that the speech events and grammatical features are successful in this film is that they are not used just as black image markers; they are used to give insight into the characters. In effect, characters use language that is appropriate for them. Given Merchy's personality, he would not be expected to use Quentin's language. Aspectual *be*, in addition to other features, is used in the film, but it is reserved for characters who can use it convincingly. The marker here is not connected so much with socioeconomic status – Lance is a famous professional football player who attended college, and Quentin's father owns a hotel with penthouse suites – as it is with the linguistic repertoire of characters and the situations in which it is used. The situation in which it occurs is one in which topics are addressed by using informal and cool language in a close-knit group.

In the films that have been addressed here, speech events, specialized vocabulary and, to some extent, syntactic features are important indicators used to alert viewers that some level of AAE is being used.

7.4   Indicators of adolescent street language

In the final section of this chapter, I briefly consider the use of specific linguistic markers, that is certain patterns, that are intended to be associated with the language used by African American male adolescents and teens. The data taken are from *Laurel Avenue* and *Fresh*, which focus, to some extent, on the street life of young African American males.

Consider the sentence from *Laurel Avenue* in which Rashawn's uncle confronts him about selling drugs, which is included to show that adults in this film also use the type of linguistic features associated with AAE:

(19)   What the hell I **be** giving you money fuh [for]?

The sentence in (19) is a rhetorical question which forces the nephew to think about his uncle's generosity and sacrifices to keep the nephew from becoming involved in drug activities. The uncle's position is that he gives Rashawn money from time to time, because he does not want Rashawn to have to resort to selling drugs as a part-time job to make money. The habitual meaning in the sentence is denoted by aspectual *be*. The uncle's question, then, can be glossed as 'Why do you think I always give you money?'

As has been noted in chapter 3, in the first analyses of preterite *had*, it was characterized as a feature in the speech of pre-adolescent speakers of AAE. Note the use of preterite *had* by the teenager Rashawn.

(20) Grandfather: Rashawn, I saw your mother's car in the parking lot, but she's not here.
      Rashawn: Oh, that's cause **I had drove** it here.

In (20) the grandfather makes an indirect request for information about Rashawn's mother's car. Rashawn explains that his mother's car is parked outside of the gym because he drove the car to the basketball game. The grandson uses the AAE preterite *had* in a simple past tense environment. As discussed in chapter 3, the preterite *had* + past verb does not denote an activity that occurred in the past before the past. As it is used here, preterite *had* may be used to associate Rashawn with a specific age, social and ethnic group.

The film *Fresh* (1994) is an interesting source of data on the way language is used to create an image of street life. It tells a story of Michael, a streetwise adolescent, and his negotiations with adults and his peers in inner-city struggles. The males (African American and Latino) who are in Michael's peer group use slang consistently in the film, so they make observations such as *I'm stupid late* and *I'm crazy late* to mean 'I'm very late.' They also use *dope* to mean very good or excellent, as in *check out that dope dog* and *I got the dope moves*. In this film, language is just as important as the drugs, violence and living conditions in creating images of the urban ghetto life that has become common in such movies. In general, features of AAE are used by characters in all age groups in the film, but I will show that one feature is especially associated with the adolescent males. Before moving to that feature, I give some general examples of linguistic features that are used by African Americans from different age groups in the film:

(21) a. A: Where Aunt Frances at?
         B: She home.
      b. They all scared to walk out the door with you to school ... I'ma miss you Michael.
      c. We gon' put it on speed today. I ain't stopping to give you lil tips either ... You ready ... You ready to be king?
      d. Kerman ain' showed up yet.
      e. Ain' nothin' gonna be protection enough around here anymore.
      f. Where I'm gon' git five thousand dollars man? Where I'm gon' git it?
      g. No woman stay here. There's no woman here.

The sentences in (21a, b, c) are examples in which there is no overt form of the auxiliary/copula *be*. The sentences in (21a, d, e, f) are used by adolescents, while (21b, c) are from adults. The sentences in (21d, e) involve negation. In (21d) *ain'* 'ain't' occurs in a present perfect context, and (21e) is an example of multiple negation. A *wh*-question has been formed without inversion of an auxiliary to the position preceding the subject *I* in (21f). Note that *stay* to mean 'live' is used in (21g). This lexical item is discussed in chapter 1.

One of the most noticeable linguistic features in the film is aspectual *be*. The first point is that the verbal marker is used regularly from the beginning of the film to the end and often by young male speakers. In fact, it was used at least fifty times by African American and Latino characters (especially adolescents) during the last one-and-a-half hours of the film. The use of aspectual *be* by the Latino characters could suggest that given their association with African Americans, they also use some of the features of black speech. It could also suggest that *be* is used by males of a certain age group who are involved in street activity. As such, street characters use aspectual *be* regardless of race or ethnicity.

Often the meaning that aspectual *be* contributes to the sentences in the film is clear, but in other instances, the marker appears to be used ungrammatically. The following are some of the *be* constructions that are used according to the rules of AAE:

(22) a. Michael, why you come home so late? You know Aunt Frances **be** getting worried when you come home so late.
      b. All his phones **be** tapped, man.
      c. My grandma **be** cookin' at home.
      d. But I know she still **be** going back there sometime for like her clothes and stuff she **be** keeping over there.

In all of the sentences, aspectual *be* has its usual function of indicating that some event or state recurs. In (22a), it is the case that Aunt Frances gets worried on those occasions when the person (i.e., Michael) arrives late. In (22b) his phones are usually tapped, and in (22c) the meaning is that grandma usually cooks at home. The first occurrence of *be* in (22d) indicates that going back there occurs on some occasions, and the second occurrence of the marker indicates that from time to time, she leaves her clothes there.

Now consider those cases in which the *be* in boldface can have the habitual meaning that has just been discussed, but its occurrence is not grammatical. I think viewers get the general idea the speakers are trying to convey; nevertheless, the *be*'s in the sentences in (23) are not used according to rules that govern the use of aspectual *be*:

(23) a. Now, am I free to do my transaction without every n----- **be** doin' some s--- behin' my back?
      b. A: I don't want nobody **be** touchin' this board.
         B: You don't own this house. You ain't hardly ever here, so you don't tell us what to do.
      c. Nikki say James tired of he **be** so small time, wanna be movin' out bigger.

The source of ungrammaticality of these sentences can be explained; in each case it has something to do with the position of *be* in the sentence. The sentence in (23a) is grammatical without the marker *be* (i.e., *Now am I free to do my transaction without...*). Aspectual *be* can precede verbs ending in *-ing*, but it cannot precede this type of *-ing* verb (*doing*) that is required for that clause. The first line in (23b) would be grammatical with *to* preceding *be* or with *be* omitted (i.e., *I don't want* *nobody to be touchin' this board* or *I don't want nobody touchin' this board.*). Aspectual *be* cannot occur in that environment, but infinitive *to be* can. I think the problem in (23c) is that the *of* requires a *be+ing* (*being*), and aspectual *be* is not in that form.[3]

The exaggerated use of *be* sends the message that the marker is associated with the inner city and language used by African Americans in that environment. It is used whenever and wherever remotely possible, regardless of the accuracy. One question about the sentences in (23a–c) is related to whether they are actually mistakes. The question is whether, due to some constraint, for example remembering lines, the actors put the wrong words together, resulting in the 'incorrect' or ungrammatical use of aspectual *be*, or whether these *be* forms were actually included in the script. In this film, aspectual *be* seemed to be used to mark the speech of adolescents, particularly boys, who are involved in inner-city street life.

7.5   Summary

Language, in connection with other devices, helps to create different types of images in films. Linguistic features from the area of speech events as well as from other parts of the grammar contribute to creating images of blackness, but it also creates images of socioeconomic, and social and ethnic class. Speech events such as rap and signification are used to create such images, as we have seen, for example, in *Do the Right Thing* and *The Best Man*. The marker aspectual *be*, which is often considered to be one of the unique features of AAE, alone suggests something about black images or more specific messages. For example, its extreme use in *Fresh* suggests that it is specifically associated with young males who are deeply entrenched in the street culture, but this is not the message that we get from characters in *The Best Man*, who have obviously had a range of experiences. A good deal can be learned from inaccurate uses of linguistic features such as the ungrammatical constructions with aspectual *be*, as has been illustrated with examples from *Fresh*.

Exercises

1. Consider the language in one of the following films: *The Brothers* (2001), *Love and Basketball* (2000), *Set it Off* (1996). (Note: There is a significant amount of explicit content and language in *Set it Off.*) What type of AAE features (e.g., specific lexical items, speech events, syntactic features) do the characters use? What images do these features help to create? Do any of the features seem to be specifically or uniquely associated with the language of African American females? African American males?

2. After reviewing *Jungle Fever* and *The Best Man*, compare the living room scene in *Jungle Fever* and the card table scene in *The Best Man*. Do the women and men use specific types of linguistic features that members of the other group do not use? Explain them.

3. After reviewing *Bulworth* and *Bamboozled*, compare the language use of Senator Bulworth (in *Bulworth*) and Thomas Dunwitty (in *Bamboozled*). Some characteristics of their speech

are given in this chapter. Consider these characteristics and others, and discuss the extent to which these characters have credibility in using these linguistic patterns.

4.   Consider a film about African Americans from the 1970s. Some examples are *Uptown Saturday Night, Buck and the Preacher* and *Sounder*. What types of linguistic patterns (syntactic, phonological, lexical, speech events) are used by African Americans in the film? In general, to what extent is the language similar to and different from language patterns of African Americans in more current (i.e, 1990s, 2000s) films?

8 Approaches, attitudes and education

Focal point In preceding chapters, general descriptions of constructions in the syntactic and phonological components of AAE were presented. These descriptions may have practical applications if they can be extended to the development of classroom strategies that are used in
teaching mainstream English proficiency. Using linguistic descriptions of AAE to develop
lessons does not in any way mean teaching AAE to school age children. Such descriptions are useful in substantiating the claim that AAE is rule-governed, but they are not
always successful in combating negative attitudes toward the linguistic system. For example, questions about whether it is right or wrong to use markers such as aspectual *be* or
resultant state *dən* usually do not just make reference to right or wrong grammatical
structure. The evaluations are connected to broader social issues, as the following passage
by Walter Mercer suggests.

Regardless of the "genuineness" of the dialect, regardless of how remarkably it may add
flavor and soul to a poem or song or novel, regardless of the solidarity it may lend to a
political rally, I say it is illogical, nonsensical, and harmful to teach an innocent black child
that it's quite all right to say 'I done gone to school.'

[Walter Mercer, from Brasch 1981]

8.1 Introduction

This chapter considers topics ranging from approaches to the study of AAE to attitudes
toward the language system. Different approaches to the study of AAE have been taken
over the years. The approach that I take in this book is one that looks at AAE as a distinct
system of language that is governed by lexical, syntactic and semantic and phonological
rules. Some researchers have focused on the similarities across varieties of nonstandard
English and have claimed that there is no distinction between AAE and other varieties
of English. In addition, AAE has been represented as consisting of two components, an
African American component and a general English component. Finally, AAE has been
approached from the standpoint of its relation to African languages. A general overview
of these approaches, all of which acknowledge that AAE is systematic, is given in this

chapter. Researchers' approaches and attitudes toward AAE have not triggered the types of debates that we have witnessed in the general public; however, it is important to know that AAE has been viewed from different angles.

The discussion of attitudes toward AAE in this chapter is divided into attitudes toward AAE as a legitimate variety, attitudes toward AAE and employment and attitudes toward AAE and education. AAE is viewed by some as illogical speech, and even those who do not deny that it is systematic agree that it has no place in certain employment and educational contexts. In discussing attitudes toward AAE and education, I consider teacher attitudes toward AAE and its speakers and classroom strategies that may be employed in teaching mainstream English proficiency. One of the major goals of this section is to highlight the importance of educational implications of studies in AAE and the role general linguistic theory can play in advancing methods that are used in teaching speakers of the variety. This chapter does not suggest that students be taught AAE; but it does suggest that understanding that the variety is valid and operates in systematic ways may be useful.

One of the major issues relating to AAE and education concerns formal instruction, strategies and intervention for teaching speakers of AAE skills that may be useful in mastering reading and mainstream English. The failure of school age children to succeed academically is an indication of the limited progress in the area of education and the need for some intervention. The general reading problems suggest that one of the barriers to success in some areas of education may be that the type of language AAE child speakers take into the classroom is different from mainstream English in systematic ways. In addition, not taking the child's language into consideration as a rule-governed system may lead to problems that could result in academic failure.

When addressing issues related to dialects of English, and in particular AAE, the discussions are seldom ever just about linguistic structure; they become socio-political in nature. Social attitudes toward AAE can be summarized by statements such as the following made by members of a talk show audience: *People should go back to their own country if they can't speak proper English. You can speak your own language, but don't force somebody else to have to suffer and listen to it.* The political side of the discussion is often linked to questions about the status of AAE: is it a dialect or a language? Perhaps concerns about its status as a language are linked to issues about funding and acceptance as a legitimate variety.

Burling (1973), in his chapter "Is Anything Wrong With It," and Labov (1972), in his paper "The Logic of Nonstandard English," set out to provide information that could be used in changing negative attitudes about AAE. In both of these works, the researchers approach AAE from the standpoint of a logical linguistic system. They echo the sentiment that nothing is wrong with AAE, as it follows rules, and is used by people in earnest communication. Nevertheless, data based on linguistic research have not always been successful in changing negative attitudes and dissipating stereotypes about AAE.

No issue related to AAE has ignited more discussion than its legitimacy and acceptance as a systematic form of communication. Specialists and non-specialists alike were engaging in heated discussions in the 1960s and 1970s, even before the explosion of the now familiar Oakland case (1996); however, the Oakland controversy sparked some of the meanest and most condescending comments about AAE that were never countered in the media. The complex concerns leading to the debates were related, in part, to the acceptance of AAE as a valid form of communication that is governed by rules and to confusion about the language system as a form of slang. There is still some distance to go in linguistic research on AAE and in framing meaningful dialogue about what it means to speak the variety. However, what we have learned about AAE over the years has served as useful information for facilitating lessons and developing intervention strategies in reading, language arts and other areas of education.

8.2   Approaches to AAE

Throughout this book, I have tried to show that speakers who know AAE know set patterns of combining sounds, morphemes and words. In comparing similar constructions and features in AAE and other varieties of English, I noted that it is necessary to study their patterns of use in answering questions about whether they are identical in the varieties or whether they have different properties. The view that I have taken here represents an approach to the study of AAE, but there are also others.

During the 1960s and early 1970s, the period during which AAE was being established as a valid system, not all language researchers were convinced that there existed a separate system of communication used almost exclusively by some African Americans. They maintained that the same features that were claimed to be associated with AAE could also be traced back to earlier stages of English and Southern white varieties. The argument, then, was that what was actually being referred to as black dialect was simply a Southern variety of English used by blacks and Southern whites alike. Williamson (1970) argued against the claim that there was a separate black dialect on the grounds that the same features that were branded as being unique to African Americans occurred freely in sources such as newspaper articles, novels and her personal files on Southern speech. She presented examples in which patterns in the speech of blacks such as the use of zero copula, marked forms of past and future, *ain't* and *don't*, and *they* for *there/their* were clearly present in the speech of white Southerners.

Farrison (1970) voiced a similar concern, noting that there were really no substantial differences between vocabulary and grammar used by black speakers and that in general English. His view was that words argued to be in the purported black dialect were also found in American English at one time or another. Researchers such as Williamson and Farrison rejected the claim that there is unique black speech on the basis that the targeted features could be traced to the speech of white speakers. The implication is that if speakers other than African Americans use the patterns, then the common source must be general English. This view runs counter to the one that suggests that the direction of spread of some features was from African American varieties to other groups in the South. Just this point is made in studies on the historical origin of AAE and features in other varieties of English. Feagin (1979) illustrates with an example of preverbal *done*, explaining the possible sources of the marker in Southern speech. She concludes the following about the source of preverbal *done* in Alabama: "I suggest that *done* was brought to Alabama by both the poorer settlers from Georgia and the Carolinas and the slaves who came with – or were later sold to – the planters" (p. 149).

Rickford (1986) examines this complex issue of whether identical lexical items in AAE and other varieties were necessarily transferred from other varieties of English to AAE as he traces the sources of the similarity between aspectual *be* in Hiberno English (Irish English, see chapter 2) and AAE. While it has been argued that the similarities are due to influence from British dialects, Rickford is careful to note that "decreolizaton and associated processes which are well-attested from the Sea Islands" may have played a role in the emergence of AAE aspectual *be* (p. 206).[1]

The more we consider linguistic features and patterns in AAE, the more we realize that the issue of its relationship to other varieties of English is very complicated. In addition to the position against a separate black dialect, there is also the claim that while some AAE features and those of other nonstandard varieties of English are similar, the varieties differ in that these features occur at greater frequency in the speech of AAE speakers. As a result, researchers focused on describing the morphological, syntactic and phonological features that were more commonly found to occur at a greater rate in AAE than in other varieties of English.

Labov (1998) delves further into the question about AAE and relation to other varieties of English. He sets up a model that includes AAE, Other American Dialects (OAD) and General English (GE).

It is proposed that AAVE consists of two distinct components: the General English (GE) component, which is similar to the grammar of OAD, and the African American (AA) component. These two components are not tightly integrated with each other, but follow internal patterns of strict co-occurrence. On the other hand, they are not completely independent structures. On the one hand, GE is a fairly complete set of syntactic, morphological, and phonological structures, which can function independently. Through the GE component, speakers of AAVE have access to much the same grammatical and lexical machinery as speakers of OAD and use it for much the same range of grammatical functions. On the other hand, the AA component allows speakers of AAVE to construct sentence types that are not available in OAD. The AA component is not a complete grammar, but a subset of all of the grammatical and lexical forms that are used in combination with much but not all of the grammatical inventory of GE . . . In the end, we will see that the distinct positive features of AAVE in this AA component are free to develop a specialized semantics that is used primarily in highly affective, socially marked interactions.

[p. 117–118]

Very simply put, Labov's model, in which AA and GE are interdependent and co-existent, is designed to account for the uniqueness of AAE on the one hand and the similarities it shares with other varieties of English on the other. In his view, the uniqueness of AAE falls under the tense-aspect system, which includes a "series of auxiliary particles found in AAVE but not in GE: *be, done, be done, been, been done, steady, come*. The semantics and syntax of those particles show only small overlap with elements found in OAD" (p. 117).

The type of system that Labov is proposing has at least two strengths: namely it opens discussion about what is unique in AAE, and it categorizes the aspectual particles as a group of elements that exhibit similar behavior. However, Labov's model leaves a number of questions unanswered. A fully developed critique of his paper goes beyond the scope of this chapter; however, some points focusing on the shortcomings are in order. Labov is correct in distinguishing markers such as *be, done* (i.e., *dən*), *be done* (i.e., *be dən*), *been* (i.e., *BIN*), *been done* (i.e., *BIN dən*), on the one hand, and forms of the auxiliary/copula *be* (e.g., *is, am, are,* etc.), *will, would* and *have*, on the other, on the basis of tense marking such that members of the latter group are marked for tense. (See chapter 2 in this book for further discussion of characteristics of members of these groups.) He suggests that members of both groups "all occur as first members of the verb phrase."[2] Indeed Labov is correct in saying that the aspectual markers can also precede verbs as in *be running*, but he misses an important point in that *have* and *ain't* can occur with *BIN* and in some cases with *dən*. As a result, there are instances in which these markers do not occur as the first members, but auxiliaries such as *is, am,* and *will* always occur as the initial elements. As Labov agrees, *do* occurs with *be* in specific environments. *Do* also occurs with the habitual resultative *be dən*, but Labov does not make this observation.

A more pressing question is related to the way Labov is able to keep the AA and GE components separate. He notes that auxiliary inversion, tag question formation and negative placement do not occur with the AA elements. (Refer to chapter 2 for a discussion of these processes.) Labov comments that "The absence of these syntactic behaviors from all clauses with AA auxiliary elements contrasts with clauses that have finite tense markers and follow the patterns of GE syntax" (p. 141). But such processes do occur in clauses with the so-called AA elements. If they did not, there would be no way of negating aspectual *be* constructions (*They don't be playing soccer during recess*), and the only way to form questions with aspectual *be* constructions would be with intonation (*They be playing soccer during recess?*); but another option in which the auxiliary *do* precedes the subject *they* is also available *(Do they be playing soccer during recess?)*. Perhaps Labov's point is that these markers themselves do not pattern as the auxiliary elements do, so aspectual *be* cannot itself host the contracted *n't* (*not*). This, of course, means that speakers do not say **ben't*; instead they say *don't be*. The point here is that although it is relatively easy to list isolated items such as aspectual markers that are used by some African Americans, it is not so easy to tease apart two systems forming AAE. There is no sharply defined evidence to support a separate AA component, no clear way of drawing such a line of demarcation between components. One question, which cannot be addressed in this chapter, is raised about the way speakers of AAE acquire the separate AA and GE components: Do they acquire the AA component in isolation? This is an important question, and it should be discussed further in the context of Labov's research. The approach to AAE which looks at the variety as consisting of two components is able to account for what distinguishes AAE from other varieties of English, but it also raises questions about how these two components are acquired by AAE speakers and then kept separate.

As noted in the Introduction to this book, AAE has been approached from its ties to African languages. Hilliard (1999) comments on the treatment of AAE by some linguists. His assessment is that "even linguists who have studied the rule-governed nature of African American speech and language are often uninformed of the antecedents or source of the rules. To understand African rules means to understand African language, history and culture. Only a handful of linguists understand this" (p. 132). If Hilliard's point is that the research necessary for fully characterizing the African origins of AAE has not been completed, then the point is well taken. Linguists working on the synchronic study of AAE simply do not focus on the diachronic aspects of the system, so they have not done the detailed historical research necessary to make strong claims about historical origins of AAE one way or the other. However, I do believe that linguists working in this area understand the type of systematic research and intense studying of documents and linguistic patterns that are prerequisites for classifying languages. Given the ties that African Americans have to Africa, there must also be some relationship between AAE and African languages, but the nature of the relationship has yet to be fully explicated beyond anecdotal comments. When researchers make historical claims without subjecting AAE to rigorous research, one major implication is that the research standards are set lower for this variety.

8.3   Attitudes toward AAE as a legitimate variety

Some members of the lay community maintain that use of AAE is a sign of deprivation – cultural, verbal or intellectual. For many, it is difficult to accept anything other than what is referred to as 'educated' English as a legitimate variety. In effect, such discussions never focus, for any length of time, on the questions about whether something is intrinsically wrong with AAE. The focal point is on the fact that the system simply deviates from the standard. For some African Americans, reference to AAE as a legitimate variety is a source of embarrassment, as it carries with it the stigma of inferiority and the stereotype that African Americans cannot speak (or learn to speak) mainstream English. On their part, the issue is simple: AAE is the incorrect use of mainstream English, and not using the standard correctly suggests that speakers are ignorant, lazy or both. Pullum (1999) addresses this key point, not just in response to African Americans, but in response to views held by the English-speaking population in general. His comment is in line with the theme of this book: "The majority of English speakers think that AAVE is just English with two added factors: some special slang terms and a lot of grammatical mistakes. They are simply wrong about this" (p. 41).

Morgan (1994), in her review of prominent issues in the study of AAE, presents an overview of African Americans' reactions to the use of the dialect. The aim of her study is to show that the reactions go beyond race to include class. She finds that a great deal of opposition to the use and acceptance of the speech variety has come from African Americans themselves. One case in point, according to Morgan, is the King case (*Martin Luther King Junior Elementary School Children* v. *Ann Arbor School District Board* [1979]). Morgan notes that some of the members of the black middle class argued against the claim that the variety was significantly different from mainstream English to the extent that it serves as a barrier to communication between teachers and students. Some of the same types of arguments were made in the Oakland controversy (1996).[3]

The King case began when the complaint that the MLK Junior Elementary School had not provided students with the education necessary to function in society was brought against the Ann Arbor, Michigan, school officials. The claim was that students (from ages five to eleven) who lived in the Green Road Housing Project in Ann Arbor and who were experiencing academic difficulty at the King School were being placed in programs for the emotionally disturbed, learning disabled and speech impaired, and some were held back or suspended from school. It was also argued that the defendants had failed to take the language of the students into consideration, a factor that contributed to their not learning to read and use mainstream English proficiently. After the students were labeled handicapped, parents responded by seeking legal advice and getting involved in litigation. In addressing communicative competence, the court ruled that the students were using a systematic linguistic variety (referred to as AAE in this book), but that a barrier to learning resulted when the school did not take into account the children's use of language.

In the Oakland controversy, which is similar to the Ann Arbor case, the Oakland School Board resolved to recognize AAE as the primary language of African American children attending schools in that district. Their proposal was to use the children's vernacular in teaching mainstream English by highlighting the contrasts between AAE and classroom English, a strategy that has been used in teaching mainstream English proficiency and improving reading skills.

What do we gain or lose by characterizing AAE as being unique and substantially different from mainstream English? For some, the characterization could suggest that, once again, African Americans are being set apart from other Americans, and this could mean buying into, if not providing more evidence for, the claim that African Americans are inferior, and language is just another deficiency. It would be hard for that group of people to see the linguistic variety as anything other than the result of too little effort and too little intelligence to produce mainstream English structures. An audience member on a 1987 *Oprah Winfrey Show* made the following observation: "Blacks give the impression that they are ignorant because they fail to see that the word is spelled 'ask' and not 'ax'." A strong judgment is levied against a group of people on the basis of the pronunciation of one word, or at least on the surface the judgment is based on some linguistic factor. But if AAE is a unique system (and not isolated occurrences of words that are pronounced differently from mainstream English counterparts), it can be classified as such and not as English mistakes.

The attitudes issue is a complex one, and quite frankly, it will be difficult to have meaningful conversations about the systematic nature of AAE if we do not address this topic in a way that gets to the source of some of these attitudes. It is true that negative attitudes have played a major role in the (mis)characterization of AAE; however, linguistic descriptions may have also left room for questions about the legitimacy of AAE in that they have not always thoroughly outlined the rules and patterns that AAE speakers use or exactly what the system looks like. In some cases, these descriptions have been in the form of a list of features without a discussion of the rules governing their use.[4] Continued research on AAE will help to fill the void resulting from limited thorough descriptions. Of course, it would be naïve to think that we could dispel all stereotypes and negative attitudes by presenting linguistic descriptions of AAE, but such descriptions would be helpful in substantiating the claim that it is a legitimate variety. For example, during the Oakland controversy, while it is true that some linguists were on hand to discuss the linguistic structure of AAE, much of the discussion focused on equating AAE and slang. Perhaps more thorough linguistic descriptions would have been somewhat helpful in responding to the uninformed claims disseminated in the media. One point that this book has tried to make is that the equation is simply wrong. Review the discussions in chapters 1, 2, 3 and 4.

8.4   Attitudes toward AAE and employment

Why speak mainstream English anyway? The most popular response to the preceding question is that it is necessary to use the standard to gain employment. The following two comments from the 1987 *Oprah Winfrey Show* just mentioned summarize this view: (1) "Speaking correctly is an indication, just a slight indication to the person who is going to hire you that perhaps maybe you can do the job. Speaking incorrectly is an indication to them that maybe you cannot. It doesn't mean it's accurate" (comment by Oprah Winfrey). (2) "In corporate America, if you want to put an extra burden, yoke on your neck, then speak slang, speak incorrect English and grammar because you're not going to get the job" (comment by a radio personality). On that same show, an employee explained how a speech consultant helped him use mainstream English more proficiently, thereby getting rid of his dialect features in the workplace – a move, according to him, that helped him enhance his chances for a successful career.

In the passages above, slang and incorrect English and grammar are actually cover terms for AAE. Unfortunately, a general argument is built on inaccurate information, to make a conservative assessment. If nothing else, it is argued that employment and improving one's chances for success in the financial marketplace should be a major incentive for AAE speakers to learn and use mainstream English, the language used in the place of business. Oprah Winfrey and the respondents on the show use speaking correctly to refer to the standard variety which is defined in Wolfram and Schilling-Estes (1998) in a slightly different way. According to that source, although it is difficult to offer a precise definition of notions such as standard American English and network standard, "they typically refer to a variety of English devoid of both general and local socially stigmatized features, as well as regionally obtrusive phonological and grammatical features. This, however, does not eliminate dialect choices altogether. We have repeatedly noted that it is impossible to speak English without speaking some dialect of English" (p. 283).

As a part of the argument goes, nonstandard English speakers should adjust their speech to the standards of their employers because, after all, they are offering services as representatives of the company, and, as a result, they should strive to be a representative voice of the company. Along these lines, employees have the obligation to speak what the employer deems appropriate for the company, and the employer has the power to demand a particular variety of language. The message is that AAE is not appropriate language for use in a professional setting.

In his review of issues related to AAE and employment, Baugh (1983a) takes a middle-of-the-road approach. On the one hand, he maintains that speaking anything other than standard English in the workplace could be evaluated or perceived as communicating ineffectively, and, on the other, he advises that "just because a person speaks street speech should not imply diminished intellectual potential. By the same token, street speakers must appreciate an employer's needs and strive to take the necessary steps to obtain the appropriate training" (p. 120).[5] According to Baugh's sources, "employers were seeking 'articulate' blacks (and other minorities) to fill management trainee positions..." (p. 118), and articulate blacks were those who were proficient in standard English. This translates into a negative judgment about AAE, as it is equated with unintelligible, incoherent, non-fluent and illogical speech. But the point that AAE is logical has been addressed over and over. Once again I refer the reader to chapters 1, 2, 3 and 4 of this book. One of the earliest treatments of this topic is in Labov's classic paper "The Logic of Nonstandard English," as noted earlier in this chapter.

Labov explains that "there is nothing in the vernacular which will interfere with the development of logical thought, for the logic of Standard English cannot be distinguished from the logic of any other dialect of English by any test that we find" (p. 229). To illustrate that a speaker can convey logical thought while speaking AAE, he uses excerpts from (L), an AAE speaker who is being interviewed by JL:

(1) JL: What happens to you after you die? Do you know?

    L: Yeah, I know. (What?) After they put you in the ground, your body turns into – ah – bones, an' s---.

    JL: What happens to your spirit?

    L: Your spirit – soon as you die, your spirit leaves you. (And where does the spirit go?) Well, it all depends . . . (On what?) You know, like some people say if you're good an' s---, your spirit goin' t'heaven . . . 'n' if you bad, your spirit goin' to hell. Well, bulls---! Your spirit goin' to hell anyway, good or bad. (p. 214)

Labov characterizes L as "a skilled speaker with great 'verbal presence of mind', who can use the English language for many purposes" (p. 217). As Labov notes, the speaker "can sum up a complex argument in a few words, and the full force of his opinions comes through without qualification or reservation" (p. 215). As logical as L's speech is, it is not packaged in a way that is accepted in certain environments. For example, while his response is direct and to the point, it would not be judged as a sufficient summary of a complex argument in school and even in some non-educational environments. L's speech is compared to that of C, an African American who speaks general American English:

(2) CR: Do you know anything that someone can do, to have someone who has passed on visit him in a dream?

    C: Well, I even heard my parents say that there is such a thing as something in dreams, some things like that, and sometimes dreams do come true. I have personally never had a dream come true. I've never dreamt that somebody was dying and they actually died, (Mhm) or that I was going to have ten dollars the next day and somehow I got ten dollars in my pocket. (Mhm). I don't particularly believe in that, I don't think it's true. I do feel, though, that there is such a thing as – ah – witchcraft.

Labov's reaction to the passage in (2) is that C "is obviously a good speaker who strikes the listener as well-educated, intelligent, and sincere. He is a likable and attractive person, the kind of person that middle-class listeners rate very high on a scale of job suitability and equally high as a potential friend. His language is more moderate and tempered than Larry's; he makes every effort to qualify his opinions and seems anxious to avoid any misstatements or overstatements" (p. 218). His overall impression is that the major characteristic of the speaker's language is verbosity, but it is in a form that follows the guidelines of mainstream English. On the other hand, L's presentation is logical, but it is not packaged in a form that is compatible with mainstream environments. An aside that I would like to make is that I do not think that even AAE speakers would use the type of language in L's passage in employment settings. So articulate, as in Baugh's use, encompasses language that is in a form that is accepted by mainstream America, and one would hope, a form that is clear and distinct.

Where does this leave speakers of AAE in the workplace? Baugh consistently maintains that speakers should do what it takes to learn mainstream English, because being proficient in the variety would give them a better chance in those professions that require it. He does note that, for some, learning the standard will not alone open all of the doors that were closed to them or guarantee them jobs, but it will break down the language barrier to employment. Nona Starks in *American Tongues*, a film that addresses dialect differences and attitudes toward dialects, gets to the center of the matter by saying that if speakers use mainstream English, then at least they will not be denied the job for not being able to speak the standard. In short, proficiency in mainstream English is necessary but not sufficient for getting and/or keeping employment. One view is that those AAE speakers who are bidialectal, that is, those who also have command of the standard or mainstream variety, will be able to compete in the professional job market. At this point, the use of standard English in the workplace is non-negotiable. Simply those who hope to participate in and "reap the benefits" of mainstream America are required to use that norm of speaking.

Jones (1982) also agrees that speaking AAE will diminish chances for employment. She notes that "It hurts me to hear black children use black English, knowing that they will be at yet another disadvantage in an educational system already full of stumbling blocks. It hurts me to sit in lecture halls and hear fellow black students complain that the professor 'be tripping dem out using big words dey can't understand'" (p. 98). But big words, especially specialized terminology, have tripped out AAE and mainstream English-speaking students alike and sent both groups running to the dictionaries. In any event, Jones contends that AAE is virtually a handicap to children and that, for her, speaking standard English means being "articulate and well-versed" (p. 97). In her discussion, it becomes clear that there is no consideration of the rules governing the use of AAE when she says, "Studies have proven that the use of ethnic dialects decreases power in the marketplace. 'I be' is acceptable on the corner, but not with the boss" (p. 98). What are the implications here? Is it that there would be a breakdown in communication between the boss and potential employee if he used 'I be'? Even for those who do not deny that producing a sequence such as 'I be' is as logical as producing 'I am usually' agree that it would still be inappropriate to use the former in a formal setting. One argument against using the former, including other AAE patterns, is that it could be another strike against an employee, and it may reduce an employee's chance of being taken seriously in the 'marketplace.' Furthermore, as I rarely see grammatical glosses of aspectual *be* in the media and other reports – which suggests that many people do not get the meaning of the marker – the employer is likely to misunderstand the speaker who uses it. Jones merely echoes the sentiment of many others, as expressed by Teepen in a *San Francisco Chronicle* article (May 8, 1991). He noted that AAE has "its own consistent usages and grammar, though it sounds merely illiterate to whites and brands every black child reared in it with a disadvantage."

In no uncertain terms, speakers are evaluated by the language they use. Indeed AAE is rule-governed; however, what is of consequence for Jones and many others is not that AAE speakers use a variety that is systematic, but that they do not consistently use mainstream English. The message is that the AAE linguistic system has no validity as a legitimate communicative system in a society in which the language of power is mainstream English.

There is nothing inherently superior about mainstream English, but it is required in the workplace because it is the language of the people of power. Those who are in power are in the position to determine which variety of a language will be used in conducting business. One choice that AAE speakers have is to be bidialectal, using AAE and mainstream English in respective settings, which does not mean that AAE should be spoken on street corners and mainstream English in other environments. Contrary to Jones's assessment of acceptability of *be* on corners, not all AAE speakers conduct transactions on street corners and those who do would conduct such business in any variety of English – mainstream or AAE. Superficially, at least, discussions such as this one are about certain types and levels of employment, but they make revealing statements about attitudes toward dialects. The topic of education and AAE, which will be addressed next, is inextricably linked to attitudes.

8.5   AAE and education

One of the most commonly discussed topics under the umbrella of AAE is research on education and methods of instruction for school age speakers of the variety. Some strides in research have been and are still being made in this area. Much of the focus has been placed on instruction in reading and language arts; however, new and much needed research is being conducted in the area of communication disorders. First, a word about research in progress in communication disorders, then I will turn my attention to issues that have been in the forefront of AAE and education over the past thirty years.

8.5.1   Over-diagnosis and assessment

A good deal of research has been conducted on the over-representation of minorities, especially African American males, in special education (Artiles and Trent 1994, Harry and Anderson 1995). These studies have not directly addressed the correlation between referral to special education and AAE although this issue was relevant in the Ann Arbor case.

A related issue is the over-diagnosing and mislabeling child AAE speakers as being communicatively impaired. According to van Keulen, Weddington and DeBose (1998), one of the reasons for mislabeling is that AAE speakers are compared to their peers "outside the developmental range or community" when, in fact, "standards of normalcy should always be the speech and language patterns of other children in the neighborhood who do not have impairments or disabilities" (p. 112). They acknowledge the major role that teachers play in referring children to speech-language pathologists. To this end, van Keulen *et al.* discuss strategies and procedures that could lead to more effective assessment. They go on to note that "the examination of phonology, syntax, and semantics can be accomplished informally or using standardized procedures as long as the child's language is judged according to the rules of the African American culture" (p. 113).

Harry Seymour, Ph.D., in the Department of Communication Disorders at the University of Massachusetts, Amherst, is currently leading a research team of communication disorders specialists and linguists whose goal is to develop a language assessment instrument for child AAE speakers. The task for the research group is to identify syntactic, semantic, phonological and pragmatic linguistic behaviors of child AAE speakers and to use the data to develop linguistic experiments that will elicit language samples from this population of speakers. The language samples will be used to establish normative data for child AAE speakers. This type of research has grown out of a response to early deficit models that branded AAE a deficient method of communication, thus children speaking it were thought to have language disorders. The University of Massachusetts project, which brings together theory and practice, is on the cutting edge of research that focuses on ways to identify disorders in the development of AAE. To date, there is limited research on the linguistic inventory of patterns used by normally developing AAE-speaking children, so the data collected in connection with this project will be useful because it will help to show what type of constructions child AAE speakers use and the extent to which it is different from and similar to adult AAE. As a result, there will be appropriate standards of normalcy to which the language of child AAE speakers can be compared. In a word, this data will make it possible to take the steps that van Keulen *et al.* advocate. It is hoped that if children are identified as developing normally linguistically according to their peers in the same speech communities or with the same type of speech patterns, then they are less likely to be over-diagnosed or mislabeled as being impaired. This research fills a void in the study of AAE, and it will answer a number of questions about the assessment of the language of speakers of AAE.

8.5.2   AAE and education from the 1960s to the twenty-first century

Over the years, work on AAE and education has been from the perspective of educators, psychologists and linguists and has concentrated on linguistics and reading, classroom practice, law and policy, attitudes and education and integrating linguistic theory and teaching AAE child speakers. A major force that served as the impetus for careful deliberation on topics related to AAE and educational issues was the challenge that children faced in public schools, in general, and learning to read, in particular.

The problem that African American youth encounter in reading has been documented in studies that show that reading scores for African Americans in inner cities are well below the mean, below the basic level or reading level for a particular grade. According to the National Center for Education Statistics, National Assessment of Educational Progress (NAEP), in the fourth grade in 1992 67% African Americans were performing below the basic level, in 1994, 69% were performing below the basic level and in 1998, 64% were below the basic level. In the eighth grade in 1992, 55% were below the basic level, in 1994, 56% were below the basic level, and in 1998, 47% were below the basic level. In the twelfth grade in 1992, 39% were below the basic level, in 1994, 48% were below the basic level and in 1998, 43% were below the basic level. While there was improvement in some grades, overall, African Americans still lagged behind their white peers. Compare these percentages to those reported for their white counterparts: In fourth grade in 1992, 29% whites were below the basic level, in 1994, 29% were below the basic level and in 1998, 27% were below the basic level. In the eighth grade in 1992, 22% whites were below the basic level, in 1994, 22% were below the basic level and in 1998, 18% were below the basic level. Finally in the twelfth grade in 1992, 14% were below the basic level, in 1994, 19% were below the basic level and in 1998, 17% were below the basic level.

The April 6, 2001, NAEP report found that African Americans are still falling behind in reading. In 2000, 63% African Americans in the fourth grade were reading below the basic level, and 27% whites were below that level. Eighth and twelfth grade assessments were not completed in 2000 (see Table 1). These data alone cannot answer questions about the extent to which language serves as a factor in the low performance of the large percentage of African Americans, and, more than likely, there are a number of factors that conspire to yield such results. In any case, factors centering around the speech and language patterns of AAE speakers have been strongly suggested to be related to their reading performance. The papers in the Baratz and Shuy (1969) volume connect reading to language as well as do other sources that will be discussed in this chapter. Research on AAE and education should directly address issues related to improving the education and performance of African Americans in reading, in particular, and in other disciplines, in general.

Table 1. *Students reading below the basic level*

Year	Grade	African Americans	Whites
1992	4th	67%	29%
	8th	55%	22%
	12th	39%	14%
1994	4th	69%	29%
	8th	56%	22%
	12th	48%	19%
1998	4th	64%	27%
	8th	47%	18%
	12th	42%	17%
2000	4th	63%	27%
	8th	—	—
	12th	—	—

Source: National Center for Education Statistics, National Assessment of Educational Progress

Baratz and Shuy (1969) introduce the papers in their volume on this issue by noting that "Reports from city after city with substantial numbers of economically deprived black children have indicated that reading achievement for this group is well below the national norm" (p. ix). In his paper in that volume, Baratz maintains that the inner-city African American child was "speaking a significantly different language from that of his middle-class teachers. Most of his middle-class teachers have wrongly viewed his language as pathological, disordered, 'lazy speech'. This failure to recognize the interference from the child's different linguistic system, and consequent negative teacher attitudes towards the child and his language, lead directly to reading difficulties and subsequent school failure" (p. 93). In general, the papers in the volume explain the differences between AAE and classroom English and how they impede reading progress. In addition the papers offer suggestions on how to use children's own language in teaching them reading. The data in these papers are based on linguistic research and/or classroom observation and interaction. Two emerging themes in the book are that the children's speech differs in systematic ways from mainstream English and their speech patterns should be taken into consideration in developing lessons that are used for reading and literacy instruction. The papers do not present fully developed lessons that teachers can use in units on reading, but they do outline specific phonological, syntactic and morphological differences between AAE and mainstream English and explain where these differences may interfere with reading progress. All the papers present ways in which linguistic principles can be used in developing teaching strategies. Also, some of the papers in the volume support the claim that children would benefit from dialect readings, which reflect general features and patterns of AAE. As Wolfram and

Fasold (1969) note in their contribution, "What appears to be needed, then, is a linguistic adaptation or translation of reading materials to a language system which more closely approximates the child's oral language behavior" (p. 141). Linguists still support this view, and I will have more to say about it in the following section. The Baratz and Shuy study marks the beginning of the type of research on AAE and education that has continued over the past thirty years. It is unfortunate that, in spite of this research, some of the same problems persist in educating African American youth.

Baugh's remarks on education and AAE point directly to the relationship between attitudes and the use of this variety of speech in the educational system. He notes that "the majority of black parents whom I have interviewed through the years, spanning both poles of the political spectrum, overwhelmingly stress the past, present, and future role of education as a means of attaining a better life for themselves and their children" (1983a, p. 108). Although AAE is a system with definable patterns, parents are nevertheless unlikely to agree that their children should be taught in an educational system that validates or accepts the variety as a legitimate means of communication by using texts and materials written in it. In fact it is the case that schools are viewed as the very places where children can and should be able to escape the nonstandard language of the street and the less educated. Some of the disapproval may stem from the incorrect assumption that the language of instruction will be strictly AAE, or that AAE will be taught; thus children will not have the opportunity to learn mainstream English, the language that will be useful in helping them become successful. On the contrary, it may be the case that reading literature in AAE would affirm that the students' variety does have a place in certain contexts in educational settings, which may have the result of encouraging them to read more.

One of the strongest criticisms against the validation of AAE is that the people who seem to be most accepting of it as a legitimate form of communication are those whose children are not directly affected by the validation and who, themselves, are speakers of mainstream English. Brasch (1981) includes the following passage from Walter Mercer, then a professor of education at Florida A&M University, a historically black university. A part of this quote is also included at the beginning of this chapter:

Regardless of the "genuineness" of the dialect, regardless of how remarkably it may add flavor and soul to a poem or song or novel, regardless of the solidarity it may lend to a political rally, I say it is illogical, nonsensical, and harmful to teach an innocent black child that it's quite all right to say 'I done gone to school.' I've also noticed that the black advocates of teaching black dialect all can use impeccable standard English.

[p. 274]

One of Mercer's points is that if the African Americans who are in support of AAE have learned to use mainstream English and are benefiting from it, then the school age children should also learn to speak the standard. Mercer represents the sentiments of many African Americans, and most certainly those referred to in Morgan's study (summarized in section 8.3). In effect, his point is that the proponents of AAE are using mainstream English as successful researchers, and they are not giving child AAE speakers the same opportunity to use the language of the marketplace, a necessary step in reaping the benefits available to them. But there are two additional issues, and the problem is how to address them both adequately. One issue is that the sequence *dən gone* (in Mercer's example, 'I done gone to school') is not accepted in educational environments, nor is it appropriate in some employment settings. The other is that the *dən gone* sequence is rule-governed and to that end grammatical; it is right, unlike the sequence **dən going*, which is wrong. I think that one of the major problems is the type of descriptions used to characterize AAE and speakers' use of it. Mercer indicates that there is something wrong with suggesting that using the *dən gone* sequence is all right. Adjectives such as *wrong* and *all right* have loaded meanings that can apply to the grammatical patterns as well as to the ethical nature related to allowing a speaker to use language that is not compatible with being upwardly mobile. For Mercer, the fact that *dən gone* is not accepted in mainstream settings overrides the grammatical nature of the construction.

8.5.2.1   *Classroom strategies*

Attitudes toward AAE influence the type of classroom practices and strategies teachers employ in instructing speakers of AAE. In reporting on early research, Labov (1995) notes that "Experimental approaches to the effects of speech on teachers' attitudes show that it is the most powerful single factor in determining teachers' predictions of student performance" (p. 49). He goes on to note that "The main effect of a child speaking AAVE was to affect teachers' attitudes toward the child, with a resultant negative expectation that affected teachers' behavior toward the child in many ways" (p. 49). The discussion will follow with an overview of teacher attitudes and strategies that have been suggested and used for teaching speakers of AAE. From the discussion, it will be clear that the strategies do not involve teaching AAE, a misconception that goes back to debates in the 60s and 70s and resurfaced in the 90s.

Brasch (1981) chronicles the scholarly research and reactions to the identification of AAE as a rule-governed system that should be respected as such. The responses to early work on AAE by linguists such as Beryl Bailey, Ralph Fasold, William Labov, Claudia Mitchell-Kernan and William Stewart ranged from labels such as bad English to a socially unacceptable way of speaking that prevented African Americans from competing in mainstream America. The copious news articles and replies to research on AAE, which began in about 1967, read much like those in response to the 1996 Oakland case. Brasch recalls a response to the Baratz and Shuy (1969) volume that has been discussed above. Gail M. Donovan, an administrative assistant to the superintendent of schools in Philadelphia, sent a memo to senior administrators noting that its contents were "intrinsically sound." It appears that the *Philadelphia Daily News* added content to the memo in an article entitled "Order to OK 'Black English' in Schools Comes Under Fire" (p. 268). The title suggested that the memo sent by Donovan was intended to endorse the use of AAE in the classroom, which was not the case. Another misinformed outcry during this period came from the National Association for the Advancement of Colored People (NAACP) in response to a Standard English Proficiency (SEP) program at Brooklyn College that was designed to help students become proficient in mainstream English. The NAACP incorrectly assumed that the program would be used to teach AAE.

AAE has not been endorsed in all classrooms in which it would be relevant, and in fact one method of approaching the variety is eradication, the goal of which is to erase its traces from the speech of children who use it. One method of eradication is subjecting the speaker to constant correction, a method which Smitherman (and others) opposes. In her essay, "English Teacher, Why You Be Doing the Thangs You Don't Do?" (2000), she explicitly shows the relation between teacher attitudes and classroom practice. The question posed in the title may be put another way: English teacher, why do you make a habit of doing what you shouldn't do? The title is essentially rhetorical, as Smitherman basically says that there really is no reasonable explanation for taking the correctionist approach in teaching English courses to speakers of AAE. She suggests that some well-intentioned teachers take such an approach under the assumption that they are equipping dialect speakers with tools that will help them in the real world. According to Smitherman, this is a misguided notion. She goes on to explain that often correcting grammar supercedes focus on and attention to meaning and sense in students' essays.

Reading and speaking instruction for speakers of AAE often includes pronunciation correction that discourages the students and inhibits them in the classroom. Smitherman (1977, pp. 217–218) recounts one case in which constant correction had a negative effect on the student's performance:

(3) Student (excitedly):   Miz Jones, you remember that show you tole us bout? Well, me and my momma 'nem –
     Teacher (interrupting with a "warm" smile): Bernadette, start again, I'm sorry, but I can't understand you.

     Student (confused):   Well, it was that show, me and my momma –
     Teacher (interrupting again, still with that "warm" smile): Sorry, I still can't understand you.
     (Student, now silent, even more confused than ever, looks at floor, says nothing.)

     Teacher: Now, Bernadette, first of all, it's *Mrs*. Jones, not *Miz* Jones. And you know it was an *exhibit*, not a show. Now, haven't I explained to the class over and over again that you always put yourself last when you are talking about a group of people and yourself doing something? So, therefore, you should say what?

     Student: My momma and me – t
     Teacher (exasperated): No! My mother and I. Now start again, this time right.
     Student: Aw, that's okay, it wasn't nothin.

One observation about this unfortunate interaction is that obviously the teacher and student were not communicating, and it is clear that the reason for lack of communication was not the one the teacher gave: "I'm sorry, but I can't understand you." There is no doubt that the message sent to the student was that the teacher was concerned more about the form of the child's response than the response itself. Evidence that the teacher followed the student and understood what she was saying comes in the form of the teacher's translating the student's 'nonstandard' speech into the more accepted variety that the student was being prodded to use. The end result was that the student eventually became frustrated and lost all interest and enthusiasm for the message she was trying to communicate. From the teacher's standpoint, the student was using an unacceptable code that did not correspond to classroom English. By correcting what was taken to be the aberrant form, the teacher tried to get the student to adjust her speech. As the exchange shows, the form took precedence over the message, so the content of the student's report was never acknowledged because the method of delivery was not in the classroom style. The student gave up and no longer tried to tell her story; the point she was trying to make must have seemed unimportant. It should be noted that AAE patterns were not addressed in particular (at least not in the excerpt); the teacher focused specifically on what was in general non-classroom English.

Also, the message the student received from the teacher probably sent a number of distressing signals to her. The student could have very well interpreted the teacher's response as an indication that what she had to say was unimportant and meaningless unless said in some particular way. In effect, the message to the student could have been that something about her speech prevented the teacher from allowing her to get through her story; her method of speaking evoked a negative response from the teacher. Every time she attempted to speak, the teacher interrupted her. Certainly this must have caused some confusion for the student, as she was relaying something that actually happened, and, no doubt, this was the speech she used in all other environments; and everyone else understood her. This type of response from the teacher could be very instrumental in silencing students in classes in subsequent stages of school years, which could result in dire consequences for children and their role and place as adults in society. John R. Rickford (1999) notes that it is no surprise that students who were interrupted and asked to repeat 'mispronounced' words over and over became withdrawn and hesitated to speak up in class.[6]

Dandy (1991, p. 2) reports a similar incident in which a student teacher, Alice, interacts with a student by engaging in incessant correction, which also silences the child. In this case, the teacher does focus on one pattern that has been identified as a feature of AAE:

(4)   At last, Alice called Joey to read. Confidently he began:
"Maxie. Maxie lived in three small rooms on the top floor of an old brownstone house on Orange Skreet.
"She ..."
"Not skreet, Joey. Say street."
"Skreet."
"Read the sentence again."
"Maxie lived in three small rooms on the top floor of an old, brownstone house on Orange Skreet. She had lived ..."
"Joey, you're not pronouncing the word correctly. I'll read it for you.

'Maxie lived in three small rooms on the top floor of an old brownstone house on Orange Street. She had lived there for many years, and every day was the same for Maxie.' Now continue, Joey."

Joey, looking puzzled, proceeded cautiously: "Every morning at exactly 7:10, Maxie's large orange cat jumped onto the middle windowsill and skretched out..."

"No, Joey. You're doing it again, Say 'stretched'."

"Skretched." Joey was speaking in a muffled tone now.

"Go ahead, Joey," coaxed Alice.

But Joey could not be coaxed. He did not read any more of the story. Suddenly, he had lost his place.

The descriptors used to characterize Joey's disposition at the outset when he began to read and when he finished are telltale signs. He began confidently, but as he continued, he "proceeded cautiously," "speaking in a muffled tone"; and ended having "lost his place." Although Alice was not yet a certified teacher, she had already begun to form her teaching philosophy, and more than likely, she had determined that her strategy was a good one. In both instances, the teachers' intentions were well placed, but the results were undesirable, and it is not clear that the students had any concrete idea about what the teachers were objecting to and correcting. Researchers agree that correcting what appear to be language errors can be very ineffective and counterproductive. According to van Keulen *et al.* (1998), "Calling on teachers to desist from correcting students' language errors is not a call for acceptance of poor performance. More than anything, it is a call for teachers to be very careful not to miscommunicate to students a dislike or disdain for an integral part of their identity and self-concept" (pp. 185–186).

Dandy (1991) concedes that mainstream English must be taught basically for similar reasons that people on both sides of the AAE argument have given: It is the language that is used in the marketplace. She contends, however, that "if children are corrected every time they open their mouths, they will become extremely self-conscious and reluctant to speak" (p. 5). According to her assessment, corrections should be made when the student's production interferes with or alters the meaning of a passage or when it distorts the content. Dandy's analysis, however, does not address the issue of non-mainstream phonological patterns such as *skr* in environments in which *str* is used in mainstream pronunciations. (See chapter 4 for a discussion of the use of *skr* in syllable-initial contexts in AAE.) If after having worked with the child, the teacher finds that she is indeed a speaker of AAE who uses rule-governed patterns such as those that have been discussed in chapters 2, 3 and 4 and if the teacher has decided to take an approach that will move the child in the direction of using corresponding mainstream English features, then she can spend some time with the child working on chosen patterns. Notice in the passage from Dandy that the teacher stopped the student when he pronounced *skreet* and *skretched*. Because the pronunciation is regular, occurring in the same environment, the teacher can compile a list of *str*-initial words that are produced with initial *skr* by some AAE speakers and work with the student's pronunciation of these words. In this way, it can be shown that one rule can apply to several words. The key here is that the child uses certain rules in producing these words, so it makes sense to use these rules when pointing out mainstream correspondences to him. This approach is one that uses AAE to teach mainstream English correspondences. There is nothing here that suggests that AAE would be taught in the classroom in this instance. Because thorough studies on reading and the acquisition of AAE have not been conducted, it is not clear at which stage AAE interferes with reading.

As Wolfram (1999) notes, "The study of various dialects hardly endangers the sovereignty of Standard English in the classroom. If anything, it enhances the learning of the standard variety through heightened sensitivity to language variation." In effect, he also notes that there are beneficial outcomes of acknowledgment of such patterns: "I have witnessed students who studied structural features of language, such as -*s* third person absence in vernacular dialects (e.g., *She go to the store*), transfer this knowledge to writing Standard English" (p. 65).

Labov (1995), based in part on Labov (1969b), explains that the phonological differences between AAE and classroom English are likely to lead to problems with reading. He focuses on the homophony that results from phonological processes in AAE. For example, *told/toll*, *mist/miss*, and *past/pass* are not usually distinguished in pronunciation due to the process of consonant cluster reduction that occurs to the final consonant clusters in the first member of each pair. In his assessment, the sound-spelling correspondences of English present problems for AAE speakers as they are learning to read. He suggests that teachers focus more on word endings (but, of course, not in the way of needless correction when students are reading), as that is often the locus of discrepancies between AAE and classroom English. However, as the passage in (4) shows, some important distinctions are made word-initially between AAE and classroom English, so teachers should be aware of them, too. It is important to know the patterns of pronunciation in AAE that correspond to classroom English regardless of whether the sound occurs initially, medially or finally. The approach that Labov considers is one that requires teachers to be aware of AAE patterns and the reading consequences for speakers using them in the classroom. In addition to focusing on ends of words, Labov gives four other principles (in addition to Principle 2) that may be useful in teaching reading to AAE speakers (pp. 57–58):

Principle 1: *Teachers should distinguish between mistakes in reading and differences in pronunciation.*
Researchers such as Dandy and Smitherman also support this principle, which makes it possible for those educators who use it to focus on content and comprehension. Delpit (1998) expresses a similar view on this issue: "Should they [teachers] spend their time relentlessly 'correcting' their Ebonics-speaking children's language so that it might conform to what we have learned to refer to as Standard English? Despite good intentions, constant correction seldom has the desired effect. Such correction increases cognitive monitoring of speech, thereby making talking difficult" (pp. 17–18).
Principle 2: *Give more attention to the ends of words.*
This principle has already been addressed above. Implementation of this strategy makes it possible to focus on the pronunciation of final sounds that may lead to confusion. Meier (1998) also notes the importance of paying attention to details about word endings. His suggestion is to discuss differences in pronunciation of words in the

vernacular and classroom English and use a variety of vernacular representations and readings as examples.

Principle 3: *Words must be presented to students in those phonological contexts that preserve underlying forms.*

Again here the focus is mainly on final consonant combinations used in environments in which they are more likely to remain intact. For example, final consonant clusters such as *-st* have been argued to be retained more often when they precede a vowel, i.e., a word beginning with a vowel sound.[7] As such, Labov suggests that using a word such as *last* in the environment in which it precedes a vowel would be more beneficial in that the chances of retaining the *-st* cluster would be greater (e.g., *last answer*).

Principle 4: *Use the full forms of words and avoid contractions.*

One reason for using full forms is that they may be helpful in avoiding confusion when teachers address students. Labov notes that contracted forms such as *'ll* for *will* and *'s* for *is* are not always easily perceived, and the auxiliaries are required in mainstream English.

Principle 5: *Grammar should be taught explicitly.*

As do the others, this principle requires some knowledge about rules of AAE; it proposes that teachers offer direct instruction in pointing out and teaching the correspondences between AAE and mainstream English.

The method of pointing out mainstream English correspondences to AAE patterns suggested above as an alternative to the correctionist approach is along the lines of what is referred to as the contrastive analysis approach. Harris-Wright (1999) reports on a program implemented in fifth and sixth grade classes in schools in DeKalb County, Georgia, which incorporates contrastive analysis in the bidialectal program. The program strives "to teach mainstream English and school communication skills to students without devaluing the language skills that they learn at home" (p. 55). In keeping with the aim of the bidialectal strategy, the DeKalb County approach embraces the importance of the child's native variety of speech as well as that of being able to use mainstream English. This program has three goals:

(1) to create in students an awareness and acceptance of the value of more than one way of communicating; (2) to create in students an awareness that American society values individuals who can use Standard English communication skills in appropriate settings and an awareness of the impact upon educational, social, and economic goals of using the vernacular for all situations; and (3) to provide opportunities for students to practice mainstream communication skills to increase their communication repertoires.

[Harris-Wright 1999, pp. 55–56]

The approach is one that "helps students analyze the differences between 'home language' and 'school language' thus providing the groundwork for integrating informal and formal language knowledge and use" (Harris-Wright 1987, p. 210). One of the tasks that students in this bidialectal program undertake is the identification of AAE and mainstream English constructions. For example, students in the program are asked to consider minimally contrastive pairs in AAE and mainstream English such as *She dɔn been here* and *She has been here*, respectively.[8] Harris-Wright (1999) reports that the program, which has been in existence for over ten years, has been successful, as "reading comprehension normal curve equivalent (NCE) scores on the Iowa Tests of Basic Skills show higher gains for students in this program than for comparable Title I students who are not in the program" (p. 58).

John R. Rickford (1999) and Wolfram and Schilling-Estes (1998) agree that the contrastive analysis approach has merit. Rickford reports the success of programs such as that conducted by Hanni Taylor (1989) and Parker and Crist (1995).[9] However, he notes that one drawback of the approach is that the type of drills used in the method may be repetitive and boring. Also, there is limited empirical research on the success of the approach, and many of the reports on contrastive analysis are outdated, summarizing studies from much earlier periods.

Wolfram and Schilling-Estes (1998) place a good deal of emphasis on the contrastive analysis approach, maintaining that it should be the basis for all programs that are designed to assist dialect speakers in becoming proficient in mainstream English. The main reason that they give in support of a contrastive-based approach is that because AAE speakers know the structure and some rules of mainstream English, there is no reason to introduce constructions in mainstream English as if they are from a foreign language with which the speakers have no familiarity. On the contrary, what speakers need are mainstream English correspondences to AAE constructions. Green (1995) considers this strategy in a paper that discusses aspectual markers and traditional auxiliaries. The paper explains the systematic differences between the two classes of items and the way these differences can be highlighted in lessons designed to teach grammatical mainstream English correspondences to AAE speakers. Also, the paper explains that it is important to highlight differences between mainstream English and AAE because the dialects use identical lexical items that may be combined in different ways to indicate different meanings. One example is be *dən*, which may be combined to give different meanings.[10] The type of information presented in the linguistic approach in Green (1995) may be useful in the contrastive analysis approach.

In implementing this strategy, it is important to understand the differences in meaning and the contexts in which lexical items are used. For example, students who use the *dən* sequences in oral responses to questions or in written assignments will understand the meaning associated with the sequence but may not always use mainstream constructions in conveying such meaning. That is to say that *dən* will be used in contexts in which general American English requires 'have usually already' or 'will have already.'

A final strategy that is used in instruction in mainstream English is introducing material written in dialect and gradually moving the vernacular speaker to mainstream English. The most commonly reported example of readings written in the vernacular is the *Bridge* series (Simpkins, Holt and Simpkins 1977). Three levels of stories were introduced in the series: (1) story in the vernacular, (2) story that served as a bridge by introducing mainstream English patterns, (3) story in mainstream English. More recently, Maroney, Thomas, Lawrence and Salcedo (1994) conducted a preliminary study to determine whether reading stories in dialect would be helpful to vernacular speakers.[11] They report that students in their preliminary study performed better on comprehension questions based on vernacular readings than on those based on the stories written in standard English. They do not present the details of the study, so issues such as the way the students responded to some of the outdated lexical items in the vernacular stories are not addressed in detail.

It is no surprise that the *Bridge* concept worked for the short time it was implemented in the school system, as initially, students were introduced to reading in a variety that was theoretically closer to what they spoke before they moved to classroom language. As Labov (1995) puts it, commenting on the *Bridge* cultural and linguistic approach: "It reduces the cultural distance between the student and his or her first reading materials, and it also reduces cognitive impediments to reading" (p. 53).

The complications that I raise here in relation to vernacular readings place some emphasis on problems with the study of AAE and should be considered carefully. One issue that should be addressed is that relating to the lexical items used in vernacular materials. As explained in chapter 1, some lexical items resist time and keep their place in the AAE lexicon, while others are more ephemeral. One of the striking features of the vernacular stories in the *Bridge* series is the vocabulary, which dates them. If such vernacular readings were used consistently as a part of teaching instruction, it would be necessary to update these stories often, given the way that some of the specialized vocabulary items change. For example, lexical items such as *split* ('leave'), *bread* ('money'), *fox* ('good looking girl') and *pad* ('place of abode') are used in the stories, as illustrated in the following excerpt:[12]

(5)   "It's beautiful, Mae. Girl, you a stone fox with your natural hairdo!" say Gloria. ("Dreamy Mae," p. 20)

Another problem with dialect readers is that it would be difficult to capture standard vernacular representations given that there is no recorded standard AAE.[13] What I am referring to here is an established or consistent code of representing words in AAE. The term standard AAE has not been used in reference to an established written form of the variety; in fact, there is no general agreement on uniform representations of written AAE. For example, as explained in chapter 1, there is no uniform spelling of *saditty*. Baugh (1983b) addresses a similar issue, expressing his views against using vernacular readings to teach mainstream English to speakers of AAE. Given the research on AAE and the agreement that researchers working in this area have reached, there is some consensus on what it means to speak AAE; however, we have not moved toward standard or uniform representations of written AAE.

Another area that has not been addressed in detail in relation to dialect readers and other material written in the vernacular is that of acquisition of patterns in AAE. In producing written material for AAE speakers, it is important to know not only the reading level of the speaker, but also the types of linguistic patterns that speakers of a certain age group are more likely to use. Consider the use of existential *it* that has been explained in chapter 3. Existential *it*, which is very salient in current AAE, is not used in "A Friend in Need" or "Dreamy Mae," two stories in the *Bridge* series, and it is not clear whether it was omitted because the feature did not occur regularly in AAE during the time the readers were written or whether it was not used regularly by speakers who were targeted by the vernacular readers. In "A Friend in Need," the narrator uses existential *there*, not *it*. Because the narrator uses aspectual *be* and *they* as the possessive marker three sentences later, it is clear that the goal was to present the narrator as a speaker of AAE. Nevertheless, the AAE sequence of existential *it* followed by some *be* form is not used. The relevant passage is given below:

(6)   "Well, anyway, **there** happen to be a young Brother by the name of Russell. He had his wheels. Soul neighborhood, you know. He had this old '57 Ford. You know how Brothers be with they wheels." (p. 1)

Also, in (7), a passage from "Dreamy Mae," the narrator uses *there*, not existential *it*:

(7)   "Mae start checking Gloria out for the first time. Gloria was a good-looking girl. **There** was something kind of different 'bout her." (p. 17)

To my knowledge, there is not a great deal of information on acquisition of AAE, so it is not clear at what ages speakers acquire certain features. Jackson (1998) begins to raise related questions in her research on aspectual *be* in child AAE. This information is tantamount in developing age- and level-appropriate vernacular reading material that will be suitable for reading instruction. There remain a number of questions and uncertainties associated with the use of vernacular readings, not the least of which is the reluctance of parents and communities to accept dialect materials as bona fide teaching material. However, as argued in research by Rickford and Rickford (1995) and John R. Rickford (1999), such material can be useful instruction tools. A beneficial outcome of integrating dialect readers into instruction is that they will legitimize AAE. If students see the language they speak in print, they may become more interested in reading in general. Also, today a wide selection of African American literature (including books, tapes and other material for instruction) is available and can be used in classes in which teachers plan to integrate prose written in AAE in the lesson. The types of questions and concerns raised here in relation to dialect reading material can be addressed in continued research on AAE. More research on AAE is available, and it will, more than likely, have a positive impact on the development of educational strategies for teaching mainstream English to speakers of AAE.

It is important to note that although classroom strategies discussed in this section are very promising, they will not be successful if teachers are not open to changing their attitudes about AAE and the students who speak it.

8.5.2.2   *The roles of teachers in implementing classroom strategies for dialect speakers*

The previous discussion reviewing different types of strategies that could be used in teaching vernacular speakers to become proficient in mainstream English is intended to show that there are different ways to approach the dialect issue in the classroom. Some teachers may have at least two main concerns in response to and misconceptions about strategies suggested for teaching reading to speakers of AAE. The first is that the strategies require teachers to teach AAE. This is not the case because children already have command of AAE when they enter school; they have already acquired it as their native form of language. The view that AAE will be taught in schools is completely unfounded especially because standard and uniform representations and rules have not been adopted for the variety. Instead of teaching AAE speakers the variety they have already acquired, teachers would be responsible for understanding and respecting students' language and providing accurate mainstream English patterns that correspond to the patterns in the child's native dialect.

A second concern is that the burden will be placed on teachers who are expected to adjust the curriculum to accommodate speakers of AAE. Teachers might be concerned that they will be expected to take responsibility for providing special instruction for speakers of every variety of English. A number of questions would follow: Is it realistic to require teachers to learn the rules of AAE? Where does this stop? If AAE gets special privileges, what happens when the majority of children in a classroom speak different varieties of English? According to Meier (1998), if it is the goal of the teacher "to help children become bidialectal or bilingual, teachers must know something about the systematic features of their students' native language" (p. 118). Teachers who know something about the children's native linguistic system are less likely to misclassify their grammatical linguistic patterns as mainstream English errors or disorders and are more likely to understand them as differences. As a result, they will take these differences into consideration when teaching mainstream English. From personal experience as an instructor of future teachers, Meier offers the following:

Although I do not require that students in my classes memorize a list of phonological and grammatical differences between Black Language/Ebonics and Standard English, we do read about and discuss these differences in some detail as well as reflect upon their implications for effective teaching practice and for the accurate assessment of African-American children's cognitive and linguistic abilities.

[p. 122]

Meier's approach in teaching classroom teachers and future teachers is not one in which teachers get detailed analytical lessons on phonological, syntactic, lexical and morphological patterns in AAE; however, they are exposed to dialect patterns. Such an introduction to AAE may be sufficient for teachers. As more and more research becomes available on AAE and classroom strategies, teachers will have more resources at their disposal that will serve as useful introductions to the study of AAE and different strategies that can be used in teaching vernacular speakers mainstream English.

The literature on suggestions and resources for teachers who work with child AAE speakers in standard language oriented programs is growing in the areas of linguistics, education and cultural studies. Also, teachers and others in the field of education who have firsthand experience in classrooms with students who use AAE have begun to discuss their strategies. Examples are the programs explained in Harris-Wright (1987) and the Academic English Mastery Program directed by Noma Lemoine in the Los Angeles Unified School District. Also of interest in this area is research and practical approaches to reading in Angela Rickford (1999).

In an interview, Carrie Secret, who teaches in the Standard English Proficiency (SEP) program in the Oakland Unified School District, discusses some of the approaches she takes in the classroom. The SEP program is designed to describe and illustrate the differences between the language children use at home and mainstream English in an environment in which the teachers and school community respect and understand the children's language. One of the questions Secret was asked during the interview was the following: How do you teach children to understand that they may be dropping consonants when they speak? She gave the following response:

I'm lucky in that I have been with these children five years and at a very early age I engaged them in listening to language for the purpose of hearing and understanding the difference between Ebonics and English. However, by the middle of second grade, they were all readers. So at that point it was easy to go to the overhead and show them exactly what they said and then call for the English translation of what they said.

Hearing the language is a crucial step. Children who speak Ebonics do not hear themselves dropping off "t" for instance. You have to teach them to hear that. So we do a lot of over enunciation when they are small. I also do a lot of dictation where I will dictate a sentence and the children write what I said, by sound only. I also try to always point out what is Ebonics speech and what is English. Children must first hear and develop an ear for both languages in order to effectively distinguish between the two.

[p. 83]

Secret also spends a great deal of time reading to her students and taking them through word flash card drills, phrase drills and sentence drills. She notes that content and comprehension are also very important in her classroom, so if students mispronounce words during a reading session, she does not stop them. The focus then is on making sure that they are comprehending what they are reading. Secret takes a number of steps to point out contrasts between sound patterns in mainstream English and AAE, but it is probably the case that her most important strategy is respecting the language the students bring to the classroom.

In discussing strategies for teaching speakers of AAE, Alexander (1985, pp. 27–28) suggests some of the same classroom activities that are discussed by Secret. From Alexander's list are the following:

(1)   Discuss reasons for the different dialects and why dialectal difference should be respected.

(2)   Discuss and role-play different situations in which AAE and standard English dialect would be used.

(3)   Use pattern practice drills to help students develop an understanding of both black English dialect and standard English dialect.

(4)   Teach new vocabulary words every day. Provide opportunities for practice of these words.

(5)   Dictate passages which contain the language constructions to be reviewed. This activity provides students with practice in punctuation, capitalization and spelling, while enlarging their vocabularies.

In order to implement strategies such as those discussed here, teachers will have to have some knowledge about AAE or access to sources on the linguistic variety, but the most important requirement is that they respect dialectal difference.

Summary

This chapter has considered attitudes toward a number of specific areas in relation to AAE. The discussion ranges from researchers' approaches to attitudes toward the use of AAE in employment and educational settings. Two of the most common topics on AAE and education are teacher attitudes and classroom strategies and instruction used in teaching AAE speakers to use mainstream English consistently in school and other environments. The type of instruction should be determined by the goal, whether it is to help the child become as proficient in mainstream English as she is in AAE or whether it is to help the student use mainstream English in the school environment. The contrastive analysis approach has received support from a number of linguists and practitioners, and it is suggested that this strategy be used as the basis for all instruction. Also, dialect reading material has been used as an instructional tool. While reports of the success of dialect reading material have been positive, its use has been met with opposition from parents and communities at large. As more research on the acquisition stages of AAE and standard representations of the variety becomes available, some of the problems facing dialect readers can be addressed. One of the major points of emphasis in this chapter is that it has not been suggested that speakers be taught AAE; however, it is useful to draw on the linguistic rules and patterns of AAE in developing plans for intervention.

Exercises

1.   Edwards (1985) argues that "the teacher should strive to make the speaker bidialectal" (p. 78). He suggests the following as a game plan for teachers of English in inner-city schools where black children speak AAE as their native variety:

(a) Learn the linguistic rules of AAE.
(b) Use the linguistic information to predict where such speakers will have pronunciation and grammatical difficulties in speaking and writing mainstream English as it is spoken and written in the region.
(c) Prepare teaching materials which address the specific difficulties that students will have or have already had.
(d) Integrate these tactics with regular methods and programs for teaching written and spoken standard English.

Now that you have considered the points in (a–d), complete the following:

(i) Discuss five linguistic rules of AAE that teachers would have to learn in following the plan proposed by Edwards.

(ii) Discuss the way in which this plan would or would not be helpful in preventing a situation such as the one in the King (Ann Arbor) and Oakland cases. It may also be a good idea to consult the additional sources on the King and Oakland cases that are given in note 3.

2.   A group of elementary and junior high school teachers have asked you to discuss with them some issues about the speech used by some African Americans in their classes. The teachers are specifically concerned about sentences such as the following that are produced by their students:

(a) The book not in my des.
(b) The spelling words be too easy.

Furthermore, the teachers are wondering if you can shed some light on why students may utter sentences such as the ones in (c) and (d):

(c) Your mother wear army boots to church.
(d) Your mother wear army boots to come out and play basketball on the court.

Provide a careful discussion of the data in (a–d), explaining the way in which you would address the issues raised by the teachers. Your discussion must include the following:

(i) General description of AAE
(ii) Explanation of the data in (a–d), which clearly shows that the examples are not just random deviations from mainstream English
(iii) Evidence to support the explanations that you give for (a–d)

3.   One of the points addressed in the Linguistic Society of America Resolution on the Oakland case issue is about the language/dialect status of AAE. The following is offered in the resolution:

The distinction between "languages" and "dialects" is usually made more on social and political grounds than on purely linguistic ones. For example, different varieties of Chinese are popularly regarded as "dialects," though their speakers cannot understand each other, but speakers of Swedish and Norwegian, which are regarded as separate "languages," generally understand each other. What is important from a linguistic and educational point of view is not whether AAVE is called a "language" or a "dialect" but rather that its systematicity be recognized.

Explain what is meant by "What is important from a linguistic and educational point of view is not whether AAVE is called a 'language' or a 'dialect' but rather that its systematicity be recognized." In your opinion, is the classification of AAE as a dialect or language important from an educational point of view? Why or why not?

4.   As discussed in Chapter 3, preterite *had* is used in narrative contexts to mark an event that occurred in the past. Its use differs from the past perfect *had*, which is used to mark the past before the past. Because preterite *had* occurs in narrative contexts, it is likely that constructions such as the following will occur in the speech and writing of students:

    (a) During the summer, I had read three books.
        'During the summer, I read three books'
    (b) We had went to the library during enrichment period.
        'We went to the library during enrichment period'
    (c) I had got strep throat on the last day of school.
        'I got strep throat on the last day of school'

What strategies would you use in teaching students the mainstream correspondences (given in single quotes) to preterite *had* constructions in AAE? Also, how would you point out the differences between the preterite *had* constructions such as (a–c) above and the pluperfect (past perfect) *had* construction (e.g., *She had eaten when I arrived*).

5.   How would you explain to someone with no background in linguistics that AAE exists and that it is not mainstream English with a bunch of errors? Are you actually convinced of the view that AAE results from a failed attempt to produce mainstream English is incorrect and uninformed? Explain your response.

6.   It has been suggested that it may be useful to use African American literature in language arts classes, especially in programs with a standard English proficiency component designed to help students master classroom English and also respect and appreciate AAE. Can you see ways in which some of the works presented in chapter 6 would be useful in such programs? Explain your answer.

Notes

1 Lexicons and meaning

1 The point about hip-hop in certain segments of mainstream America is a separate issue.

2 Refer to Fromkin *et al.* (2000) for an introductory overview of principles of word learning.

3 Abbreviations such as DCU (Drug culture use), JBWU (Jazz and Blues world use), NECU (Northeastern city use), SU (Southern use) and SNU (Southern and northern use) are used.

4 The term *funeralize* is also included as an entry in the *Dictionary of American Regional English*. It was used in the South and the South Midland areas by black and white speakers.

5 William Wells Brown is the author of *Clotel, or the President's Daughter*, known as the first novel by an African American. Charles W. Chesnutt is the author of works including *The House Behind the Cedars* and *The Marrow of Tradition*. The representation of black speech in *Clotel* and *The House Behind the Cedars* will be discussed in chapter 6.

6 *Get over* is still commonly used today and recognized in texts about specialized words and phrases that are a part of the hip-hop culture such as Brathwaite (1992). In that work, entries for *get over* are the following: (1) to obtain a goal, (2) to trick someone.

7 The use of language in the works of Zora Neale Hurston, who wrote during the Harlem Renaissance, will be discussed in the chapter on the representation of AAE in literature (chapter 6).

8 Turner presents a thorough discussion of African sound patterns, tones and words that are identified in Gullah. Some of these words are listed below:

	Gullah	African origin
(a)	guba 'peanut'	nguba (Kimbundu)
(b)	kuʃ 'cornmeal dough'	kuskus 'cassava shredded into meal, sweetened and fried' boiled, and dipped in oil (Efik)
(c)	nana 'mother'	nanã 'grandmother, elderly woman' (Twi)
(d)	wudu 'witchcraft'	vodu 'a good or bad spirit, sorcery' (Fon)
(e)	yam 'sweet potato'	ya:mu 'a species of yam that is planted early' (Gã)

See Turner's *Africanisms in the Gullah Dialect* for many more examples and for an inventory of African languages from which some Gullah words have descended.

9   This issue raises the question of coexistent systems that is discussed in Labov (1998). I discuss Labov's view in chapter 8.

10   Symbols from the phonetic alphabet are used in representing the pronunciation of the lexical items.

Vowel sound in:

[I]	hit
[o]	hope
[ə]	**about**
[ɔ]	law
[ɛ]	bless
[i]	beat
[ʌ]	run
[e], [ei]	gate
[æ]	ash

Consonant sound in:

[ʃ]	**sh**ip
[D]	bu**tt**er

11   Agreement and number marking on verbs will be discussed in chapter 3. Note that *call* as opposed to the third singular *calls* is used in the example.

12   The case of pronouns will be discussed in the following chapter.

13   It has also been noted that *mash* is used similarly by speakers in the Caribbean. John R. Rickford discussed this use of *mash* in a course on African American English at Stanford University, spring 1994.

14   At the January 2000 Linguistic Society of America meeting, Arthur Spears discussed the use of stressed *stay* by African American adolescents and adults in New York.

15   The *be* form in this sentence is referred to as aspectual *be*, and it is distinguished from the copula/auxiliary *be* (*is*, *are*, etc.) by the meaning it assigns to predicates. This marker will be discussed in more detail in the next chapter.

16   Baugh (1984) notes that the restriction is that *steady* cannot occur with an indefinite subject. This restriction is too strong, as *steady* can occur with the weak indefinite *a* followed by a noun if additional descriptors are given (a, b). Also, *steady* can occur with other weak indefinites (c). The following examples are good although the subjects are indefinite noun phrases:

(a) **A basketball player sitting way in the back** was steady talking.
(b) **Some student I couldn't see** was steady singing.
(c) I couldn't follow the lecture because **some student** was steady talking.

17   One exception is the entry for aspectual *be* in the *Dictionary of American Regional English*.

18   The marker *BIN* will be represented in capital letters to indicate that it is stressed, and *dən* will be spelled with a schwa (ə) throughout this book, to indicate that it is unstressed.

19   The term 'eventuality' is used in the most general sense as a cover term for states and activities.

20   Specific terms of address may also be used for specialized groups within the African American population. The Five Percenters, an Islamic organization based in New York, refer to one another as god, and use "Peace god" as a greeting. (See Brathwaite (1992) for a brief discussion of Five Percenters.)

21   Brathwaite (1992) is a compilation of terms that were used in and popularized by the hip-hop culture. In the Introduction to the book, James Bernard notes that "hip-hop culture is driven by clever wordplay and skillful delivery . . . The words and phrases may have been familiar but their meaning took flight on new paths." The point here is that the words and phrases probably had meanings that were common to the general public, but they came to have different meanings.

2   Syntax part I: verbal markers in AAE

1   This *be* is also referred to as invariant *be* and *be$_2$* in the literature.

2   An attempt has been made to represent the paradigms in general AAE forms. There are a number of constraining factors: 1) pronunciations may differ due to regional and other type of variation in AAE, and 2) there is no standard official written AAE, so some inconsistencies, especially in spellings, are inevitable.

3   See the following references for discussions of variation in AAE: Labov (1969a), Wolfram (1969, 1974), Fasold (1972), Baugh (1983), Rickford, Ball, Blake, Jackson, Martin (1991), Mufwene (1992) and Rickford (1999).

4   In some environments, the form preceding the verb is pronounced [In], as in *He In eat*. The form may be a reduced version of *didn't or ain't*. Also, see Weldon (1995) for a discussion of such issues related to *ain't*.

5   Coles (1996) discusses future interpretations of *I'ma* in AAE.

6   It is not general consensus that *it's* is a contracted form of *it is* (and likewise that *that's* and *what's* are contracted forms of *that is* and *what is*, respectively). DeBose and Faraclas (1993) argue that *I'm, that's* and *what's* are variants of the pronouns *I, that* and *what*, respectively. Blake (1997) also considers similar issues.

7   In standard orthography, aspectual markers may be spelled the same way auxiliaries are spelled, but there may be differences in pronunciation, as indicated by the representation of the stressed and unstressed vowels in these markers here.

8   The meanings associated with aspectual markers *be*, *BIN* and *dən* are discussed in Déchaine (1993) and Green (1993, 1998a, b, 2000).

9   The form is written as *bes* or *bees* in some works and *be's* in others.

10   See Bailey and Maynor (1987) for a discussion of aspectual *be*. In that work, they argue that the use of aspectual *be* in certain environments is an innovation in AAE, and they also compare it to auxiliary *be*.

11   Green (2000) gives a semantic analysis of aspectual *be* that focuses on its function of coercing a state to have temporary properties.

12   *BIN* is written in capitals letters to indicate that it is stressed or accented when it is pronounced. Rickford (1975) uses *BÍN* as a notation for the marker.

13   In Green (1998b), *BIN* is defined as a remote past marker that relates "some eventuality expressed by the following predicate to a time in the remote past" (133). The account uses parts of Parsons's (1990) events analysis in accounting for *BIN*. The interested reader is referred to that discussion.

14   *BIN* followed by an adverb or preposition is also attested in conversation:

(a) They BIN around. (attested)
(b) I BIN out there. (attested)

However, *BIN* followed by a noun occurs less often in my data.

15   Janna Oetting, Ph.D., who conducted this research, is in the Department of Communication Sciences and Disorders at Louisiana State University. The project is supported by a grant from the National Institute on Deafness and Other Communication Disorders. Some of the findings are in Oetting and McDonald (2001). The examples from Oetting's data are given below:

(a) We BIN having a car.
(b) Because I BIN knowing how to make them with legos.

16   This sentence can also mean 'I bought it a long time ago.'

17   This is the only example of a present tense verb form of an irregular verb in the BIN_{COMP} construction that I have in my data.

18   The notions in-progress state and resultant state are from Parsons's (1990) events analysis.

19   See Terry (2000) for a treatment of *dən* sequences as the perfect in AAE.

20   See Green (1998a) for a discussion about the parallels between *dən* constructions and the present perfect. They are similar in that they disallow some of the same types of adverb phrases. The following italicized adverb phrases are ungrammatical with *dən* constructions as well as with perfect constructions:

(a) *I *dən* went back to visit *two months ago*. (cf. I have gone back to visit two months ago.)
(b) *I *dən* went back to visit *last weekend*. (cf. I have gone back to visit last weekend.)
(c) *I *dən* went back to visit *yesterday*. (p. 48, cf. I have gone back to visit yesterday.)

21   Some uses of *done* in the ex-slave narratives are similar to the uses in Feagin's data. For example, the following is reported in *Gabr'l Blow Sof: Sumter County, Alabama, Slave Narratives*.

When I heard from her atter surrender she done dead and buried. (p. 23)

22   For more discussion of this *be dən* sequence, see Dayton (1996) and Labov (1998). Also see Baugh (1983a) for discussion of *be dən* sequences.

23   Myhill (1991) discusses this notion of attitude for aspectual *be*, and Labov (1998) argues that a range of feelings is associated with *dən*.

24   Jaeggli and Hyams (1993) look at cases of aspectual *come* and *go* in mainstream varieties of English, which may slightly resemble the *come* discussed here.

3   Syntax part 2: syntactic and morphosyntactic properties in AAE

1   The analyses in some of these works are in the syntactic frameworks of Government and Binding Theory, Head Phrase Structure Driven Grammar and Optimality Theory. Reading them requires background in syntax.

2   The construction in (8d) is given without an overt copula *be* form, but it is difficult to tell whether or not one is present because the word that would follow the *be* form (*'s*) begins with an *s*. That is, it is not easy to distinguish *Dey's some . . .* and *Dey some . . .* . If the *'s* form ever existed, it may have merged with the *s* sound at the beginning of *some*. The curious reader will ask whether sentences such as *Dey a cup in the kitchen* and *Dey's a cup in the kitchen*, in which the word following the putative *'s* does not begin with an *s*, are acceptable. The extent to which both are actually acceptable is not clear.

3   It is not clear whether the speaker actually used *dey* or *they*.

4   It is interesting to note that some people take *dey got* to be *they got* as in ownership. It is clear that there in no ownership in this particular example. The sentence was used in a context in which five girls were sitting at a table reading a book in a summer reading program. After a fly continued to

fly around one student, she uttered the sentence in (10n). Nobody owned the fly, so a possessive reading of *dey got* in this instance does not fit the context. Also, one person (B) who had argued strongly that *dey got* could only be used to refer to ownership had the following exchange with me:

A: Dey had a bus?
B: Yes, dey had a bus.
A: Who had a bus?
B: I don't know. There was a bus.

B agreed that a school bus picked up children who lived near his house when he was younger, and he also admitted that he was not saying that someone in particular owned the bus. He meant that a bus that took those children to school existed. It is clear that ownership was not intended.

As the examples in (10) show, an overwhelming majority of the existential sentences are introduced by *it*. *It* occurs with all forms of *be*, but it is not clear that *dey* does.

5   One account of the sentence in (21) is that both *if* and the inverted auxiliary target the same position, but only a single element can occupy the position. The sentences in (20a–p) are grammatical because either *if* or the inverted auxiliary occupies the targeted position.

6   *One girl* in (24j) certainly looks like an object, but there is one interpretation in which *one girl* is actually a predicate nominative. Consider the case in which the sentence means 'There is one girl [Ø be here every night].'

7   It is also necessary to consider the production of *-ed* in the discussion of phonology, because it is not always pronounced. As a result, *jumped* may be pronounced as *jump* (without *-ed*). We will return to this issue in the next chapter.

8   Poplack and Tagliamonte (1989) base their findings on data from AAE in Myhill and Harris (1986) and Samaná English in Tagliamonte and Poplack (1988).

9   This form of *test* (*tes*) will be discussed in chapter 4 in the section on consonant clusters.

10   Of course, it may also be the case that verbal *-s* reflects hypercorrection, in the speakers' attempt to use patterns in mainstream English. Poplack and Tagliamonte (1989) argue against hypercorrection as a source for verbal *-s* in early AAE.

11   Speakers also use genitive pronouns such as *yours, yourn, y'all's, hern* and *mines*.

4   Phonology of AAE

1   "Variationist treatments of phonological processes typically provide precise quantitative accounts of the effects of conditioning environmental factors on the occurrence of the process, and these effects have been shown to be robust for several well-studied processes" (Guy 1991, p. 1).

2   Phonetic transcription key

Consonant sounds

p-pill	f-fine	t-tip	ʃ-ship	k-kill
b-bill	v-vine	d-dip	ʒ-measure	g-gill
m-mat	θ-thin	s-sip	tʃ-chip	ŋ-sing
w-witch	ð-then	z-zip		
		n-note	dʒ-judge	
		l-lip	y-yes	
		r-rip		

Vowel sounds

i-feet	ə-about
I-fit	ʌ -cup
e-bait	U-put
ɛ-bet	u-boot
æ-ash	ɔ-bought
	o-boat
	a-pot

3 He based his findings on classroom correction tests in which his informants were not successful in correcting the -ed elements in sentences such as in (4).

4 Wolfram and Fasold (1974, p. 130) give the following list of consonant clusters in which the final consonant may be absent.

Phonetic cluster	Type I	Type II
[st]	test, post, list	missed, messed, dressed
[sp]	wasp, clasp, grasp	
[sk]	desk, risk, mask	
[ʃt]		finished, crashed
[zd]		raised, composed, amazed
[dʒd]		judged, charged, forged
[ft]	left, craft, cleft	laughed, stuffed, roughed
[vd]		loved, lived, moved
[nd]	mind, find, mound	rained, fanned, canned
[md]		named, foamed, rammed
[ld]	cold, wild, old	called, smelled, killed
[pt]	apt, adept, inept	mapped, stopped, clapped
[kt]	act, contact, expect	looked, cooked, cracked

Type II clusters result from adding the suffix -ed to the word.

5 It has been suggested that some speakers produce words such as *postes*; however, I have not heard this pronunciation used regularly. Interestingly, the following sentence occurs in Zora Neale Hurston's novel *Jonah's Gourd Vine*:

Dis heah mus' be de cotton-gin wid all dem folks and hawses and buggies tied tuh de hitchin' postes. (p. 15)

6 Rickford (1999) mentions deletion of *d* and *g* in auxiliaries in his list of phonological and grammatical features for AAE. As noted in chapter 2, *I'ma* is a variant of *I'm gonna/gon*.

7 Mary Ziegler, Ph.D., in a presentation at the 2001 annual meeting of the Linguistic Society of America, discussed related data for African American speakers in Atlanta, GA.

8 The final *r* is not represented here. *r* sounds will be discussed in section 4.5.

9 But see chapter 1, in which it is noted that *ting* ('thing') occurs in Gullah.

10 The consonant sounds *r* and *l* are referred to as liquids. "The term liquid is a nontechnical, impressionistic, expression indicating that the sound is smooth and flows easily (Akmajian, Demers, Farmer, Harnish 1995, p. 72).

11 For example, McCarthy (1991) discusses processes with *r* in a variety of English spoken in Eastern Massachusetts, and Sledd (1958) also discusses similar processes with *r* in varieties of English.

12   The *nd* cluster is not necessarily produced in this environment. This issue is addressed in section 4.2.

13   As a reviewer noted, another example is *guitar* (GUItar), in which the first syllable is stressed.

5   Speech events and rules of interaction in AAE

1   Dandy's (1991) model of the system of communication in black communications. Reprinted with permission of African American Images.

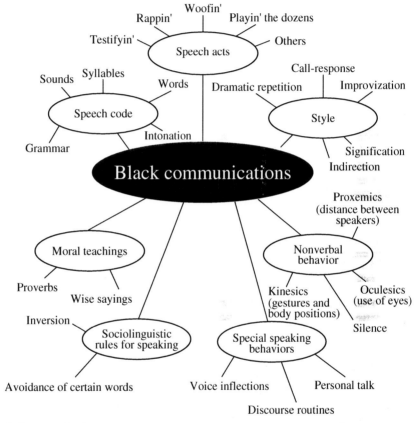

Black communications

2   Nonverbal communication occurs in all cultures, so it is not restricted to African Americans. The readers can judge the extent to which the nonverbal communication that is being described here differs from that in other cultures. Here I use black to avoid restricting this behavior to African Americans. As Rickford and Rickford (1976) note, similar nonverbal behavior is observed in the Caribbean.

3   I have made particular reference to African American, but there may also be some similarities between African American church services described here and church services by other people of African origin. The African American church service is indeed complex and cannot be discussed adequately here because the goal is to consider issues that relate to speech events. See Pitts (1993) and references in that book for more thorough discussions of African American church services.

4   The call and response strategy is also used in church songs. The congregation gets involved with song leaders who "raise" hymns. For example, the song leader may call out the lines of the song "I Love the Lord."

Leader: I love the Lord; He heard my cry and pitied my every groan.
Congregation: I love the Lord; He heard my cry and pitied my every groan.

This continues with the leader calling out or speaking the lines and the congregation singing the repetition in long, drawn-out notes.

5   Not all of the congregation's responses are captured. What I give are some of the most salient ones.

6   The passage including the second line is provided here:

Pastor: ...The brother said I press toward the mahk [mark]. I, I remember when I was a boy an' I was slow about growin. Everybody had outgrew me. I was a runt. I was eighteen. I was about like that [*raises hand to show height*] an' I was lookin like a ol man...Are you gon pray wit me? Tha's what my uncles use to call me, ol man, 'cause I wadn't growin...

7   See chapter 7 for a discussion of AAE in the media. Questions about the representation of AAE will be addressed there.

8   Smitherman (1995) also refers to the 'war council' in her 1995 paper on signifying and the dozens ("If I'm Lyin, I'm Flyin: The Game of Insult in Black Language"). I return to Lee's *Jungle Fever* in chapter 7.

9   Much of the bragging in current commercial rap is about material possession (e.g., clothes, jewelery, cars, sexual conquests).

10   Baugh (1983a) discusses this notion of continuum and the African American English-speaking population. For Baugh, those speakers who have minimal contact with the "Black Vernacular Street Culture" will speak more standard English, while those who have more contact with the "Black Vernacular Street Culture" will speak more of what he refers to as Black Street Speech.

6   AAE in literature

1   The ex-slave narratives were collected as a part of the Federal Writer's Project from 1936–1938. The collection consists of over 2,000 interviews with ex-slaves from seventeen states.

2   Green (1987) is a preliminary discussion of the *for to* sequence as it is used by some speakers in parts of southwest Louisiana. Many speakers of AAE reject sentences with the *for to* sequence, but they do occur in speech. Some speakers use sentences such as the following: *He gave me that money for to buy all the water with.* The issues surrounding the occurrence of this sequence are interesting in that it is definitely attested but used only by a small number of speakers in that area. *For to* occurred in earlier stages of English.

3   See Chomsky and Lasnik (1977) and Henry (1992, 1995) for a syntactic analysis of this sequence.

4   Eye dialect is used to indicate "that the speech of a character in some way differs from normal conventional speech" (Bowdre 1971, p. 179). The author uses quasi-phonetic spellings which look different from the standard but are very close, if not identical, to the reader's pronunciation. One argument for the use of eye dialect is as follows: "It is better to use Eye Dialect than to burden the reader with outlandish forms intended to represent all the intricacies of regional speech or substandard speech" (Bowdre 1971, p. 179).

5   See Walters (1999) for a discussion of rhetorical strategies in Hurston's writings.

6   Another possible reading of (22i) is "You could have already been to get the water." In this reading, *been* does not indicate remote past.

7   Note that the singular *secret* (as opposed to the plural *secrets*) is used here following *no.*

8   The Simple stories were written in the 1950s, later in Hughes's career.

9   Some characters refer to Simple by the name Semple.

7   AAE in the media

1   This line is from Paskman (1976).

2   In some studies of AAE, this zero plural marking (e.g., *three dog, fifty cent*) is included as a feature of AAE. I find that this pattern occurs most often with *cent.*

3   I have given very brief statements about the use of *be* in (23a–c), but further linguistic detail can be provided to explain the problems with these sentences.

8   Approaches, attitudes and education

1   Rickford uses the Sea Islands to refer to the coastal Carolinas and Georgia, where Gullah is spoken. See the section on aspectual *be* in chapter 2. Also, see the section on the historical origins in the introduction to this book. By decreolization, Rickford means losing those properties that are distinctively creole and becoming more like English.

2   Labov must mean "verb phrase" in the most general sense because it has been shown that auxiliaries are not a part of the verb phrase (VP). Tests such as VP-ellipsis have been used to make this point in mainstream English. See Green (1998a) for discussion of this issue with respect to AAE.

3   Detailed arguments will not be reproduced here. See overviews and bibliographies in sources such as Whiteman (1980), Smitherman (1981), Brooks (1985) and Smitherman (2000) for a review of the King case. See Adger, Christian and Taylor (1999), Baugh (2000), Perry and Delpit (1998), John R. Rickford (1999), and Smitherman (2000) for a review of the Oakland case.

4   Feature lists such as the following have been useful as quick reference guides, but they have not provided the type of information that highlights the systematic nature of AAE:

> Aspectual *be*
> Multiple negation
> Remote past *BIN*
> Absence of auxiliary/copula *be*
> Final consonant cluster reduction
> Production of *f*, *v* in the environments of *th*
> Initial syllable forestressing
> *Skr* for *str* at the beginning of words

5   Baugh defines street speech in the following terms: "It is largely for ethnographic reasons that I have adopted the term "black street speech," because it conveys a similar meaning to most of the black consultants whom I have interviewed, regardless of their social or regional background. Street speech is the nonstandard dialect that thrives within the black street culture, and it is constantly fluctuating as new terminology flows in and out of colloquial vogue" (p. 16).

6   Rickford provides an overview of Piestrup's (1973) study in addressing interruption and correction. The Piestrup study involved over 200 first grade African American students in Oakland, CA. Two teaching methods were evaluated in the program: the Black Artful approach and the interrupting approach.

7   See chapter 4 for a discussion of environments of final consonant cluster reduction.

8   In presenting the two examples, Harris-Wright uses *done* instead of *dən*.

9   Taylor (1989) is a contrastive analysis study conducted at Aurora University in Aurora, IL.

10   See chapter 2 for a discussion of the different meanings and syntactic properties of *be dən*.

11   Maroney *et al*, conducted this study as a course project in Linguistics 73: African American Vernacular English, a course at Stanford University.

12   Also, the stories, which were written over twenty years ago, feature some lexical items from the slang component that are still used today. Words such as *cat* (male), *slick* (very nice) and *tighten up* (to get together or fix) are used in "A Friend in Need" and "Dreamy Mae."

13   The term standard AAE has been used to refer to the level of AAE in which intonational patterns of the variety are used. It is suggested that, at that level, syntactic, morphological and phonological features that are traditionally associated with AAE do not occur. Meier's (1998) characterization of the standard is given below:

While proficiency in Standard Black English requires that speakers and writers conform to the grammatical conventions of the standard code, it allows for the incorporation of many stylistic features associated with Black oral and written traditions – for example, characteristic intonational patterns; metaphorical language; concrete examples and analogies to make a point; rhyme, rhythm, alliteration, and other forms of repetition, including word play; use of proverbs, aphorisms, biblical quotations and learned allusions; colorful and unusual vocabulary; arguing *to* a main point (rather than *from* a main point); making a point through indirection.

(p. 99)

What Meier is describing is virtually a code that adheres to mainstream English grammatical patterns (e.g., sentence structure) and segmental phonological patterns (e.g., pronunciation of final consonant clusters, initial *str* versus *skr*) and that may be enhanced by AAE rhetorical stylistic patterns. If dialect readers are designed to approximate the familiar speech of child vernacular speakers, the 'standard' AAE in which they will be written must be more broadly defined to include the grammatical and phonological patterns of AAE.

References

Abrahams, Roger 1972, 'Talking my talk: black English and social segmentation in black communities,' *The Florida FL Reporter*, 10: 29–35.

1976, *Talking Black*, Rowley, MA: Newbury House.

Adger, Carolyn Temple, Donna Christian and Orlando Taylor (eds.) 1999, *Making the Connection: Language and Academic Achievement among African American Students*, McHenry, IL: Center for Applied Linguistics and Delta Systems Co., Inc.

Akmajian, Adrian, Richard A. Demers, Ann K. Farmer and Robert M. Harnish 1995 (4th edn), *Linguistics: an Introduction to Language and Communication*, Cambridge, MA: MIT Press.

Akmajian, Adrian, Susan M. Steele, and Thomas Wasow 1979, 'The category AUX in universal grammar,' *Linguistic Inquiry*, 10: 1–64.

Alexander, Clara Franklin 1985, 'Black English dialect and the classroom teacher,' in Charlotte K. Brooks (ed.), *Tapping Potential: English and Language Arts for the Black Learner*, Urbana, IL: National Council of Teachers of English, pp. 20–29.

Alvarez, Louis and Andrew Kolker 1987, *American Tongues*, New York: Center for New American Media.

Andrews, William L. [1980] 1992, 'Charles W. Chesnutt (1858–1932),' in James P. Draper (ed.), *Black Literature Criticism: Excerpts from Criticism of the Most Significant Works of Black Authors Over the Past 200 Years*, vol. I, Detroit, MI: Gale Research Inc., pp. 389–396.

Artiles, Alfredo. J. and Stanley C. Trent 1994, 'Overrepresentation of minority students in special education: a continuing debate,' *The Journal of Special Education*, 24: 410–437.

Babcock, C. Merton 1963, 'A word-list from Zora Neale Hurston,' *Publication of the American Dialect Society*, 40: 1–11.

Bailey, Guy and Natalie Maynor 1987, 'Decreolization?' *Language and Society*, 16: 449–473.

Bailey, Guy and Cynthia Schnebly 1988, 'Auxiliary deletion in black English Vernacular,' in Kathleen Ferrara, Becky Brown, Keith Walters and John Baugh (eds.), *Linguistic Change and Contact: NWAV-XVI*, Texas Linguistic Forum, pp. 34–41.

Bailey, Guy, Tom Wikle, Jan Tillery and Lori Sand 1991, 'The apparent time construct,' *Language Variation and Change*, 3: 241–264.

Baker, Jr., Houston A. 1993a, *Black Studies: Rap and the Academy*, University of Chicago Press.

1993b, 'Spike Lee and the commerce of culture,' in Manthia Diawara (ed.), *Black American Cinema*, New York: Routledge, pp. 154–173.

1984, *Blues, Ideology, and Afro-American Literature: a Vernacular Theory*, University of Chicago Press.

Baran, Jane and Harry Seymour 1976, 'The influence of three phonological rules of black English on the discrimination of minimal word pairs,' *Journal of Speech and Hearing Research*, 129: 467–474.

Baratz, Joan C. and Roger Shuy (eds.) 1969, *Teaching Black Children to Read*, Washington, DC: Center for Applied Linguistics.

Baugh, John 1978, 'The politics of black power handshakes,' *Natural History*, October 1978.

1980, 'A re-examination of the black English copula,' in William Labov (ed.), *Locating Language in Time and Space*, New York: Academic Press, pp. 83–106.

1983a, *Black Street Speech*, Austin: University of Texas Press.

1983b, 'Survey of Afro-American English,' *Annual Review of Anthropology*, 12: 335–354.

1984, '*Steady*: progressive aspect in black vernacular English,' *American Speech*, 59: 1–12.

1988, 'Discourse functions for *come* in black English vernacular,' in Kathleen Ferrara, Becky Brown, Keith Walters and John Baugh (eds.), *Linguistic Change and Contact: NWAV-XVI*, Texas Linguistic Forum, pp. 42–49.

1999, *Out of the Mouths of Slaves: African American Language and Educational Malpractice*, Austin: University of Texas Press.

2000, *Beyond Ebonics*, New York: Oxford University Press.

Bernard, James 1992, "Introduction," in Fred Brathwaite (ed.), *Words & Phrases of the Hip Hop Generation: Fresh Fly Flava*, Stamford, CT: Longmeadow Press.

Bickerton, Derek 1981, *Roots of Language*, Ann Arbor: Karoma.

Binnick, Robert I. 1991, *Time and the Verb: a Guide to Tense & Aspect*, New York: Oxford University Press.

Blake, Renée 1997, 'Defining the envelope of linguistic variation: the case of 'don't count' forms in the copula analysis of African American vernacular English,' *Language Variation and Change*, 9: 55–80.

Bogle, Donald 1995 (3rd edn), *Toms, Coons, Mulattoes, Mammies & Bucks: an Interpretative History of Blacks in American Films*, New York: Continuum.

Bowdre, Jr., Paul Hall 1971, 'Eye dialect as a literary device,' in Juanita V. Williamson and Virginia M. Burke (eds.), *A Various Language: Perspectives on American Dialects*, New York: Holt, Rinehart and Winston, Inc., pp. 178–186.

Bradley, F. W. 1950, 'A word-list from South Carolina,' *Publication of the American Dialect Society*, 14: 1–73.

Brasch, Walter M. 1981, *Black English in the Mass Media*, Amherst: University of Massachusetts Press.

Brathwaite, Fred. 1992, *Words & Phrases of the Hip-Hop Generation: Fresh Fly Flava*, Stamford, CT: Longmeadow Press.

Brinton, Laurel 1988, *The Development of English Aspectual Systems: Aspectualizers and Post-Verbal Particles*, Cambridge University Press.

Brooks, Charlotte K. (ed.) 1985, *Tapping Potential: English and Language Arts for the Black Learner*, Urbana, IL:, National Council of Teachers of English.

Brown, Alan and David Taylor (eds.) 1997, *Gabr'l Blow Sof': Sumter County, Alabama, Slave Narratives*, Livingston, AL: Livingston Press.

Brown, H. Rap 1972, 'Street talk,' in Thomas Kochman (ed.), *Rappin' and Stylin' Out: Communication in Urban Black America*, Urbana, IL: University of Illinois Press, pp. 205–207.

Brown, William Wells 1853, *Clotel; or the President's Daughter: a Narrative of Slave Life in the United States*, in Henry Louis Gates, Jr. (ed.), *Three Classic African-American Novels*, New York: Vintage Books, pp. 7–164.

Burford, Michelle 2000, 'Retreat to health: One sister's meatless and mellow vacation,' *Essence*, 30: 116–117.

Burling, Robbins 1973, *English in Black and White*, New York: Holt, Rinehart and Winston, Inc.

Butters, Ronald R. 1989, *The Death of Black English: Divergence and Convergence in Black and White Vernaculars*, New York: Verlag Peter Lang.

Callahan, John F. 1988, *In the African-American Grain*, Urbana: University of Illinois Press.

Carroll, Susanne 1983, 'Remarks on FOR-TO infinitives,' *Linguistic Analysis*, 12: 415–451.

Carter, Delores, Rev. and Rev. Nolan E. Williams (eds.) 2001, *African American Heritage Hymnal: 575 Hymns, Spirituals, and Gospel Songs*, Chicago, IL: GIA Publications Inc.

Cassidy, Frederick (ed.) 1985, *Dictionary of American Regional English*, Cambridge, MA: Harvard University Press.

Chesnutt, Charles W. [1900] 1993, *The House Behind the Cedars*, New York: Penguin Books.

Chomsky, Noam and Howard Lasnik 1977, 'Filters and control,' *Linguistic Inquiry*, 8: 425–504.

Christian, Donna 1991, 'The personal dative in Appalachian speech,' in Peter Trudgill and J. K. Chambers (eds.), *Dialects of English: Studies in Grammatical Variation*, London: Longman, pp. 11–17.

Coles, D'Jaris 1996, 'Immediate and remote future interpretations of *Ima* among African American English speakers,' talk presented at the Memphis Research Symposium, June 1996.

Comrie, Bernard 1976, *Aspect*, Cambridge University Press.

Cruttenden, Alan 1986, *Intonation*, Cambridge University Press.

Dalby, David 1972, 'The African element in American English,' in Thomas Kochman (ed.), *Rappin and Stylin Out: Communication in Urban Black America*, Urbana, IL: University of Illinois Press, pp. 170–186.

Dandy, Evelyn B. 1991, *Black Communications: Breaking Down the Barriers*, Chicago, IL: African American Images.

Dayton, Elizabeth 1996, 'Grammatical categories of the verb in African American vernacular English,' Ph.D. diss. University of Pennsylvania.

DeBose, Charles and Nicholas Faraclas 1993, 'An Africanist approach to the linguistic study of black English: getting to the roots of tense-aspect-modality and copula systems in Afro-American,' in Salikoko S. Mufwene (ed.), *Africanisms in Afro-American Language Varieties*, Athens, GA: University of Georgia Press, pp. 364–387.

Déchaine, Rose-Marie 1993, 'Predicates across categories: towards a category neutral syntax,' Ph.D. diss., University of Massachusetts.

Delpit, Lisa 1998, 'Ebonics and culturally responsive instruction,' in Theresa Perry and Lisa Delpit (eds.), *The Real Ebonics Debate: Power, Language and the Education of African-American Children*, Boston: Beacon Press, pp. 17–28.

Diawara, Manthia (ed.) 1993, *Black American Cinema*, New York: Routledge.

Dillard, J. L. 1972, *Black English: its History and Usage in the United States*, New York: Vintage House.

1977, *Lexicon of Black English*, New York: Seabury Press.

1992, *A History of American English*, New York: Longman.

Dollard, John 1939, 'The dozens: dialectic of insult,' *The American Imago*, 1: 3–25.

Dunn, Ernest F. (1976), 'Black-Southern white dialect controversy,' in Deborah S. Harrison and Tom Trabasso (eds.), *Black English: A Seminar*, Hillsdale, NJ: Erlbaum, pp. 105–122.

Edwards, Walter F. 1985, 'Inner-city English,' in Charlotte K. Brooks (ed.), *Tapping Potential: English and Language Arts for the Black Learner*. Urbana, IL: National Council of Teachers of English, pp. 78–80.

1991, 'A comparative description of Guyanese Creole and black English preverbal aspect marker *don*,' in Walter F. Edwards and Donald Winford (eds.), pp. 240–255.

2000, 'The northern cities chain shift in black and white Detroit speech,' talk presented at the Linguistic Society of America, Chicago, January 2000.

2001 'Aspectual *dən* in African American Vernacular English in Detroit,' *Journal of Sociolinguistics*, 5: 413–427.

Edwards, Walter F. and Donald Winford (eds.) 1991, *Verb Phrase Patterns in Black English and Creole*, Detroit, MI: Wayne State University Press.

Ellison, Ralph 1952, *Invisible Man*, New York: Vintage Books.

[1955] 1999, 'The Art of Fiction: An Interview,' in Hazel Arnett Ervin (ed.), *African American Literary Criticism, 1773 to 2000*, New York: Twayne Publishers, pp. 105–110.

Ewers, Traute 1996, *The Origin of American Black English: Be Forms in HOODOO Texts*, New York: Mouton de Gruyter.

Faelton, Shannon (ed.) 1999, 'Celebrate Your Beauty: 200 Secrets for Radiant Skin,' in *Prevention Health Books*, Emmaus, PA: Rodale Inc.

Farrison, W. Edward 1970, 'Dialectology versus Negro dialect,' *CLA Journal* 13: 21–27.

Fasold, Ralph W. 1972, *Tense Marking in Black English*, Arlington, VA: Center for Applied Linguistics.

Favor, J. Martin 1999, *Authentic Blackness: the Folk in the New Negro Renaissance*, Durham, NC: Duke University Press.

Feagin, Crawford 1997, 'The African contribution to southern states English,' in Cynthia Berstein, Thomas Nunnally and Robin Sabino (eds.) *Language Variety in the South Revisited*, University of Tuscaloosa, AL: Alabama Press, pp. 123–139.

1979, *Variation and Change in Alabama English: a Sociolinguistic Study of the White Community*, Washington, DC: Georgetown University Press.

Fishkin, Shelley Fisher 1993, *Was Huck Black? Mark Twain and African American Voices*, New York: Oxford University Press.

Folb, Edith A. 1980, *Runnin' Down Some Lines: the Language and Culture of Black Teenagers*, Cambridge, MA: Harvard University Press.

Fordham, Signithia 1996, *Blacked Out: Dilemmas of Race, Identity, and Success at Capital High*, University of Chicago Press.

Foreman, Christina G. 1999, 'Identification of African-American English dialect from prosodic cues,' in Nisha Merchant Goss, Amanda Doran and Anastasia Coles (eds.), *Salsa VII, Proccedings of the Seventh Annual Symposium about Language and Society*, Austin, TX: Texas Linguistic Forum 43, pp. 57–66.

Fromkin, Virginia (ed.) 2000, *Linguistics: an Introduction to Linguistic Theory*, New York: Blackwell.

Fromkin, Virginia and Robert Rodman 1998 (6th edn), *An Introduction to Language*, New York: Harcourt Brace College Publishers.

Gaines, Ernest 1968, *Bloodline*, New York: The Dial Press.

1968, 'A long day in November,' in Gaines (1968), pp. 3–79.

1968, 'Three men,' in Gaines (1968), pp. 121–155.

1968, 'The sky is gray,' in Gaines (1968), pp. 79–117.

Gates, Jr., Henry Louis 1988, *The Signifying Monkey: a Theory of Afro-American Literary Criticism*, New York: Oxford University Press.

1990, 'Introduction,' in Henry Louis Gates, Jr. (ed.), *Three Classic African-American Novels*, New York: Vintage Books, pp. vii–xvii.

George, Nelson 1998, *Hip Hop America*, New York: Penguin Books.

Gibson, Kean 2001, *Comfa Religion and Creole Language in a Caribbean Community*, Albany, NY: State University of New York Press.

Goodman, Morris 1993, 'African substratum: some cautionary words,' in Salikoko S. Mufwene (ed.), *Africanisms in Afro-American Language Varieties*, Athens, GA: University of Georgia Press, pp. 64–73.

Green, Lisa 1987, 'An overview of the occurrence of *for-to* in a Southern English dialect,' mimeo, University of Massachusetts.

1990, 'Intonational patterns of questions in black English: some observations,' mimeo, University of Massachusetts.

1991, 'Consonant cluster reduction and suffix interface in African American English,' mimeo, University of Massachusetts.

1993, 'Topics in African American English: the verb system analysis,' Ph.D. diss., University of Massachusetts.

1995, 'Study of verb classes in African American English,' *Linguistics and Education*, 7: 65–81.

1998a, 'Aspect and predicate phrases in African-American vernacular English,' in Salikoko S. Mufwene, John R. Rickford, Guy Bailey and John Baugh (eds.), 1998, *African-American English: Structure, History and Use*, New York: Routledge, pp. 37–68.

1998b, 'Remote past and states in African-American English,' *American Speech* 73: 115–138.

2000, 'Aspectual *be*-type constructions and coercion in African American English,' *Natural Language Semantics*, 8: 1–25.

2001, 'Negative concord and negative inversion in African American English,' mimeo, Austin: University of Texas.

Guy, Gregory 1991, 'Explanation in variable phonology: an exponential model of morphological constraints,' *Language Variation and Change*, 3: 1–22.

Harris, John 1985, 'Expanding the superstrate: habitual aspect markers in Atlantic Englishes,' *Sheffield Working Papers in Linguistics*, 2: 72–97.

Harris, M. A. 1974, *The Black Book*, New York: Random House.

Harris, Joel Chandler [1880] 1955, *The Complete Tales of Uncle Remus*, Boston, MA: Houghton Mifflin Company.

'Uncle Remus initiates the little boy,' in Harris ([1880] 1955), pp. 3–6.

'The wonderful tar-baby story,' in Harris ([1880] 1955), pp. 6–8.

Harris-Wright, K. 1987, 'The challenge of educational coalescence: teaching nonmainstream English-speaking students,' *Journal of Childhood Communication Disorders*, 11: 209–215.

1999, 'Enhancing bidialectalism in urban African American students,' in Carolyn Temple Adger, Donna Christian and Orlando Taylor (eds.), *Making the Connection: Language and Academic Achievement among African American Students*, McHenry, IL: Center for Applied Linguistics and Delta Systems Co., Inc., pp. 53–60.

Harry, Beth and Mary G. Anderson 1995, 'The disproportionate placement of African-American males in special education programs: a critique of the process,' *Journal of Negro Education*, 63: 602–619.

Henderson, Stephen E. [1973] 1999 'From the forms of things unknown in understanding the new black poetry and black music,' in Hazel A. Ervin (ed.), *African American Literary Criticism, 1773 to 2000*, New York: Twayne Publishers, pp. 141–152.

Henry, Alison, 1992, 'Infinitives in a *for-to* dialect,' *Natural Language and Linguistic Theory*, 10: 279–301.

1995, *Belfast English and Standard English: Dialect Variation in Parameter Setting*, New York: Oxford University Press.

Hilliard III, Asa G. 1999, 'Language, diversity, and assessment – ideology, professional practice, and the achievement gap,' in Carolyn Temple Adger, Donna Christian and Orlando Taylor (eds.), *Making the Connection: Language and Academic Achievement among African American Students*, McHenry, IL: Center for Applied Linguistics and Delta Systems Co., Inc., pp. 125–136.

Holloway, Karla F. C. 1978, 'A critical investigation of literary and linguistic structures in the fiction of Zora Neale Hurston,' Ph.D. diss., Michigan State University.

1987, *The Character of the Word: The Texts of Zora Neale Hurston*, West Port, CT: Greenwood Press.

Holm, John 1984, 'Variability of the copula in black English and its creole kin,' *American Speech*, 59: 291–309.

Holt, Grace Sims 1972, 'Stylin' outta the black pulpit,' in Thomas Kochman (ed.), *Rappin' and Stylin' Out: Communication in Urban Black America*, Urbana, IL: University of Illinois Press., pp. 189–204.

Holton, Sylvia Wallace 1984, *Down Home and Up Town: the Representation of Black Speech in American Fiction*, London: Associated University Press.

Hopkins, Pauline E. [1900] 1991, 'General Washington: a Christmas story,' in Elizabeth Ammons (ed.), *Short Fiction by Black Women, 1900–1920*, New York: Oxford University Press, pp. 69–82.

Hoover, Mary 1985, 'Ethnology of black communications,' *Journal of Black Reading/ Language Education*, 2: 2–4.

Howe, Darin M. 1997, 'Negation and the history of African American vernacular English,' *Language Variation and Change*, 9: 267–294.

Howe, Darin M. and James A. Walker 2000, 'Negation and creole-origins hypothesis: evidence from early African American English,' in Shana Poplack (ed.), *The English History of African American English*, Malden, MA: Blackwell, pp. 109–140.

Huggins, Nathan Irvin 1971, *Harlem Renaissance*, New York: Oxford University Press.

Hughes, Langston [1926] 1999, 'The Negro artist and the racial mountain,' in Hazel A. Ervin (ed.), *African American Literary Criticism, 1773 to 2000*, New York: Twayne Publishers, pp. 44–48.

1961, *The Best of Simple*, New York: Hill and Wang.

1961, 'Bones, bombs, chicken necks,' in Hughes, pp. 199–202.

1961, 'Last whipping,' in Hughes, pp. 74–78.

1961, 'Seven rings,' in Hughes, pp. 94–100.

1961, 'Springtime,' in Hughes, pp. 72–74.

1961, 'What can a man say?' in Hughes, pp. 100–103.

Hurston, Zora Neale [1934] 1990, *Jonah's Gourd Vine*, New York: Harper & Row. [1942] 1984 (2nd edn), *Dust Tracks on a Road: an Autobiography*, New York: Harper & Row.

1983, 'Characteristics of Negro expression,' in Zora Neale Hurston, pp. 41–78.

1983, *The Sanctified Church*, Turtle Island, Berkeley.

Hymes, Dell 1972, 'Models of the interaction of language and social life,' in J. Gumperz and D. Hymes (eds.), *Directions in Sociolinguistics: Ethnography of Communication*, New York: Holt, Rinehart and Winston, Inc., pp. 35–71.

Jackson, Janice E. 1998, 'Linguistic aspect in African-American English speaking children: an investigation of aspectual *be*,' Ph.D. diss., University of Massachusetts.

Jaeggli, Osvaldo and Nina M. Hyams 1993, 'On the independence and interdependence of syntactic and morphological properties: English aspectual *come* and *go*, *Natural Language and Linguistic Theory*, 11: 313–346.

Jones, Rachel [1982] 1992, 'What's wrong with black English,' in Gary Goshgarian (ed.), *Exploring Language*, New York: HarperCollins Publishers, pp. 96–99.

Jun, Sun-Ah and Christina Foreman 1996, 'Boundary tones and focus realization in African-American English intonation,' talk presented at the third joint meeting of ASA and ASJ.

Kallen, Jeffrey L. 1985, 'The co-occurrence of *do* and *be* in Hiberno-English,' in John Harris, David Little and David Singleton (eds.), *Perspectives on English Language in Ireland*, Proceedings of the First Symposium on Hiberno-English, Dublin: Trinity College, pp. 133–147.

Kochman, Thomas (ed.), 1972, *Rappin' and Stylin' Out: Communication in Urban Black America*, Urbana, IL: University of Illinois Press.

1972, 'Toward an ethnography of black American speech behavior,' in Thomas Kochman (ed.), pp. 241–264.

Labov, Teresa 1992, 'Social and language boundaries among adolescents,' *American Speech*, 67: 339–366.

Labov, William 1969a, 'Contraction, deletion, and inherent variability in the English copula,' *Language*, 45: 715–776.

1969b, 'Some sources of reading problems for Negro speakers of nonstandard English,' in Joan C. Baratz and Roger Shuy (eds.), *Teaching Black Children to Read*, Washington, DC: Center for Applied Linguistics, pp. 29–67.

1972, *Language in the Inner City: Studies in the Black English Vernacular*, Philadelphia: University of Pennsylvania Press.

1987, 'Are black and white vernaculars diverging?' Papers from the NWAVE XIV panel discussion, *American Speech*, 62: 5–12.

1991, 'The three dialects of English,' in Penelope Eckert (ed.), *New Ways of Analyzing Sound Change*, New York: Academic Press. pp. 1–44.

1995, 'Can reading failure be reversed: a linguistic approach to the question,' in Vivian Gadsden and Daniel A. Wagner (eds.), *Literacy Among African-American Youth: Issues in Learning, Teaching, and Schooling*, Cresskill, NJ: Hampton Press, Inc., pp. 39–68.

1998, 'Coexistent systems in African-American vernacular English,' in Salikoko S. Mufwene, John R. Rickford, Guy Bailey and John Baugh (eds.), *African-American English: Structure, History and Use*, New York: Routledge, pp. 110–153.

Labov, William, Paul Cohen, Clarence Robbins and John Lewis 1968, *A Study of Non-Standard English of Negro and Puerto Rican Speakers in New York City*, 2 vols, Philadelphia: US Regional Survey.

Ladefoged, Peter 1993 (3rd edn), *A Course in Phonetics*, New York: Harcourt Brace Jovanovich College Publishers.

Lewis, Shirley A. 1981, 'Practical aspects of teaching composition to bidialectal students: the Nairobi method,' in Marcia Farr Whiteman (ed), *Writing: the Nature, Development, and Teaching of Written Composition*, Hillsdale, NJ: Erlbaum, pp. 189–196.

Lott, Eric 1993, *Love and Theft: Blackface Minstrelsy and the American Working Class*, New York: Oxford University Press.

1996, 'Blackface and blackness: the minstrel show in American culture,' in Annemarie Bean, James Vernon Hatch and Brooks McNamara (eds.), *Inside the Minstrel Mask: Readings in Nineteenth-Century Blackface Minstrelsy*, London: University Press of New England, pp. 3–32.

Luelsdorff, Phillip 1973, *A Segmental Phonology of Black English*, The Netherlands: Mouton.

McCarthy, John J. 1991, 'Synchronic rule inversion,' in L. Sutton, C. Johnson and R. Shields (eds.), *Proceedings of the Seventeenth Annual Meeting of the Berkeley Linguistics Society*, Berkeley: University of California, pp. 192–207.

McCloskey, James 1992, 'Adjunction, selection and embedded verb second,' mimeo, Santa Cruz: University of California.

McManis, Carolyn, Deborah Stollenwerk and Zhang Zheng-Sheng (eds.) 1987, *Language Files: Materials for an Introduction to Language*, Reynoldsburg, OH: Advocate Publishing Group.

Major, Clarence 1994, *Juba to Jive: a Dictionary of African-American Slang*, New York: Penguin Books.

Mao, Charmaine 2000, 'Tales of whoa!' *Vibe*, 8, 5: 161–164.

Margolick, David 1995, 'Simpson witness saw a white car,' *The New York Times National*, July 13, 1995.

Maroney, Oahn, Tracey Thomas, Gerard Lawrence and Susan Salcedo 1994, 'Black dialect vs. standard English in education,' in *The AAVE Happen in'*, John R. Rickford, Lisa Green, Jennifer Arnold, Renée Blake (compilers),1994: 3–45, Stanford, CA: Stanford University Department of Linguistics.

Martin Luther King Junior Elementary School Children v. Ann Arbor School District Board, July 12, 1979. Civil Action No. 7-71861 (E. D. Mich).

Martin, Stefan E. 1992, 'Topics in the syntax of nonstandard English,' Ph.D. diss., University of Maryland.

Meier, Terry 1998, 'Teaching teachers about black communications,' in Theresa Perry and Lisa Delpit (eds.), *The Real Ebonics Debate: Power, Language and the Education of African American Children*, Boston: Beacon Press, pp. 117–125.

Menand, Louis 1997, 'Johnny be good: ebonics and the language of cultural separatism,' *The New Yorker*, 72: 4–5.

Meredith, Scott and Caroline Hinton, (no date) 'Transcriptions and analysis of the prosody of a black vernacular English Idiolect,' mimeo.

Miller, Michael 1986, 'The greatest blemish: plurals in *-sp, -st, -sk*,' in Michael Montgomery and Guy Bailey (eds.), *Language Variety in the South*, Tuscaloosa, AL: University of Alabama Press.

Mitchell-Kernan, Claudia 1972, 'Signifying, loud-talking and marking,' in Thomas Kochman (ed.), *Rappin' and Stylin' Out: Communication in Urban Black America*, Urbana, IL: University of Illinois Press, pp. 315–335.

Montgomery, Michael and Margaret Mishoe 1999, 'He bes took up with a Yankee girl and moved up there to New York: the verb *bes* in the Carolinas and its history,' *American Speech*, 74: 240–281.

Morgan, Marcyliena 1996, 'Conversational signifying: grammar and indirectness among African American women,' in E. Ochs, E. Schegloff and S. Thompson (eds.), *Interaction and Grammar*, Cambridge University Press, pp. 405–434.

1994, 'The African-American speech community: reality and sociolinguistics,' in Marcyliena Morgan (ed.), *The Social Construction of Identities in Creole Situations*, Los Angeles: Center for Afro-American Studies, pp. 121–148.

Mufwene, Salikoko S. 1992, 'Ideology and facts on African American English,' *Pragmatics* 2: 141–166.

1996, 'The founder principle in creole genesis,' *Diachronica*, 13: 83–134.

2000, 'Some sociohistorical inferences about the development of African American English,' in Shana Poplack (ed.), *The English History of African American English*, Malden, MA: Blackwell, pp. 233–263.

Mufwene, Salikoko S., John R. Rickford, Guy Bailey and John Baugh (eds.) 1998, *African-American English: Structure, History and Use*, New York: Routledge.

Myhill, John 1991, 'The use of invariant *be* with verbal predicates in BEV,' in Walter Edwards and Donald Winford (eds.), *Verb Phrase Patterns in Black English and Creole*, Detroit, MI: Wayne State University Press, pp. 101–113.

Myhill, John and Wendell A. Harris 1986, 'The use of verbal *-s* inflection in BEV,' in D. Sankoff (ed.) *Diversity and Diachrony*, Amsterdam: John Benjamins, pp. 25–32.

Nathan, Hans 1996, 'The performance of the Virginia minstrels,' in Annemarie Bean, James V. Hatch and Brooks McNamara (eds.), *Inside the Minstrel Mask: Readings in Nineteenth-Century Blackface Minstrelsy*. Hanover, NH: University Press of New England.

The Nation's Report Card, Fourth Grade Reading 2000, National Assessment of Educational Progress, April 6, 2001, US Department of Educational Research and Improvement.

Nesteby, James R. 1982, *Black Images in American Films, 1896–1954: the Interplay Between Civil Rights and Film Culture*, Washington, DC: University Press of America.

Oetting, Janna B. and Janet L. McDonald 2001, 'Nonmainstream dialect use and specific language impairment,' *Journal of Speech, Language, and Hearing Research*, 44: 207–223.

O'Grady, William, Michael Dobrovolsky and Mark Aronoff 1993 (2nd edn), *Contemporary Linguistics: an Introduction*, New York: St. Martin's Press.

Ostrom, Hans 1993, *Langston Hughes: A Study of the Short Fiction*, New York: Twayne Publishers.

Parker, Henry H. and Marilyn I. Crist 1995, *Teaching Minorities to Play the Corporate Language Game*, Columbia: National Resource Center for the Freshman Year Experience and Students in Transition, University of South Carolina.

Parsons, Terence 1990, *Events in the Semantics of English: a Study in Subatomic Semantics*, Cambridge, MA: MIT Press.

Paskman, Dailey 1976, '*Gentlemen, Be Seated!*': *a Parade of the American Minstrels*, New York: Clarkson N. Potter, Inc..

Percelay, James, Stephan Dweck and Monteria Ivey 1994, *Snaps*, New York: William Morrow & Company.

Percelay, James, Monteria Ivey and Stephan Dweck 1995, *Double Snaps*, New York: William Morrow & Company.

Perry, Theresa and Lisa Delpit 1998, 'Embracing ebonics teaching standard English: an interview with Oakland teacher Carrie Scott,' in Theresa Perry and Lisa Delpit (eds.), *The Real Ebonics Debate: Power, Language and the Education of African-American Children*, Boston: Beacon Press, pp. 79–88.

Pierrehumbert, Janet 1980, 'The phonology and phonetics of English intonation,' Ph.D. diss., MIT.

Pierrehumbert, J. and J. Hirschberg 1987, 'The meaning of intonational contours in the interpretation of discourse,' mimeo, AT&T Bell Laboratories.

Piestrup, Anne McCormick 1973, *Black Dialect Interference and Accommodation of Reading Instruction in First Grade*, monographs of the Language Behavior Research Laboratory, no. 4, Berkeley: University of California.

Pitts, Jr., Walter F. 1993, *Old Ship of Zion: the Afro-Baptist Ritual in the African Diaspora*, New York: Oxford University Press.

Pollock, Karen 1998, 'Clinical implications,' talk presented at the American Speech Language and Hearing Association, San Antonio,TX: November 1998.

Poplack, Shana (ed.) 2000, *The English History of African American English*. New York: Blackwell.

Poplack, Shana and Sali Tagliamonte 1989, 'There's no tense like the present: verbal *-s* inflection in early black English,' *Language Variation and Change*, 1: 47–84.

Potter, Russell A. 1995, *Spectacular Vernaculars: Hip Hop and the Politics of Postmodernism*, Albany, NY: State University of New York Press.

Pullum, Geoffrey K. 1999, 'African American vernacular English is not Standard English with mistakes,' in Rebecca S. Wheeler (ed.), *The Workings of Language: From Prescriptions to Perspectives*, Westport, CT: Praeger, 39–58.

Pullum, Geoffrey and Deirdre Wilson 1977, 'Autonomous syntax and the analysis of auxiliaries,' *Language*, 53: 741–788.

Radford, Andrew 1988, *Transformational Grammar: a First Course*, Cambridge University Press.

Rickford, Angela Marshall 1999, *Teaching Narratives and Reading Comprehension to African American and Other Ethnic Minority Students*, New York: University Press of America.

Rickford, John R. 1972, ' "Sounding" black or "sounding" white: a preliminary investigation,' mimeo, University of Pennsylvania.

1973, '*Been* in black English,' mimeo, University of Pennsylvania.

1975, 'Carrying the new wave into syntax: the case of black English *been*,' in Ralph W. Fasold (ed.), *Variation in the Form and Use of Language*, Washington, DC: Georgetown University Press, pp. 98–119.

1977, 'The question of prior creolization in black English,' in A. Valdman (ed.), *Pidgin-Creole Linguistics*, Bloomington: University of Indiana Press, pp. 199–221.

1986, 'Social contact and linguistic diffusion: Hiberno-English and new world black English,' *Language*, 62: 245–289.

1987, *Dimensions of a Creole Continuum: History, Texts and Linguistic Analysis of Guyanese Creole*, Stanford University Press.

1998, 'The creole origin of African American vernacular English: evidence from copula absence,' in Salikoko S. Mufwene, John R. Rickford, Guy Bailey and John Baugh (eds.), *African-American English: Structure, History and Use*, New York: Routledge, pp. 154–200.

1999, *African American Vernacular English: Features, Evolution, Educational Implications*, New York: Blackwell.

Rickford, John R., Arnetha Ball, Renee Blake, Raina Jackson and Nomi Martin 1991, 'Rappin' on the copula coffin: theoretical and methodological issues in the analysis of copula variation in African-American vernacular English,' *Language Variation and Change*, 3: 102–132.

Rickford, John R. and Angela E. Rickford 1976, 'Cut-eye and suck teeth: African words and gestures in new world guise,' in J. L. Dillard (ed.), *Perspectives on American English* New York: Mouton Publishers, pp. 347–365.

1995, 'Dialect readers revisited,' *Linguistics and Education*, 7: 107–128.

Rickford, John R. and Russell John Rickford 2000, *Spoken Soul*, New York: John Wiley & Sons, Inc.

Rickford, John R. and Christine Théberge-Rafal 1996, 'Preterite *had* in the narratives of African American preadolescents,' *American Speech*, 71: 227–254.

Rose, Tricia 1994, *Black Noise: Rap Music and Black Culture in Contemporary America*, Hanover, NH: University Press of New England.

Santa Ana, Otto A. 1992, 'Chicano English evidence for exponential hypothesis: a variable rule pervades lexical phonology,' *Language Variation and Change*, 4: 275–288.

Schneider, Edgar W. 1989, *American Earlier Black English*, Tuscaloosa: University of Alabama Press.

Selkirk, Elisabeth O. 1982, *The Syntax of Words*, Cambridge, MA: MIT Press.

Sells, Peter, John R. Rickford and Thomas Wasow 1996, 'An optimality approach to variation in negative inversion in AAVE,' *Natural Language and Linguistic Theory*, 14: 591–627.

Seymour, Harry 1998, 'Development and validation of a language test for children speaking non-standard English: a study of children who speak African American English,' NIH Contract N01-DC8-2104, Amherst: University of Massachusetts.

Shannon, Sandra G. 1999, 'Blues, history and dramaturgy: an interview with August Wilson (1994),' in Hazel A. Ervin (ed.), *African American Literary Criticism, 1773 to 2000*, New York: Twayne Publishers, pp. 44–48.

Simmons, Donald C. 1963, 'Possible West African sources for the American Negro "dozens",' *Journal of American Folklore*, 76: 339–340.

Simpkins, Gary A., G. Holt and Charlesetta Simpkins 1977 (1st edn), *Bridge: a Cross-Cultural Reading Program*, Boston: Houghton Mifflin.

Singler, John Victor 1991, 'Copula variation in Liberian settler English,' in Walter F. Edwards and Donald Winford (eds.), *Verb Phrase Patterns in Black English and Creole*, Detroit, MI: Wayne State University Press, pp. 129–164.

Sledd, James 1958, 'Some questions of English phonology,' *Language*, 34: 252–258.

Smith, Carlota S. 1997, *The Parameter of Aspect* (2nd edn), Dordrecht: Kluwer Academic Press.

Smith, Ernie 1998, 'What is black English? What is Ebonics?' in Theresa Perry and Lisa Delpit (eds.), *The Real Ebonics Debate: Power, Language, and the Education of African-American Children*, Boston: Beacon Press, pp. 49–58.

Smitherman, Geneva 1977, *Talkin and Testifyin: the Language of Black America*, Detroit, MI: Wayne State University Press.

1981, 'What go round come round: King in perspective,' *Harvard Eduational Review*, 51: 40–56.

1985, 'It bees dat way sometime: sounds and structure of present-day black English,' in Virginia P. Clark (ed.), *Language: Introductory Readings*, New York: St. Martin's Press, pp. 552–568.

1994, *Black Talk: Words and Phrases from the Hood to the Amen Corner*, Boston: Houghton Mifflin.

1995, 'If I'm lyin', I'm flyin': an introduction to the art of the snap,' in J. Percelay, S. Dweck, and M. Ivey (eds.) *Double Snaps*, New York: Morrow and Company.

2000, 'English teacher, why you be doing the thangs you don't do?' in Smitherman, pp. 123–131.

2000, *Talkin that Talk: Language, Culture and Education in African America*, New York: Routledge.

Spears, Arthur K. 1982, 'The black English semi-auxiliary *come*,' *Language*, 58: 850–872.

2000, 'Stressed *stay*: a new African-American English aspect marker,' talk presented at the Linguistic Society of America Annual Meeting, Chicago, IL: January 2000.

2001, 'Standard African-American English: race, grammar, and ideology,' talk presented at the Linguistic Society of America Annual Meeting, Washington, DC: January 2001.

Stockman, Ida J. and Fay Vaughn-Cooke 1982, 'Semantic categories in the language of working class black children,' *Proceedings of the Second International Child Language Conference*, 1: 312–327.

Tagliamonte, Sali and Shana Poplack 1988, 'How black English past got to the present: evidence from Samaná,' *Language in Society*, 17: 513–533.

Tarone, Elaine E. 1972, 'Aspects of intonation in vernacular white and black English speech,' Ph.D. diss., University of Washington.

1973, 'Aspects of intonation in black English,' *American Speech*, 48: 29–36.

Taylor, Hanni U. 1989, *Standard English, Black English, and Bidialectalism: a Controversy*, New York: Peter Lang.

Taylor, Mikki, Amy Dubois Barnett and Angela Burt-Murray 1999, 'Looking through the glass reflections of timeless beauty rituals,' *Essence* 30: 21–28, December 1999.

Taylor, Orlando 1971, 'Response to social dialects and the field of speech,' in R. Shuy (ed.), *Sociolinguistic Theory: Materials and Practice*, Washington DC: Center for Applied Linguistics, pp. 13–20.

Teepen, Tom 1991, 'Talking the talk, in black and white,' *San Francisco Chronicle*, May 8, 1991.

Terry, J. Michael 2000, 'On the semantics of *dən* in African American English,' in Kiyomi Kusumoto and Elizabeth Villalta (eds.), *UMOP 23*, Issues in Semantics, 225–249.

Tottie, Gunnel and Dawn Harrie 2000, 'It's all relative: relativization strategies in early African American English,' in Shana Poplack (ed.), *The English History of African American English*, Malden, MA: Blackwell, pp. 198–230.

Turner, Lorenzo Dow 1949, *Africanisms in the Gullah Dialect*, Ann Arbor: University of Michigan Press.

van Keulen, Jean E., Gloria Toliver Weddington and Charles E. DeBose 1998, *Speech, Language, Learning, and the African American Child*, Boston: Allyn and Bacon.

Viereck, Wolfgang 1988, 'Invariant *be* in an unnoticed source of American early black English,' *American Speech*, 63: 291–303.

Walters, Keith 1999, '"He can read my writing but he sho' can't read my mind": Zora Neale Hurston's revenge in *Mules and Men*,' *Journal of American Folklore*, 112: 334–371.

Warner, Anthony 1993, *English Auxiliaries: Structure and History*, Cambridge University Press.

Watkins, S. Craig 1998, *Representing: Hip Hop Culture and the Production of Black Cinema*, University of Chicago Press.

Weldon, Tracey 1995, 'Variability in negation in African American vernacular English,' *Language Variation and Change*, 6: 359–397.

Whiteman, Marcia Farr (ed.) 1980, *Reactions to Ann Arbor: Vernacular Black English and Education*, Washington, DC: Center for Applied Linguistics.

Wideman, John Edgar 1984, *Brothers and Keepers*, New York: Penguin Books.

Williams, Robert, (ed.) 1975, *Ebonics: the True Language of Black Folks*, St Louis, MO: The Institute of Black Studies.

Williamson, Juanita 1970, 'Selected features of speech: black and white,' *CLA Journal*, 13: 420–433.

Wilson, August 1986, *Fences*, New York: Penguin Books.

Winford, Donald 1997, 'On the origins of African American English – a creolist perspective part I: the sociohistorical background,' *Diachronica*, 14: 305–344.

1998, 'On the origins of African American English – a creolist perspective part II: linguistic features,' *Diachronica*, 15: 99–154.

Wolfram, Walt 1969, *A Sociolinguistic Description of Detroit Negro Speech*, Washington, DC: Center for Applied Linguistics.

1974, 'The relationship of white southern speech to vernacular black English,' *Language*, 50: 498–527.

1991, *Dialects and American English*, Englewood Cliffs, NJ: Prentice-Hall.

1994, 'On the sociolinguistic significance of dialect structures: The [NPi Call NPi V-ing] construction in African-American vernacular English,' *American Speech*, 69: 339–360.

1999, 'Repercussions from the Oakland ebonics controversy – the critical role of dialect awareness programs,' in Carolyn Adger Temple, Donna Christian and Orlando Taylor (eds.), *Making the Connection: Language and Academic Achievement among African American Students*, McHenry, IL: Center for Applied Linguistics and Delta Systems Co., Inc., pp. 61–80.

Wolfram, Walter A. and Ralph W. Fasold 1969, 'Toward reading materials for speakers of black English: three linguistically appropriate passages,' in Joan C. Baratz and Roger Shuy (eds.), *Teaching Black Children to Read*, Washington, DC: Center for Applied Linguistics, pp. 138–155.

1974, *Social Dialects in American English*, Englewood Cliffs, NJ: Prentice-Hall.

Wolfram, Walt and Natalie Schilling-Estes 1998, *American English: Dialects and Variation*, Malden, MA: Blackwell.

Woodard, C. M. 1946, 'A word-list from Virginia and North Carolina,' *Publication of the American Dialect Society*, 6.

Wyatt, Toya 1991, 'Linguistic constraints on copula production in black English child speech,' Ph.D. diss., University of Massachusetts.

  1995, 'Language development in African American English child speech,' *Linguistics and Education*, 7: 7–22.

Yetman, Norman R. (ed.) 1970, *Voices from Slavery*, New York: Holt, Rinehart and Winston.

Ziegler, Mary B. 2001, '"Cause I likedid it that way": sound and meaning in the AAL past tense,' talk presented at the Linguistic Society of America Annual Meeting, Washington, DC: January 2001.

Acknowledgments

Illustrations

Black communications ©1991, EAB Dandy. Reprinted with permission of African American Images.
Larynx: state of the glottis, by permission of Ohio State University Press.

Music

extract from "The Art of Easing," Digable Planets 1994, ©Capitol Records, Alruby Music Inc.
extract from "Bananas," Queen Latifah 1998, ©Motown Records, EMI Music Publishing.
extract from "Bling, Bling," B. G. 1999, ©Cash Money Records, Inc.
extract from "Can't Nobody Do Me Like Jesus," ©1982, Bud John Songs, Inc.
extract from "Get Your Roll On," Cash Money 2000, ©Cash Money Records, Inc.
extract from "Git Up, Git Out," OutKast 1994, © Arista Records.
extract from "I Can' Live Without My Radio," L. L. Cool J 1985, ©Sony Music Entertainment, EMI Music Publishing.
extract from "I Love the Lord," ©1990, Oak/Richwood Music.
extract from "I'm Every Woman," Chaka Kahn 1979, ©Warner Brother Records.
extract from "I Used to Love H. E. R," by Rashid Lonnie Lynn (common) and Ernest D. Wilson, used by permission of Songs of Universal, Inc. (BMI).
extract from "Jesus is Mine," by Donnie McClerkin, performed by Florida Mass Choir, Savgos Music, Inc.
extract from "Leader of the Pack," UTFO 1984, © Select Records, EMI Music Publishing.
extract from "Rapper's Delight," Sugar Hill Gang 1979, © Bernard's Other Music, Warner Chapel Publishing.
extract from "Thieves in the Night," Black Star 1999, ©Priority Records, Firststars Music.
extract from "This Morning When I Rose," ©1996, Malaco Music, Savgos/Jonan/Arisav.

Films

Bamboozled, 2000, Spike Lee, New Line Cinema.
The Best Man, 1999, Malcolm Lee, Universal Pictures.
Bulworth, 1998, Warren Beatty, Twentieth Century Fox.
Do the Right Thing, 1988, Spike Lee, Universal Pictures.
Fresh, 1994, Boaz Yakin, Miramax Films.

Imitation of Life, 1934, John M. Stahl, Universal Cinema.
Jungle Fever, 1991, Spike Lee, Universal Studios Home Video.

Plays

Extract from *Fences* by August Wilson, © 1986 by
August Wilson. Used by permission of Dutton Signet, a
division of Penguin Putnam Inc.

Television Shows

Comic View, Black Entertainment TV.
The Fresh Prince of Bel Air, Stuffed Dog Company.
Judge Joe Brown, Paramount Pictures.
Laurel Street, HBO Independent Productions.
Oprah Winfrey Show, Harpo Productions Inc.
What's Happening, Toy Productions.

Every effort has been made to contact the copyright holders of
material reproduced in this book by the time it goes to press;
if any have been overlooked the publisher will be pleased
to add the relevant details when the book is reprinted.

Index

AAE in the index refers to African American English.